2007 Microsoft® Office System Plain & Simple

M000199138

Jerry Joyce
Marianne Moon

PUBLISHED BY

Microsoft Press

A Division of Microsoft Corporation

One Microsoft Way

Redmond, Washington 98052-6399

Library of Congress Control Number: 2006937717

Printed and bound in the United States of America.

12 13 14 15 16 17 18 19 20 21 QGT 5 4 3 2 1 0

Distributed in Canada by H.B. Fenn and Company Ltd.

A CIP catalogue record for this book is available from the British Library.

Microsoft Press books are available through booksellers and distributors worldwide. For further information about international editions, contact your local Microsoft Corporation office or contact Microsoft Press International directly at fax (425) 936-7329. Visit our Web site at www.microsoft.com/mspress. Send comments to mspinput@microsoft.com.

Microsoft, ActiveX, Aero, AutoSum, Excel, Hotmail, Internet Explorer, OneNote, Outlook, PivotChart, PivotTable, PowerPoint, SharePoint, Windows, and Windows Vista are either registered trademarks or trademarks of Microsoft Corporation in the United States and/or other countries. Other product and company names mentioned herein may be the trademarks of their respective owners.

The example companies, organizations, products, domain names, e-mail addresses, logos, people, places, and events depicted herein are fictitious. No association with any real company, organization, product, domain name, e-mail address, logo, person, place, or event is intended or should be inferred.

This book expresses the author's views and opinions. The information contained in this book is provided without any express, statutory, or implied warranties. Neither the authors, Microsoft Corporation, nor its resellers, or distributors will be held liable for any damages caused or alleged to be caused either directly or indirectly by this book.

Acquisitions Editor: Juliana Aldous Atkinson
Developmental Editor: Sandra Haynes
Project Editor: Kathleen Atkins
Technical Editor: Jerry Joyce

Manuscript Editor: Marianne Moon
Typographers: Kari Fera and Kat Marriner
Proofreader/Copy Editor: Alice Copp Smith
Indexer: Jan Wright, Wright Information

Body Part No. X12-65190

*In memory of C. Christopher Stern, Microsoft Press's first typographer,
and esteemed preservationist of the craft of letterpress printing.*

Contents

Acknowledgments . . . . *xv*

1 **About This Book**   **1**

No Computerspeak! 1
A Quick Overview 2
What's New in Office 2007? 4
A Few Assumptions 5
A Final Word (or Two) 6

2 **Working in Office**   **7**

What's What in Office? 8
Dialog Box Decisions 9
Using the Ribbon 10
Using Menus and Toolbars 12
Using Only the Keyboard 14
Moving and Copying Content 16
Getting Help 18
Saving Your Work 19
Office's File Formats 20

3 **Common Tasks in Office**   **21**

Working with Old Documents 22
Inserting Special Characters 23
Inserting Pictures 24
Changing the Size of a Picture 25
Editing a Picture 26

Adding Shapes 28
Adding Clip Art 29
Formatting a Shape 30
Inserting the Date and Time 31
Creating Stylized Text 32
Inserting a Relational Diagram 34
Researching a Subject 36

4 Viewing and Editing Text in Word   37

What's Where in Word 2007? 38
Creating a New Document 40
Composing Different Types of Documents 41
Word's Views 42
Reading a Document 44
Editing Text 45
Finding Text 46
Replacing Text 47
Correcting Your Spelling and Grammar 48
Correcting Text Automatically 50
Adding Page Numbers 51
So Many Ways to Do It 52
Marking and Reviewing Changes in a Document 54
Comparing Documents Side by Side 56

5 Formatting in Word   57

Controlling the Look: Themes, Styles, and Fonts 58
Setting the Overall Look 59
Formatting Text 60
Using Any Style 61

Changing Character Fonts 62
Setting Paragraph Alignment 63
Adjusting Paragraph Line Spacing 64
Indenting a Paragraph 66
Formatting with Tabs. 67
Adding Emphasis and Special Formatting 68
Copying Your Formatting 69
Creating a Bulleted or Numbered List 70
Formatting a List 71
Creating a Table from Scratch 72
Using a Predesigned Table 73
Creating a Table from Text 74
Adding or Deleting Rows and Columns. 75
Formatting a Table. 76
Improving the Layout with Hyphenation. 77
Laying Out the Page 78
Changing Page Orientation Within a Document 80
Flowing Text into Columns. 81
Creating Chapters 82
Wrapping Text Around a Graphic 83
Creating a Running Head. 84
Sorting Your Information 85
Reorganizing a Document 86

6 Working with Special Content in Word — 87

Inserting a Cover Page 88
Numbering Headings 89
Adding Line Numbers. 90
Inserting Information with Smart Tags. 91
Inserting an Equation 92

Adding a Sidebar or a Pull Quote 93

Inserting a Watermark 94

Creating Footnotes and Endnotes. 95

Inserting a Citation 96

Creating a Table of Contents 98

Printing an Envelope. 99

Printing a Mailing Label 100

Mail Merge: The Power and the Pain 101

Creating a Form Letter 102

Finalizing Your Document 104

7 Working in Excel 105

What's Where in Excel?. 106

Entering the Data. 107

Editing the Data. 108

Excel's Eccentricities. 109

Using a Predefined Workbook. 110

Formatting Cells. 111

Changing the Overall Look 112

Formatting Numbers. 113

Moving and Copying Data. 114

Adding and Deleting Columns and Rows 116

Creating a Series 118

Hiding Columns and Rows. 119

Formatting Cell Dimensions. 120

Organizing Your Worksheets 122

Setting Up the Page 124

Printing a Worksheet. 126

Adding and Viewing Comments 128

Analyzing and Presenting Data in Excel 129

Creating a Table 130
Cell References, Formulas, and Functions 132
Doing the Arithmetic 134
Summing the Data 136
Creating a Series of Calculations 137
Making Calculations with Functions 138
Troubleshooting Formulas 140
Sorting the Data 142
Filtering the Data 143
Separating Data into Columns 144
Creating Subtotals 145
Summarizing the Data with a PivotTable 146
Displaying Relative Values 148
Automatically Highlighting Certain Data 149
Customizing Conditional Formatting 150
The Anatomy of a Chart 151
Charting Your Data 152
Formatting a Chart 154
Customizing a Chart 156
Reviewing the Data 158

Creating a PowerPoint Presentation 159

What's Where in PowerPoint? 160
Creating a Presentation 162
Inserting a Table 164
Converting Text into a SmartArt Graphic 165
Converting Text into WordArt 166
Including a Slide from Another Presentation 167
Inserting Multimedia 168

Formatting a Slide 170
Animating Items on a Slide 172
Customizing Your Animation 174
Adding an Action to a Slide 175
Editing a Presentation 176
Repeating Content on Every Slide 178
Adding Transition Effects to Slides 179
Modifying the Default Layout 180
Creating a Photo Album 182

10   Presenting a PowerPoint Slide Show   183

Adding Speaker Notes 184
Printing Handouts 186
The Perils of Presentation 187
Running a Slide Show 188
Running a Slide Show with Dual Monitors 190
Customizing the Presentation 191
Recording a Narration 192
Timing a Presentation 193
Creating Different Versions of a Slide Show 194
Creating a Show for Distribution 195
Taking Your Show on the Road 196
Using Navigation Buttons 197
Creating Pictures of Your Slides 198
Reviewing a Presentation 199
Changing Slide-Show Settings 200

11   Working with Messages in Outlook   201

What's Where in Outlook Messages? 202
Sending E-Mail 204

Receiving and Reading E-Mail 206
Replying to and Forwarding a Message 207
Sending or Receiving a File 208
Formatting E-Mail Messages 210
Managing Messages 212
Signing Your E-Mail 214
Setting Up RSS Subscriptions 215
Reading RSS Items 215
Setting Up E-Mail Accounts 216
E-Mailing Your Schedule 218
Understanding E-Mail Encryption 220

12 Organizing with Outlook 221

What's Where in Outlook? 222
Keeping Track of Your Schedule 224
Sharing Calendars 226
Viewing Your Group's Schedule 228
Scheduling a Meeting 230
Managing Your Contacts 232
Keeping Track of Your Tasks 234
Assigning Tasks 236
Tacking Up Notes 237
Creating and E-Mailing Contact Business Cards 238
Customizing Outlook 240

13 Creating a Publication in Publisher 241

What's Where in Publisher? 242
Creating a Publication from a Design 243
Creating a Publication from Scratch 244

Adding Text. 245
Flowing Text Among Text Boxes 246
Tweaking Your Text 248
Adding a Table. 249
Repeating Objects on Every Page 250
Modifying a Picture. 251
Formatting an Object 252
Adding a Design Object 253
Arranging Objects on the Page 254
Stacking and Grouping Objects. 256
Flowing Text Around an Object 257
Reusing Content. 258
Inserting Your Business Information 259
Creating a Web Site in Publisher. 260
Double-Checking Your Publication. 262
Sending a Publication as E-Mail 263
Printing Your Publication 264

14 Working in Access   265

What's Where in Access? 266
What is a Relational Database? 268
Using an Existing Database 269
Creating a Database from a Template 270
Adding a Table to a Database 272
Modifying a Table 273
Adding Data to a Table. 274
Access File Formats 275
Importing Data. 276
Exporting Data. 278
Defining Relationships Among Tables 279

Creating a Form...280
Creating a Report from the Data...282
Extracting Information from a Database (Queries)................................284
Analyzing Data with a PivotChart..286
Collecting Data Using E-Mail..288
Customizing Access..290

15 Exchanging Information Among Office Programs 291

Inserting Excel Data into a Document, Publication, or Presentation..............292
Inserting an Excel Chart into a Document, Publication, or Presentation 294
Analyzing a Word Table in Excel..295
Using Word to Prepare PowerPoint Text 296
Preparing PowerPoint Handouts in Word 297
Inserting a PowerPoint Slide Show into a Document, Worksheet, or Publication..298
Using Publisher to Present a Word Document 299
Using Word to Prepare Publisher Text 300
Using Word to Present Access Data 301
Analyzing Access Data in Excel 302
Adding Excel Data to an Access Database......................................303
Using Access Data in a Mail Merge...304
Using Your Contacts List in a Mail Merge 305
Creating PDF or XPS Documents..306
Creating an Image of Your Work..308
Viewing and Annotating a Scanned Image or a Fax 309
Converting a Scanned Document into Text.....................................310
Scanning a Document..311
Managing and Editing Your Pictures 312
Linking to a File or to a Web Page 313
Managing Pictures, Videos, and Sound Files...................................314

16 Customizing and Securing Office   **315**

Customizing the Quick Access Toolbar 316
Customizing the Window 318
Customizing Your Editing 320
Changing Your User Information 321
Customizing the Spelling and Grammar Checkers 322
Customizing Your Spelling Dictionaries 323
Changing the Location and Type of Saved Files 324
Safeguarding a Document 325
Protecting a Document, Workbook, or Presentation with a Password 326
Signing a Document or Workbook with a Visible Signature 328
Signing a Document, Workbook, or Presentation with a Digital Certificate 330
Controlling Macros, Add-Ins, and ActiveX Controls 331
Downloading Add-Ins and Other Free Software 332
Adding or Removing Office Components 333
Checking the Compatibility 334
Fixing Office 335

Index 337

Acknowledgments

This book is the result of the combined efforts of a team of skilled professionals whose work we trust and admire and whose friendship we value highly. Kari Fera and Kat Marriner, our talented typographers, proved to us once again that they're the best in the business. They collaborated graciously on this, our 15th book, refining and producing the graphics, laying out the complex design, and wrestling with problems ranging from limited space to logical arrangement of numbered steps. We sincerely appreciate their excellent work. Our dear friend Alice Copp Smith has helped us improve every one of the books we've written. Alice does so much more than proofread and copyedit: Her gentle and witty chiding on countless yellow sticky notes makes us groan (and laugh) but teaches us to write better and, always, to get rid of those danglers! And we are fortunate indeed to be able to work with indexer *par excellence* Jan Wright, whose index reveals in microcosm the soul of the book. We thank this dedicated and hardworking team for their exceptional work and their unwavering good humor in the face of grueling deadlines.

We also thank Jim Boyce and Beth Sheresh for writing the Outlook sections, and Curt Frye for writing the Access section. Thanks also to the other people who worked on these three sections: Joell Smith-Borne (technical editor/copyeditor/proofreader); Kelly Henthorne (copyeditor/proofreader); Chris Pichereau (technical editor); and, especially, Debbie Berman (compositor/layout artist), who helped greatly with the coordination and integration of these sections.

At Microsoft Press we thank Lucinda Rowley and Juliana Aldous Atkinson for asking us to write this book, and we thank Kathleen Atkins for her valuable insight and helpful suggestions. Thanks also to Jim Kramer, Sandra Haynes, Victoria Thulman, Bill Teel, and Sally Stickney.

We also thank, in spirit, Oscar Tschirky, longtime *maître d'hôtel* at The Waldorf (now The Waldorf-Astoria) in New York City, whose book *The Cook Book by "Oscar" of The Waldorf*, first published in 1896, is a family heirloom and the source of the sample text in many of our screen shots.

On the home front, we thank our beautiful grandchild, Zuzu, for love, laughter, and many hours of Monopoly, at which she routinely beats both of us and winds up with more money than the bank.

Last but not least, we thank each other—for everything.

1

About This Book

In this section:

- No Computerspeak!
- A Quick Overview
- What's New in Office 2007?
- A Few Assumptions
- A Final Word (or Two)

If you want to get the most from your computer and your software with the least amount of time and effort—and who doesn't?—this book is for you. You'll find *2007 Microsoft Office System Plain & Simple* to be a straightforward, easy-to-read reference tool. With the premise that your computer should work for you, not you for it, this book's purpose is to help you get your work done quickly and efficiently so that you can get away from the computer and live your life.

No Computerspeak!

Let's face it—when there's a task you don't know how to do but you need to get it done in a hurry, or when you're stuck in the middle of a task and can't figure out what to do next, there's nothing more frustrating than having to read page after page of technical background material. You want the information you need—nothing more, nothing less—and you want it now! *And* it should be easy to find and understand.

That's what this book is about. It's written in plain English, with no technical jargon and no computerspeak. No single task in the book takes more than two pages. Just look up the task in the index or the table of contents, turn to the page, and there's the information you need, laid out in an illustrated step-by-step format. You don't get bogged down by the whys and wherefores: Just follow the steps and get your work done with a minimum of hassle. Occasionally you might have to turn to another page if the procedure you're working on is accompanied by a *See Also*. That's because there's a lot of overlap among tasks, and we didn't want to keep repeating ourselves. We've scattered some useful *Tips* here and there, pointed out some features that are new in this version of Office, and thrown in a *Try This* or a *Caution* once in a while. By and large, however, we've tried to remain true to the heart and soul of the book, which is that the information you need should be available to you at a glance and it should be *plain and simple!*

Useful Tasks...

Whether you use the programs in Microsoft Office for work, school, personal correspondence, or some of each, we've tried to pack this book with procedures for everything we could think of that you might want to do, from the simplest tasks to some of the more esoteric ones.

...And the Easiest Way to Do Them

Another thing we've tried to do in this book is to find and document the easiest way to accomplish a task. The Office programs often provide a multitude of methods for achieving a single end result—and that can be daunting or delightful, depending on the way you like to work. If you tend to stick with one favorite and familiar approach, we think the methods described in this book are the way to go. If you like trying out alternative techniques, go ahead! The intuitiveness of Microsoft Office invites exploration, and you're likely to discover ways of doing things that you think are easier or that you like better than ours. If you do, that's great! It's exactly what the developers of Office 2007 had in mind when they provided so many alternatives.

A Quick Overview

First, we're assuming that Office 2007 is already installed on your computer. If it isn't, Windows makes installation so simple that you won't need our help anyway. We're also assuming that you're interested in the most popular of the Office programs: Word, Excel, PowerPoint, Outlook, Access, and Publisher. Some of the other programs that are part of the Office 2007 suite—Microsoft OneNote, for example—are so intuitive that you're unlikely to need any guidance; you'll just jump right in and start using them. Others, such as Microsoft Project, are complex enough that you'll want to find a specialized book devoted to that program.

Next, you don't have to read this book in any particular order. It's designed so that you can jump in, get the information you need, and then close the book and keep it near your computer until the next time you need it. But that doesn't mean we scattered the information about with wild abandon. We've organized the book into some sections that deal with the individual programs in Office, and some that show you how to use the programs together. If you're new to Office or if you're stymied by the Ribbon, we recommend that you first read sections 2 and 3, "Working in Office" and "Common Tasks in Office," for an introduction to the ways in which the programs look and work alike. Try out the step-by-step procedures that are common to most of the programs: working with the Ribbon; using dialog boxes, menus, and toolbars; saving, copying, and moving content; working with pictures and diagrams; doing some research; and getting help if you need it. Regardless of which program you're working in, you'll find that the tasks you want to accomplish are always arranged in two levels. The overall type of task you're looking for is under a main heading such as "Inserting a Picture" or "Formatting a Worksheet." Then, under each of those headings, the smaller tasks within each main task are arranged in a loose progression from the simplest to the more complex.

OK, so what's where in this book? As we said, sections 2 and 3 cover the basic tasks—and a few slightly more complex ones—that are common to all the Office 2007 programs.

Sections 4, 5, and 6 are dedicated to Microsoft Office Word 2007, and they'll take you step by step through the basics to some of the more complex tasks. If you're new to Word, section 4 is where you'll learn how to create different types of documents; edit your text; use Word's find-and-replace feature to take care of document-wide changes; correct your spelling and grammar; add page numbers to your documents, and so on. In section 5, you'll move on to some slightly more complex tasks: using the Track Changes feature to mark changes in your documents; reading and accepting or rejecting the changes made to a document you've sent out to be reviewed; formatting text, lists, and tables; creating a layout, and dividing a long document into sections or chapters; working with running heads; and wrapping text around a graphic. Section 6 takes you well beyond the basics and focuses on designing and formatting your documents, using themes, styles, and fonts to create letters, memos, and other types of frequently used documents. You'll see how simple it is to create and design a sophisticated cover page, and add sidebars, pull quotes, and watermarks to liven up a document. If your work involves technical or scholarly documents, you'll learn how to number headings and lines, create footnotes or endnotes, insert citations, and create a table of contents. And, if you need to send a bunch of letters to a large group of people, Word's mail merge feature is the way to go.

Sections 7 and 8 are about Microsoft Office Excel 2007. Section 7 introduces you to the program and covers the basics to get you started: the column/row/cell composition of the worksheets and workbooks; entering, editing, and replacing data; formatting numbers and cells; adding and deleting columns and rows; formatting and organizing your worksheets; and setting up and printing your worksheets. In section 8, which is about analyzing and presenting your data, we'll cover some of Excel's more complex features. You'll learn about *cell notation* and *functions,* and create a *PivotTable* that will help you examine the relationships among your data. We'll discuss filtering the data to display only the items you want to work with; using the *AutoFill* feature to create a series of calculations; sorting your data, and more. And, if you'll be presenting your data at a meeting or in a report, we'll show you how to turn your boring old worksheets into snazzy, professional-looking charts that hold your audience's interest and make the results of the data immediately understandable to everyone.

Sections 9 and 10 are about Microsoft Office PowerPoint 2007, an immensely popular slide-presentation program. Section 9 introduces you to the various components of the program—its views, tabs, buttons, working area, and so on—and then takes you through the creation of your presentation. You'll choose among ready-made themes and layouts and learn how to add tables, SmartArt graphics, WordArt, and multimedia items—videos and sounds—to your slides. And, of course, if you're not satisfied with the themes and layouts just as they come, you can create your own designs. Section 10 takes you to the next level: the presentation of your slide show. You might have seen (or even given) a slide show that turned out to be a complete disaster. Everything went wrong, and both the presenter and the audience were mightily embarrassed. That won't happen again—PowerPoint and Windows Vista provide easy-to-use tools to ensure that your show will run smoothly. In this section, you'll learn how to create and print speaker notes and handouts; rehearse and time your show to fit into a specific time slot; run the show from a projector or from dual monitors; and, if your work involves traveling, take your presentation on the road.

Sections 11 and 12 cover Microsoft Office Outlook 2007, Office's e-mail program. (These two sections were written by Jim Boyce and Beth Sheresh, who graciously brought their knowledge and expertise to our book.) Section 11 walks you through the basics: creating and sending e-mail messages;

reading the e-mail messages you receive; replying to those messages and/or forwarding them to someone else; attaching a file to a message you're sending; and opening the *attachments* you receive. You can indicate which messages you've read and which are unread, and you can set up as many other e-mail accounts as you want. Section 12 takes a look at Outlook's other useful features, including the Calendar and the Contacts folder. You can use the Calendar to schedule your business or personal appointments on an hourly, daily, weekly, or monthly basis; and, if you're using Outlook with Exchange Server, you can schedule meetings and even reserve a meeting room. Your Contacts folder stores the names and e-mail addresses of your contacts, with as much or as little other information as you want to include—telephone numbers, home or work addresses, and so on. You can also create customized electronic business cards that you can exchange via e-mail with your business partners.

Section 13 walks you through the creation of various publications in Microsoft Office Publisher 2007. Publisher is a page-layout program that provides a vast array of well-designed, ready-made publications such as newsletters, reports, business cards, brochures, award certificates, banners, menus, résumés, and so on. You select the type of publication you want, choose a design, and then insert your own text, pictures, and other items. If you have the time and you're feeling creative, you can, of course, modify any of the existing designs or create your own and save them for reuse.

Section 14 concentrates on Microsoft Office Access 2007—a relational database program. (This section of the book was written by Curt Frye, who was kind enough to lend his in-depth knowledge of the program to our book.) If you need to understand and work with a database program, this is a good place to start. You'll find basic information about databases, tables, and forms; and you'll learn how to add data to tables, add tables to a database, extract information from your database, analyze the data with a PivotChart, and define relationships among tables.

Section 15 discusses the *interoperability* of all the Office programs—that is, their ability to work together to enhance each other's performance. Let's say you're preparing a PowerPoint slide show. You'll find it easiest to write and format your text in Word and then send the completed text to PowerPoint. You can insert a PowerPoint slide show into a Word document, and you can have Excel analyze the data in a Word table. These are just a few of the many other ways in which you'll find that using certain Office programs together can often achieve better results than using one program alone.

Section 16 is about customizing and securing Office. You can customize just about anything in all the Office programs—the Quick Access toolbar, the window, the status bar, your user information, the spelling and grammar checkers, and more. We'll also talk about an extremely important topic: your computer's security. We'll discuss all the precautions you can and should take to protect your files and guard against the bad stuff we all know is out there in cyberspace We'll show you how to add or remove Office components and how to run some easy-to-use automatic diagnostics should you encounter any problems with your Office programs and your computer.

What's New in Office 2007?

Much of Microsoft Office 2007 has been built on an entirely new structure, and you'll find that some of its features look different from those of earlier versions and work quite a bit differently too. The first conspicuously new feature you'll encounter when you start Word, Excel, PowerPoint, and Access, or create a new message in the Outlook Editor, will undoubtedly be the *Ribbon*. And where are the menus and toolbars? That's the beauty of the Ribbon. No longer do you have to wander through the maze of menus, submenus, and toolbars searching for what you want—they're all right there, in plain sight, at a glance. On the Ribbon are all the commands, styles, and resources you need, arranged on task-oriented tabs. Click the Page Layout tab to see the tools and resources you need to lay out your document's pages. Click the Insert tab to insert something into your file—how simple, and how sensible! The one and only menu remaining from earlier versions of the programs is the Office menu—hidden until you click the big, round Office button—which gives you access to most of your file-management commands. The one remaining toolbar is the Quick Access toolbar, where you can place your most frequently used commands and resources for easy access, regardless of which tab of the Ribbon is active.

Another aspect of replacing the menus was the development of the *galleries*. These are the graphical equivalents of drop-down menus, except that they show you samples of all the choices that are available for you to "try on." There are many different galleries—for styles, for themes, for page numbers, and so on. The galleries provide you with the ability to look before you leap, so to speak. With *Live Preview*, you can see how the formatting you choose will change your text, pictures, or other content; or how the overall look of your document will change when you switch the theme simply by pointing to the different items in the galleries.

So what else is new in these programs other than the entire interface? Plenty! Some of the biggest changes you'll encounter are the new file types. Word, Excel, PowerPoint, and Access use a whole new file structure that, unfortunately, isn't directly compatible with earlier versions of these programs. Of course, you can open and use files from earlier versions, but people who are using any earlier version of Word, Excel, or PowerPoint will need to download and install a converter so that they can open the files you create using the Office 2007 file format. However, the good news is that the new file format is what enables many of the improvements in these Office 2007 programs.

Word, Excel, PowerPoint, and the Outlook Editor also include an entirely new graphics tool, *SmartArt graphics,* designed to help you create diagrams and lists that not only present your information graphically but take the finished product to a new level of professionalism. However, even if you don't use SmartArt graphics, you'll find that the formatting and special effects you can apply so easily to shapes, text boxes, and pictures can produce some amazing results. And it's not only all the new stuff that expands your capabilities; some existing features have been greatly enhanced too. In Word and PowerPoint, and in the Outlook Editor, the ability to check your spelling has become much more accurate and comprehensive. Now you can check the contextual use of words: for example, should it be "to" or "too," "there" or "their"? You get the picture. If you're involved in mathematics, science, or engineering, you'll appreciate the enhanced Equations feature, which not only supplies some predesigned equations that you can edit but also makes it easy to create your own equations and save them for future use.

In Outlook and Publisher—two of the programs that don't use the Ribbon—you'll find some changes that are less dramatic than those in the Ribbon-based programs but that substantially improve the programs nevertheless. In Outlook, for example, you'll see the new To-Do Bar that helps you keep track of your appointments and tasks but stays out of the way when you don't need it. In Publisher, creating attractive publications is easier than ever with the simple switching of designs and easy-to-apply layouts. A really useful addition to Publisher is the Content Library, where you can keep all sorts of content that you can use over and over again.

Despite the differences among the programs that we've pointed out, what all the 2007 Office programs have in common is greatly improved file safety and security. You'll be better able to control access to your files—for example, you can indicate when a file is completed and specify that no further changes may be made to it. You can easily check for and remove any sensitive or personal information in your files that you don't want other people to have access to. You can digitally sign a file to provide verification in the electronic file that it really *was* you who signed it. With Office's improved file-recovery system, your files are now not only more secure from loss than ever before, but the new file system also assists you in being able to recover files if they've become corrupted. And, if you end up with any system problems involving the Office programs and your computer, you can easily run a series of diagnostics that can determine the problem and either fix it or get you the help you need to get it fixed.

The appearance of Office 2007 is extremely dynamic, so be aware that the look of the Ribbon will change depending on the screen resolution you're using. That is, with a high resolution, you'll see many more individual items on the Ribbon than you will if you're using a low resolution. With a low resolution, you'll find that items are contained under a button, and only when you click the button are the items then displayed. To see this effect, resize the width of a window in Word, Excel, PowerPoint, or in an Outlook message, and note that items are hidden when you decrease the size of the window and that they appear when you increase the size of the window. The programs in Office 2007 were designed using a screen resolution of 1024 by 768 pixels, so this is the resolution we've used in the graphics you'll see throughout this book.

A Few Assumptions

We had to make a few educated guesses about you, our audience, when we started writing this book. Perhaps your computer is solely for personal use—e-mail, the Internet, and so on. Or you might run a small business or work for a giant corporation. After taking these quite varied possibilities into account, we assumed that you'd be familiar with computer basics—the keyboard and your little friend the mouse, for example—and that you're connected to the Internet and/or a company intranet. We also assumed, if you're working on a corporate network, that you're familiar with the specialized and customized tools, such as a SharePoint site or a file-management system, that are being used on the network. We also assumed that you're using and that you're familiar with the basics of Windows Vista, and that you have the Aero glass appearance enabled. However, if you're running Microsoft Windows XP, you'll still be able to use this book, although you might find that the look and function of the windows and dialog boxes on your screen are a bit different from those shown in this book. Whichever version of Windows you're using, we'd like to recommend two other books we've written that you'll find helpful: *Windows Vista Plain & Simple* and *Microsoft Windows XP Plain & Simple—2nd Edition*.

A Final Word (or Two)

We had three goals in writing this book:

- Whatever you want to do, we want the book to help you get it done.
- We want the book to help you discover how to do things you *didn't* know you wanted to do.
- And, finally, if we've achieved the first two goals, we'll be well on the way to the third, which is for our book to help you *enjoy* using Office 2007. We think that's the best gift we could give you to thank you for buying our book.

We hope you'll have as much fun using *2007 Microsoft Office System Plain & Simple* as we've had writing it. The best way to learn is by *doing,* and that's how we hope you'll use this book.

2 Working in Office

In this section:

- What's What in Office?
- Dialog Box Decisions
- Using the Ribbon
- Using Menus and Toolbars
- Using Only the Keyboard
- Moving and Copying Content
- Getting Help
- Saving Your Work
- Office's File Formats

In this section of the book, we'll discuss the various programs in the 2007 Microsoft Office System—their similarities and differences, and the ways they work separately and together. Depending on which version of Office you're running, you might have some or all of the programs installed on your computer. All the Office programs have elements in common, but there are two big differences that you'll notice right away. Some programs use the new design, which features the *Ribbon* and the *command tabs* and does away with all the menus and toolbars except for one solitary menu and one lone toolbar. Other programs use the menu-based design that you're familiar with if you're an Office aficionado, and one program—Microsoft Outlook—uses a combination of both designs. We'll describe on a case-by-case basis the different ways in which each program works.

We'll take a quick look at the basics that are common to all the Office programs: dialog boxes that you use to choose among various options; shortcut menus that appear when you right-click an item; keyboard shortcuts that speed up your work; the Office Clipboard and the Windows Clipboard that you use to cut, copy, and move text from one place to another; the Help system; and, of course, the process of saving your work. You'll also find a listing of Office's many file formats.

What's What in Office?

Here's a listing of the most common programs in the 2007 Microsoft Office System, with a brief description of each program's purpose. Depending on which version of Office 2007 you have and whether you purchased any additional Office programs, you might have some or all of these programs installed on your computer. Take a look at the different designs for the programs. Microsoft Word, Excel, PowerPoint, and Access all use the new Ribbon design, with tabs to display the different tools for specific types of tasks. Microsoft Publisher and the Office Tools programs use the more traditional menu-based design. Microsoft Outlook is a hybrid—some of its parts use the traditional design and others use the Ribbon design. As you become familiar with the different designs, you'll find that it's easy to understand the way the programs work as you switch from one to another.

Microsoft Office 2007 Programs

Microsoft Office Access is a relational database program for storing, retrieving, and analyzing data.

Microsoft Office Excel is a worksheet program for organizing, analyzing, and graphing data.

Microsoft Office Outlook is an e-mail program and a great way to manage your contacts, tasks, and schedules.

Microsoft Office PowerPoint is a program for developing and presenting electronic slide shows with accompanying lecture notes and supporting printed handouts, to be shown on a computer screen, projected onto a screen, or displayed on the Web.

Microsoft Office Publisher is a desktop publishing program for intricate placement of text and graphics on the printed page or on the Web.

Microsoft Office Word is a powerful word processing program for doing everything from writing a letter to writing a novel to creating mass mailings.

Microsoft Office Tools are programs you can use in conjunction with the main Office programs:

- **Microsoft Clip Organizer** provides easy access to Clip Art and similar content.
- **Microsoft Office 2007 Language Settings** control the languages identified and used in your programs.
- **Microsoft Office Diagnostics** provides a suite of diagnostics to determine the source of problems when Office isn't performing correctly, and either fixes the problem or provides information so that you can figure out how to fix it.
- **Microsoft Office Picture Manager** organizes and creates quick access to your pictures.
- **Microsoft Office Document Imaging** and **Microsoft Office Document Scanning** scan and view documents and recognize text in scanned images and faxes.

Dialog Box Decisions

You'll be seeing a lot of *dialog boxes* as you work with your Office programs, and if you're not familiar with them now, you soon will be. Dialog boxes appear when a program, or Windows, needs you to make one or more decisions about what you want to do. Sometimes all you have to do is click a Yes, a No, or an OK button; at other times, there'll be quite a few decisions to make in one dialog box. The Print dialog

box, shown below, is typical of many dialog boxes and is one you'll probably be seeing frequently, so take a look at its components and the way they work. If you're using Windows Vista, you'll also be seeing windows that work like dialog boxes and some dialog boxes that work like windows. Whatever they're called, you use them to make your decisions and get on with your work.

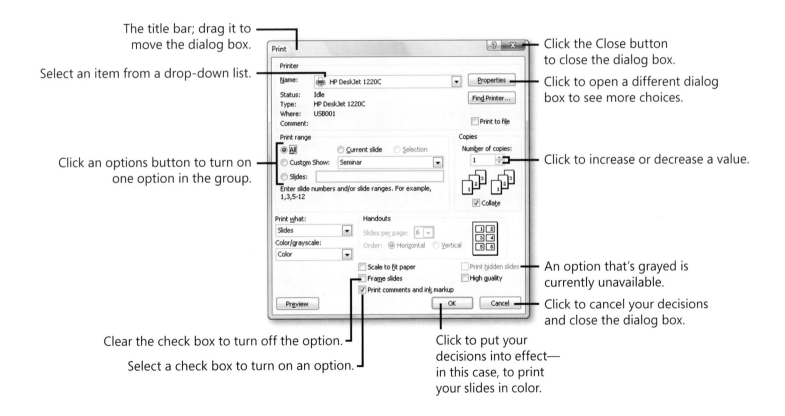

The title bar; drag it to move the dialog box.

Select an item from a drop-down list.

Click an options button to turn on one option in the group.

Clear the check box to turn off the option.

Select a check box to turn on an option.

Click the Close button to close the dialog box.

Click to open a different dialog box to see more choices.

Click to increase or decrease a value.

An option that's grayed is currently unavailable.

Click to cancel your decisions and close the dialog box.

Click to put your decisions into effect— in this case, to print your slides in color.

Using the Ribbon

Microsoft Word, Excel, PowerPoint, and Access, and some parts of Outlook, use the Ribbon and its different tabs instead of the standard menu structure to access the programs' commands and features. With the Ribbon, you can switch among the task-oriented tabs and see all the available options. Additionally, many items provide a live preview: You point to something on the Ribbon—a style or a font, for example—and see immediately how it affects the content of your document.

Explore the Ribbon

1. Open one of the programs that uses the Ribbon.

2. If you see the command tabs but no commands, click a command tab to display the Ribbon temporarily.

3. Do any of the following:
   - Click a button to execute a command.
   - Click a down arrow to open a gallery, a drop-down menu, or a drop-down list.
   - Point to an item in a gallery to see its effect on the content of your document.

4. Click another tab and explore those items.

5. Click the Office button to see the commands for opening, saving, printing, or otherwise managing your document.

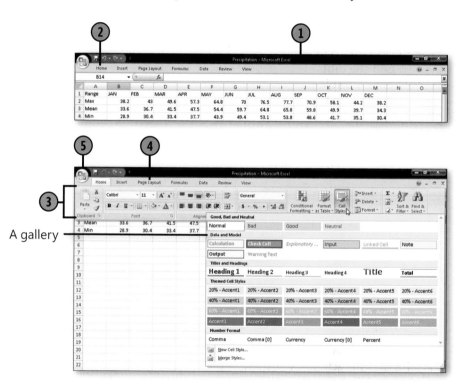

A gallery

Tip

The Ribbon is composed of tabs and commands. When the Ribbon is minimized, you see only the tabs.

Set the Ribbon Display

1 With the Ribbon displayed, click the down arrow at the right of the Quick Access toolbar, and, on the Customize Quick Access Toolbar menu, click Minimize The Ribbon.

2 When you want to display the Ribbon, click the tab you want to use, and the Ribbon will appear and will remain displayed until you click a command on the Ribbon or click in your document.

3 To have the Ribbon constantly displayed, click the down arrow at the right of the Quick Access toolbar, and click Minimize The Ribbon again.

Try This!

With the Ribbon in its displayed state, double-click the active tab to minimize the Ribbon, and then click any tab to display the Ribbon temporarily. Click in your document to minimize the Ribbon again. Double-click the active tab to have the Ribbon always displayed. Press Ctrl+F1 to hide the Ribbon, and press Ctrl+F1 again to have the Ribbon always displayed.

1

2
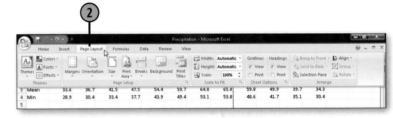

3

Using Menus and Toolbars

If menus are gateways to the power of your programs, toolbars are shortcuts to the most frequently used features that you access from the menus. Stored within the menus are *keyboard shortcuts* that speed up your work. And there are even special context-sensitive *shortcut menus* that pop up right in the middle of your work when you right-click the mouse button. To make your work quick and easy in Publisher and in parts of Outlook, the menus and toolbars all use the same basic structure, with customizations for each program.

Explore the Menus

① In an Office program that uses the standard menu structure, click to open the File menu.

② Click a command that has a right-pointing arrow to see the contents of the submenu.

③ Click a menu name to open another menu, and take a look at the items listed. The icon at the left of a menu item is the toolbar button you can use to execute that command. The text at the right of the command is the keyboard shortcut for the command.

④ Continue exploring the different menus in this and other Office programs.

⑤ To execute any command, click it.

⑥ To close a menu without executing a command, click outside the menu.

Tip

To open a menu without using the mouse, press and release the Alt key, and then press the underlined letter in the menu name. Then, to execute a command, press the underlined letter in the command name.

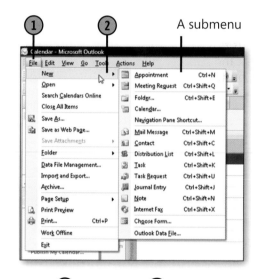

A submenu

Use the Toolbars

① Point to a button on the toolbar and wait for a ScreenTip, showing the button's name, to appear. Click the button to execute that action.

② If a button looks "pressed," click it again if you want to turn off that feature.

③ If the toolbar shares a single line with another toolbar and is truncated—that is, part of it isn't visible—click the right-pointing arrows to display the hidden buttons.

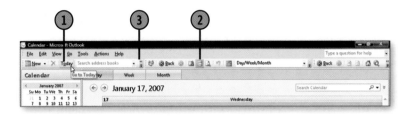

See Also

"Customizing the Quick Access Toolbar" on pages 316–317 for information about modifying the Quick Access toolbar in Word, Excel, PowerPoint, and Access, and in the Outlook Editor.

Use the Shortcut Menus

① Right-click any content or location in your program where you want to execute an action.

② Choose the action you want from the context-sensitive shortcut menu that appears.

Tip ✓

Items that are grayed on menus or toolbars are items that aren't available at the moment. For example, if you haven't copied anything, the Paste button is grayed because there's nothing to paste.

Using Only the Keyboard

If you prefer to keep your hands on the keyboard instead of using the mouse, you can do almost everything using Office and program-specific keyboard shortcuts. By activating the command tabs and the Ribbon, you can use the displayed keys to navigate and to execute commands and activities. There are also many keyboard shortcuts you can use to execute some of the most common commands and activities.

Browse the Ribbon with Your Keyboard

① Press and release the Alt key to display the KeyTips for access to the tabs and the Ribbon.

② Type the letter for the tab you want. You can also type the letter for any item on the Quick Access toolbar or to open the Office menu.

③ Type the letter or the keyboard shortcut to access the item you want on the Ribbon. If a gallery or a drop-down menu appears, use the arrow keys to select the item you want, and then press Enter.

④ If you want to access items on the status bar, press the F6 key until an item on the status bar becomes selected. Use the arrow keys to select items on the status bar, and press Enter to execute your choice.

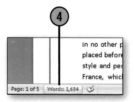

Tip

If you decide you don't want to execute an action after you've pressed the Alt key, press the Esc key to return to your work.

Use Keyboard Shortcuts

① Use the keyboard shortcuts shown in the table at the right to execute the action you want. Not all shortcuts are appropriate for all programs all the time.

② If you want to switch from mouse methods to keyboard methods, point to the button or other item you want to work with, and note the keyboard shortcut in the ScreenTip. Then use that keyboard shortcut.

③ If you don't see the keyboard shortcut you want in the table or in a ScreenTip, search Help for "keyboard shortcuts."

See Also

"Getting Help" on page 18 for information about using Office's Help system.

Common Keyboard Shortcuts

Action	Keyboard shortcut
Copy and delete (cut) selected content	Ctrl+X
Copy selected content	Ctrl+C
Paste content	Ctrl+V
Hide or minimize Ribbon	Ctrl+F1
Apply/remove bold formatting	Ctrl+B
Apply/remove italic formatting	Ctrl+I
Apply/remove underline formatting	Ctrl+U
Align paragraph left	Ctrl+L
Align paragraph center	Ctrl+E
Align paragraph right	Ctrl+R
Add/remove space before paragraph	Ctrl+0 (zero)
Apply double line spacing	Ctrl+2
Apply single line spacing	Ctrl+1
Apply Normal style	Ctrl+Shift+N
Apply Heading 1 style	Alt+Shift+1
Apply Heading 2 style	Alt+Shift+2
Apply Heading 3 style	Alt+Shift+3
Change case	Shift+F3
Undo last action	Ctrl+Z
Redo last action	Ctrl+Y
Open shortcut menu	Shift+F10
Check spelling	F7
Save document	Ctrl+S
Save As	F12
Print (show Print dialog box)	Ctrl+P
Open Help	F1

Moving and Copying Content

Office programs, and most other programs, use a tool called the *Clipboard* as a temporary holding area for content that you want to move or copy to another part of your document, to another document in the same program, or to a document in another program. You simply park your text on the Clipboard and then, when you're ready, you retrieve it and "paste" it into its new location. Office programs use two different Clipboards: the Windows Clipboard, which stores the item most recently cut or copied; and the Office Clipboard, which can store as many as 24 different items, including the most recently cut or copied item. You'll probably use the Paste button (or press Ctrl+V) when you're pasting the last item you cut or copied, and the Windows Clipboard when you want to move several different pieces of text from one place to another.

Cut or Copy Text

① Select the text you want to cut or copy.

② Do either of the following:

- Click the Cut button (or press Ctrl+X) to delete the selected text and store it on the Clipboard.

- Click the Copy button (or press Ctrl+C) to keep the selected text where it is and place a copy on the Clipboard.

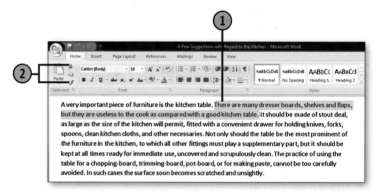

See Also

"Customizing Your Editing" on page 320 for information about modifying the default settings for the way items are cut and pasted in your document, and to display the Paste Options button.

Tip

You can use both the Windows Clipboard and the Office Clipboard to store items other than text, including pictures, tables, and even data from Microsoft Excel worksheets.

Tip

Although the Windows Clipboard is limited to storing only one item at a time, you can use it to transfer information among many different programs. The Office Clipboard works only with Office programs.

Paste the Cut or Copied Text

1 Click in your document where you want to insert the text.

2 Click the Paste button (or press Ctrl+V).

3 If the inserted text looks strange because it doesn't match the look (that is, the formatting) of the surrounding text, click the Paste Options button that appears and, from the menu, choose to match the destination formatting.

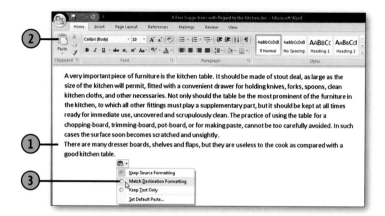

Copy and Paste Multiple Items

1 In Word, Excel, PowerPoint, or Access, click the Clipboard button on the Home tab. In Publisher or Outlook, choose Office Clipboard from the Edit menu. In a new Outlook message, click the Office Clipboard on the Message tab. Select and cut or copy the items you want to copy to one or more different locations in your document, or in any other Office document.

2 If necessary, switch to the document into which you want to paste some or all of the items you cut or copied. Click where you want to insert one of the items.

3 Click the item to be inserted. Continue inserting, cutting, and copying text as necessary.

4 To paste all the items you copied into one location, click Paste All.

5 Click Clear All when you no longer need any of the copied items and want to empty the Clipboard to collect and store new items.

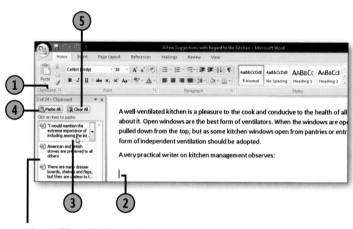

The Office Clipboard

Getting Help

Nothing can replace this book, of course, but Office does provide you with other resources to help solve problems you might encounter. We're using Word Help here to illustrate the ways you can get help in all your Office programs.

Browse for Help

1. In your program, press the F1 key to display the Help window for that program.

2. Click a category to expand the list.

3. Click an appropriate topic, and then click an article that seems relevant to your question.

4. If the font size is too small or too large, click the Change Font Size button, and choose a font size from the menu.

5. To print the topic, click the Print button.

6. To return to either the list or the articles, click the Back button. To return to the list of categories, click the Back button again.

Search for Help

1. Type your Search text.

2. If you want to specify which Help resources you want, click the Search down arrow, and then click the resource.

3. Click Search.

4. Click a search result that seems relevant. If there's more than one page of results, click the Next button at the top of the search results to see any additional pages.

5. Close the window when you've finished.

Go back and forth between topics you've already opened.

Click to keep window on top.

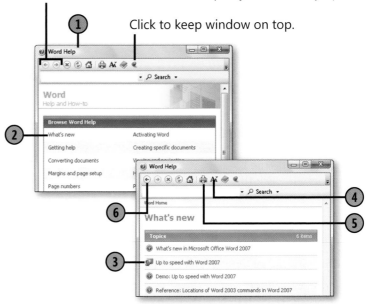

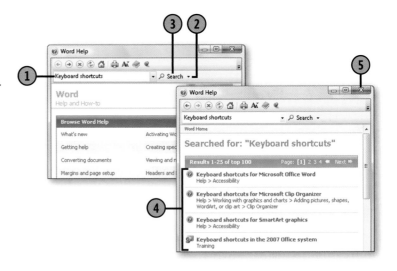

Saving Your Work

While you're working on your document, you'll want to save it frequently to make sure that it's preserved for posterity—or at least until you've completed it, printed it, or sent it off for someone to read or comment on. After you've named and saved the file, the Save As dialog box won't appear for subsequent saves.

Save the File

① In Word, Excel, and PowerPoint, click the Save button on the Quick Access toolbar. In Publisher, click the Save button on the Standard toolbar. In Access, the file is saved automatically when you create it; click the Save button to save individual items, such as a new table.

② Type a name for the file in the File Name box if you don't want the name that the program proposes. File names can be as long as 250 characters and can include spaces, but you can't use the \ / * ? < > and | characters.

③ If you'll always want to save the file to your default location, click Hide Folders.

④ If you don't want to save the file in the suggested format, select the format you want.

⑤ Select this check box (if it's available) if you want to see a preview of the file in a folder window.

⑥ Click Save.

⑦ Work on the file, saving your work frequently by clicking the Save button or pressing the keyboard shortcut Ctrl+S.

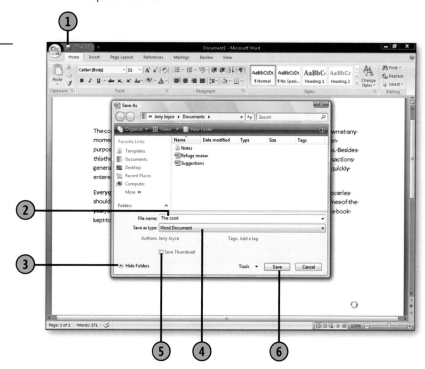

Tip

If you're running Windows XP instead of Windows Vista, the Save As dialog box looks different from the one shown here but functions in a similar way.

Office's File Formats

Microsoft Word, Excel, PowerPoint, and Access use some file formats that are different from those of previous versions, but whether or not to use them is your choice. If you decide not to use the new formats, however, be aware that you won't be able to use some of the programs' very cool new features. Review the descriptions of the formats used in Word, Excel, and PowerPoint to see which formats work best for you. To see the list of all available formats, choose Save As from the Office menu, and, in the Save As dialog box, scroll through the Save As Type list. To see a description of the Access file format choices, see "Access File Formats" on page 275.

- **Document, Workbook, or Presentation:** This is the new format that enables all of the programs' new features. Files in this format can't be opened in earlier versions of their respective programs unless you've downloaded and installed a special translating filter program. The new format has the standard file extension with an added "x" (for example, .docx, .xlsx, .pptx).

- **Macro-Enabled Document, Workbook, or Presentation:** This is the same format as the Document, Workbook, or Presentation format, except that it contains macros.

- **XML Document or Presentation:** This is a plain Text file that includes all the text and the XML coding. This format is used primarily in a corporate setting where transforms are created to extract and/or reformat information that will be stored for reuse.

- **Word, Excel, or PowerPoint Template:** This new form of template also enables the new features of the program.

- **Word, Excel, or PowerPoint Macro-Enabled Template:** This is the same format as the Template format, except that it can contain macros.

Other File Formats for Office Programs

- **Word, Excel, or PowerPoint 97–2003 format**: This is the binary file format used in previous versions of these programs. Although it provides compatibility with earlier versions, saving in this format disables some of the advanced features of the 2007 programs.

- **Word, Excel, or PowerPoint 97–2003 Template:** This is the binary file format for templates used in previous versions of Word.

- **Single File Web Page:** This format creates a Web page and stores all the graphics in the same file.

- **Web Page:** This format creates a standard HTML-format Web page whose graphics are stored in a separate folder.

- **Rich Text Format:** This is a binary file that contains the text and formatting information but little else. It provides compatibility with many programs.

- **Plain Text:** This text file contains only the text of the document and no formatting.

And There's More

Many Office programs have their own special formats. Excel has a new Binary Workbook format that enables the new features and is optimized to speed your work. Word has a Web Page Filtered format that creates a standard HTML-format Web page but deletes Word-specific information that isn't needed to display the Web page. In PowerPoint, you can save the file as a PowerPoint show, with or without macros. In most cases, however, you'll probably want to use the default 2007 file formats.

3

Common Tasks in Office

In this section:

- Working with Old Documents
- Inserting Special Characters
- Inserting Pictures
- Changing the Size of a Picture
- Editing a Picture
- Adding Shapes
- Adding Clip Art
- Formatting a Shape
- Inserting the Date and Time
- Creating Stylized Text
- Inserting a Relational Diagram
- Researching a Subject

In this section of the book, we'll cover some of the step-by-step procedures that are common among most of the programs in the 2007 Microsoft Office System. Even though there are some differences among the programs that use the Ribbon and those that don't, you'll still find that most features work in similar ways, whether you're adding special characters, such as accented letters in other languages, or currency or mathematical symbols; or pictures, such as photographs and drawings. After you've placed your pictures, you can edit them, crop them, add special effects, and so on. You can put text inside an assortment of shapes to create pull quotes, advertising blurbs, and other interesting effects; and, using the alchemy of WordArt, you can transmute words into wonderfully colorful three-dimensional art.

You can have your Office program insert the date and/or time that you created your document or presentation; you can describe your topics visually using Office's new diagramming system; and you can use Office's built-in research feature to look up definitions of words or get information about just about anything simply by clicking a word or a name.

As varied as these tasks are, most of them work in just about the same way as each other—and if there are any significant differences, we'll point them out as we go along.

Working with Old Documents

When you open a file that was created in an earlier version of Microsoft Office Word, Excel, PowerPoint, or Access, you're working in Compatibility mode, which means that some of the new features of your program won't be available. To use these features, you'll need to convert the file to the program's 2007 format.

Convert the Document

1 With your Office 97–2003 format file open, choose Convert from the Office menu.

2 If you see a dialog box asking you whether you want to convert the file, click OK. The original file won't be overwritten because its file extension is different from that of the updated file.

3 Work on the file, using all the features of your program.

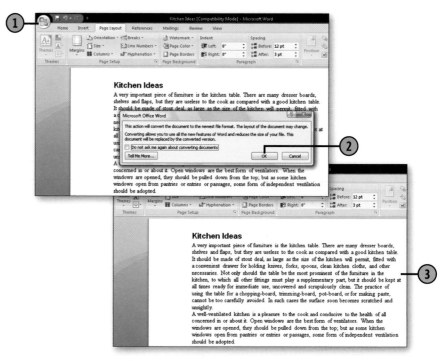

Tip

If you need to send an upgraded file to someone who has an earlier version of the Office program but doesn't have the Office Compatibility pack, point to the arrow at the right of the Save As command on the Office menu, and choose the Office program's 97–2003 Format from the gallery that appears. You might lose some advanced features in your file, but at least the other person will be able to read it.

Inserting Special Characters

With at least 101 keys at your fingertips, you'd think that every character you could possibly need would be available on your keyboard. But what about the accented characters in other languages? Different currency symbols? Mathematical symbols? You'd need a keyboard with thousands of keys!

As you can see in the illustrations, Microsoft Word, Excel, PowerPoint, Publisher, and the Outlook Editor all provide a huge assortment of symbols and special characters, as well as several ways to insert them into your documents.

Insert a Character

1. On the Insert tab, with the insertion point located where you want to insert the symbol into your document, click the Symbol button. In Publisher, choose Symbol from the Insert menu. In Excel, PowerPoint, and Publisher, skip to step 4.

2. In Word and Outlook, in the Symbol gallery that appears, click the character you want if it's displayed, or click More Symbols to display the Symbol dialog box.

3. If the symbol you want is displayed, select it, and then skip to step 7.

4. Click Normal Text to insert a character from the font you're currently using, or click a specific font. Click one of the symbol fonts for nonstandard characters.

5. Select the character's category if it's displayed.

6. Click the character you want to use.

7. Click Insert. To add more characters, click in your document to activate it, click where you want to insert each special character, and then select and insert the character.

8. To insert a typographic character or a special mark, click the Special Characters tab, and double-click the character you want to insert. Click Close after you've inserted the special characters and symbols you want.

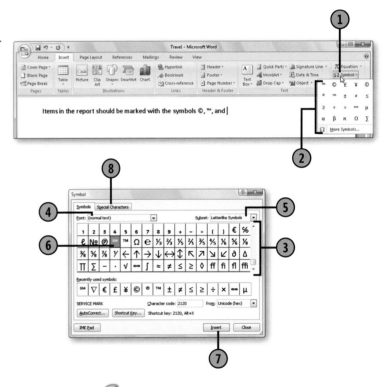

Tip

The Symbol dialog box in Word and Outlook has extra features that let you assign a keyboard shortcut to the symbol and add it to the program's AutoCorrect list.

Inserting Pictures

In Word, Excel, PowerPoint, Publisher, and the Outlook Editor, you can add different types of picture files to a single document—photographs and drawings, for example— provided the pictures are in one of the many different file formats that can be used. Once you've added the picture file, you can add effects and can even edit the picture.

Insert a Picture

(1) Click in your document where you want to insert the picture.

(2) On the Insert tab, click the Picture button to display the Insert Picture window. In Publisher, point to Picture on the Insert menu and choose From File from the submenu that appears.

(3) Navigate to the folder that contains the picture you want, and select the picture file from the list.

(4) Do either of the following:

- Click Insert to place the picture in your document.

- Click the down arrow at the right of the Insert button, and choose to link to the file only or to insert and link to the file.

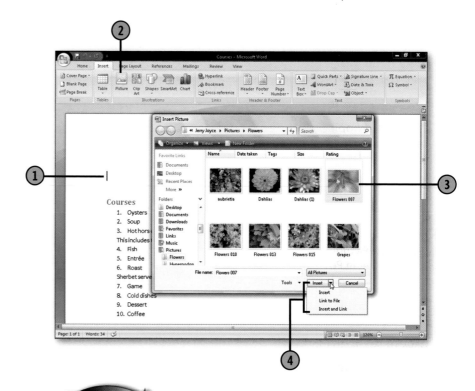

Tip

If you link to the picture, the image in your document will be updated if the picture is updated. Linking without inserting the entire file can substantially reduce the file's size.

See Also

"Managing and Editing Your Pictures" on page 312 for information about organizing and editing your picture files using the Microsoft Office Picture Manager, and "Managing Pictures, Videos, and Sound Files" on page 314 for information about including your pictures in the ClipArt collections.

Changing the Size of a Picture

Your inserted picture doesn't always look exactly right—the subject might be too far to one side, or the picture might be too big or too small in proportion to the page. You can easily fix both problems: You can crop the picture to keep only the content you want, and you can decrease or increase the size of the picture.

Trim It

1. Click to select the picture if it isn't already selected and to activate the Picture Tools Format tab.

2. On the Picture Tools Format tab, click the Crop button.

3. Place the cropping mouse cursor over a Cropping handle, and drag the sides, top, or bottom of the picture to crop off the parts you don't want.

4. Click the Crop button again to turn off cropping.

See Also

"Modifying a Picture" on page 251 for information about editing pictures in Publisher.

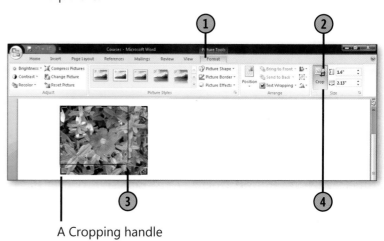

A Cropping handle

Size It

1. Click to select the picture if it isn't already selected.

2. Drag a Sizing handle on the picture to modify the size of the picture.

Tip

When you drag a Sizing handle, your picture can become distorted. To change its size but keep its original aspect, adjust the picture's size in the Size section of the Picture Tools Format tab.

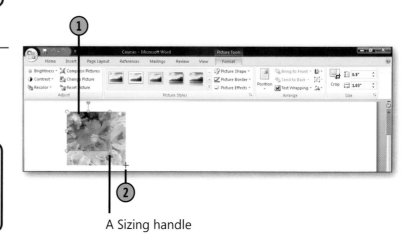

A Sizing handle

Editing a Picture

After you've placed a picture in your document, workbook, presentation, or mail message, you can make substantial changes and add many different effects to the picture to make it look exactly the way you want.

Change Its Appearance

1. Click to select the picture if it isn't already selected, and click the Picture Tools Format tab if it isn't already displayed.

2. Click the Brightness, Contrast, and Recolor buttons in turn, and drag your mouse through each gallery that appears to see how the settings affect the picture. Click the settings to produce the effects you want.

See Also

"Modifying a Picture" on page 251 for information about editing a picture in Publisher.

Rotate It

1. Click to select the picture if it isn't already selected.

2. Drag the Rotation handle to rotate the picture.

Tip

When you edit a picture, you're editing only the copy of it that you've inserted into your document. If you want to change the original picture file, you'll need to edit it in a separate program—for example, in the Windows Photo Gallery that comes with Windows Vista.

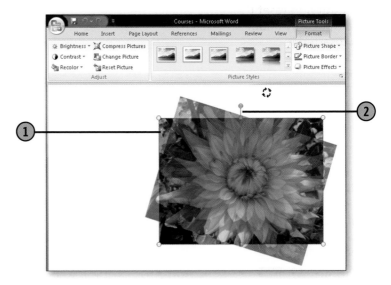

Add an Effect

① Move your mouse though the different styles in the Picture Styles section of the Ribbon to see how your picture looks when you apply that style, and then click the style you want.

② Click the Picture Border button, and move your mouse through the gallery to see the effects of a different picture-border color, weight, or pattern. Click any effects you want.

③ Click Picture Effects to add or change the 3-D rotation, shadow, reflection, glow, or soft edges.

④ If, after all that hard work, you don't like the result, click the Reset Picture button to reset the entire picture to the way it looked when you first inserted it.

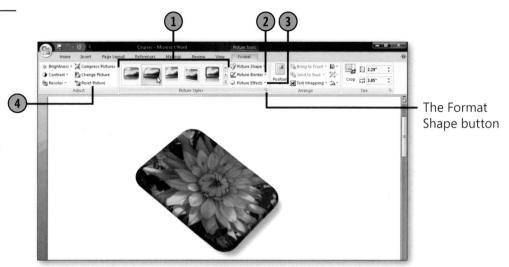

The Format Shape button

Adding Shapes

Shapes are drawing objects that you can manipulate in many ways to create unusual and eye-catching effects. You can also use shapes as containers for text, which allows you to create callouts, pull quotes, advertising blurbs, and so on, producing all sorts of interestingly shaped special effects. Shapes are available in Word, Excel, PowerPoint, and Publisher, and in the Outlook Editor.

Draw a Shape

① Click in your document where you want to insert the shape. On the Insert tab, click Shapes, and click the shape you want in the gallery that appears. In Publisher, click AutoShapes on the Objects toolbar, point to a type of shape, and then choose the shape you want from the submenu that appears.

② Hold down the left mouse button, and drag out the shape.

③ Adjust the shape by dragging

- The Sizing handles to change the size of the drawing.

- The Adjustment handle to reshape the drawing.

- The Rotation handle to rotate the drawing.

④ Drag the shape to place it where you want it.

⑤ In any of the programs except Publisher, use the tools on the Drawing Tools Format tab to customize the appearance of the shape.

> **See Also**
>
> "Formatting a Shape" on page 30 for information about modifying the appearance of a shape.
>
> "Formatting an Object" on page 252 for information about formatting an AutoShape in Publisher.

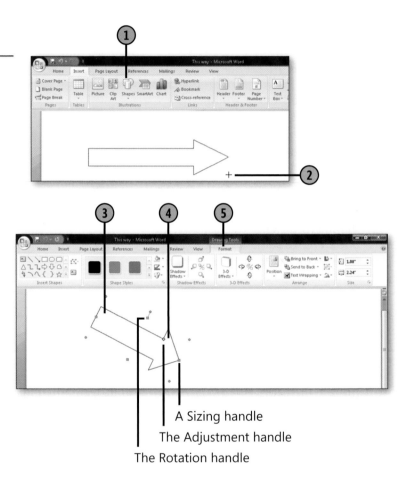

A Sizing handle

The Adjustment handle

The Rotation handle

Adding Clip Art

When you're looking for just the right piece of clip art to illustrate a story, an article, or a presentation, you can hunt through different categories or conduct a search using keywords. When you add a picture to a document, the picture becomes part of the document.

Find and Insert Clip Art

① Click in your document where you want to place the clip art.

② On the Insert tab, click the Clip Art button. In Publisher, point to Pictures on the Insert menu, and choose Clip Art from the submenu.

③ In the Clip Art pane, type a keyword or keywords to describe the type of picture you want.

④ In the list, click the clip-art collection you want. To select only certain categories, expand the list under the collection, and select the check box for each category you want to look through.

⑤ Specify the type of clip you want.

⑥ Click Go to view the items that match your criteria.

⑦ Click to insert the picture into your document. Add any other clip art you want, and close the Clip Art pane when you've finished.

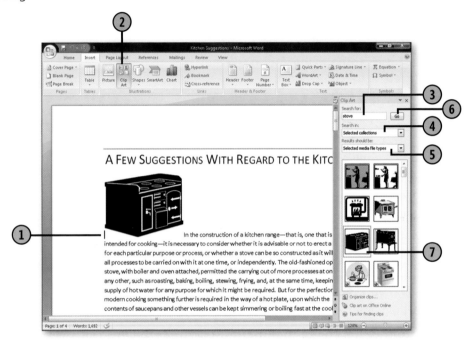

See Also

"Managing Pictures, Videos, and Sound Files" on page 314 for information about customizing the content of the Clip Art collections.

Formatting a Shape

Shapes are useful tools for illustrating your content. However, in Word, Excel, PowerPoint, and in the Outlook Editor, you can often add extra impact to a document by creating a formatted shape rather than using a plain black-and-white-outlined shape.

Format the Shape

(1) Click to select the shape if it isn't already selected.

(2) Point to different shape styles, and click the style you want.

(3) Click the Shape Fill button if you want to customize the color of the fill.

(4) Click the Shape Outline button if you want to customize the color, thickness, and style of the outline.

(5) Use the Shadow or 3-D Effects galleries to add any special effects you want.

(6) If you want to add text to the shape, click the Edit Text button to insert a text box, and then enter your text. Note, however, that all the Callouts shapes automatically contain a text box.

(7) To add special effects, such as a fill pattern, a fill transparency, or arrow styles, adjust the properties of the text box; or, for other advanced customizations, click the More button to open the Shape Styles gallery, and click Advanced Tools to display the Format AutoShape dialog box.

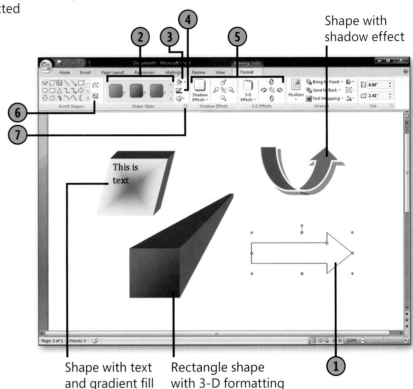

Shape with shadow effect

This is text

Shape with text and gradient fill

Rectangle shape with 3-D formatting

See Also

"Formatting an Object" on page 252 for information about formatting an AutoShape in Publisher.

Inserting the Date and Time

If you want to indicate the date and/or time that you created your document or presentation, or if you want the current date and/or time shown, you can have Word, PowerPoint, Publisher, or the Outlook Editor insert either or both for you.

Insert the Date and/or Time

(1) Click in the document where you want the date and/or time to appear.

(2) On the Insert tab, click the Date & Time button to Display the Date And Time dialog box. In Publisher, choose Date And Time from the Insert menu to display the dialog box.

(3) Select the format you want and the information to be included.

(4) Specify the language you want to use if it isn't your default language. If the selected language supports more than one type of calendar, select the calendar you want to use.

(5) Select this check box to have the date and/or time updated each time you open, save, or print the document. Clear the check box if you want the original date and/or time to be displayed.

(6) Click OK.

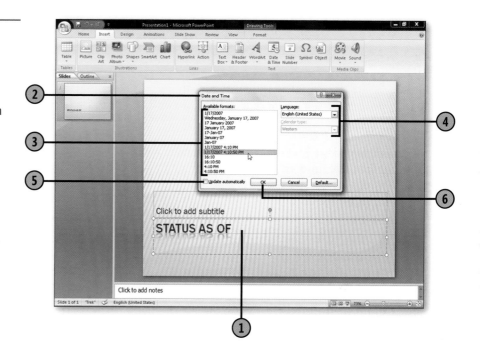

Tip ✔
The date and/or time are often placed in a document as part of the running head. Use the header and/or footer features that are unique to each program to insert the date and/or time in the running head.

Tip ✔
The Date And Time dialog box is slightly different in each individual program. For example, the Calendar list isn't available in Word or Outlook unless a language with more than one calendar appears. Also, for no apparent reason, the location of the Update Automatically check box is moved around in the different programs.

Creating Stylized Text

You can achieve some spectacular effects by creating text as art in Word, Excel, PowerPoint, and Publisher, and in the Outlook Editor. WordArt lets you twist your text into weird and wonderful shapes and three-dimensional configurations, and then inserts the result into your document as an object.

Although the way you work with WordArt is a bit different in some of the Office programs, the main method and the end results are similar. The steps in the procedure below walk you through the process of creating WordArt in Word and in the Outlook Editor.

Create Some WordArt

1. On the Insert tab, click the WordArt button to display the WordArt gallery.

2. Click the WordArt style you want.

3. In the Edit WordArt Text dialog box, specify a font, a font size, and any character emphasis you want. The same formatting will apply to all the text in this piece of WordArt.

4. Type your text. Note that WordArt text doesn't wrap automatically; you have to press Enter to start a new line. (To transform existing text into WordArt, select the text before you click the WordArt button.)

5. Click OK.

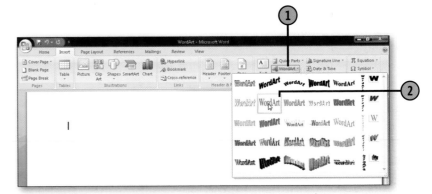

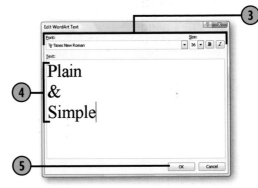

Try This!

Create some WordArt, select it, and then use the tools on the WordArt Tools Format tab to change the shape, character spacing and height, and text alignment. Use the WordArt Styles gallery to apply a three-dimensional effect. Use the 3-D Effects tools to change the color, depth, direction, lighting, surface type, and 3-D angle. Amazing, isn't it? And so much fun!

See Also

"Formatting a Chart" on pages 154–155 for information about using WordArt in Excel and PowerPoint.

Fine-Tune the Result

① Click to select the WordArt if it isn't already selected, and use the Sizing handles to change the size of the WordArt.

② If you want to arrange the WordArt in relationship to your text, on the WordArt Tools Format tab, click Text Wrapping, and specify the way you want the text to wrap around the WordArt.

③ Point to different WordArt styles, and click the style you want.

④ Use the text tools to edit the WordArt text, modify the letter spacing, and change the text orientation and alignment.

⑤ Use the Shape Fill or the Shape Outline button to customize the color of the fill effects or the outline thickness.

⑥ Click the Change Shape button, and select the type of shape you want the text arranged in.

⑦ Add any shadow or 3-D effects.

⑧ Use the Rotation and Adjustment handles if you want to modify the angle or shape.

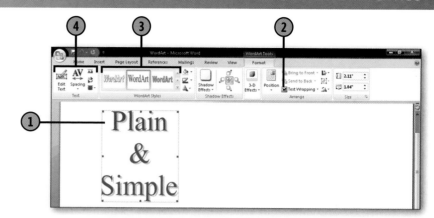

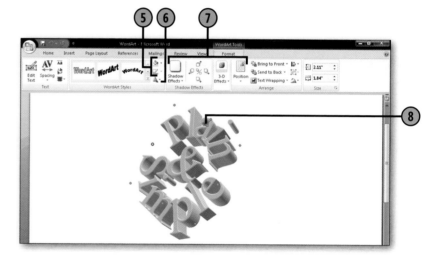

Tip

To change the colors of dual-colored or multicolored WordArt, on the WordArt Tools Format tab, click the Shape Fill button, point to Gradient on the drop-down menu, click More Gradients, and modify the colors on the Gradient tab of the Fill Effects dialog box.

Tip

The steps you take to create WordArt in Publisher are similar to those on this page, except that you insert the WordArt from the Objects toolbar and use the WordArt toolbar to adjust the style and formatting.

Inserting a Relational Diagram

The new diagramming system in Word, Excel, and PowerPoint, and in the Outlook Editor, provides a great opportunity for you to describe your topic visually, whether your diagram illustrates the command structure at your workplace, the flow diagram of a project, or the interrelationship among different activities. After you've inserted a diagram, you'll find that it's extremely customizable.

Create a Diagram

1. On the Insert tab, click the SmartArt button to display the Choose A SmartArt Graphic dialog box.

2. Select the type of diagram you want.

3. Click a diagram type, and review the information about that diagram.

4. Click OK to create the diagram type you want.

5. Click the first item in the Text pane, and type the text for that item.

6. Continue entering text, doing any of the following:

   - Press the Tab key to make the entry a subentry of the previous item (or click Demote), or Press Shift+Tab to elevate the entry one level (or click Promote).

   - Press Enter to finish the current item and insert a new line for text.

   - Press the Down arrow key to move to the next item.

   - Press Delete to remove entries you don't want.

Click here if the
Text pane isn't
displayed.

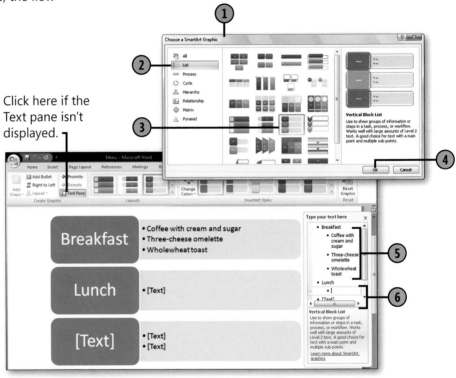

Tip

You must use the new file formats to create SmartArt graphics. When you save a document that contains SmartArt in the 97–2003 file format, the SmartArt is converted into a picture that you can't modify.

Modify the Diagram

1. On the SmartArt Tools Design tab, point to different layouts and click the one that works best for your content.

2. Point to the different Quick Styles and click the one you want.

3. Click an item in the diagram to select it.

4. On the SmartArt Tools Format tab, point to the different Shape Styles, and click the one you want.

5. Click the Shape Fill, Shape Outline, and Shape Effects buttons to modify the fill color, modify the outline color and style, or add special effects, such as a shadow or a glow.

6. Point to different WordArt Styles to see how the text in the shape is affected. Click a style you like if you want to use WordArt.

7. Drag a selected shape to move it into a new location, or use a Sizing or a Rotation handle to change the dimensions or rotation of the diagram.

8. Click the frame of the diagram, and use a Sizing handle to change the diagram's size.

See Also

"Converting Text Into WordArt" on page 166 for information about converting text into a SmartArt graphic in PowerPoint.

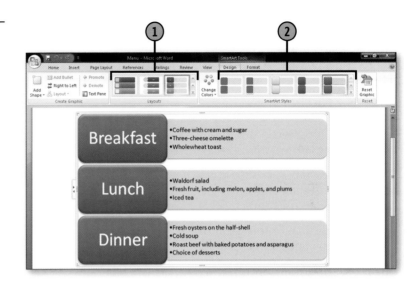

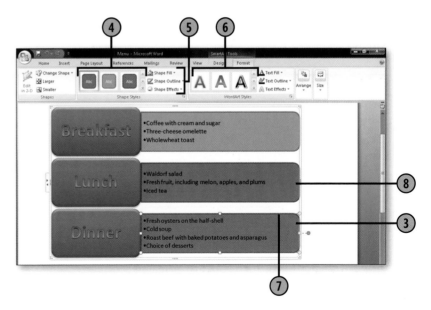

Researching a Subject

Wouldn't it be great to look up the definition of a word directly from your computer? Or to get information about something simply by clicking a word or a name? Well, you can do this in Word, Excel, PowerPoint, and Publisher, and in the Outlook Editor, by using the built-in research feature and access to the Internet.

Do Some Research

① Click a word (or select a group of words) that you want information about.

② On the Review tab, click the Research button. In Publisher, choose Research from the Tools menu.

③ Select the resource or the types of resources you want to use.

④ Review the results.

⑤ If you want to look up something more, type the word or words, and press Enter.

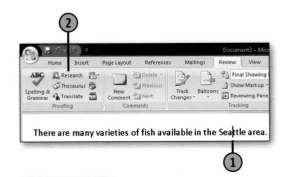

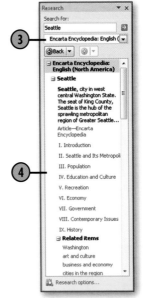

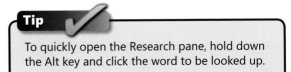

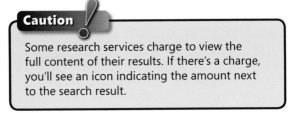

Tip

To quickly open the Research pane, hold down the Alt key and click the word to be looked up.

Caution

Some research services charge to view the full content of their results. If there's a charge, you'll see an icon indicating the amount next to the search result.

Viewing and Editing Text in Word

In this section:

- What's Where in Word 2007?
- Creating a New Document
- Composing Different Types of Documents
- Word's Views
- Reading a Document
- Editing Text
- Finding and Replacing Text
- Correcting Your Spelling and Grammar
- Correcting Text Automatically
- Adding Page Numbers
- Marking and Reviewing Changes in a Document
- Comparing Documents Side by Side

The new design of Microsoft Office Word 2007 makes creating professional-looking documents faster and easier than ever. If you're new to Word, the logical layout of its tools and the ease of finding just what you need for the job at hand will quickly make you feel like an expert. If you're a longtime user, you'll probably say, as we did, *"Why didn't they think of this before?"*

In this section, we'll introduce that new interface and cover the basic skills you'll use every day: creating different kinds of documents using Word's templates; editing, copying, and moving text, and adding page numbers; correcting your spelling and grammar; and using Word's Track Changes feature to mark document revisions. If you're not familiar with Word, step through the first few tasks and see just how easily you can produce great-looking documents. If you're already a Word aficionado, you'll quickly see how the new design eliminates that all-too-familiar "Now *which* menu was that command on?" Hallelujah! No more digging through menu after menu looking for that elusive command.

Turn the page for a short visual tour of Word's new interface. Then jump right in! If you get stuck in some way, you'll find the answers to most of your questions in other sections of this book, or in Word's Help system.

What's Where in Word 2007?

Microsoft Word 2007 has many faces and can be customized in countless ways. The pictures on these two pages show some of the common features you'll see when you're working in Word, and they also introduce just a few of the customizations you can use. We've identified many of the screen elements for you, but it's a good idea to explore Word's interface while you're looking at these two pages. For example, click each of the tabs and familiarize yourself with what's on the different parts of the Ribbon. If you're not sure what the buttons are used for, point to one of them. In a moment or two, you'll see a *ToolTip* that tells you the button's name and gives you a pretty good idea of that particular tool's function.

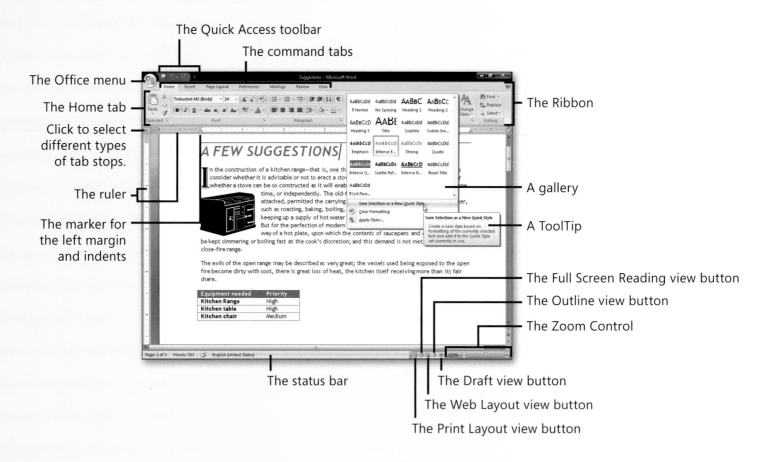

The Quick Access toolbar

The command tabs

The Office menu

The Home tab

Click to select different types of tab stops.

The ruler

The marker for the left margin and indents

The Ribbon

A gallery

A ToolTip

The Full Screen Reading view button

The Outline view button

The Zoom Control

The Draft view button

The status bar

The Web Layout view button

The Print Layout view button

The picture below shows more of Word's new interface. As you experiment with it, you'll find that Word has different tabs for different tasks, toolbars that you can customize, items that appear exactly when you need them for the job you're doing right that minute, and many more features that you'll discover as you work in Word.

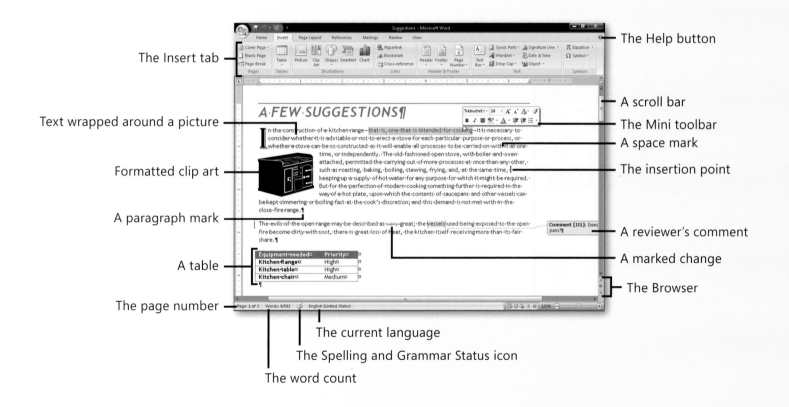

The Insert tab

Text wrapped around a picture

Formatted clip art

A paragraph mark

A table

The page number

The word count

The Spelling and Grammar Status icon

The current language

The Help button

A scroll bar

The Mini toolbar

A space mark

The insertion point

A reviewer's comment

A marked change

The Browser

Creating a New Document

You can start Word in several different ways, depending on how it was installed, but the tried-and-true method is to choose Microsoft Word from the Windows Start menu. When Word starts, it automatically opens a new blank document for you. If you've been experimenting and Word is already running, you can open a new blank document with a few mouse-clicks.

Start Word and Enter Some Text

1. If Word is already running and you've entered some text, choose New from the Office menu to display the New Document dialog box, and double-click Blank Document to create a new blank document. If Word isn't running, start it from the Windows Start menu.

2. To show paragraph marks and other formatting marks such as spaces and tabs, on the Home tab, click the Show/Hide ¶ button. Click the button again if you want to hide the marks.

3. Type your text. When you reach the end of a line, continue typing. Word automatically moves, or *wraps*, your words onto the next line.

4. Press Enter to start a new paragraph.

5. Click Save on the Quick Access toolbar, enter a name for the file, and click Save. To quickly save the document while you're working, press Ctrl+S.

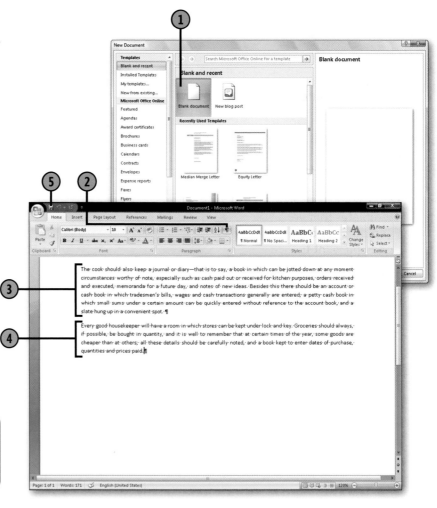

Tip

To better see the formatting marks, as well as your text, use the Zoom Control at the bottom of the window to increase the magnification, as shown here.

Composing Different Types of Documents

You can use templates to quickly create all kinds of documents. Word 2007 comes with numerous templates, and you can download many more. When you start a new document based on a template, the document contains its own design elements, and the template's predefined styles ensure that all your paragraphs work harmoniously together. Templates are completely customizable and can come from a variety of sources, so you're likely to encounter substantial differences both in design and in ways to complete a document that's based on a template.

Start the Document

1. Choose New from the Office menu to display the New Document dialog box.

2. If you see the template you want, select it to preview it, and then click Create.

3. If you don't see the template you want, do any of the following:

   • Click Installed Templates to see the Microsoft templates that you've either installed on your computer or downloaded, and double-click the one you want to use.

   • Click My Templates to display the New dialog box and your custom templates. Double-click a template to create a document.

   • Click a topic to see templates of that type that are available for download, and double-click the one you want to use.

   • Click New From Existing to open an existing document as a template.

4. In the new document that appears, replace any placeholder text with your own text, and add any other elements you want.

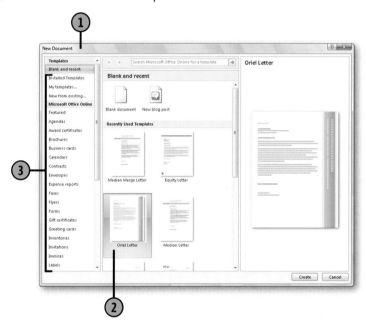

Word's Views

Word gives you several ways to view your document as you work on it, and you'll find that your efficiency increases and your work becomes easier when you use the optimal view for the task at hand. You can use either the View tab on the Ribbon or any of the five view buttons at the bottom-left of the window to change your view.

Print Layout View

The standard working view for print documents, Print Layout view shows you how your document will look when it's printed—the page and line breaks, the placement of pictures, the way text wraps around pictures or other items, the arrangement of columns, the distance of the text from the edge of the page, and so on.

Full Screen Reading View

Full Screen Reading view makes it easy to read documents on your screen. The text is laid out in long vertical pages (or screens), just like those you see in most books. If you increase the size of the text for better readability, the content simply flows from one screen to the next. To maximize the area of the screen that's available for the document's content, the elements you normally see in the other views—the tabs, the Ribbon, and the status bar, for example—are no longer visible.

Web Layout View

Web Layout view is exclusively for working with online documents as if they were Web pages. That is, all the elements are displayed, but font size, line length, and page length all adjust to fit the window, just as they do on many Web pages.

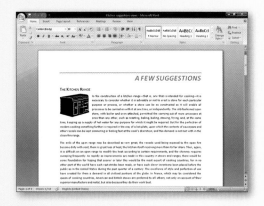

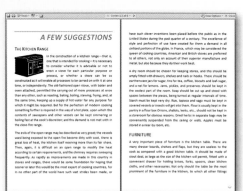

Although the six views shown on these two pages are the ones you'll probably use most often, there are other views and options that are useful in various circumstances: Thumbnails, Document Map, draft font, picture placeholders, and more.

You'll find information about many of these items elsewhere in this book, in the discussions of the tasks and procedures where their use is the most relevant.

Outline View

Outline view displays your document as an outline, with the paragraph formatting defining the levels of the outline. By default, Word's standard heading styles have corresponding outline levels—Heading 1 is level one, Heading 2 is level two, and so on—and other paragraph styles, such as Normal, are treated as regular text. You can use Outline view to organize your topics before you start writing, or you can use it to reorganize an existing document.

Draft View

Draft view is designed for speed of entry and editing. It's based on the commercial publishing technique of creating *galleys*. You place the text and other elements in one long, continuous column that flows from one page to the next, and you deal with the placement of elements after you've ironed out any content problems. (Draft view was called Normal view in earlier versions of Word.)

Print Preview

Print Preview is designed to show you just how your document will look when you print it. You can see a close-up view, one page at a time, or two or more pages at once. Use Print Preview to make sure your document's layout is exactly the way you want before you go ahead and print it. Unlike Word's other views, you switch to this view by pointing to Print on the Office menu and choosing Print Preview from the gallery that appears.

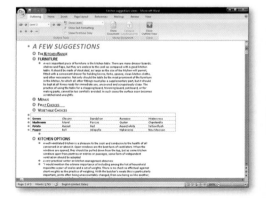

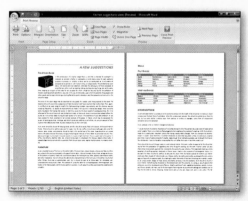

Reading a Document

To help you cut down on the amount of paper that piles up in the so-called "paperless office," Word's new Full Screen Reading view is designed to make it simple and pleasant to read documents without printing them. If you like it, that's great—you'll save some trees, as well as some clutter.

Read

1. If you're not already in Full Screen Reading view, click the Full Screen Reading button on the status bar to display your document for easy reading.

2. Move the mouse to the left or right edge of the screen until the cursor turns into a little hand. Click to move to the previous page or pair of pages (left edge) or to the next page or pair of pages (right edge).

3. Click the View Options button, and specify how you want to view the page or pages, whether you want to do some typing in the document, and whether you want tracked changes and comments to be shown.

4. Click the Page button to go to a specific page, location, or heading, or to display the Document Map or the Thumbnails pane.

5. When you've finished, press the Esc key or click the Close button to exit Full Screen Reading view.

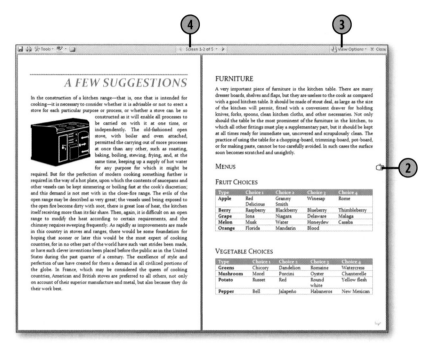

Tip

Word is set to display any Word attachments in your e-mail in Full Screen Reading view. If you prefer not to use this view, you can turn it off from the View Options gallery.

Editing Text

Whether you're creating a business letter, a financial report, or your master's thesis, it's a sure bet that you're going to need to go back into your document and do some editing.

Select and Modify Text

① Click at the beginning of the text you want to delete.

② Drag the mouse over all the text to select it, and then release the mouse button.

③ Press the Delete key. The selected text is deleted.

④ Select some text that you want to replace with new typing.

⑤ Type the new text. The selected text is automatically deleted and replaced by the new typing.

⑥ Click Save.

See Also

"So Many Ways to Do It" on page 52 for more information about different ways to select text.

Tip

If you prefer to type over text without selecting it, use Overtype mode. To turn it on, choose Word Options from the Office menu, and, in the Advanced section, select the Use The Insert Key To Control Overtype Mode option. Click OK, and then press the Insert key to turn on Overtype mode; press Insert again to turn off overtyping.

Word provides a great variety of ways to edit. To edit existing content, you simply select it and make your changes, or, if you prefer, you can type over some existing text to replace it.

A very important piece of furniture is the kitchen table. There are many dresser boards, shelves and flaps, but they are useless to the cook as compared with a good kitchen table. It should be made of stout deal, as large as the size of the kitchen will permit, fitted with a convenient drawer for holding knives, forks, spoons, clean kitchen cloths, and other necessaries.

A very important piece of furniture is the kitchen table. It should be made of stout deal, as large as the size of the kitchen will permit, fitted with a convenient drawer for holding knives, forks, spoons, clean kitchen cloths, and other necessaries.

A very important piece of furniture is the kitchen table. It should be made of stout deal, as large as the size of the kitchen will permit, fitted with a convenient drawer for holding knives, forks, spoons, clean kitchen cloths, and other necessaries.

⑤

A very important piece of furniture is the kitchen table. It should be made of pine planks, as large as the size of the kitchen will permit, fitted with a convenient drawer for holding knives, forks, spoons, clean kitchen cloths, and other necessaries.

Tip

If you accidentally delete some text, immediately click the Undo button on the Quick Access toolbar to restore the deleted text.

Finding Text

If you're not sure where to find some text in your document, Word can locate it for you. You can broaden the search so that Word finds similar words, or you can narrow the search to a designated part of the document or to text that uses specific formatting.

Find Text One Instance at a Time

1 On the Home tab, click Find (or press Ctrl+F) to display the Find And Replace dialog box.

2 Type the text you want to find.

3 Click Find Next. Continue to click Find Next as you move through the document, finding each instance of the text.

4 If you want to refine the search criteria, click the More button, and select your conditions.

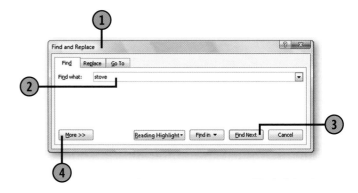

Tip

To limit the search to a specific part of a document, select that part of the document before you open the Find And Replace dialog box.

Find All Instances of Text

1 Do either of the following:

- Click Reading Highlight, and choose Highlight All from the drop-down menu if you want to highlight all the words that match the search. To remove highlighting from the text, click the Reading Highlight button again, and choose Clear Highlighting from the menu.

- Click Find In, and, on the drop-down menu, specify where to search to select all instances of the search text in that part of the document; then click Find Next.

2 Click Close when you've finished.

Replacing Text

When you need to replace a word or phrase with a different word or phrase in several places in your document, let Word do it for you. It's a great way to use Word's speed and power to make quick work of those tedious document-wide changes.

Replace Text

① On the Home tab, click the Replace button (or press Ctrl+H) to display the Find And Replace dialog box. Click the More button, if it's displayed, to show the full dialog box.

② Type the text you want to find.

③ To narrow the search, click Format, and specify the formatting of the text you're searching for.

④ To replace non-text items, click Special, and specify any element that's associated with the text.

⑤ Type the replacement text. Click the Format button to specify any formatting the replacement text should have. Use the Special button to specify a non-text element.

⑥ Click one of the following:

  • Replace to replace the found text and find the next instance of the search text

  • Replace All to replace all instances of the search text with the replacement text

  • Find Next to find the next instance of the search text without replacing it

⑦ Click Close when you've finished.

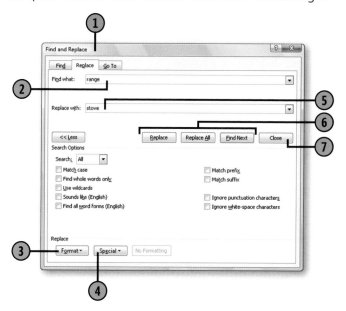

See Also

"Finding Text" on the facing page for information about broadening or narrowing a search.

Tip

If you used the Replace All button and the results aren't quite what you expected, click the Undo button on the Quick Access toolbar. You can then try the replacement again, this time with more specific search parameters.

Correcting Your Spelling and Grammar

You can avoid the embarrassment of distributing a document full of misspellings, incorrectly used words, or poor grammar even if you don't have a proofreader or an editor at your disposal. Word comes to the rescue by discreetly pointing out your spelling errors, word usage problems, and grammatical no-no's. When you see one of those helpful little squiggles under a word or phrase, you can choose what you want to do to correct the mistake—if it really is a mistake.

Correct a Spelling Error

(1) Right-click a red squiggle to see one or more suggestions for correcting the error.

(2) Click the suggestion you want to use.

(3) If you believe that what you have isn't an error but is something that Word doesn't recognize, click Ignore to have Word ignore this one instance; click Ignore All to have Word ignore the word throughout this document; or click Add To Dictionary to have Word ignore the word throughout all your documents.

Tip ✓

If Word didn't offer any suggestions when you right-clicked a squiggle, return to your document and try to correct the error yourself. If the squiggle remains, right-click it, and see whether there are any suggestions now.

Correct a Contextual Spelling Error

(1) Right-click a blue squiggle to see one or more suggestions for fixing improper word usage.

(2) Click the suggestion you want, or choose to ignore this error or this word throughout the document.

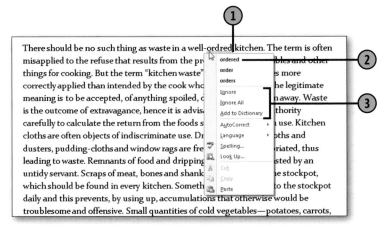

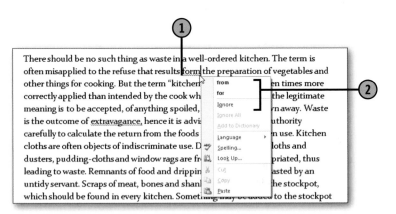

Correct the Grammar

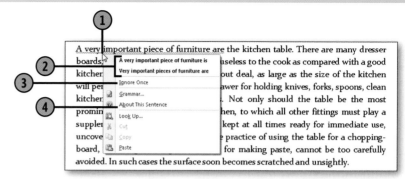

① Right-click a green squiggle.

② If the shortcut menu suggests alternative phrasing, click to use the alternative. If only a description of the problem is shown, click in the document and edit the text as suggested.

③ If you're sure your grammar is correct, click Ignore Once.

④ If you want to know why the text was marked, click About This Sentence for an explanation of the grammar rules involved.

Automatically Correct Your Misspellings

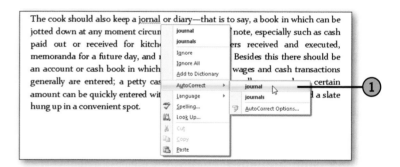

① Right-click one of your own common misspellings, point to AutoCorrect on the shortcut menu, and choose the correct spelling from the list of suggestions.

② Check your document, and observe that the correct spelling has replaced your misspelling.

③ Continue composing your document. Note that if the same misspelling occurs again, Word corrects it for you.

Tip

Word uses blue squiggles to mark formatting incon-sistencies as well as contextual spelling errors.

See Also

"Customizing the Spelling and Grammar Checkers" on page 322 for information about modifying the way Word checks your spelling and grammar, and "Customizing Your Spelling Dictionaries" on page 323 for information about using and editing custom dictionaries.

Correcting Text Automatically

Word provides an exceptionally useful feature called AutoCorrect that you can use to correct common misspellings of certain words. You can also customize the AutoCorrect feature to include your own common repetitive typing errors and misspellings, and you can make AutoCorrect work even harder for you by defining special AutoCorrect entries.

Add Entries

① Choose Word Options from the Office menu, select the Proofing category, and click the AutoCorrect Options button.

② On the AutoCorrect tab of the AutoCorrect dialog box, with the Replace Text As You Type check box selected, enter the abbreviated or misspelled text that you often type.

③ Type the text that you want to replace the incorrect or abbreviated text you typed.

④ Click Add.

⑤ Add any other entries you want. When you've finished, click OK, and then click OK again to close the Word Options dialog box.

⑥ In your Word document, type the text you entered in the Replace box, type a space, and make sure your corrected entry has been inserted.

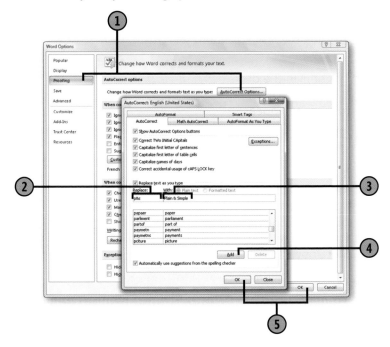

Tip

To modify the way the AutoCorrect feature works, open the AutoCorrect dialog box, and clear or select check boxes to specify what you want AutoCorrect to do.

Adding Page Numbers

It's a wise practice to add page numbers to any document that's more than a few pages long. We all know what a time-consuming hassle it is to try to put the unnumbered pages of a long document back in the right order after they've gone flying all over the place. Don't let this happen to you!

Insert Page Numbers

① On the Insert tab, click the Page Number button. On the drop-down menu, point to the location where you want the page number to appear.

② Click the page-numbering design you want in the gallery that appears.

③ If you want to change the numbering format or the way the pages are numbered in a multi-section document, click Page Number again, and choose Format Page Numbers from the menu that appears.

④ In the Page Number Format dialog box, select the numbering format you want.

⑤ If you have more than one section in your document, specify whether you want the page numbering to be continuous or to restart at the beginning of each section.

⑥ Click OK.

⑦ If you don't like the way the page number looks or where it's positioned, click Page Number, choose Remove Page Numbers, and then choose a different numbering format.

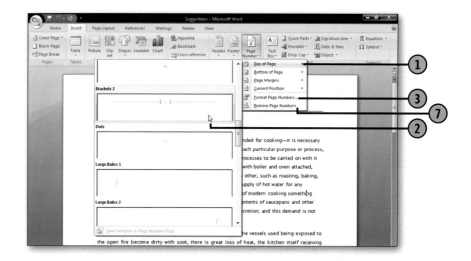

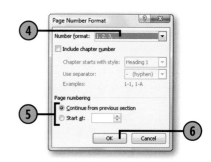

See Also

"Setting the Overall Look" on page 59 for information about changing the appearance of the page numbers by changing the theme.

"Creating a Running Head" on page 84 for information about incorporating page numbers with other information.

So Many Ways to Do It

Word offers you a variety of ways to do most things. You might, for example, be able to use a button, a menu item, a keyboard shortcut, a task pane, or a mouse-click to accomplish the same result. Why are there so many choices? Well, one reason is that we all work differently. Given several choices, we usually do some experimenting, find the way that works best for us and that we're most comfortable with, and then stick with it. Another reason is that certain methods work best in certain situations.

You can accomplish two frequently used procedures—selecting text and moving or copying it—using quite a few different methods, some of which might cause you a bit of difficulty if you use them in the wrong situation. The tips we offer here will help you choose which method to use in which circumstances.

Try these common methods of selecting text to see which work best for you. Of course, there are other ways to select text, and, depending on whether and how you've customized Word, some selection methods might work a bit differently from those described here. For information about customizing Word, see "Customizing Your Editing" on page 320.

Text-Selection Methods

To select	Use this method
Characters in a word	Drag the mouse over the characters.
A word	Double-click the word.
Several words	Drag the mouse over the words.
A sentence	Hold down the Ctrl key and click anywhere in the sentence.
A line of text	Move the pointer to the far left of the window, and click when you see a right-pointing arrow.
A paragraph	Move the pointer to the far left of the window, and double-click when you see a right-pointing arrow.
A long passage	Click at the beginning of the passage, and then hold down the Shift key and click at the end of the passage.
Noncontiguous blocks of text	Drag the mouse to select the first block. Hold down the Ctrl key and drag the mouse to select the second block.
A vertical block of text	Click at the top-left corner of the text block. Hold down the Alt key and drag the mouse over the text block.
The entire document	Press Ctrl+A.

After you've selected the text, your next step might be to move it or copy it. Again, some methods are better than others, depending on the situation.

The process of moving or copying contents uses different tools, depending on what you want to do. When you use the F2 key or the Shift+F2 key combination, the selected material is stored in Word's short-term memory, where it's remembered only until you paste it into another location or execute any other Word activity.

The Cut and Copy buttons on the Clipboard store the selected material on the Office Clipboard, from where you can retrieve the information once or numerous times. The Office Clipboard stores up to 24 items, which you can retrieve one at a time or all at once. For more information about the Office Clipboard, see "Moving and Copying Content" on pages 16–17.

If these seem like an overwhelming number of ways to accomplish the same tasks, get ready for a surprise—there are even more ways! If you really want to explore the full range of different ways to do these tasks, take a stroll through Word's Help and try out some of the other methods.

Copying and Moving Methods

To do this	Use this method after you've selected the text
Move a short distance	Drag the selection to the new location.
Copy a short distance	Hold down the Ctrl key, drag the selection to the new location, and release the Ctrl key.
Move a long distance or to a different document or program	Click the Cut button, click at the new location, and click the Paste button. OR press Ctrl+X, click at the new location, and press Ctrl+V.
Copy a long distance or to a different document or program	Click the Copy button, click at the new location, and click the Paste button. OR press Ctrl+C, click at the new location, and press Ctrl+V.
Copy several items and insert all in one place	Open the Office Clipboard, click the Copy button, select the next item, click the Copy button again, and repeat to copy up to 24 items. OR hold down the Ctrl key, select multiple items, and then click the Copy button. Click at the new location, and then click the Paste All button on the Clipboard.
Move a long or short distance	Press the F2 key, click at the new location, and press Enter.
Copy a long or short distance	Press Shift+F2, click at the new location, and press Enter.

Marking and Reviewing Changes in a Document

When you have a document that needs to be reviewed or changed and you want to mark the changes you or others make, you can use the Track Changes feature in Word. When this feature is turned on, additions, deletions, moves, and even formatting changes are marked. You can also add comments.

When you're reviewing the edited document, you can accept or reject any change or comment, view the changes made by individual reviewers, and even view the document as it was before the changes were made. You can also view the document as it would look if you accepted all the changes.

Review a Document

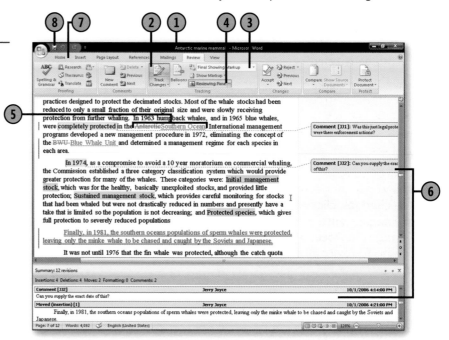

① Open the document to be reviewed.

② On the Review tab, click the Track Changes button if it isn't already selected.

③ Click Final Showing Markup so that you can see your changes.

④ If you want to monitor your changes, click Reviewing Pane, and specify whether you want the pane to be displayed on the left side or at the bottom of the window.

⑤ Edit the content as usual. Note that text you insert is underlined, and text you delete has strikethrough formatting.

⑥ To insert a comment, select the text you want to comment on, and click the New Comment button. Type your comment in the balloon that appears or in the Reviewing pane, depending on your settings.

⑦ To highlight text without adding a comment, on the Home tab, click the Highlight button, and drag the mouse pointer over the content you want to highlight.

⑧ Switch to Final view, review the document for any errors, and then save and close it.

Tip

In Draft view, all your changes are marked in the document, and the descriptions and comments are displayed in the Reviewing pane at the left side or at the bottom of the window. In Page Layout view, click the Balloons button to select the content that's placed in the balloons.

Review a Review

1. Open a document that has been reviewed and edited. If it's marked as Read-Only, save it using a different name.

2. On the Review tab, click the Track Changes button, if it's selected, to turn off marking changes.

3. Switch to Final Showing Markup view if it isn't already selected.

4. Click Show Markup, and specify the types of changes you want to be displayed. If you don't want to see the markup from every reviewer, specify which reviewers' changes you do want to see.

5. Choose to accept, reject, or locate each change in the document. To accept all the changes, click the down arrow on the Accept button and choose Accept All Changes In Document from the drop-down menu. To reject all changes, click the down arrow on the Reject button, and choose Reject All Changes In Document.

6. When you've finished, switch the view to Final, review the document for any errors, and then save and close it.

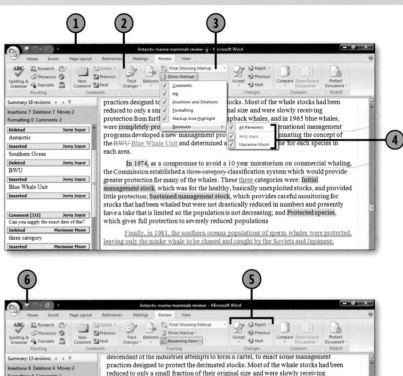

Tip

Note that paragraphs you've moved are indicated by a double underline, and that their original location is indicated by a double strikethrough.

Tip

To compare two versions of the same document and mark the changes, click the Compare button on the Review tab, and choose Compare from the drop-down menu. To combine separate files that contain marked changes by different reviewers, click the Compare button, and choose Combine from the drop-down menu.

Comparing Documents Side by Side

When you want to look at two documents at the same time to compare their content, Word will place the documents in adjacent windows. If the documents are similar enough, you can have Word scroll through both of them at the same time, or you can scroll through the documents at your own pace.

View the Documents

1 Open the two documents you want to view and compare.

2 In one document, on the View tab, click the View Side By Side button.

3 If a dialog box appears and asks you which documents you want to view, select the documents you want, and click OK.

4 If you don't want the documents to scroll together, on the View tab, click the Window button to expand the window section (if it's collapsed), and click the Synchronous Scrolling button to turn off the scrolling. Click Synchronous Scrolling again to resume the coordinated scrolling.

5 Scroll through the documents. When you've finished, click the Window button again, and click the View Side By Side button to turn off that view.

Tip ✓

If the two windows don't start at the same part of the document when you scroll through them, turn off Synchronous Scrolling, scroll through one window until it displays the same top line as the other window, and then turn Synchronous Scrolling back on.

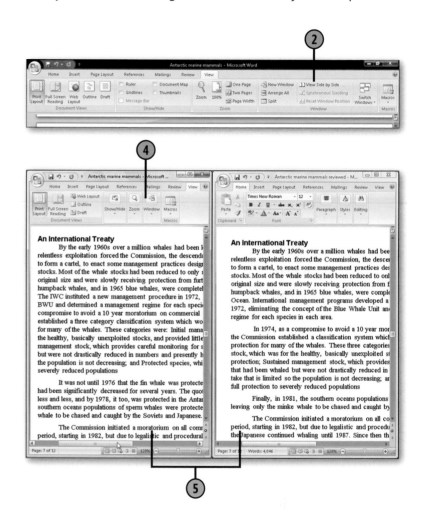

5

Formatting in Word

In this section:

- **Controlling the Look: Themes, Styles, and Fonts**
- **Formatting Text**
- **Formatting Paragraphs**
- **Formatting with Tabs**
- **Adding Emphasis and Special Formatting**
- **Copying Your Formatting**
- **Creating and Formatting Lists**
- **Creating and Formatting Tables**
- **Laying Out the Page**
- **Flowing Text into Columns**
- **Creating Chapters**
- **Creating a Running Head**

Even if you don't have the time, inclination, or experience to design the documents you use every day, you can still produce professional-looking, well-designed letters, reports, memos, and even the Great American Novel. You do this by using the themes, styles, fonts, colors, borders, shading, decorative lines, and other design elements that Microsoft Office Word 2007 provides to help you create, design, and maintain consistency throughout the documents you produce at work, at school, or at play. Depending on your desired end result and how little or how much involvement you want in the design, you can use the predesigned themes and style sets just as they come, without changing a thing; you can modify the existing ones a little or a lot; or, with a bit of time and experimentation, you can create your own highly individual designs.

We'll cover a lot of topics in this section, including creating, formatting, and working with lists and tables; laying out your pages, and using automatic hyphenation to improve the overall look of the layout; setting up a long document such as a book or report that you intend to have bound, dividing it into chapters or sections, and adding running heads; flowing text into columns like those in a newspaper or magazine; and wrapping text around a graphic for a very professional look.

Controlling the Look: Themes, Styles, and Fonts

Microsoft Office Word 2007 provides powerful tools that make it possible for you to easily create professional-looking documents. To simplify the design process—and thereby avoid the chaos that's often a problem in heavily formatted documents—Word's tools help you build consistent layouts with a minimum of hassle.

Themes: The master controllers of the design, themes set many elements, including the default fonts; the color schemes for text, horizontal and vertical lines, and backgrounds; and the shading and shadow effects in graphics. When you change a theme, you change the entire appearance of your document. You can change the whole theme or only individual elements—the default fonts, for example, or the color scheme or shading effects. Word comes with many built-in themes, but you can also design and save your own themes. See "Setting the Overall Look" on the facing page for information about choosing and changing themes.

Paragraph Styles: These styles define the layout of your paragraphs—line spacing, indents, tab spacing, borders, and so on.

Character Styles: These styles define the look of individual text characters—for example, boldfaced, italicized, or underlined emphasis; strikethrough, superscript, color, and shadow effects; and spacing between characters. If you specify the font as something other than the theme's default font, the character style can also define the font and font size. Otherwise, the font is determined by the chosen theme.

Linked Styles: These styles define both paragraph and character formatting—for example, in a single style you can define the paragraph layout, including the alignment and line spacing, as well as the appearance of the characters for the entire paragraph, including font, font size, emphasis, and effects. See the Tip on page 60 for information about creating your own styles.

Table Styles: These styles define the appearance of your tables—for example, the shading of rows or columns and the thickness of the gridlines. See "Formatting a Table" on page 76 for information about using table styles.

List Styles: These styles determine the appearance of your bulleted and numbered lists—for example, the kind of bullet used and how far the paragraph is indented. See "Formatting a List" on page 71 for information about using list styles.

Direct Formatting: You can use direct formatting to create customized words, paragraphs, or blocks of text. For example, you can apply bold formatting to a couple of words for emphasis, or select a quotation and add italics to it. Although you'll want to use styles most of time to maintain a consistent look, direct formatting is a useful tool in certain instances. If you use direct formatting and later want to use the same formatting again, you can either use that formatting to create a new style or copy the formatting and apply it elsewhere with the Format Painter tool. See "Copying Your Formatting" on page 69 for information about using the Format Painter tool.

Setting the Overall Look

Themes define the look of your entire document—the color scheme, the pairing of the default fonts used for body and heading text, and even the shading effects on graphics. Once you've selected a theme, you can use the font pairing and the color palette in your formatting to apply a unified look to your document design.

Choose a Theme

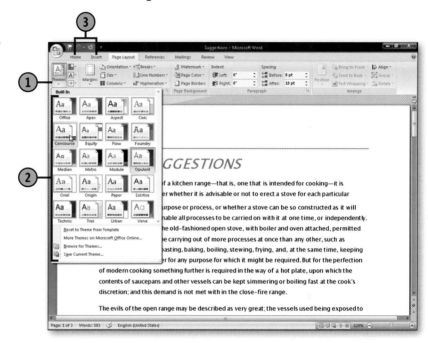

1. On the Page Layout tab, click the Themes button to display the Themes gallery.

2. Do any of the following:

   • Point to a theme to see how your document will look if you use that theme.

   • Click the theme you want to use.

   • Click More Themes on Microsoft Office Online to find more themes on line, and select the theme you want.

   • Click Browse For Themes to display the Choose Theme Or Themed Document dialog box. Select a theme or a document that contains the theme you want, and click Open.

   • Click Reset To Theme From Template to revert to the original theme for the document.

3. Use the tools on the Home and Insert tabs as you normally would, selecting from the theme fonts and colors displayed or selecting non-theme fonts and colors for special effects.

Tip

If you don't see a preview of the changes when you point to different themes, choose Word Options from the Office menu, and, with the Popular item selected, select the Enable Live Preview check box. Click OK.

Formatting Text

Rarely, unless it's a short note, is a document composed of just plain old text, with all the paragraphs in the same font and font size and with the same indents and line spacing. In Microsoft Word, you can quickly add formatting to selected text, or set all the formatting for the paragraphs to give your documents a consistent and professional look. You can apply formatting whenever you want—before you type, while you're typing, or after you've typed all your text.

Apply a Quick Paragraph Style

① Click in the paragraph that you want to format, or select multiple paragraphs to which you want to apply the same formatting.

② On the Home tab, point to a style to preview it. Click the style if you want to use it.

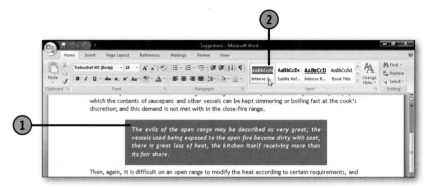

Apply Character Formatting

① Select the text you want to format.

② On the Home tab, point to any style that isn't a paragraph style—that is, one that doesn't have a small paragraph mark (¶) at the left of its name—to preview it. Click the style if you want to use it.

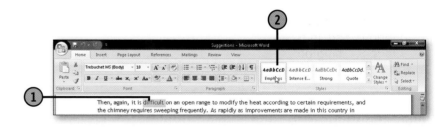

Tip

To create a style, format your text or paragraph so that it looks the way you want, and then select it. On the Home tab, open the Styles gallery, and click Save Selection As A New Quick Style. In the Create New Style From Formatting dialog box that appears, type a descriptive name for the style, and click OK. Presto! You've created your own style.

Using Any Style

Sometimes there are styles you want that aren't part of the Quick Styles set you can see at a glance on the Home tab.

You can easily access these other styles and use them wherever you want.

Access Your Styles

① On the Home tab, click the Show The Styles Window button at the bottom-right of the Styles group.

② Select the Show Preview check box if it isn't already selected.

③ Click in a paragraph, or select the text, paragraphs, or table cells to which you want to apply the same formatting.

④ In the Styles list, click the style you want to apply.

⑤ If the style you want isn't listed, click Options, and, in the Styles Gallery Options dialog box, under Select Styles To Show, click All Styles, click OK, and then click the style you want.

Try This!

Open the Quick Styles gallery, and click Apply Styles to display the Apply Styles window. Click in a paragraph, or select the text you want to format. Click the Apply Styles window, and start typing the name of the style you want. Press Enter when the name of the style you want is displayed.

Changing Character Fonts

The combination of font and font size largely determines the look of your document. You can easily set both of these elements for all or part of your content with just a few clicks. Font and font size affect the selected character or characters.

Change the Font

1. Select the text whose font you want to change.
2. On the Home tab, click the Font list down arrow.
3. Click the font you want to use.

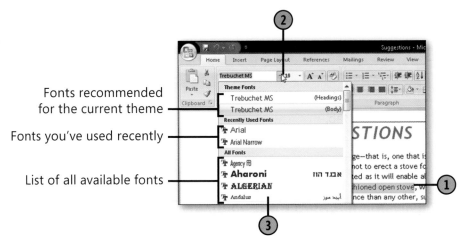

Fonts recommended for the current theme

Fonts you've used recently

List of all available fonts

Change the Font Size

1. Select the text whose font size you want to change.
2. On the Home tab, do any of the following:
   - Click the Font Size down arrow, and select a font size from the drop-down list that appears.
   - Click the Font Size list, and type the font size you want.
   - Click the Grow Font button or the Shrink Font button to increase or decrease the font size.

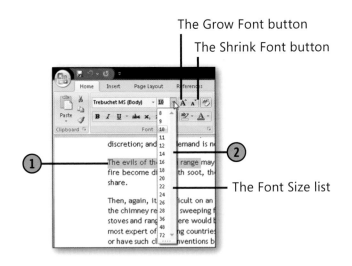

The Grow Font button

The Shrink Font button

The Font Size list

Setting Paragraph Alignment

The alignment you choose for a paragraph results in a distinctive appearance, and you can experiment with the various alignments to achieve just the right look for the way you'll be using that particular paragraph. With Word, you can adjust the alignment of an individual paragraph, several paragraphs, or even all your paragraphs.

Set the Alignment

① Click in a paragraph, or select all the paragraphs whose alignment you want to set.

② On the Home tab, click any of the following:

- The Align Left button to align the paragraph with the left margin or left indent, creating a ragged right edge

- The Center button to center each line of the paragraph, creating both a ragged left edge and a ragged right edge

- The Align Right button to align the paragraph with the right margin or right indent, creating a ragged left edge

- The Justify button to align the paragraph with both the left margin or left indent and the right margin or right indent by adding any necessary space between words

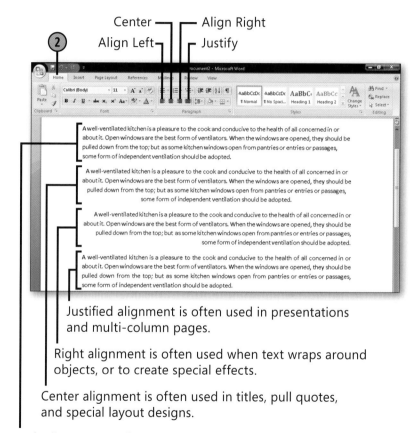

Center ——— ┐ ┌— Align Right
Align Left—┐ ┌ Justify

Justified alignment is often used in presentations and multi-column pages.

Right alignment is often used when text wraps around objects, or to create special effects.

Center alignment is often used in titles, pull quotes, and special layout designs.

Left alignment is often used in standard paragraphs for ease of reading.

Tip ✓

Consider using a style instead of direct formatting to ensure consistency in your document if you're going to use this formatting more than once.

Adjusting Paragraph Line Spacing

You can improve the readability of your text by adjusting the spacing, or *leading* (pronounced "ledding"), between the lines. Too little space makes the lines of text looked squashed together and difficult to read; too much space also makes the text difficult to read because the reader's eye has to search for the beginning of the next line.

Set the Line Spacing Within a Paragraph

① Click in a paragraph, or select all the paragraphs whose line spacing you want to set.

② On the Home tab, click the Line Spacing button.

③ Select the line spacing you want.

④ If you don't see the spacing you want, click Line Spacing Options.

⑤ On the Indents And Spacing tab of the Paragraph dialog box, select the line spacing you want:

- Exactly to create a specified space between lines regardless of the font size used

- At Least to create a minimum space between lines, which can increase if you use large font sizes

- Multiple to specify how many lines of space you want between the lines of text

⑥ Use the arrows or type a value. For Exactly and At Least settings, this is a distance measurement, usually in points; for Multiple, this is the number of lines of space. Click OK.

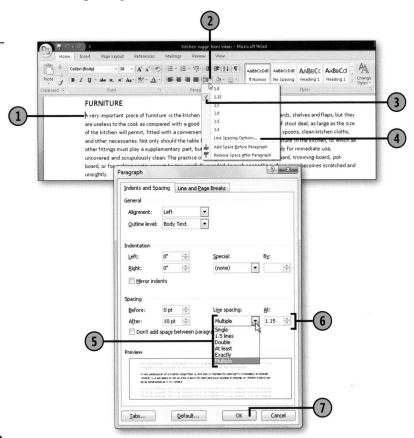

Tip

The default measure for spacing is the *point*, abbreviated as "pt." A point is a typographic measure: 72 points equal one inch (or about 28.57 points equal one centimeter).

Set the Line Spacing Between Paragraphs

① Click in a paragraph, or select all the paragraphs for which you want to set the spacing.

② On the Home tab, click the Line Spacing button.

③ Click the option for adding space before or after the paragraph or paragraphs.

④ If you want to customize the spacing, click Line Spacing Options to display the Paragraph dialog box.

⑤ In the Before and After boxes, use the arrows or type a value for the space before (above) the first line of the paragraph and for the space after (below) the last line of the paragraph.

⑥ Select this check box if you don't want space between paragraphs of the same style.

⑦ Click OK.

⑧ If you want to remove the space before or after the selected paragraph or paragraphs, click the Line Spacing button again, and choose Remove Space Before Paragraph or Remove Space After Paragraph from the menu.

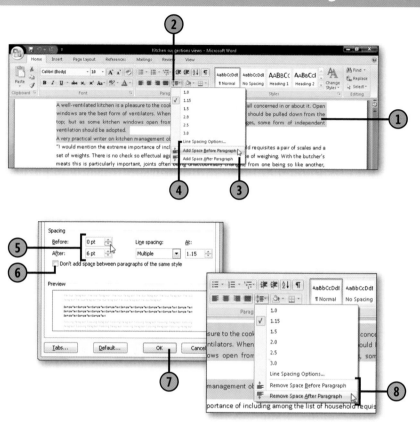

Caution

Note that the distance between two paragraphs is the sum of the space below the first paragraph and the space above the second paragraph. Keep this in mind so that you don't end up with a bigger space between paragraphs than the space you intended.

Tip

Some commonly used keyboard shortcuts are for line spacing and "space-before" spacing. Press Ctrl+1 for single spacing, Ctrl+5 for 1.5 line spacing, Ctrl+2 for double spacing, and Ctrl+0 (zero) for 1 line before the paragraph. Ctrl+0 is a toggle, so you can use it to change a paragraph from 1 line before to no lines before.

Indenting a Paragraph

An *indent* is the distance a paragraph or a first line is moved in from the left and/or right margin. Indenting a paragraph sets it off from other paragraphs. The indention can be as simple as slightly indenting the first line to indicate the start of a new paragraph, or as complex as indenting both the left and right sides of the paragraph to create a separate block of text.

Indent the Paragraph

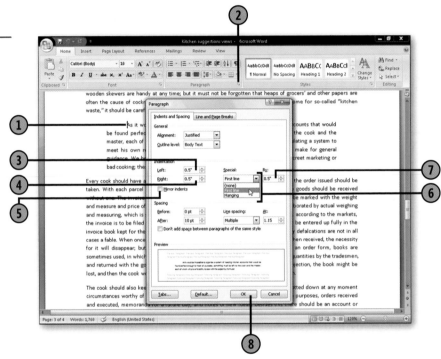

(1) Click in a paragraph, or select all the paragraphs for which you want to set a first-line indent.

(2) On the Home tab, click the Paragraph button to display the Paragraph dialog box.

(3) Click in the Left box, and use the arrows or type a value for the distance you want the text indented from the left margin.

(4) Click in the Right box, and set the distance for the right indent from the right margin.

(5) Select this check box if you want the left and right indents to switch depending on whether they're on odd- or even-numbered pages. This option is designed for two-sided documents, so you'll notice that the Left label changes to Inside and the Right label changes to Outside.

(6) Click in the Special box, and select

- First Line to indent the first line.

- Hanging to indent all lines in the paragraph except the first line.

(7) Click in the By box, and use the arrows or type a value to specify the size of the indent.

(8) Click OK.

Tip

Using the ruler, you can easily set the indents by dragging the Left Indent, First Line Indent, and Right Indent markers. You can also create a left indent in a paragraph by clicking the Home tab and then clicking the Increase Indent button. When you set indents using the Paragraph dialog box, however, you can specify precise values for all the indents.

Formatting with Tabs

Although using a table is generally the easiest way to position text horizontally, there are times when setting tab stops and pressing the Tab key work best. All you need to do is specify the location of each tab and the alignment you want for the tab stop. If you don't set any tab stops, however, Word provides default tab stops that are usually set at 0.5 inch all the way across the line of text. You can change this default value in the Tabs dialog box.

Set Your Tabs

① If the ruler isn't already displayed, click the View Ruler button to display the ruler.

② Click in a paragraph, or select all the paragraphs in which you want to set the tabs.

③ Click to select the type of tab you want. Each click selects a different type of tab or other ruler marker.

④ Click in the ruler where you want the tabs. If necessary, drag a tab stop to a new location to adjust it. Drag a tab stop off the ruler to delete that tab stop.

⑤ If you want to modify a tab stop or set a tab leader—a dotted, dashed, or solid line—double-click any tab stop on the ruler to display the Tabs dialog box.

⑥ Make the changes you want.

⑦ Click Set.

⑧ Make any changes you want to other tabs, and then click OK.

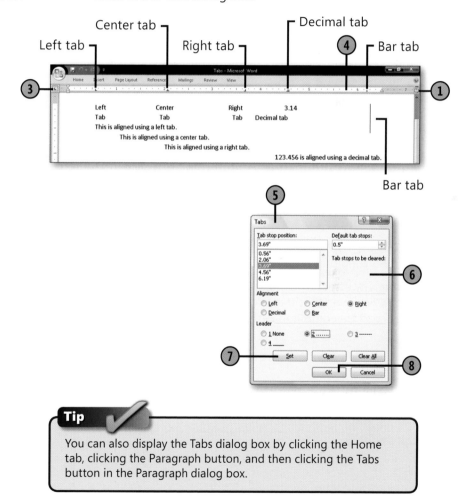

Tip

You can also display the Tabs dialog box by clicking the Home tab, clicking the Paragraph button, and then clicking the Tabs button in the Paragraph dialog box.

Adding Emphasis and Special Formatting

You'll often want to add special formatting to some text: for example, italics to use in a reference, bold to draw attention to a particular element, strikethrough to show what has been deleted, and so on. Word gives you a large array of special formatting options.

Format the Text

1. Select the text you want to format.

2. On the Home tab, use any combination of the formatting buttons to add the formatting you want. Click a button a second time to remove that formatting.

3. If there isn't a button for the formatting you want, click the Font button to display the Font dialog box.

4. Do any of the following:

   • Select a font color.

   • Select the type of underline and the underline color you want.

   • Select any effect or combination of effects. Note, however, that there are some effects that can't be combined with others.

5. Click OK.

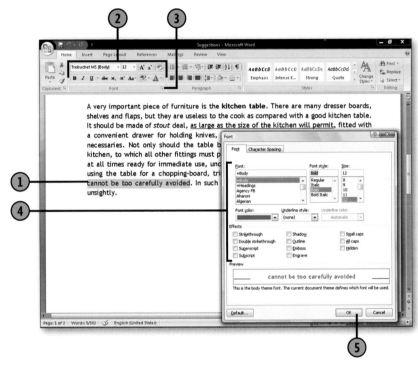

See Also

"Formatting Text" on page 60 for information about using Quick Styles to add emphasis.

Tip

If you're not sure what a formatting button does, point to it, and wait for the ScreenTip to appear. In addition to describing the button's function, the ScreenTip shows you which keyboard shortcut you can use instead of clicking the button with the mouse.

Copying Your Formatting

If you've created some formatting that you like, you can copy it and apply it to any text or paragraph that you want to have the same look. On the other hand, if you've created some formatting that you don't like or that looks really weird, you can replace it with a copy of any of your good formatting.

Copy the Formatting

1. If paragraph marks aren't displayed in your text, click the Home tab, and then click the Show/Hide ¶ button.

2. Select the text whose formatting you want to copy. If you want to copy paragraph formatting, make sure your selection includes the paragraph mark at the end of the paragraph.

3. On the Home tab, click the Format Painter button.

4. Drag the Format Painter over the selected text to apply the formatting, and then release the button.

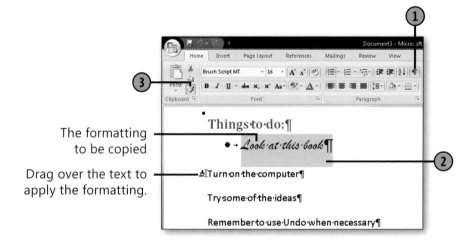

The formatting to be copied

Drag over the text to apply the formatting.

Tip
To copy formatting to several locations, double-click the Format Painter button after you've selected your text. You can then copy the formatting to as many places as you want. When you've finished, press the Esc key or click the Format Painter button again.

Tip
To copy only paragraph formatting, select only the paragraph mark before you click the Format Painter button.

Caution
You can't copy multiple types of formatting at one time. For example, in a selection where the first word is formatted in bold and the next word is in italics, only the bold formatting will be applied when you use the Format Painter.

Creating a Bulleted or Numbered List

A great way to provide information clearly is to present it in a numbered or bulleted list. Not only does Word add numbers or bullets to your list, with consistent spacing between the number or bullet and the text, but it keeps track of your list so that if you move an item within a numbered list, Word will renumber the list to keep the items in the correct order. You can also have the numbering skip paragraphs and can even split a list by restarting a series at 1.

Create the List

① Start typing the first line of your list. Make sure you're using the paragraph style you want for the list.

② On the Home tab, click the Numbering button for a numbered list or the Bullets button for a bulleted list.

③ After completing the first line, press Enter to start the second list item.

④ When you've completed the list, press Enter twice to create an empty paragraph and to turn off the list formatting.

Tip ✓

Sometimes, between the items in a numbered list, you need to insert unnumbered paragraphs that aren't part of the list. To restart numbering, right-click the paragraph following the unnumbered paragraph, and click either Restart Numbering or Continue Numbering.

Tip ✓

To create a multi-level list, press the Tab key to indent and demote an item in the list, or press Shift+Tab to promote the item.

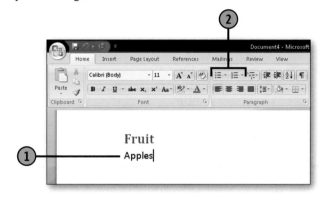

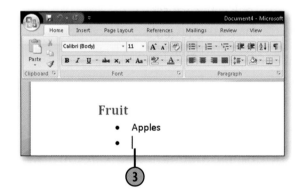

Formatting a List

The standard bulleted or numbering system is fine for a simple document, but if you want to give your work some extra pizzazz, or if you need to create a document with a specific outline-numbering scheme, you can adjust the look of the list.

Change the Format

1. Select your list.

2. On the Home tab, click the down arrow at the right of either the Bullets, Numbering, or Outline Numbering button to display the gallery for that button.

3. Move the mouse pointer over the different bulleted or numbering schemes, and preview the way your list will look with each scheme.

4. Click the bulleted or numbering scheme you want.

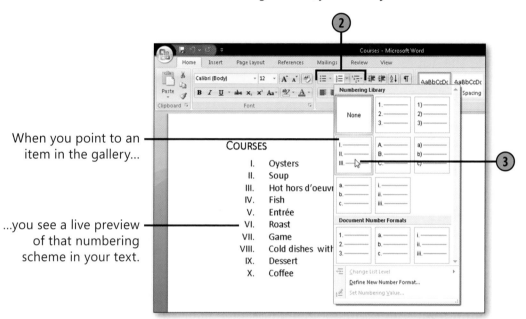

When you point to an item in the gallery...

...you see a live preview of that numbering scheme in your text.

See Also

"Formatting Text" on page 60 for information about applying different styles, and "Adding Emphasis and Special Formatting" on page 68 for information about applying special formatting.

Creating a Table from Scratch

If you tend to think of tables merely as containers for numbers, think again. Tables provide an excellent way to lay out and organize almost any kind of information. There are many ways to create a table, but the simplest and most versatile is to create an empty, unformatted table with a prescribed number of rows and columns. You can easily add content, and you can format and modify the table contents and layout later.

Create the Table

1. On the Insert tab, click the Table button. Move the mouse pointer to select the number of rows and columns you want in your table, and then click to insert the table.

2. Click in the first cell, and insert your content.

3. Press Tab to move to the next cell, and add your content. (Press Enter only to start a new paragraph inside a table cell.) Continue pressing Tab and entering content to complete your table.

4. If you've reached the end of your table but you still need to enter more items, press Tab, and Word will create a new row.

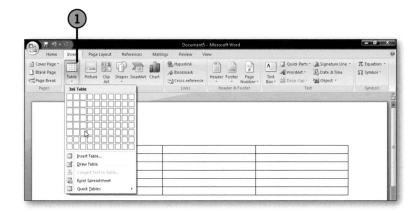

Tip

To move to the previous cell, press Shift+Tab. To insert a tab inside a cell, press Ctrl+Tab.

See Also

"Creating a Table from Text" on page 74 for information about converting existing text in paragraphs into text in a table.

Using a Predesigned Table

In the same way that you use templates for creating specialized types of documents, you can use a table template to create a specialized type of table, complete with formatting and related material—a title or a caption, for example.

Choose a Table

(1) Click in your document where you want the table to appear.

(2) On the Insert tab, click the Table button, point to Quick Tables, and click the type of table you want.

(3) Drag the mouse over the content of the table, and press the Delete key to remove the sample text.

(4) Click in the top-left cell, and type your information. Use the Tab key to move through the cells, and enter the rest of your content.

Tip

After you've created the table, you can modify its appearance by applying table styles or other formatting.

See Also

"Formatting a Table" on page 76 for information about formatting a table.

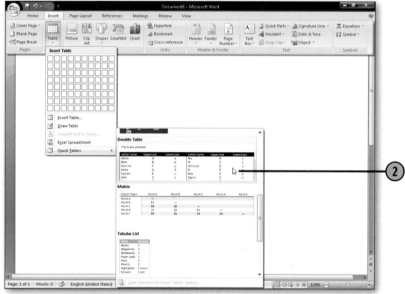

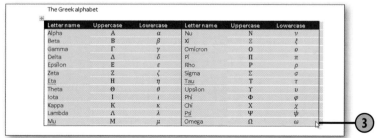

Creating a Table from Text

Many people still use tabs to create columns for a table, but doing so means that the content can get seriously messed up if you decide to reformat the document with different fonts, margins, and layouts. One way to avoid this problem is to convert your text into a table. That way, not only is the formatting so much simpler, but you can use the table tools to organize your information more easily.

Convert the Text

① Examine the text to make sure that the information is correctly separated by tabs, commas, paragraphs, or other marks. Delete any extra tabs (more than one tab between columns, for example) even if this affects the current alignment.

② Select all the text.

③ On the Insert tab, click the Table button, and click Convert Text To Table to display the Convert Text To Table dialog box.

④ Select the type of mark you've used to separate the columns of text.

⑤ Verify the number of columns you want. If there are more columns than you had in the text, repeat steps 1 through 4.

⑥ Click OK.

⑦ If you're not happy with the way the table looks, click the Undo button, and repeat steps 1 through 6.

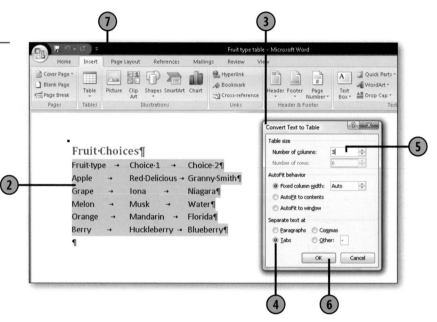

Tip
To convert text in a table to regular text, click in the table and, on the Table Tools Layout tab, click Convert To Text.

Tip
You can convert regular text to text in a table for many reasons other than just aligning columns. When the information is contained in a table, you can sort it, add or delete columns, and even do some math with it. To do some simple math in the table, click the Formula button on the Table Tools Layout tab.

Adding or Deleting Rows and Columns

You can modify the layout of an existing table by adding or deleting rows and columns anywhere in the table.

Add to the Table

① Click in the table next to where you want to add a row or column.

② On the Table Tools Layout tab, choose what you want to add.

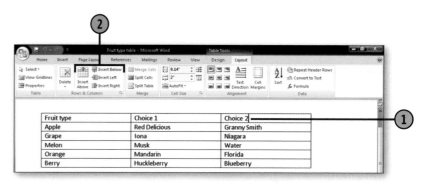

Try This!

Create a table with three columns and three rows. Click in the top-left cell. Drag the mouse to the right to select the first two cells. Click the Table Tools Layout tab, and then click Insert Left. With the new columns selected, click Insert Above. Note that the number of rows and columns that are inserted is based on the number of rows and columns in which cells were selected. Now try deleting rows and columns to revert to the size of the original table.

Tip

To delete the content of a row or column without deleting the row or column itself, select the row or column, and press the Delete key.

Caution

If you want to delete content from a row or column without deleting the row or column itself, make sure your selection doesn't extend above or below the table. If it does, you'll delete whatever part of the table is selected, as well as its content.

Delete from the Table

① Click in a table cell that's in the row or column you want to delete.

② On the Table Tools Layout tab, click Delete, and choose what you want to delete.

Formatting a Table

A table provides a superb way to organize almost any kind of information, and you can add interest and clarity to any table with the styles and formatting options Word provides. For example, you can use shading to delineate certain cell groupings, add borders to draw attention to particular cells, or use the formatting tools to vary the dimensions and alignment of the text.

Format the Table

1. Click anywhere inside the table.

2. On the Table Tools Design tab that appears, select a style for the table.

3. Select or clear the check boxes to turn the various formatting options on or off, as desired.

4. Select the cell or cells to which you want to add or from which you want to remove shading, click the Shading button, and select a color to add shading, or select No Color to remove shading.

5. Select the cell or cells to which you want to add or from which you want to remove borders, click the Borders button, and select the borders you want, or select No Borders to remove the borders.

6. Click the Layout tab, and use the tools to add or delete rows or columns, to set the dimensions of the rows and columns, and to set the text alignment, the text direction—that is, horizontal or vertical—and the margins.

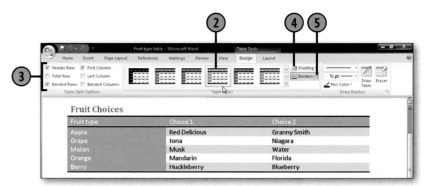

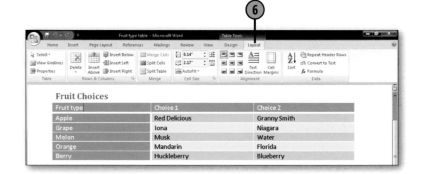

See Also

"Using a Predesigned Table" on page 73 for information about using a template to create a preformatted table.

Improving the Layout with Hyphenation

Sometimes the ragged right edges of left-aligned paragraphs look way too uneven. And sometimes justified paragraphs can contain big white spaces between words, especially in columnar text. You can easily repair these common problems by having Word automatically hyphenate the document.

Set Automatic Hyphenation

① On the Page Layout tab, click the Hyphenation button, and choose Automatic from the gallery that appears.

② If you don't like the way Word hyphenates, click the Hyphenation button again, and choose Hyphenation Options from the gallery to display the Hyphenation dialog box.

③ Specify whether or not you want to allow hyphenation of capitalized words.

④ Specify the maximum distance between the end of the last word and the edge of the column.

⑤ Specify whether you want to limit the number of consecutive end-of-line hyphens. (In many books, including this one, a limit of two consecutive end-of-line hyphens is customary.)

⑥ Click OK.

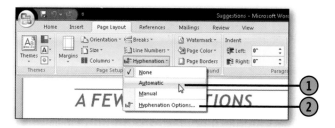

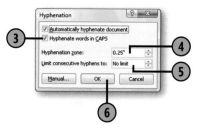

> **Tip**
>
> If you want to use automatic hyphenation in a document but want a few specific paragraphs to remain unhyphenated, create and use a separate paragraph style (or use direct paragraph formatting) for those paragraphs, making sure that, on the Line And Page Breaks tab of the Paragraph dialog box, you've selected the Don't Hyphenate check box.

Laying Out the Page

When you create a document that will be printed, you need to tell Word how you want the page to be set up—what size paper you're using, whether the page will be printed in landscape or in portrait orientation, the size of the margins, and so on. If the document will be printed on both sides of the paper or is going to be bound, you can tell Word to accommodate those design elements. A good template will usually set up the specifics for you, but you might need to readjust the settings a bit to get everything exactly right.

Set Up a Standard Page

① On the Page Layout tab, click the Size button, and, in the gallery that appears, select the size of the paper you want. If that size isn't listed, click More Paper Sizes, and specify your paper size on the Paper tab of the Page Setup dialog box.

② Click the Margins button, and select the margins you want. If that size isn't listed, click Custom Margins, and specify your margins on the Margins tab of the Page Setup dialog box.

③ Click the Orientation button, and select the orientation you want for the page: Portrait (longer than wide) or Landscape (wider than long).

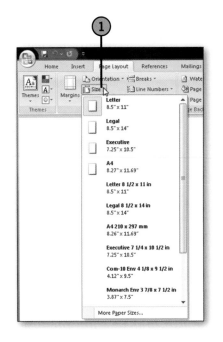

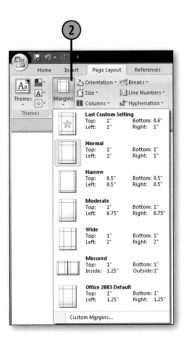

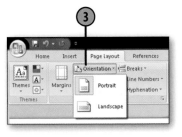

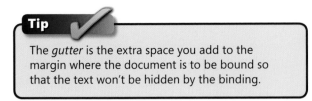

Tip

The *gutter* is the extra space you add to the margin where the document is to be bound so that the text won't be hidden by the binding.

Set Up a Two-Sided Document

① On the Page Layout tab, click the Margins button, and choose Custom Margins from the gallery to display the Page Setup dialog box.

② On the Margins tab, click Mirror Margins in the Multiple Pages list.

③ Set the document's side margins using the Inside and Outside boxes. The Inside margin will be on the left side of odd-numbered (right-hand, or *recto*) pages and will be on the right side of even-numbered (left-hand, or *verso*) pages.

④ Click OK.

Tip

You can apply a gutter to any document layout. For a document that's set up for one-sided printing, you can specify the gutter location as the left side of the paper or the top of the paper. For a multiple-page layout, Word uses the default location of the gutter for the type of layout you choose. Use the preview to see the placement of the gutter.

Set Up a Bound Document

① Click the Margins button, and choose Custom Margins from the gallery to display the Page Setup dialog box.

② On the Margins tab, specify a value for the gutter.

③ If the Multiple Pages list is set to Normal, specify whether the gutter (and therefore the binding) should be on the left side or at the top of the page. For other Multiple Pages settings, the gutter position is set automatically.

④ Click OK.

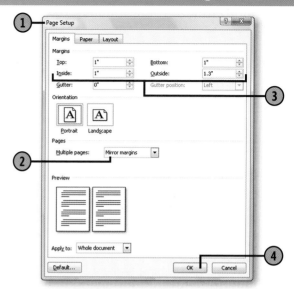

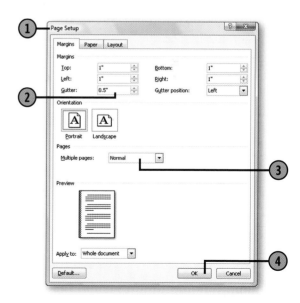

Changing Page Orientation Within a Document

Different parts of a long document sometimes require different layouts. For example, although most of the document's text is in portrait orientation, one or two pages might contain tables, figures, or other special elements that need to be set up in landscape orientation because of their width. By dividing the document into sections, you can set up each section with its own orientation.

Change the Page Orientation

① Select the part of the document whose page orientation you want to change.

② On the Page Layout tab, click the Margins button, and choose Custom Margins from the gallery to display the Page Setup dialog box.

③ Click the orientation you want.

④ Specify Selected Text.

⑤ Click OK.

⑥ Use the Zoom Control on the status bar to see your pages in detail, and verify that the layout is what you want.

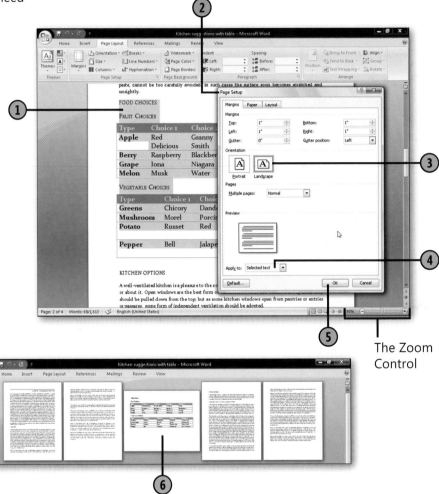

The Zoom Control

Tip ✔

When you change the orientation of selected text, you're actually creating two new sections: one for the selected text and another for the text that follows the selection.

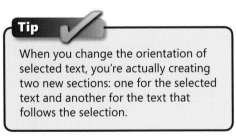

Flowing Text into Columns

You can flow text into multiple columns on a page, like the columns in a newspaper or magazine. By dividing a page into separate sections, you can even vary the number of columns in each section of the page.

Change the Number of Columns

① Without worrying about the layout just yet, complete the content of your document. Make sure the page orientation and the margins are set correctly for the document.

② On the Home tab, click the Show/Hide ¶ button if it isn't already turned on.

③ Select the text that you want to flow into columns.

④ On the Page Layout tab, click the Columns button, and select the layout you want. Word makes the selected text into a separate section by inserting Continuous section breaks before and after the selected text.

⑤ If you want to adjust the columns, click anywhere in the section that has the columns.

⑥ Click the Columns button again, and click More Columns in the Columns gallery to display the Columns dialog box.

⑦ If you don't want even-width columns, clear this check box, and then specify the width you want for each column.

⑧ Select this check box if you want a vertical line centered between adjacent columns.

⑨ Make sure the settings are applied only to the selected text, and then click OK.

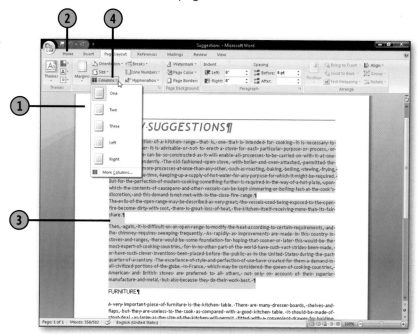

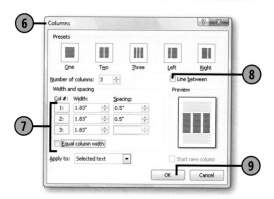

Creating Chapters

A long document is usually divided into chapters or sections, each of which should begin on an odd-numbered (right-hand, or *recto*) page. Word will start your chapters or sections on odd-numbered pages, and will create running heads to your specifications.

Start a New Chapter

① In the document you want to divide into different chapters, place the insertion point at the beginning of the paragraph that starts a new chapter.

② On the Page Layout tab, click the Breaks button, and click the Odd Page section-break option in the gallery. Word inserts the section break in front of the insertion point.

Change the Running Heads

① On the Insert tab, click the Header button, and click Edit Header in the gallery.

② On the Header & Footer Tools Design tab that appears, click the Link To Previous button to turn it off and to disconnect the header from any previous header.

③ Replace the old header text, if any, with the text for your new running head.

④ Click the Go To Footer button to move to the footer, and repeat steps 2 and 3 for the footer. If the document is set for a different running head on the first page, or for different running heads on odd- and even-numbered pages, repeat steps 2 and 3 for those running heads.

⑤ Click Close Header And Footer when you've finished.

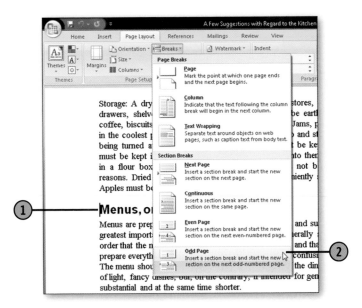

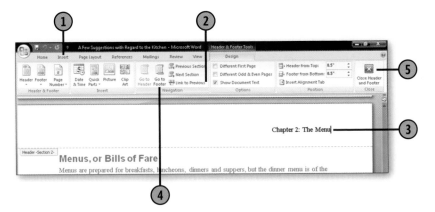

Wrapping Text Around a Graphic

Wrapping text around an item can add another level of polish to the professional look of your document. However, using one of the standard text-wrapping configurations doesn't always produce the desired effect. As you might expect, you can customize the way Word wraps the text.

Set the Text Wrapping

1. Click the graphic to select it.

2. On the appropriate Format tab for that item (for example, the Picture Tools Format tab or the Drawing Tools Format tab), click the Text Wrapping button, and specify the text-wrapping option you want.

3. Drag the graphic to set its position in the paragraph and to specify the way you want the text to wrap around it.

4. If the text wrapping still doesn't look the way you want, click the Text Wrapping button again, choose More Layout Options from the menu, and make your custom layout settings in the Advanced Layout dialog box. Click OK when you've finished.

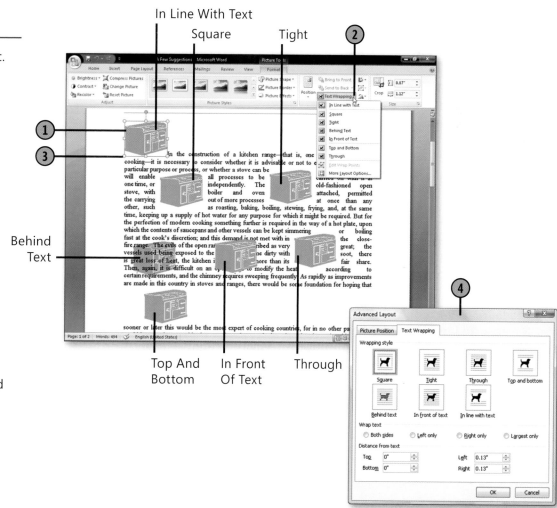

In Line With Text

Square

Tight

Behind Text

Top And Bottom

In Front Of Text

Through

Creating a Running Head

In addition to page numbers, a long document usually has some type of identifying text—called a *running head*—at the top or bottom of each page of the document. All you do is create the running head once, and Word places it on the pages you designate. For the sake of consistency, we're using the term *running head* for the heading itself, and the terms *header* and *footer* to indicate the running head's position on the page. Note that on the screen you can see the headers and footers on your page only in Print Layout view or Print Preview.

Create a Header and a Footer

① On the Insert tab, click the Header button, and, in the gallery that appears, select the layout and content you want in the header.

② If there are placeholders in the header, click the placeholder field or text, and select or type your information.

③ Click the Footer button, select the layout and content you want, and enter the footer information.

④ Click the Close Header And Footer button to return to the main part of your document.

⑤ If you want to edit the contents of the header or footer, double-click it to activate the area, and make your changes.

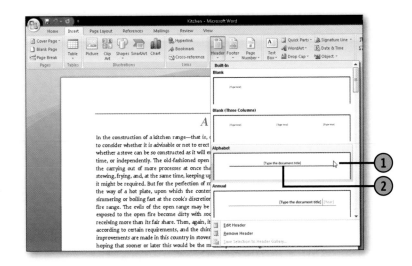

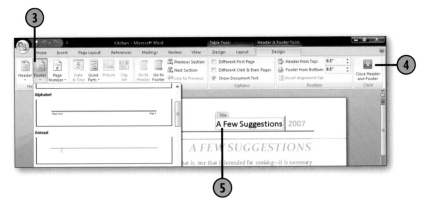

Sorting Your Information

Tables and lists are invaluable tools for presenting information briefly and clearly, and you can make them even more useful by organizing their contents as efficiently as possible. If you have a table or a list that you want to rearrange so that it's presented in alphabetic or numeric order, all you need to do is tell Word to sort it for you.

Sort a Table

(1) With the insertion point anywhere in the table, on the Table Tools Layout tab, click the Sort button.

(2) In the Sort dialog box, specify whether the table will contain a header row (a row that shows the column titles).

(3) Specify the title of the column you want to use to sort the table, the type of content in the column, and whether you want the information to be sorted in ascending or descending order.

(4) If you want to conduct a second- or third-level sort, enter the criteria.

(5) Click OK.

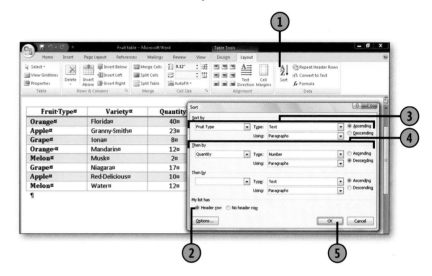

Sort a List

(1) Select the entire list.

(2) On the Home tab, click the Sort button.

(3) In the Sort Text dialog box, specify the type of information that's in the list, whether you want to sort by words or by paragraphs, and whether you want the information to be sorted in ascending or descending order.

(4) Click OK.

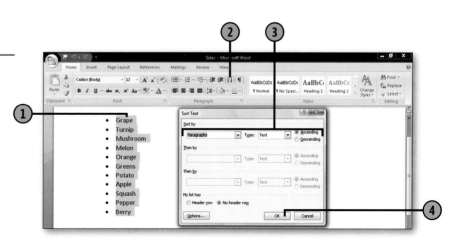

Reorganizing a Document

Outline view provides a powerful way for you to view the structure of your document and to rearrange the order of presentation of the topics. The outline structure assumes that you've used specific heading and body styles to organize your document into a hierarchy of topics and subtopics.

View a Document's Outline

① Click the Outline View button at the bottom-right of your screen to switch to Outline view.

② On the Outlining tab, specify the lowest level of heading to be displayed.

③ Click to expand or collapse the content under the selected heading.

④ Click to change the outline level of the selected text by promoting it one level or demoting it one level, or to change body text to a heading or a heading to body text.

⑤ To move a section, click the plus sign to select the entire section, and drag the section up or down.

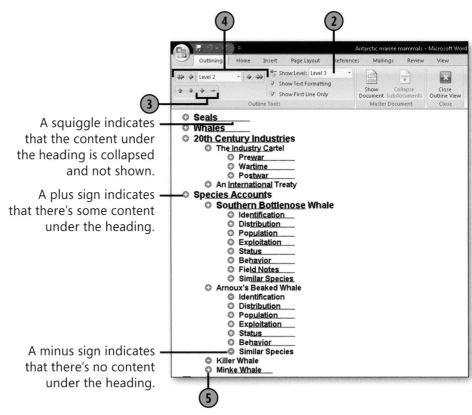

A squiggle indicates that the content under the heading is collapsed and not shown.

A plus sign indicates that there's some content under the heading.

A minus sign indicates that there's no content under the heading.

Try This!

Drag a topic's plus or minus sign to the left to quickly promote the topic's outline level, to the right to demote it, or to the far right to turn it into body text. Changing the outline level also changes the style that's assigned to that paragraph.

Tip

To quickly expand or collapse a section, double-click the plus sign next to the heading.

6

Working with Special Content in Word

In this section:

- Inserting a Cover Page
- Numbering Headings and Lines
- Inserting Information with Smart Tags
- Inserting an Equation
- Adding a Sidebar or a Pull Quote
- Inserting a Watermark
- Creating Footnotes and Endnotes
- Inserting a Citation
- Creating a Table of Contents
- Printing Envelopes and Mailing Labels
- Mail Merge: The Power and the Pain
- Creating a Form Letter
- Finalizing Your Document

This section of the book deals with the special content required in certain types of documents. Something many documents need is a well-designed cover page, and in Microsoft Office Word 2007 you'll find a wide selection of predesigned cover pages that you can use as is or customize to better coordinate with your needs.

It's a common practice to number heading levels—and often individual lines—in scientific or legal documents for convenience when the documents are being reviewed, and it's a snap to do in Word. We'll talk about inserting equations, using text boxes to create sidebars and pull quotes, and creating watermarks. If your document needs footnotes or endnotes, Word not only numbers them automatically but updates the numbers for you if you add or delete a note, and even figures out their exact placement on the page. We'll also discuss adding citations, creating a table of contents, and finalizing your document.

And then there's the mail merge feature—a great time-saver when you need to send the same information to a few individuals or to a large group of people. You provide a *main document* and a *data source,* and Word combines, or merges, the information into a new, personalized document.

Inserting a Cover Page

First impressions count! A well-designed cover page can provide the incentive that makes your readers want to see what's inside your document.

Insert the Cover Page

(1) On the Insert tab, click the Cover Page button, and, in the gallery that appears click the cover page you want.

(2) Switch to Print Layout view if you aren't already in that view, press Ctrl+Home to move to the beginning of your document, click in an area that needs to be completed, and type the required information. Repeat for all the other areas that need to be completed.

(3) If you're not happy with the design of the cover page, do any of the following:

- On the Insert tab, click Cover Page, and choose another design.

- On the Page Layout tab, click Themes, and choose a different theme.

- Add a picture, a drawing, fields, text, or other items to customize the page.

- On the Insert tab, click Cover Page, and choose Remove Current Cover Page to delete the cover page.

(4) Save your document.

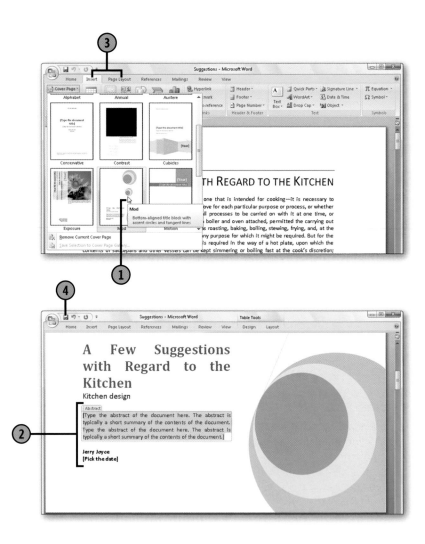

Numbering Headings

It's a commonly accepted practice to number each heading level in certain long documents so that when the document is being reviewed or is under discussion at a meeting, it's easy to refer to the relevant sections. Word uses the outline-level setting for each style as the basis for the numbering hierarchy.

Number the Headings

① Verify that you've applied the correct styles to all the headings.

② Click in the first heading paragraph.

③ On the Home tab, click the Multilevel List button, and click one of the heading-numbering schemes.

④ Verify that your document headings are numbered correctly. If you don't like the look of the numbering scheme, click the Undo button on the Quick Access toolbar.

The Multilevel List button

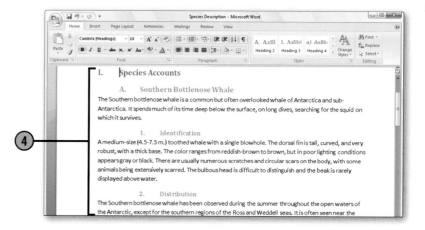

Tip

If a paragraph that you want to number as a heading isn't included when you use a heading-numbering scheme, you haven't assigned it the proper outline level. To correct this problem, you can either modify the style and assign it the correct outline level, or switch to Outline view, click in the paragraph, and select the outline level on the Outlining tab.

Adding Line Numbers

Numbering lines is a convenient—and sometimes required—way to provide references in a document that is going to be reviewed. Word will automatically number the lines for you and will also skip the numbering of any lines that you don't want numbered.

Number the Lines

① On the Page Layout tab, click the Line Numbers button, and choose the type of line numbering you want from the drop-down menu.

② If you want to change the starting number or the interval at which line numbers are shown (every fifth line, for example), click Line Numbers again, choose Line Numbering Options from the menu, and, on the Layout tab of the Page Setup dialog box, click the Line Numbers button to display the Line Numbers dialog box.

③ Select this check box, if it isn't already selected, to turn on line numbering.

④ Specify the options you want.

⑤ Click OK, and then click OK in the Page Setup dialog box.

The Paragraph button

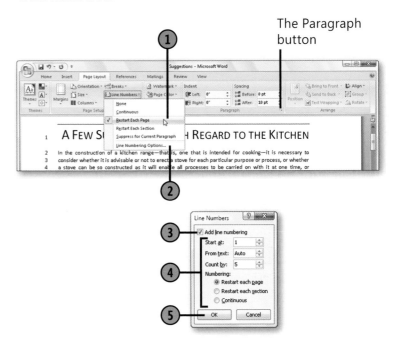

Tip

If there's a paragraph whose lines you don't want to be included in the line-numbering process, click in the paragraph, click the Line Numbers button on the Page Layout tab, and choose Suppress For Current Paragraph.

Tip

The line numbers are visible on your screen only in Page Layout view and Print Preview.

Inserting Information with Smart Tags

Word searches through your document for certain text that it recognizes (names, phone numbers, stock symbols, and so on) and, when it finds that text, attaches a *smart tag* to it. You use the smart tag to obtain additional information about an item or to perform some type of action. Because smart tags are add-ins, there are many different types available, depending on which ones are installed on your computer.

Insert a Character

① Look through your document for text with the purplish-red dotted underline that indicates a smart tag.

② Point to the text and wait for the Smart Tag Actions button to appear.

③ Click the Smart Tag Actions button.

④ In the drop-down list that appears, click the action you want to take. The actions listed depend on the type of data represented by the text (an address or a name, for example) and the type of smart tag being used.

A date smart tag

A telephone-number smart tag

A financial-symbol smart tag

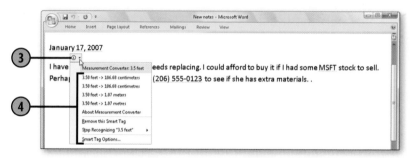

Try This!

Click the Office button, and then click the Word Options button to display the Word Options dialog box. Click the AutoCorrect Options button in the Proofing category. On the Smart Tags tab, select the check boxes for the smart tags you want to use and clear the check boxes for the tags you don't want to use. Make sure the Label Text With Smart Tags check box is selected. Click More Smart Tags to see whether there are other tags you want to use. In the Word Options dialog box, click Recheck Document, and then click OK.

Tip

Note the difference between smart tags and Actions buttons. A smart tag identifies a certain type of text. An Actions button lists the actions you can perform. Some Actions buttons, such as the AutoCorrect and Paste Options buttons, aren't associated with smart tags.

Inserting an Equation

Few tasks have been as difficult as displaying mathematical equations in a document—until now. Word 2007 provides powerful equation-writing tools that allow you to insert a prepackaged equation as is, modify one as you want, or create a new one from scratch. Remember, however, that any equation you insert is the current version of that equation only; Word is unable to do any math with that equation.

Insert the Equation

1 Click in the document where you want to insert the equation.

2 On the Insert tab, click the down arrow at the right of the Equation button, and, in the gallery that appears, click the equation you want.

3 Use standard editing techniques, such as formatting text size and emphasis; or use the tools on the Equation Tools Design tab to insert different symbols, letters, or numbers or to change the equation into a linear form or to plain text.

4 Click outside the equation when you've finished working with it.

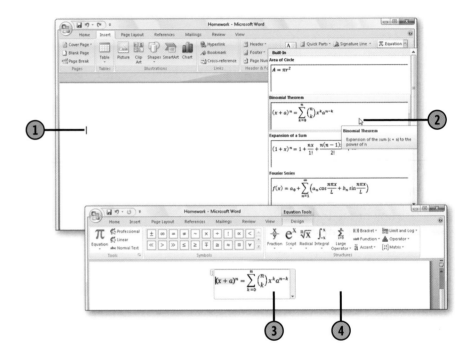

Tip ✓

To create your own equation from scratch, click the Equation button to insert a blank equation *content control,* and use the tools on the Equation Tools Design tab to build your equation.

Tip ✓

A *content control* is an object that Word uses to hold special content and to keep that content as one unit. Click the content to display the content control; click outside the control to show only the content and not the control.

Adding a Sidebar or a Pull Quote

Sidebars and pull quotes are useful features that add interest to a design and break up the sea of text on a page while drawing attention to special pieces of information. Word provides a variety of predesigned text boxes that you can use for sidebars and pull quotes.

Insert a Predesigned Text Box

1. Switch to Print Layout view if you aren't already in that view.

2. On the Insert tab, click the Text Box button, and, in the gallery that appears, click the text-box design you like.

3. Select any sample text in the text box, and paste or type your replacement text.

4. Click the outer boundary of the text box, and drag it to the location you want.

5. Use any of the tools on the Text Box Tools Format tab to modify the text box itself, or use the formatting tools on the Home tab to modify the text.

6. Click outside the text box to resume working on the main content of your document.

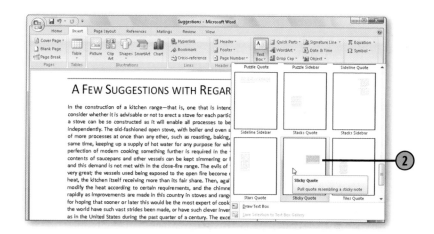

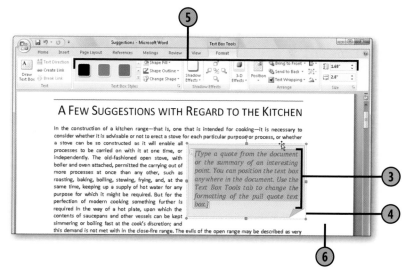

Tip

To create your own custom text box, click Draw Text Box in the Text Box gallery, and use your mouse to drag out the dimensions of the text box.

Inserting a Watermark

A *watermark* is a picture or some text (a company logo, for example) that sits "behind" the main text. It appears on every printed page as if it were part of the paper. You can create a picture watermark or a text watermark, but you can't have both on the same page.

Create the Watermark

(1) On the Page Layout tab, click the Watermark button, and choose the watermark you want from the gallery that appears.

(2) If none of the existing watermarks is what you want, choose Custom Watermark from the gallery to display the Printed Watermark dialog box.

(3) To create a text watermark, select Text Watermark, type the text, choose your formatting options, and click OK.

(4) To create a picture watermark, select Picture Watermark, locate and select the picture file you want to use, choose your formatting options, and click OK.

(5) If you decide you don't want a watermark after all, click the Watermark button on the Page Layout tab, and choose Remove Watermark from the gallery.

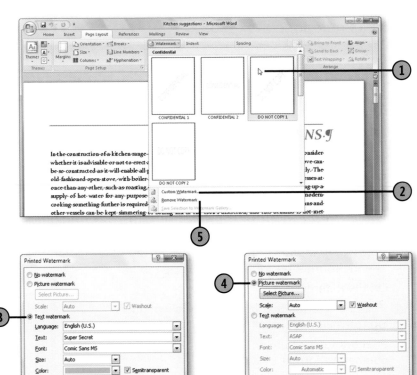

Tip

To have the same watermark appear automatically in every document that you create using a particular template, create the watermark in that template. To have the watermark available to all your documents, add it to the Watermark gallery.

Tip

The watermark appears in Print Layout and Full Screen Reading views, and in Print Preview. It also appears, of course, in the printed document.

Creating Footnotes and Endnotes

Word makes it so easy to add footnotes and/or endnotes to a document! Endnotes are just like footnotes, except that endnotes appear all together at the end of a document (or the end of a section) instead of at the foot of each page. Word will number the footnotes for you in one number series and the endnotes in a different number series or format.

Whenever you add or delete a footnote or an endnote, Word automatically renumbers the appropriate series. For a footnote, Word also figures out how much space is required at the bottom of the page for the footnote, and, when a footnote is too long for the page, Word automatically continues it on the next page.

Insert the Footnote or Endnote

(1) In Page Layout view, with the insertion point located where you want the footnote or endnote reference mark to appear in your document, click the Insert Footnote button on the References tab for a footnote or the Insert Endnote button for an endnote.

(2) Type your footnote or endnote text.

Change the Reference Mark

(1) On the References tab, click the Footnote & Endnote button.

(2) Specify where you want the footnotes or endnotes to appear, and click the numbering format you want.

(3) Click to display the Symbol dialog box, choose a symbol for the footnote or endnote reference mark, and click OK.

(4) Click Apply to change the location of the footnotes or endnotes and/or the number format, or click Insert to use the selected symbol as the reference mark for this footnote or endnote.

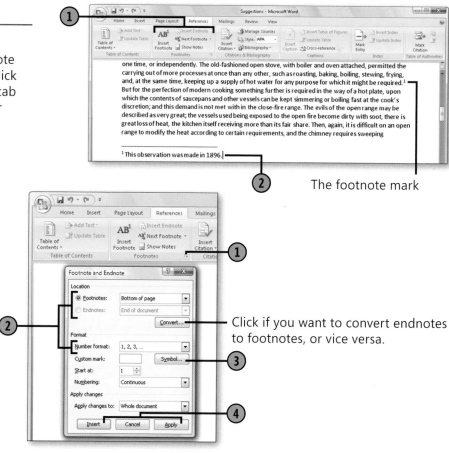

The footnote mark

Click if you want to convert endnotes to footnotes, or vice versa.

Inserting a Citation

When your writing references outside sources and/or works by other people, including books, articles, legal decisions, or other items, you'll need to cite these sources. Word provides a rich environment for entering, compiling, formatting, and inserting citations into your documents. If you're working in a company, a school, or an agency that frequently creates documents that include citations, you probably already have the data entered in bibliographies, ready to be dropped in. However, if you don't have access to existing bibliographies, you can enter the data once and then save it for future use.

Add Existing Citations

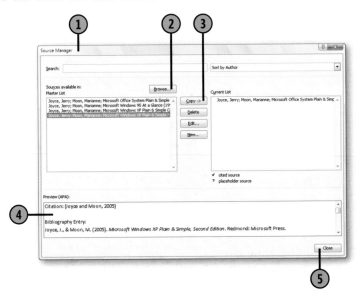

① On the References tab, click the Manage Sources button to display the Source Manager dialog box.

② If the default source file isn't the one you want, click Browse. Use the Open Source List dialog box to locate the source file you want, and then click OK. You can use numerous source files to copy citations into your document.

③ If citations exist in the source document that aren't already in your document, and you'll eventually want to add them, select the citations you want, and click Copy. Use the Sort and Search tools if you need to find citations in a large source file, and add those you want to your document.

④ Select any citation you're not sure of to inspect the information, and then decide whether or not to add it to your document.

⑤ Click Close when you've finished.

Tip ✔

All citations are tagged as fields, and you can easily modify their styles by changing the Citations & Bibliography style on the References tab.

Try This! 🖱

If you need to cite a source but don't currently have the citation information, don't worry. Click in the document where you want to place the citation, click Insert Citation, and choose Add New Placeholder. When you eventually have the information, double-click the placeholder, and enter the information in the Edit Source dialog box.

Insert a Citation

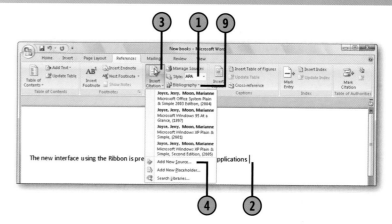

① Select the citation style you want for all of your citations.

② Click in your document where you want the citation to appear.

③ On the References tab, click the Insert Citation button, and, if the citation you want is listed, click it.

④ If the citation isn't listed, click Add New Source to display the Create Source dialog box.

⑤ Select the type of citation you want.

⑥ Enter the information for the citation.

⑦ Either use the proposed citation tag name or enter a unique name.

⑧ Click OK.

⑨ If you want to insert a bibliography of your citations or a list of works cited, place the insertion point where you want the item to appear, click the Bibliography button, and click the item you want in the gallery that appears.

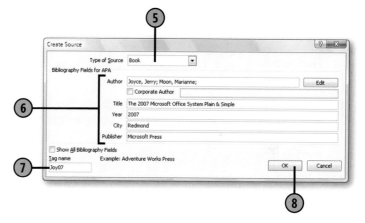

Tip

The citation is placed inside a *content control* in your document. To edit the citation or the source, or to convert the citation into static text, point to the content control, click the down arrow that appears, and choose what you want to do from the drop-down menu.

Tip

To edit a citation, double-click it, and change the information in the Edit Source dialog box.

Creating a Table of Contents

Provided your document is organized by styles or you've assigned outline levels to your heading paragraphs, it's a snap to have Word create a well-organized table of contents for you. Word comes with predesigned table-of-contents layouts. The table is inserted as a field in a *content control*, so after you've created the table, you can change its layout by choosing a different design. You can also update the table if you change the content of your document.

Set the Outline Text

1. In Outline view, scroll through the document, verifying that any paragraph you want to appear in the table of contents has a style that uses the appropriate level 1, level 2, or level 3 outline level, and that any paragraph you don't want to include has an outline level of 4 or below or a Body Text outline level. If a paragraph you want to include doesn't have a style with the appropriate outline level assigned to it, click in the paragraph and apply the appropriate style.

2. If you want to include or exclude a paragraph but don't want to change its style, click the Add Text button on the References tab, and click the outline level you want to apply.

3. Switch to Print Layout view, and click in the document where you want the table of contents to appear.

4. On the References tab, click the Table Of Contents button, and select the style and type of table of contents you want to insert.

5. If you make changes to the document that affect the pagination or the heading content, click the Update Table button on the References tab.

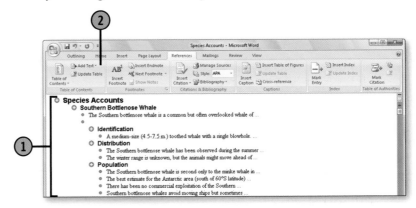

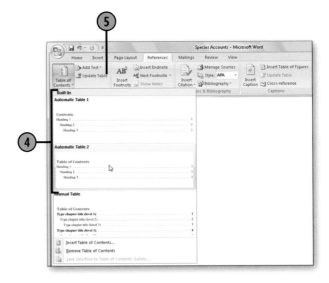

Printing an Envelope

When you've taken the time and trouble to create a professional-looking letter or some other document for mailing, you don't want to ruin the good impression with a handwritten envelope! Word makes it easy for you to create crisp, businesslike printed envelopes. You can easily include your return address, and, in the United States, you can add electronic postage. If you already have the mailing address in your letter, Word usually detects it and copies it to the Envelopes And Labels dialog box. You can also type the address directly in the dialog box.

Add the Address

① On the Mailings tab, click the Envelopes button to display the Envelopes And Labels dialog box.

② If a delivery address is displayed on the Envelopes tab, verify that it's correct.

③ If no delivery address is shown, or if you want to use a different address, type the address. If the address is in your Microsoft Outlook Contacts list, click the Insert Address button.

④ Verify that the return address is correct. If you're using an envelope with a preprinted return address, select the Omit check box so that the return address won't be printed.

⑤ Click Options to display the Envelope Options dialog box.

⑥ On the Envelope Options tab, specify the envelope size and the fonts and positions for the addresses.

⑦ On the Printing Options tab, specify how the envelope is to be loaded and printed. Click OK.

⑧ If you have Electronic Postage (E-Postage) software installed, select this check box to use electronic postage.

⑨ If you need to make changes to your E-Postage setup, click the E-Postage Properties button.

⑩ Click Print to print the envelope.

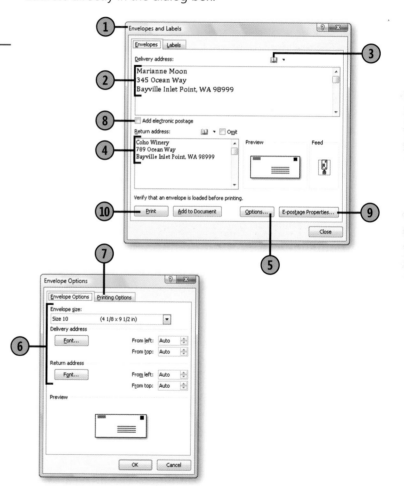

Printing a Mailing Label

Whether you need to print a single mailing label or a full page of labels, Word provides a tool that takes care of most of the details for you. All you need to do is specify the type of label you're using, the address, and the way you want the label to be printed. That's it! Word obligingly does the rest for you.

Print the Label

1. Make a note of the manufacturer and the design number of the labels you'll be using. If you're planning to print only one label, figure out which label on the sheet of labels is the one you're going to use. Later in the process, you'll need to specify the label by row (the horizontal line of labels) and by column (the vertical line of labels). Insert the sheet of labels into your printer (usually into the manual feed tray, if there is one).

2. On the Mailings tab, click the Labels button to display the Envelopes And Labels dialog box.

3. On the Labels tab of the Envelopes And Labels dialog box, use the proposed address, type a new one, or click the Insert Address button to insert an address from your Outlook Contacts list. To insert your return address, select the Use Return Address check box.

4. If the type of label shown isn't the one you're using, click Options to display the Label Options dialog box, specify the label you're using, and click OK.

5. If you're using a full sheet of labels, click the appropriate option to print a whole page of identical labels or only one label on the sheet of labels. If you want to print only one label, specify the label by row and column.

6. Click Print to print the label or labels.

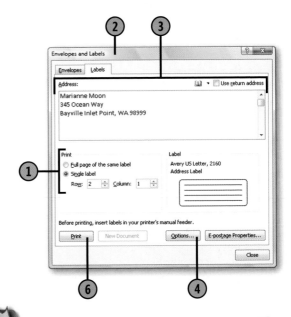

See Also

"Managing Your Contacts" on pages 232–233 for information about adding or modifying address information in your Outlook Contacts list.

"Changing Your User Information" on page 321 for information about modifying your return address.

Tip

If you need to print a large number of different mailing labels, consider using the mail merge feature.

Mail Merge: The Power and the Pain

Mail merge is a tool that combines two different parts into a sleek and well-crafted whole: that is, a series of identical printed documents (form letters, for example) with the appropriate information (individual names and addresses) inserted automatically into each document. The two parts are the *master document* and a *data source*. The master document is the template (although not a template in the Word-document sense) that lays out your document and contains text or other items that never change. The master document also contains instructions for inserting data from a data source into each document. The data source is a uniform collection of information from one of a number of sources.

Mail merge is an almost unbelievable time-saver once you've set it up, and its power can be awesome. But—and here's the rub—you have to be willing to deal with all the complexities of *fields* and *conditional expressions*. The good news is that the mail merge feature is extremely *scalable*—that is, it's easy to do a simple, basic mail merge, but the process becomes increasingly demanding as your mail merge becomes more complex. If, for example, you simply want to address a stack of envelopes to people whose addresses are contained in a Word table, a Microsoft Excel worksheet, or your Microsoft Outlook Contacts list, you can just jump in and do it with little preparation and a great likelihood of success.

Setting Conditional Content

One of the real powers of mail merge is the ability it gives you to tailor the content of a document based on some data stored in your mailing list. For example, you might offer a tour of your company to individuals who have invested a large amount of money in the company, but offer only a free monthly newsletter to the small investors. If you have an entry in your data file for the level of investment, you can use that data to control the content of your document.

You control conditional content by using the IF Word field. To use this field, you place it in your document where you want the conditional content to appear by clicking Rules on the Mailings tab, and then clicking If...Then...Else in the list that appears. In the Insert Word Field: IF dialog box, you specify the data field that lists the value to be tested (for example, amount of investment), the comparison (Greater Than Or Equal To), and the value (5000). Then you insert the text to be used if the comparison is true ("Please call to arrange a tour.") or untrue ("Please call to receive your monthly newsletter.").

It's More than Letters

The mail merge feature can do more than create form letters and address envelopes. You can save the merged documents as a file so that you can edit them or send them by e-mail. You can create almost any type of document by using a specific template or designing the document from scratch. All Word needs is a data document with some data fields in it. You can create mailing labels and address books, awards, parts lists, different versions of exams, and catalogs designed for specific geographical areas or demographic populations. The uses for mail merge are limited only by your creativity, your willingness to experiment with different data fields and Word fields, and your decision as to whether mail merge would be faster than manually creating individual documents.

Creating a Form Letter

"Mail merge"—a dreaded phrase in the world of word processing! Not only does it conjure up an image of piles of junk mail, but associated terms such as "fields" and "conditional expressions" add to the intimidation factor.

However, with just a little effort—and a lot of help from Word—when you need to send nearly identical letters to numerous people, you can create your own mail-merged documents and personalized form letters.

Set Up Your Letter

1. Create your letter as you would any other letter, leaving blank any parts that you want to be completed with data from your mailing list. Save the letter.

2. On the Mailings tab, click the Start Mail Merge button, and choose Letters from the drop-down menu.

3. Click the Select Recipients button, and specify the type of data you want to use for your mailing list:

   • Type New List to enter your data in the New Address List dialog box.

   • Use Existing List to use data that exists in a file Word can read. To see which type of data sources you can use, open the Files Of Type list in the Select Data Source dialog box, and review the list.

   • Select From Outlook Contacts to use data from your Outlook Contacts list.

4. Click Edit Recipient List to display the Mail Merge Recipients dialog box.

5. Select or clear check boxes to designate whom you want to include in the mail merge.

6. Click an arrow for the field you want to sort or filter by, and select your action from the list that appears. Click OK when you've finished.

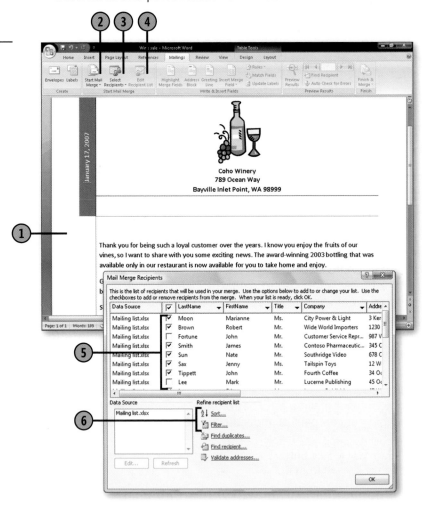

Specify the Data to Be Merged

① In your document, click where you want to add information from your data source.

② Click the type of information you want to insert.

③ In the dialog box that appears, specify the options you want, and then click OK. Continue adding items to the letter.

④ Click the Preview Results button to display your data in the document.

⑤ Use the buttons to see how your form letters will look when they're merged with the different data records.

⑥ Click Edit Recipient List if you see that the form letter you're previewing is addressed to someone you don't want to include in this mailing. In the Mail Merge Recipients dialog box, clear the check box for that individual, and click OK.

⑦ Click Auto Check For Errors, and choose to do a simulated merge to check the document for errors. Correct any errors.

⑧ Click Finish & Merge, and specify how you want your letters to be completed.

Tip

If you're familiar with conducting a mail merge using the Mail Merge Wizard that steps you through the process, and if you want to use the wizard, click the Start Mail Merge button, and choose Step By Step Mail Merge Wizard from the drop-down list.

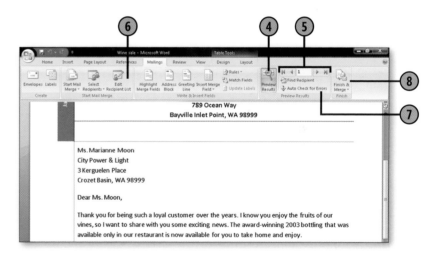

Finalizing Your Document

If you've ever released a final version of a document, only to find that there are still revisions marked on it or that it contains information you don't want others to see, you know that you don't want to do that again! And if you've ever released a document whose wording makes you cringe because someone has edited it without your permission, you don't want that to happen again either. Fortunately, Word provides tools to prevent these embarrassing events from happening again.

Prepare Your Document

(1) With your document completed and saved, click the Office button. On the Office menu, point to Prepare, and choose Inspect Document from the gallery to display the Document Inspector dialog box.

(2) Clear the check boxes for the items you want to keep in the document, select the check boxes for the items you don't want to appear in the document, and then click the Inspect button at the bottom of the dialog box.

(3) In the Document Inspector dialog box, click the Remove All button for each type of item you want to remove. Close the dialog box when you've finished.

(4) If you don't want other people who have access to your document to edit it, open the Office menu, point to Prepare, and choose Mark As Final from the gallery. Click OK to confirm that you want to mark the document as final.

(5) Close and distribute the document.

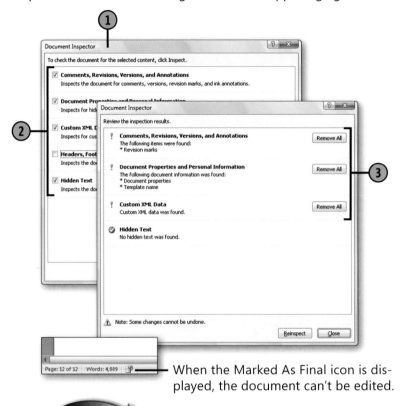

When the Marked As Final icon is displayed, the document can't be edited.

> **Tip** ✔
>
> To edit a document that has been marked as Final, choose Mark As Final again from the Prepare submenu.

> **See Also**
>
> "Protecting a Document, Workbook, or Presentation with a Password" on page 326 for information about using additional security settings to prevent changes to your document.

7

Working in Excel

In this section:

- What's Where in Excel?
- Entering and Editing the Data
- Excel's Eccentricities
- Using a Predefined Workbook
- Formatting Cells
- Changing the Overall Look
- Formatting Numbers
- Moving and Copying Data
- Adding and Deleting Columns and Rows
- Creating a Series
- Organizing Your Worksheets
- Printing a Worksheet
- Adding and Viewing Comments

If you've never used it before, open up Microsoft Office Excel 2007 and take a look. You'll see a worksheet that contains a seemingly endless grid of columns and rows—16,384 columns and more than a million rows! The space at the intersection of each column and row is a *cell,* so, although you'll probably never need them all, you have billions of cells ready to hold whatever types of data you'll be working with. You can use a single work-sheet if that's all you need, or you can use multiple worksheets for large projects. You can organize several worksheets that all pertain to one set of data into their own *workbook.* If you work on several large projects, you can give each project its own work-book. When you start a new workbook, you'll see that it contains three worksheets, but you can add more if you need them.

In this section of the book, you'll learn how to enter and edit data and how to add visual appeal and clarity to your work-sheets by formatting them with fonts, colors, borders, and so on. You can create your own look, or use templates that quickly apply predefined styles to your worksheets or workbooks. You'll learn how to format numbers in various ways—as currency, per-centages, or decimals—for readability. We'll also show you how to update, change, move, or copy your data, and how to print your worksheets.

What's Where in Excel?

Microsoft Office Excel 2007 has one purpose—to help you get the most out of your data. Although Excel can display many different appearances and elements, the most common of these are illustrated below.

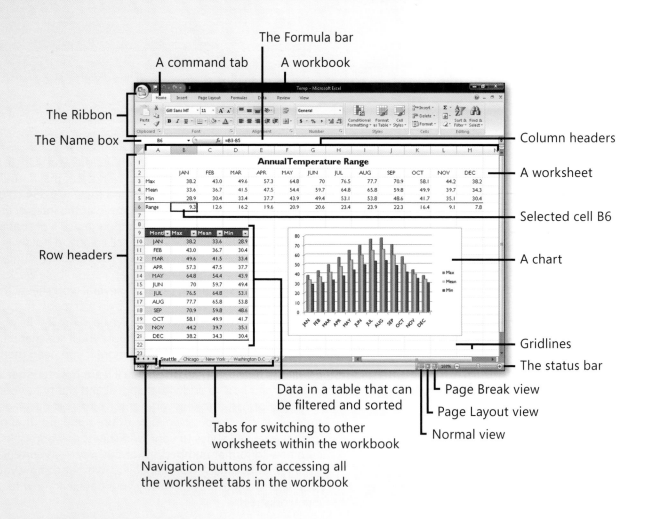

- The Formula bar
- A command tab
- A workbook
- The Ribbon
- The Name box
- Column headers
- A worksheet
- Selected cell B6
- Row headers
- A chart
- Gridlines
- The status bar
- Page Break view
- Page Layout view
- Normal view
- Data in a table that can be filtered and sorted
- Tabs for switching to other worksheets within the workbook
- Navigation buttons for accessing all the worksheet tabs in the workbook

Entering the Data

Because Excel is all about working with data, whether the items are numbers or names, you'll need to enter the data before Excel can start working its magic. To enter your data, place one data item in each cell, arranged in the way that works best for you.

Enter Your Data

(1) Start a new workbook if you don't already have a blank worksheet open. Save the workbook with a new file name.

(2) Type the header (the title) of the first column, press Tab, and type the header of the next column. Continue across the top row until all your columns have headers. Press Enter after you've typed the last item.

(3) Click in the beginning of the second row, and enter your data. Press Tab, and continue entering your data. Press Enter after you've typed the last item.

(4) Continue entering your data row by row, and be sure to save the file periodically.

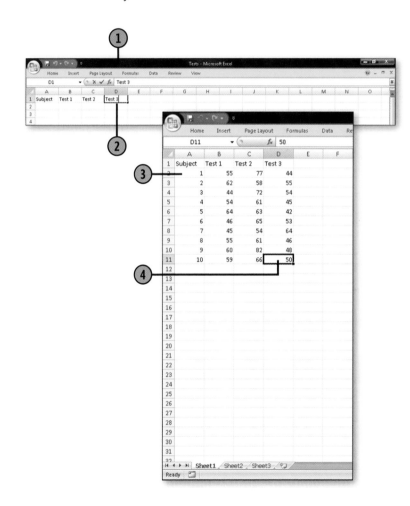

Tip ✓
To move backward in a row, press Shift+Tab. You can also use your keyboard's arrow keys or the mouse to move to any cell.

Editing the Data

Sometimes you need to go back into a worksheet and make changes to your data. You can correct the data quickly and easily, either by replacing the contents of an entire cell or by editing the existing content.

Replace the Data

1. Click in the cell, or use the arrow keys to select the cell whose data you want to replace.

2. Type the new data, and press Enter.

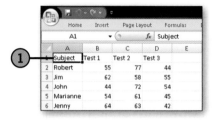

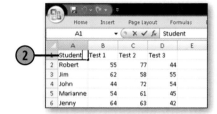

Edit the Existing Data

1. Double-click the cell to activate it for editing, or select the cell and press F2.

2. Click or use the arrow keys to move the insertion point to where you want to do your editing.

3. Use the Backspace or the Delete key to remove the data you don't want, and type the new information. Press Enter when you've finished.

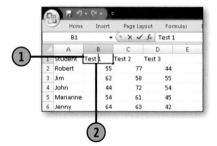

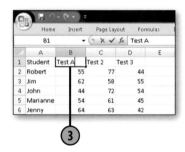

Tip

To select an adjacent cell and set the direction in which the selection moves when you press Enter, choose Excel Options from the Office menu, and, in the Advanced category, select the After Pressing Enter, Move Selection check box. Then, in the Direction list box, select the direction in which you want the selection to move.

Excel's Eccentricities

If you're familiar with the way a program such as Microsoft Office Word works, your first reaction to Excel's idiosyncratic behavior might be "Huh?" or "What happened?" To become comfortable with Excel, you need to understand that it's a completely different creature from Word. It behaves differently because it's designed for the organization and analysis of data.

Excel is made up of vertical columns and horizontal rows. At the intersection of a column and a row is a *cell*. This grid structure is designed to help you organize your data. Look at the worksheet below, and you'll see that all the items in column A are related—that is, each cell contains the name of a student. Similarly, all the items in columns B, C, and D are related—they represent scores for different tests. The items in each row are related too. All the items in row 2 are related to each other—that is, each is about Robert's exam scores. So, at the intersection of a column and a row is a single piece of data—a *data point*. At the intersection of column C and row 2 is the data point indicating that in Test 2 (column C), Robert (row 2) scored 77. In Excel's *cell notation*—its shorthand language—this data point is located in cell C2.

Keep in mind that Excel is all about data. Unlike Word, it cares little about presentation. You can, with a little work, make a fine-looking presentation in Excel, but Excel might occasionally stymie you because its priority is to preserve the integrity of the data when it's being edited. This means that if you click in a cell and start typing, you'll be replacing the existing data rather than adding to it. Why? Because, to Excel, each cell contains that single piece of data. When you click in a cell that contains data, Excel thinks that you want to either update or correct the data. This can definitely throw you off when you're used to the normal Office protocol of selecting something before you change it! You'll see the same thing when you copy or move columns, rows, or cells. Unlike Word, for example, Excel doesn't automatically add columns or rows to a table to compensate for your actions—you have to manage the columns, rows, and cells yourself.

It might take you a little while to get used to Excel's differences, but, as you start crunching your data, you'll find that what seems like Excel's quirky behavior actually helps you get accurate results very efficiently. Of course, Excel does have many other complexities, such as using *relative* or *absolute* references to cells, and building complex formulas that contain sophisticated functions. However, these features really are designed to make working with your data as precise and accurate as possible. We'll go into detail about cell references, formulas, and functions in "Cell References, Formulas, and Functions" on pages 132–133.

	A	B	C	D
1	Student	Test A	Test B	Test C
2	Robert	55	77	44
3	Jim	62	58	55
4	John	44	72	54
5	Marianne	54	61	45
6	Jenny	64	63	42
7	Rob	46	65	53
8	Beth	45	54	64
9	Jerry	55	61	46
10	Rick	60	82	48
11	Roberta	59	66	50

Using a Predefined Workbook

Wouldn't it be great to have a workbook all set up and formatted for you so that all you'd have to do would be enter your information? Well, dream no more! When you use one of Excel's existing templates, you don't have to worry about structure and formatting—they're already taken care of for you. Not only that, but many templates provide an extensive array of formulas and relationships already built into them that provide some powerful methods of data analysis.

Open and Use a Template

① Choose New from the Office menu to display the New Workbook dialog box.

② If you see a template you want, select it to preview it, and then click Create.

③ If you don't see a template you want, do any of the following:

- Click Installed Templates to see the Microsoft templates that you've either installed on your computer or downloaded, and double-click the one you want to use.

- Click My Templates to display the New dialog box and your custom templates. Double-click a template to create a document.

- Click New From Existing to open an existing workbook as a template.

- Click a topic to see templates of that type that are available for download, and double-click the one you want to use.

- In the new workbook that appears, replace any placeholder text or data with your own, and add any other elements you want.

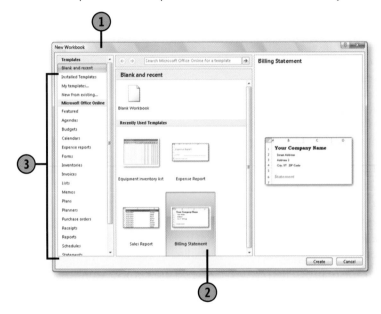

Tip

To change the number of worksheets included in the new workbook, the default font and font size, and the default view, choose Excel Options from the Office menu, and, with the Popular category selected, modify the settings in the When Creating New Workbooks section.

Formatting Cells

Reviewing or working with the data in your worksheets might not be high on the list of tasks you do with great enthusiasm, but you can make your work in Excel visually interesting by formatting the cells in your worksheets. To add continuity to the design, you can use the predefined formats that match the main theme used in the document. You can also modify the formatting by choosing different fonts and adding emphasis such as italicized or bold type, adding borders and color to the cells, and aligning your data for the greatest clarity.

Format Some Cells

① Select the cells you want to format with the same formatting.

② On the Home tab, click Cell Styles, and point to the different styles to see how your selected cells look using that style. Click the style you want.

③ To customize any existing formatting or to create your own formatting, use the buttons and galleries on the Home tab to format the cells with fonts, emphasis, alignment, borders, and colors; and specify whether you want the text to wrap onto more than one line if it's too long to fit into its cell.

Click a column header to select a column.

Click to select the entire worksheet.

Click a row header to select a row.

Drag the mouse over the cells to select them.

Hold down the Ctrl key, and click or drag to select nonadjacent areas.

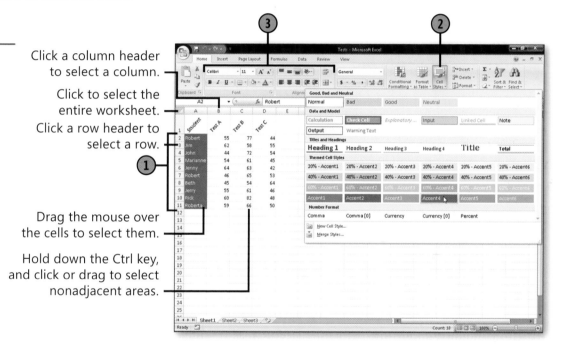

Tip ✓

To select a large range of cells, select the first (top-left) cell of the selection, scroll down and/or over to the end of the area to be selected, hold down the Shift key, and then click the last (bottom-right) cell of the selection.

Changing the Overall Look

Themes define the look of your entire workbook—the color scheme, the pairing of the default fonts used for body and heading text, and the color scheme for charts and graphics.

Once you've selected a theme, you can use the font pairing—fonts that work well together—and the color palette in your formatting to apply a unified look to your document design.

Choose a Theme

① On the Page Layout tab, click the Themes button to display the Themes gallery.

② Do any of the following:

- Point to a theme to see how your work-sheet will look if you use that theme.

- Click the theme you want to use.

- Click More Themes On Microsoft Office Online to find more themes on line, and select the theme you want.

- Click Browse For Themes to display the Choose Theme Or Themed Document dialog box. Select a theme, or select a document that contains the theme you want, and click Open.

③ Use the tools on the Home and the Insert tabs as you normally would, selecting from the theme fonts and colors shown or selecting non-theme fonts and colors for special effects.

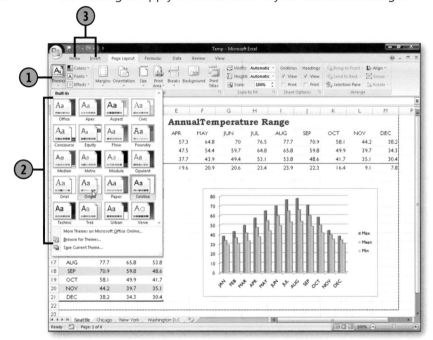

Tip

You're not limited to the fonts or colors of your theme. The theme fonts and colors are suggested and usually appear at the top of your formatting choices, but you can choose any fonts and colors you want.

Formatting Numbers

When you look at columns and rows stacked full of numbers, it isn't always immediately clear what those numbers represent. Do they indicate currency? Are they percentages of something? You can improve the readability of your workbook by using standard numeric formatting to make everything as clear as possible.

Format Some Numbers

1 Select the columns, rows, or cells that contain numbers that will all be formatted in the same way.

2 Select the type of numbering format to be used.

3 Use the buttons on the Formatting toolbar to modify the numeric formatting.

4 If the formatting isn't what you want, click the Format Cells: Number button.

5 On the Number tab of the Format Cells dialog box that appears, select the type of formatting you want.

6 Select any available options you want to use to customize the formatting.

7 Click OK when you've finished.

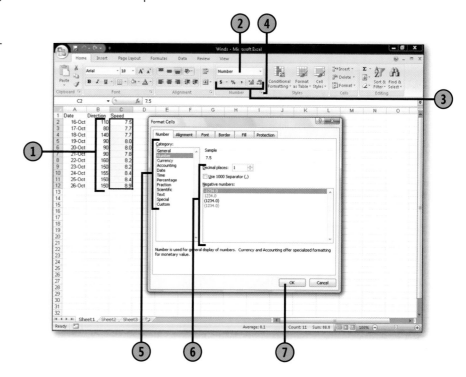

Tip

If you're applying an accounting number format (currency), click the down arrow at the right of the Currency button, and choose the type of currency you want from the drop-down menu.

Tip

To select non-adjacent rows or columns, hold down the Ctrl key as you click each row or column header.

Moving and Copying Data

As with most Office programs, you can move the existing information around by copying or cutting it. However, when you copy data in Excel, you'll need to have a blank area ready to receive the data, or else Excel will overwrite any existing data. You can also tell Excel to copy the contents of a cell to a group of adjacent cells.

Move Some Content

① Select all the cells you want to move.

② Move the mouse pointer over an edge of your selection until the pointer turns into a four-headed arrow.

③ Drag the selection to a blank location.

> **See Also**
>
> "Adding and Deleting Columns and Rows" on pages 116–117 for information about adding blank columns or rows.

Copy or Cut Some Content

① Select all the cells you want to copy or cut.

② Click either the Copy button (or press Ctrl+C) or the Cut button (or press Ctrl+X).

③ Click in the first cell of the destination, and do either of the following:

- Press the Enter key to paste a single copy of the content.

- Click the Paste button (or press Ctrl+V) to paste one copy; move to another location, and click the Paste button again. Continue until you've pasted all the copies you want. Press Esc to end the copying.

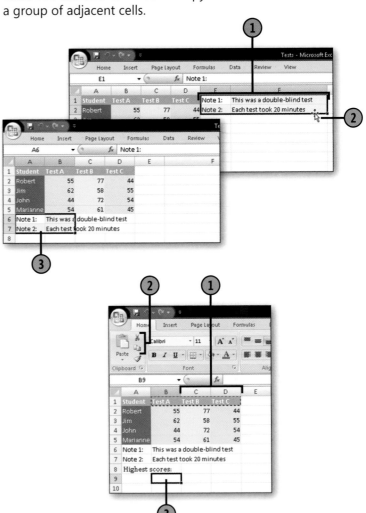

Copy Content to Adjacent Cells

(1) Select the cell whose content you want to copy.

(2) Move the mouse pointer to the bottom-right corner of the cell until the pointer turns into a cross (the Fill handle).

(3) Drag the Fill handle either vertically or horizontally. Note that the ScreenTip shows the value for each cell. When you release the mouse button, the selected cells are filled.

(4) If the results aren't what you expected, click the AutoFill Options button, select the Copy Cells option, and click outside the selection to have the contents of the first cell copied to all the other selected cells instead of creating a calculated series.

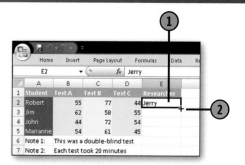

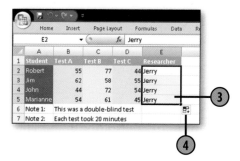

Tip ✓

To copy only a part of the cell contents—the formatting, a comment, or a value, for example—copy the item, click where you want to put it, click the down arrow at the bottom of the Paste button, and either choose the action you want from the drop-down menu or choose Paste Special from the menu. Select the action you want from the Paste Special dialog box to paste the element you want.

Tip ✓

You can copy in any direction—up or down, left or right. You're not limited to copying only values—you can copy formulas too.

Tip ✓

If you can't drag selected cells to a new location or if the Fill handle doesn't appear, choose Excel Options from the Office menu, click the Advanced category, and select the Enable Fill Handle And Cell Drag-And-Drop check box. (Catchy title!)

See Also ➤

"Creating a Series" on page 118 for information about having Excel insert a series of values based on the first selected cell instead of just copying the contents of that cell.

Adding and Deleting Columns and Rows

It might take a little time to get your worksheet laid out perfectly, but getting it exactly right is simple enough and very satisfying. You'll probably need to rearrange some columns or rows, delete empty or useless columns or rows, or add new

ones. You might need to make room for some data that you want to move. If you find that you need an existing row or column but that its current content is useless, you can simply delete the content but leave the empty row or column intact.

Add a Column

① Right-click the column header at the right of where you want the new column.

② Choose Insert from the shortcut menu.

> **Tip**
>
> To add or delete several rows or columns at one time, or to clear the contents of multiple rows or columns at one time, select multiple column or row headers before you right-click. To select nonadjacent rows or columns, hold down the Ctrl key as you click each row or column header.

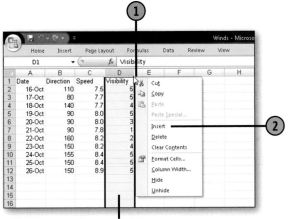

Excel will create a new column D.

Add a Row

① Right-click the row header below where you want the new row.

② Choose Insert from the shortcut menu.

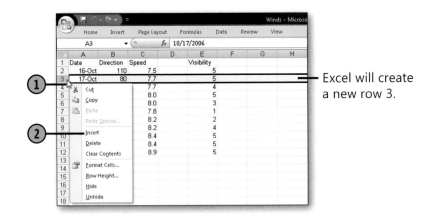

Excel will create a new row 3.

Delete a Column or a Row

(1) Right-click the column header or the row header.

(2) Choose Delete from the shortcut menu.

See Also

"Hiding Columns and Rows" on page 119 for information about hiding columns or rows without deleting them.

Delete Some or All Content of Cells

(1) Select the cells to be cleared.

(2) On the Home tab, click the Clear button and, from the submenu, choose what you want to delete.

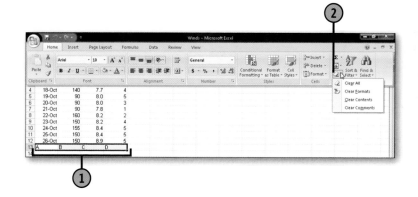

Tip

To quickly clear the content of a selected cell or cells without removing any formatting, press the Delete key. Remember that you can use the Undo button on the Quick Access toolbar to restore any content that you deleted unintentionally.

Creating a Series

When you're working with a *series*—that is, a particular set of data such as a series of dates or a list of consecutive numbers—numbering or labeling all the items in the series can be quite time consuming. Why not put your time to better use by letting Excel do the work for you? All you need to do is make sure that Excel recognizes the data as a series.

Create a Series

① Type the first item in the series.

② Point to the bottom-right corner of the cell until the mouse pointer turns into a cross (the Fill handle).

③ Drag the Fill handle to fill the cells that you want to be included in the series.

④ If Excel copied the cell instead of creating a series, or didn't fill the series as you expected, click the AutoFill Options button, and select Fill Series or any other appropriate option.

⑤ Make sure the series is correct. If it isn't, click the Undo button on the Standard toolbar and try again.

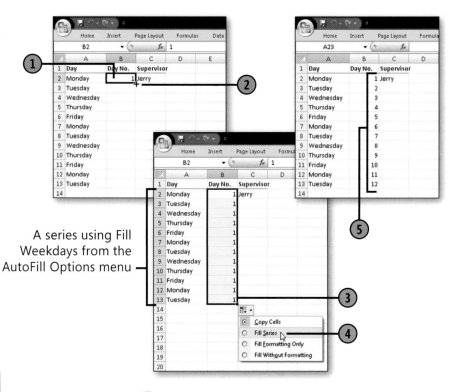

A series using Fill Weekdays from the AutoFill Options menu

Tip ✓

If the Fill Series option isn't listed on the AutoFill Options shortcut menu, Excel doesn't recognize the data as a series. You can define your own series by choosing Excel Options from the Office menu, and, with the Popular category selected, clicking the Edit Custom Lists button. In the Custom Lists dialog box, define your list, and click OK.

Tip ✓

To define a numeric or date series that is nonlinear, that doesn't use a single-step value, or that is very long, click the Fill button on the Home tab, choose Series from the drop-down menu, and use the Series dialog box to set the parameters for your series.

Hiding Columns and Rows

When you create a worksheet, it sometimes contains columns and rows of data that aren't relevant for every review or for every use of the worksheet, even though they're important in various analyses. You can hide these columns and rows from view when they're not needed and reveal them again when you or someone else wants to review or work with them.

Hide Columns or Rows

① Select the columns or rows that you want to hide.

② Right-click one of the selected headers, and choose Hide from the shortcut menu.

Reveal Hidden Columns or Rows

① Select the columns or rows that are adjacent to the hidden columns or rows.

② Right-click one of the selected headers, and choose Unhide from the shortcut menu.

Tip

To make sure that you don't accidentally distribute a workbook that contains information you don't want to share with others, make sure there are no hidden rows or columns in your final version of the workbook. To check for hidden rows or columns, run the Document Inspector by pointing to Prepare on the Office menu and clicking Inspect Document in the gallery.

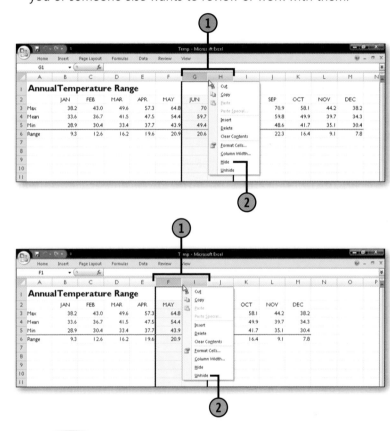

See Also

"Finalizing Your Document" on page 104 for information about using the Document Inspector.

Formatting Cell Dimensions

Your worksheet can contain many different types of data that occupy different amounts of space. Excel creates all worksheets using a default setting for the width of the columns and the height of the rows. As you start entering your information, you might find that some columns are too narrow, resulting in truncated content. In other columns, you might find that some columns are too wide, resulting in

wasted space. Similarly, you might want to increase the height of the rows to increase the readability of the content. Although a row will automatically increase in height if you increase the font size of its content, you might want to increase the height of the row and then change the vertical alignment of the text to add space above or below the content.

Set the Column Width

1. Select the columns whose widths you want to change.

2. Right-click one of the selected column headers, and choose Column Width from the shortcut menu to display the Column Width dialog box.

3. Specify the width of the columns, calculated by the number of characters of the default font that can be displayed on one line.

4. Click OK.

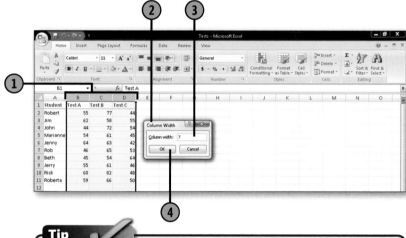

Tip ✓

To change the vertical alignment of text in one or more rows, select the cells to be adjusted, and then click the Top Align, Middle Align, or Bottom Align button in the Alignment section of the Home tab.

Tip ✓

To select the entire worksheet, click the blank header between the "1" row header and the "A" column header. If the cells in the area you want to format are contiguous—that is, all the cells are adjacent to one another—just click in any one of the cells before you choose AutoFormat, and Excel will figure out the area to be formatted.

Try This!

On the Page Layout tab, click the Background button. Find a picture that you like or that's relevant to your data, and click Open. Format your data so that it's easily readable on top of your picture. Now that's adding some *real* interest to your formatting!

Set the Row Height

① Select the rows whose heights you want to change.

② Right-click one of the selected row headers, and choose Row Height from the shortcut menu to display the Row Height dialog box.

③ Specify the height of the rows in points.

④ Click OK.

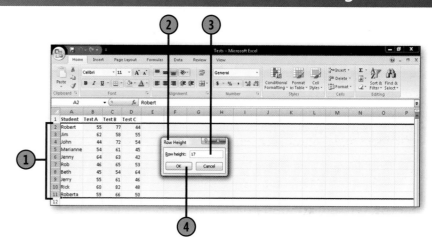

Adjust the Height or Width to Fit the Content

① Select the cells that you want to format.

② On the Home tab, click the Format button, and choose AutoFit Row Height from the drop-down menu.

③ Click the Format button again, and choose AutoFit Column width from the drop-down menu.

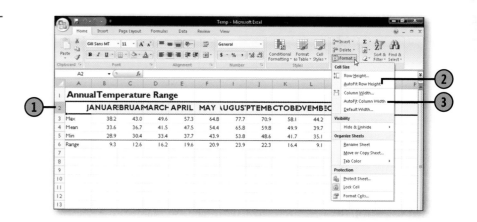

Organizing Your Worksheets

When you're working on a big project, you can spend so much time deep in your Excel workbook that it becomes an alternate universe. You can do a lot to make that workbook universe a comfortable place in which to work. Give your worksheets descriptive names—rather than Sheet 1, Sheet 2—to make them easy to recognize; reorganize them into a logical order; add new worksheets if you need to, or delete unused ones to get rid of any unnecessary clutter.

Name the Worksheets

1 Double-click a worksheet tab, type a descriptive name for the worksheet, and press Enter.

2 Repeat for any other worksheet tabs you'd like to rename.

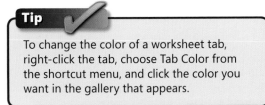

Tip

To change the color of a worksheet tab, right-click the tab, choose Tab Color from the shortcut menu, and click the color you want in the gallery that appears.

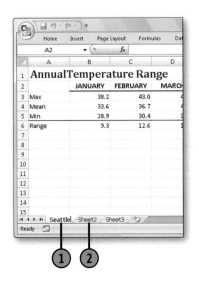

Change Their Order

1 Click the tab of the worksheet you want to move.

2 Drag the tab to the desired location.

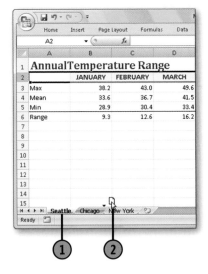

Insert a Worksheet

① Click the Insert Worksheet button.

② Rename the new worksheet, and move it to a different position among the tabs if you want.

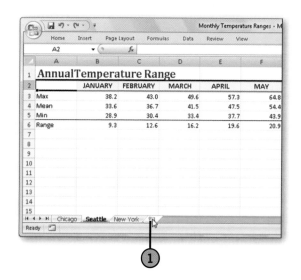

Delete a Worksheet

① Right-click the tab for the worksheet you want to delete, and choose Delete from the shortcut menu.

② When you're asked to confirm the deletion, click Delete.

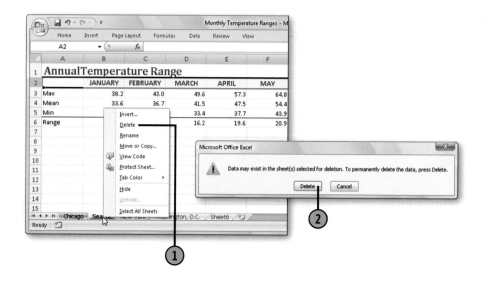

Setting Up the Page

You don't really need to worry about page setup in Excel until you're ready to print or distribute your worksheet, but at that point it's crucial that you attend to several details so that you get the results you want.

Set the Dimensions

① Switch to Page Layout view if you aren't already in that view, and adjust the zoom, if necessary, to see the layout of your page.

② On the Page Layout tab, click the Margins button, and select the margin settings you want. To create different margins, click Custom Margins, make your settings on the Margins tab of the Page Setup dialog box, and click OK.

③ Click the Orientation button, and click either the Portrait (longer than wide) or the Landscape (wider than long) printing orientation in the gallery that appears.

④ Click the Size button, and select the paper size you'll be using.

⑤ Specify the scaling to change the size of the printed worksheet or to force the worksheet to fit onto a set number of pages.

⑥ Specify whether you want to display and/or print the gridlines and the headings.

⑦ On the Office menu, point to Print, and click Print Preview in the gallery that appears. Review the pages as they'll look when printed, and then click Close Print Preview to return to Page Layout view. Make any other necessary layout adjustments.

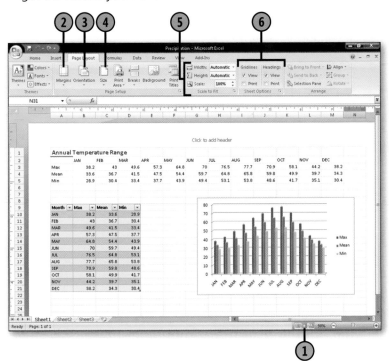

Tip

If you're going to print more than one worksheet at a time, step through these procedures for each worksheet.

Set the Header and Footer

① Switch to Page Layout view if you aren't already in that view.

② On the first page of your worksheet, click in the first section of the header.

③ On the Header & Footer Tools Design tab, specify whether you want to have a separate first-page header and/or different odd- and even-page headers.

④ Click the Header button if you want to choose one of the predesigned headers.

⑤ If you want to create your own header, with the insertion point in the first of the three sections of the header, click any buttons to automatically include specific information and/or type any information you want.

⑥ Click in the center section and add your content, and then click in the last section and add your content.

⑦ Click the Go To Footer button, and add your content to the three sections of the footer.

⑧ Click in your worksheet. If you chose to have a different first-page header and/or different odd- and even-page headers, move to the next page, click in the header area, and repeat steps 2 through 7. Repeat for any other headers that you want to add.

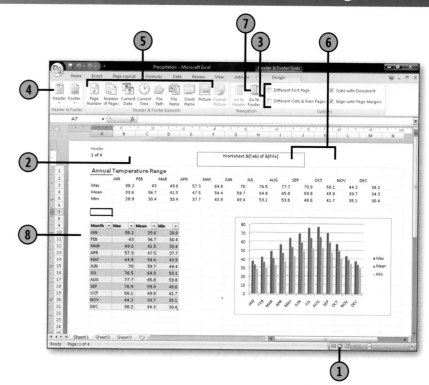

Printing a Worksheet

If you don't set it up exactly right, printing an Excel worksheet can be a trip down a rocky road, as well as a waste of paper. To avoid such calamities, you'll need to preview the page before you print it, make a few adjustments, and then preview it again and again—as many times as you need to until you're satisfied that the final product will live up to your expectations.

Specify What's to be Printed

① Select the area to be printed.

② On the Page Layout tab, click the Print Area button, and choose Set Print Area from the drop-down menu.

③ If your worksheet will occupy more than one page and you want to have the column and/or row headings repeated on each page, click the Print Titles button on the Page Layout tab to display the Sheet tab of the Page Setup dialog box.

④ Click to minimize the dialog box (yes, this is one of Excel's eccentricities), select any rows that you want to repeat at the top of each printed page, and press Enter.

⑤ Click to minimize the dialog box, select any columns that you want to repeat at the left side of each printed page, and press Enter.

⑥ Select the check boxes for the items you want to print and clear the check boxes for the items you don't want to print.

⑦ Select the way you want the worksheet to be printed

⑧ Click OK.

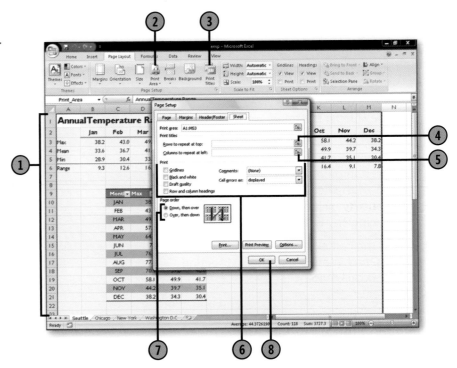

Tip

If the data area of your worksheet is made up of contiguous cells, Excel will automatically print only the part of the worksheet that contains your data. If you want to print only a specific section of the worksheet's data area, however, you'll need to set the print area manually.

Check the Layout

1 Switch to Page Layout view, and examine the way the pages will appear.

2 If you want some of the content to start on a new page, click in the cell where you want the new page to start, click the Breaks button on the Page Layout tab, and choose Insert Page Break from the drop-down menu.

3 If the page breaks aren't where you want them, click the Page Break Preview button. Drag a page break to a new position, and adjust other page breaks if necessary.

4 On the Office menu, point to Print, and click Print Preview in the gallery that appears. Review the pages as they'll look when printed. Click Close Print Preview, make any modifications to the layout, and recheck the document.

5 Choose Print from the Office menu, make your printing settings in the Print dialog box, and then print the worksheet or worksheets.

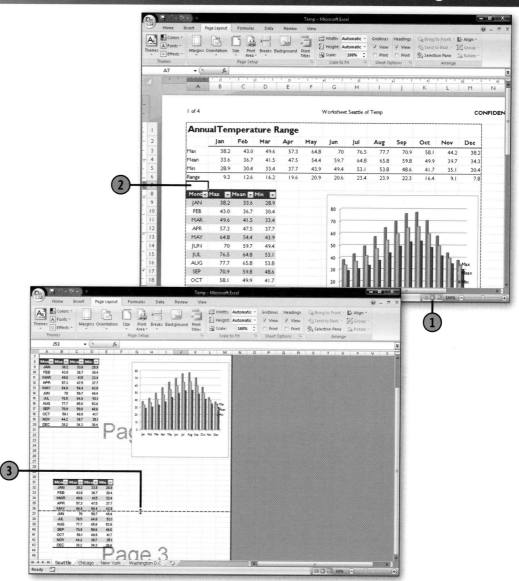

Adding and Viewing Comments

You can use comments in a workbook in a couple of ways. You can add an explanatory comment to an item to track what you did or clarify it to others, or you can use a comment when you're reviewing a worksheet to add any concerns or suggestions.

Create a Comment

1 Click the cell to which you want to attach your comment.

2 On the Review tab, click the New Comment button.

3 Type your comment. Press Enter only if you need to start a new paragraph in the note. Click outside the note when you've finished it.

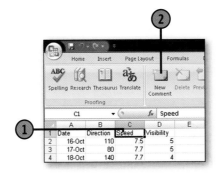
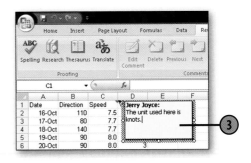

Review the Comments

1 Move the mouse pointer over a cell that contains a red triangle in the top-right corner. Read the comment that appears.

2 If you can't find a comment, or if you want to review several comments, on the Review tab, do any of the following:

• Click Previous or Next to find and display a comment.

• Click Show All Comments to display all the comments in the worksheet.

• With a comment displayed, click Edit Comment to modify the comment. (The New Comment button changes to the Edit Comment button when a comment is selected and displayed.)

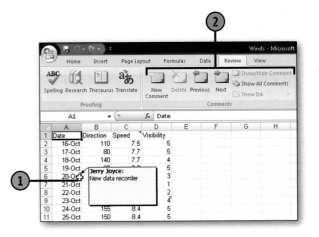

8

Analyzing and Presenting Data in Excel

In this section:

- Creating a Table
- Cell References, Formulas, and Functions
- Doing the Arithmetic
- Creating a Series of Calculations
- Making Calculations with Functions
- Troubleshooting Formulas
- Sorting and Filtering the Data
- Summarizing the Data with a PivotTable
- Displaying Relative Values
- Customizing Conditional Formatting
- The Anatomy of a Chart
- Working with Charts
- Reviewing the Data

There's more to working with your data than organizing the information in worksheets and making it look pretty, and this is where you'll unleash the real power of Microsoft Office Excel 2007: its ability to make complex statistical, financial, and mathematical computations. In this section, we'll examine *cell notation*—the conventions by which Excel references individual cells and ranges of cells—and the way you use cell notation to create formulas that do the calculations for you. We'll also talk about *functions*—ready-made bits of code that do the math for you.

There's some fairly advanced stuff in this section: creating a *PivotTable* that lets you look at relationships among your data, filtering the data to display items that meet the criteria you specify, troubleshooting formulas, using the AutoFill feature to create a series of calculations, and more. If you're going to present your data—at a company meeting, for example—the most effective way to do so is with a chart, whose visual appeal holds your audience's interest more closely than the dry columns and rows of the worksheet on which the chart is based, even though both represent the same data. Excel does more than make your chart look attractive with colors, 3-D effects, and so on—you can plot trendlines to show how your sales figures have improved over time or how your company's bottom line is on an upward trend.

Creating a Table

It's true that Excel is all about data, but data can include more than just numbers. Excel's column-and-row format lends itself smoothly to creating and reviewing lists by placing them in tables. Excel provides special features that make short work of sorting your table by specific criteria; filtering it—that is, viewing only part of the list; or summarizing the data in the list.

Create a Table

1. In a worksheet, enter the data for your table, making sure that you add descriptive titles for the columns and saving the file as you work.

2. Select your entries.

3. On the Home tab, click the Format As Table button.

4. In the gallery that appears, click the table style you want to use.

5. In the Format As Table dialog box that appears, confirm the range of cells that you want to be included in the table.

6. Select this check box if your list has column headings; otherwise, clear the check box if you want Excel to insert generic headings.

7. Click OK.

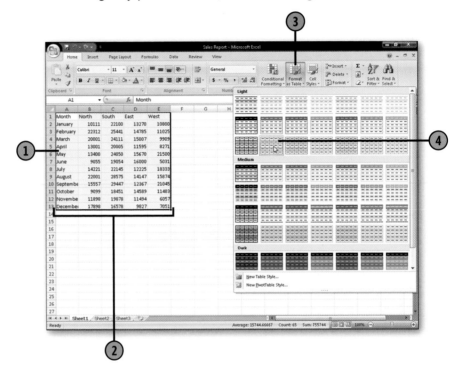

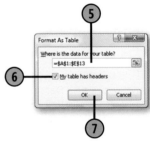

> **See Also**
>
> "Excel's Eccentricities" on page 109 and "Cell References, Formulas, and Functions" on pages 132–133 for information about the notation Excel uses to describe ranges of cells.

Use the Table

1. Click in the table, and, on the Table Tools Design tab, select the check boxes for the items you want displayed and clear the check boxes for the items you don't want displayed.

2. If you've included a totals row, click in the cell that has the totals, click the down arrow that appears, and select the type of total you want. Use the AutoFill feature to copy the totals setting to any other cells that you want to display the total.

3. Click Summarize With PivotTable if you want to create a PivotTable based on the data in the table.

4. Click Remove Duplicates if you want to remove duplicated information from selected columns.

5. Click the down arrow at the top of the column that you want to use to sort or to filter the list; then select the action you want to take. Repeat for any other columns whose data you want to sort or filter.

6. Click Convert To Range if you want to convert the table back to standard data in your worksheet.

See Also

"Creating a Series of Calculations" on page 137 for information about using AutoFill.

"Summarizing the Data with a PivotTable" on pages 146–147 for information about using a Pivot-Table to examine your data.

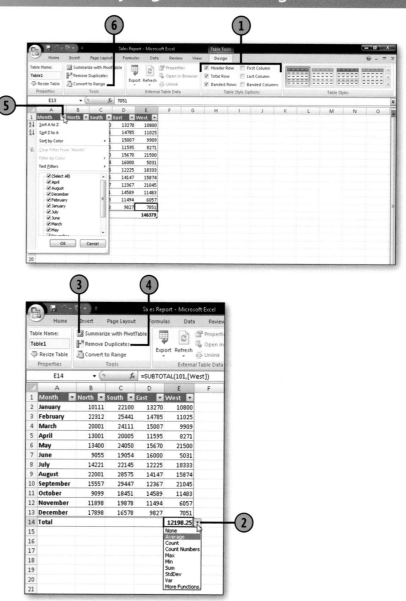

Cell References, Formulas, and Functions

Every cell in an Excel worksheet has its own *label,* or address. For example, if you go to the third column (column C) and work your way down to the fourth row, that cell's label, or address, is C4 (column C, row 4). To quickly determine a *cell reference,* click in the cell, and look in the Name Box at the left of the Formula bar.

A selected *range* of cells is listed from the top-left cell to the bottom-right cell, so if you select cells from the afore-mentioned C4 to the sixth column (column F) and the ninth row, the selection goes from cell C4 to cell F9, and, in Excel's cell notation method, this selected range is designated as C4:F9. Excel also uses this method of notation to designate when whole rows or columns are selected. Select row 12, and Excel calls it 12:12; select columns G and H, and their designation is G:H.

Before we go further in this discussion about ranges, there are three special situations you need to be aware of. Occasionally, to make working in Excel more user friendly, someone will give a cell or a range of cells a name, and will use the name instead of the cell reference. Excel also automatically names some components, such as tables. So, if you click in a cell and see a name in the Name Box instead of a cell refer-ence, you'll know why. However, you can ignore the name and use the cell reference if you prefer—just pretend the name doesn't exist.

The second situation you might encounter is a style of cell referencing that you're not familiar with. If you notice that the columns in a workbook use numbers instead of letters as their labels, or headers, the workbook has been set up to use the R1C1 reference style. This is an old style of cell referenc-ing that some people prefer, but it isn't Excel's default style. In this style, what was cell C4 is referred to as cell R4C3 (row 4 column C). If you want to switch back to Excel's default reference style, choose Excel Options from the Office menu,

and, in the Formulas category, clear the R1C1 Reference Style check box; then click OK.

The third situation is simple and logical. Because your workbook typically contains more than one worksheet, cell references often include the name of the worksheet as well as the cell references in that worksheet. When your references are exclusively within one worksheet, you can simply omit the worksheet reference. However, if you're including data from more than one worksheet, you'll need to reference each work-sheet so that Excel can understand which cells you're referenc-ing. For example, the cell in reference Sheet1!C4 is a different cell from the one in reference Sheet2!C4. Fortunately, in most cases, Excel adds the sheet reference for you when necessary.

You'll use cell references frequently in Excel—when you designate the area of a worksheet you want to print, for example. One of the most important uses of cell references, however, is in *formulas.* A formula is what you use to put Excel to work by making calculations for you. A formula can be just a little arithmetic (=4.201*12.8), or it can use values already in the worksheet (=C4/B3). Note that all formulas begin with an equal sign (=). The asterisk (*) symbol indicates multiplication; the forward slash (/) symbol indicates division. The complexity of your formulas is limited only by your mathematical and log-ical abilities and by the way you need to manipulate the data.

Another component of a formula can be a *function.* A function is a bit of computer programming code that does the math for you. What you have to do is insert the correct function and provide the necessary data for the function. For example, if you want to know the total for cells C4 through C20, instead of creating a formula of =C4+C5+C6, and so on, all the way up to +C20, you can simply use the Sum function and create the formula =Sum(C4:C20).

Of course, now that you've got this all figured out, Excel makes it a bit more complicated! There are actually a couple of additional ways to reference cells. You probably won't need to deal with them too often, and, when you do, they'll make more sense to you and can often solve some problems. The cell reference we just described is called a *relative reference*. The other method is called an *absolute reference*. An absolute reference always references a particular cell, and it's useful when you always want to reference the same constant value in that cell. A relative reference is useful when you're working on a series and want to reference a relative position. So, for example, when you reference cell C4 from cell D6, and you're using the absolute reference, you're actually saying, "I don't care what you copy or move or how you fill other cells with this reference; this reference is always to the value in cell C4." When you use the relative reference, you're saying, "I want the value from the cell that's up two rows and over one column; so, from cell D6, I'm referencing cell C4." However, if you copy this relative reference or use it to fill other cells, the cell you'll be referencing is not cell C4 but the cell that's two rows up and one column over. Got it?

Take a look at the two views of the worksheet below; it uses both relative and absolute references. The first view shows the first three rows of a standard invoice, with the sales-tax rate listed in cell B1, making it easy to modify the numbers if the tax rate goes up or (however unlikely!) down. The second view shows the formulas in this part of the invoice. Note that all the references are relative except the one in cell E3.

If we use Excel's AutoFill feature to fill row 4 with formulas, as shown in the worksheet below, the formulas relate to items in row 4 and not to those in row 3, except for the absolute reference. That's because when you create the series, AutoFill sees the formula in column D as being the value of the cell two cells to the left plus the value of the cell one cell to the left. If all the references were absolute, each row would have the same values in columns D, E, and F. However, if cell E3 used a relative reference for the tax, the formula in cell E4 would be D4*B2—a meaningless value.

Now that the formulas have the correct references and the cells are filled with the correct formulas, Excel will generate a correct invoice. For information about calculating totals, see "Summing the Data" on page 136. For more information about creating formulas with AutoFill, and about using absolute references, see "Creating a Series of Calculations" on page 137. For information about displaying formulas, see "Troubleshooting Formulas" on pages 140–141.

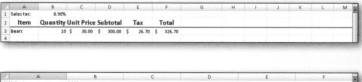

Doing the Arithmetic

Working with math in Excel is similar to working on paper, except that you actually do less work! All you have to do is type the values and the arithmetic operators and then leave it to Excel to do all the calculations. You can easily change the values you've entered if necessary, or make the values equal to a value in another cell or series of cells.

Calculate a Value

1 In the cell in which you want the result of the calculation to be displayed, type an equal sign and then the numbers and operators for your calculation.

2 Press Enter to see your result.

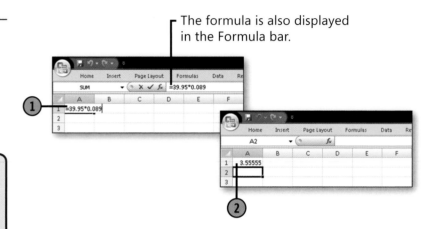

The formula is also displayed in the Formula bar.

Tip

Excel makes its calculations based on the standard order of precedence for arithmetic operators—that is, negation, percentage, exponentiation, multiplication and division, and addition and subtraction. If two operators have the same precedence, Excel makes the calculation from left to right. To change the order of calculation, you use parentheses to group portions of the formula.

Try This!

In an empty cell, type **=10+5*30+6/3** and press Enter. Copy the formula to a new cell, and then press the F2 key to activate editing of the cell. Add a pair of parentheses to the formula so that it's now **=(10+5)*30+6/3** and press Enter. Note that adding the parentheses changed the order of the operations and thus the result. Continue adding, moving, or deleting pairs of parentheses in the formula to see the effects on the final result.

Arithmetic Operators

Action	Operator
Addition	+ (plus sign)
Subtraction	- (minus sign)
Negation	- (minus sign)
Multiplication	* (asterisk)
Division	/ (forward slash)
Percentage	% (percent sign)
Exponentiation	^ (caret)
Set order of actions	( ) (opening and closing parentheses)

Calculate the Value of Cells

① In the cell where you want the result to be displayed, type an equal sign.

② Click in the cell whose value you want to use.

③ Type the arithmetic operator you want to use.

④ Click in the next cell whose value you want to use in the calculation.

⑤ Continue typing the operators and clicking in cells until you've completed the formula, and then press Enter.

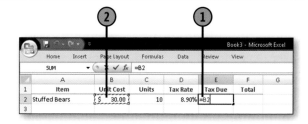

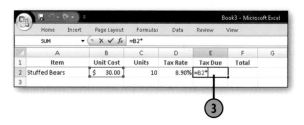

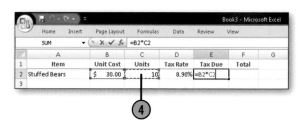

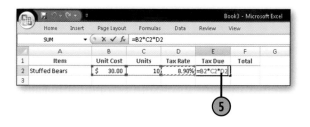

Tip

You can mix cell references and numeric values in a cell—for example, a formula might be =C1+C3+10. You can also reference cells in other worksheets or in other workbooks.

Caution

Don't assume that a formula contains an error just because it uses different operators from those you're familiar with. Some formulas are logical tests that return a true or false value, while others are used to manipulate text. For example, a formula of =C3=10 would display TRUE if the value in cell C3 was equal to 10, and would display FALSE otherwise.

Summing the Data

It's probable that one of the most frequent calculations you'll make in Excel is to *sum*, or add up, a series of numbers. Luckily, summing is also one of the easiest calculations to make, with the AutoSum feature just a click away.

Sum the Numbers

① Click in a cell below or at the right of the series of cells you want to sum.

② On the Formulas tab, click the AutoSum button.

③ Make sure the selection rectangle encloses all the cells you want to sum. If you've accidentally included any unwanted cells or omitted any desired cells, move the mouse pointer over a corner of the selection until a two-headed arrow appears, and then drag the selection rectangle to resize it so that it includes all the cells you want. You can also move the entire selection rectangle by pointing to a side of the rectangle and dragging it to a new location.

④ Press Enter to sum the cells and see the result.

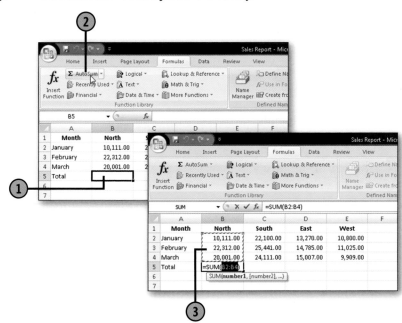

> **Tip**
>
> To quickly find the average, count, and sum of a series, select the series, and note the values on the status bar.

Creating a Series of Calculations

When you reference cells in a formula and then use the AutoFill feature, Excel modifies the reference to cells relative to the newly filled cells. That means you can create a whole series of calculations simply by creating a single calculation and then filling cells with the formula. And if you need to use a single constant value in all the calculations, you can use an absolute reference to a cell instead of a relative reference.

Create the Series

 Create the first formula, referencing the cells.

 Drag the Fill handle to fill adjacent cells.

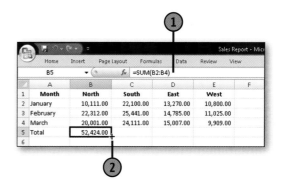 Click in a filled cell.

 Verify that the formula is correct.

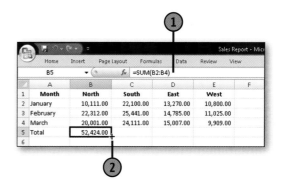

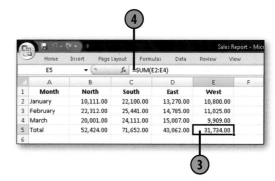

Tip

To include a reference to the same cell in all the formulas, make the reference to the cell absolute instead of relative. Press the F4 key to switch from a relative to an absolute reference.

See Also

"Cell References, Formulas, and Functions" on pages 132–133 for information about the difference between relative and absolute references.

See Also

"Copy Content to Adjacent Cells" on page 115 for information about using the Fill handle to copy the contents of a cell instead of creating a series.

Making Calculations with Functions

Excel is jam-packed with functions that can make you look like a financial wizard or a mathematical genius (if you aren't either or both of those already, of course!). Do you want to know the standard deviation of a series of numbers? What about the sum of the squares? How about calculating the number and amount of the payments needed to retire a loan over a certain period? If you're a real stickler for precision, you can even use a function that returns the value of *pi*, accurate to 15 digits.

Find a Function

1. Click in the cell in which you want the results of the function to be displayed.

2. Click the Insert Function button. If the Formula bar isn't displayed, click the Insert Function button on the Formulas tab.

3. In the Insert Function dialog box, type the name of the function or a description of the action you want to take, and press Enter.

4. Select the function you want in the list.

5. If the function isn't listed, select a different category, and then select the function in the list.

6. Verify that the function will do what you want it to do.

7. Click OK.

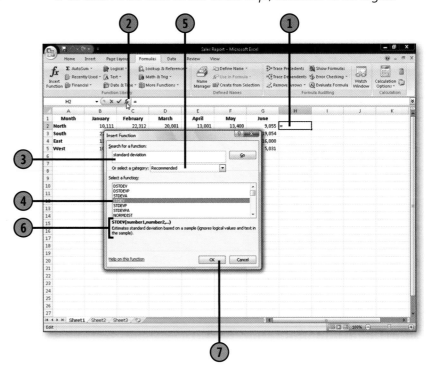

> **Tip**
>
> If you know the name of the function you want to use, click the button on the Formulas tab for the type of function, and then choose the function from the drop-down menu. To use a function that you used recently, click the Recently Used button on the Formulas tab, and choose the function from the drop-down menu.

Add Your Arguments

① In the Function Arguments dialog box that appears, if a range is proposed, make sure it's the one you want. If it isn't, type any values that you want to enter directly, or type the cell references.

② To select cell ranges, click to minimize the dialog box and return to the worksheet. In the worksheet, select the cell or range of cells you want to use as an *argument*, or parameter, for the function, and then click the button again to restore the dialog box to its normal size.

③ Complete any other arguments that are required for the function.

④ Click OK.

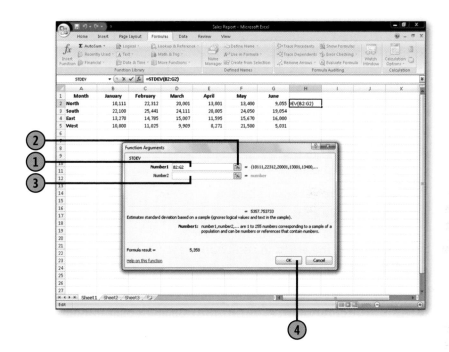

Tip ✓

You can integrate more than one function into a formula, or you can include other elements—for example, standard arithmetic operations such as adding or multiplying by a number or a value in another cell.

Tip ✓

Numerous functions don't return a value but are logical tests instead. The powerful IF function, for example, returns one value you've set if the logical test is true and a second value if the logical test is false. Many other functions, such as ISBLANK, return true or false values only.

Tip ✓

A function requires specific types of data, delivered in a specific order; these are the arguments for the function. Some functions don't have any arguments—for example, NOW( ); some have a single argument—SQRT(*number*); and some have multiple arguments—NPER(*rate,pmt,pv,fv,type*). For information about the arguments for a function, click Help On This Function in the Function Arguments dialog box.

Troubleshooting Formulas

Formulas are extremely powerful tools, especially when they include functions, and constructing valid formulas can be a bit tricky. Fortunately, Excel provides a group of formula-auditing tools that can help you find and fix errors such as circular references, incorrect syntax in a formula, or a referenced cell that has been deleted.

Review the Errors

① On the Formulas tab, click the Show Formulas button to display all the formulas in the worksheet.

② Click the Error Checking button.

③ In the Error Checking dialog box, use the Next and the Previous buttons to find and review the errors in your worksheet.

④ Click the Edit In Formula Bar button if you see the mistake and want to correct the formula.

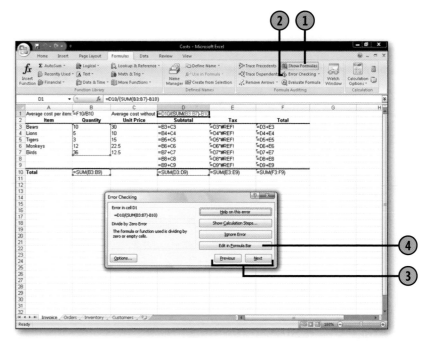

Evaluate a Formula

(1) If you can't figure out the error, click the Show Calculation Steps button in the Error Checking dialog box to display the Evaluate Formula dialog box.

(2) Note the formula and the underlined item.

(3) Click the Evaluate button to see the formula with the result of the underlined item included.

(4) Inspect the formula and try to identify the source of the error. If the error is shown but you can't determine its source, click the Restart button.

(5) Continue clicking the Evaluate button and inspecting the formula until the entire formula is solved, noting any errors as they occur.

(6) Click Close, and make any changes necessary to correct the formula.

(7) On the Formulas tab, click the Show Formulas button to hide the formulas and display their results instead.

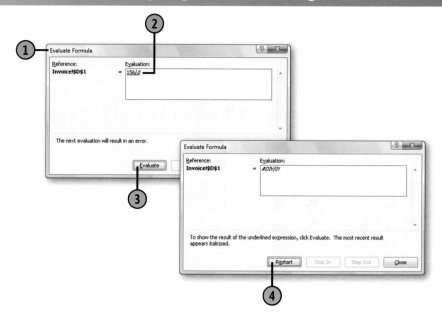

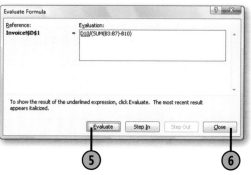

Tip

To modify the error-checking rules that Excel uses, choose Excel Options from the Office menu, and, in the Excel Options dialog box, click the Formulas category. Review the rules, and select or clear check boxes to change which rules are used.

See Also

"Doing the Arithmetic" on pages 134–135 for information about the order in which Excel makes calculations and how you can change the order.

Sorting the Data

One of the easiest ways to organize or evaluate your data is to use Excel's Sort feature. There are a couple of ways to control the sort—you can do a simple ascending or descending sort, or you can specify which data you want to sort and the type of sort you want to conduct.

Conduct an Alphabetic or a Numeric Sort

1. Select the columns or the portions of columns whose contents you want to sort.

2. On the Data tab, click the Sort button to display the Sort dialog box.

3. Specify whether or not the columns have header labels.

4. Specify which column you want to sort by.

5. Select Values if it isn't already selected.

6. Specify whether the data will be sorted A to Z, Z to A, or based on a custom list (alphabetic); or from smallest to largest, largest to smallest, or based on a custom list (numeric).

7. If you want to refine the sort by also sorting by a second column, click the Add Level button, and enter the search parameters. Repeat for any further level of search. You can use up to 64 levels in your search.

8. Click the Options button if you want to change to a case-sensitive sort for text or if you want to sort by rows instead of by columns.

9. Click OK to sort the data.

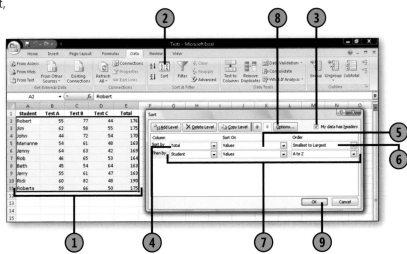

When the first sort was done by the Total column and then by the Student column, people who had the same score were sorted by the alphabetic order of their names.

Tip

To do a quick alphabetic sort without setting any sort parameters, click the Sort A To Z or the Sort Z To A button on the Data tab; or, if you've selected numbers, click the Sort Smallest To Largest or the Sort Largest To Smallest button at the left of the Sort button.

Filtering the Data

Filtering, or *querying,* is a quick and easy way to find and work with a subset of data so that you can display only the rows in your worksheet that meet the criteria you specify— for example, rows that contain specific text, or numbers that are greater than or less than a specific number. Filtering

temporarily hides the rows that don't meet your criteria so that you see only the data you're interested in. Excel simplifies the power of filtering your data without your having to use a separate database. All you do is set up the filtering and select the items you want to display.

Filter the Data

① Select the data you want to filter.

② On the Data tab, click the Filter button.

③ Click the down arrow for the column you want to use as the filter, and select the item you want to use as the filter.

④ To filter by another column, click the down arrow for that column, and select the item you want to use as the filter. It's easy to see which columns have filtering applied—they show a little filter icon instead of a black down arrow.

⑤ When you've finished with the filtered data and want to return it to its unfiltered state, click the Filter button on the Data tab again.

Tip

If your data is arranged so that you want to filter by rows, you must transform the data so that the rows become columns and the columns become rows. To make this happen, select the data and click Copy. Click in a blank area where you want to place the transformed data, click the down arrow at the bottom of the Paste button, and click Transpose in the drop-down list.

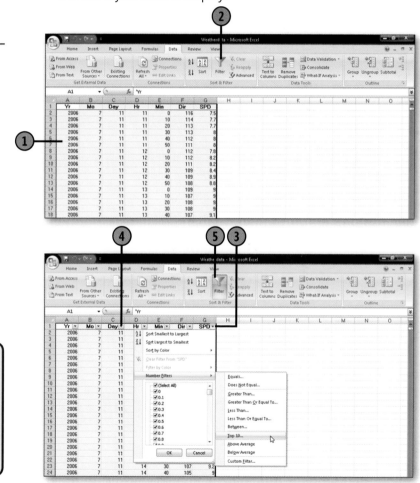

Separating Data into Columns

You might find that some data has been collected in a way that isn't designed for what you want to do with it. For example, let's say you have a mailing list in which people's first and last names are lumped together in one column. What do you do if you want the first name in one column and the last name in a second column? Easy! You just tell Excel to divide this type of information into separate columns.

Separate the Data

① Select the data that is to be separated.

② On the Data tab, click the Text To Columns button to start the Convert Text To Columns Wizard.

③ Specify whether the data is currently separated by a character such as a tab, a space, or a comma (Delimited), or whether the data is in text columns of specific widths (Fixed Width).

④ Click Next, and step through the wizard to specify how you want the data to be separated; whether the data should be formatted as numbers, text, or dates; and where the new column or columns should be placed.

⑤ Inspect the result. If it's not what you want, click the Undo button on the Quick Access toolbar, and use the wizard again, setting different values this time.

Tip ✔

If you choose to replace the existing data, make sure there's a blank column for each new column that you create.

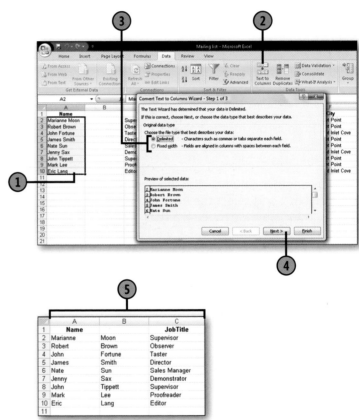

Creating Subtotals

When you've accumulated a mass of data, you can leave it to Excel to calculate the subtotals in your worksheets—how many boxes of crayons you sold in January, for example, or the number of different songbirds you've seen in your back yard. All you need to do is group the data by the items to be subtotaled and tell Excel to outline—that is, to classify and prioritize—your data, and to calculate the subtotals. You'll need to sort the data before you tell Excel to create the subtotals.

Create the Subtotals

① Select and sort the data by the columns for which you want to create the subtotals.

② On the Data tab, click the Subtotal button to display the Subtotal dialog box.

③ Select the column that you want to be subtotaled.

④ Select the function to be used to calculate the subtotal.

⑤ Select the column or columns in which you want the results to be displayed.

⑥ Select any other options you want.

⑦ Click OK.

⑧ Review the results, hiding or displaying the details.

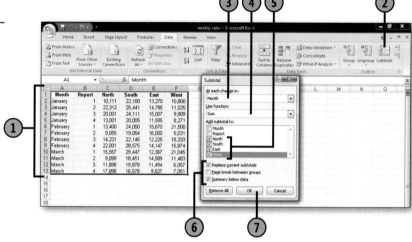

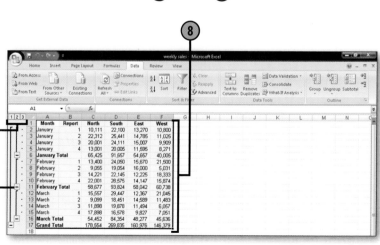

Click the outline-level symbols to display or hide the details.

Click a minus button to hide the details, or click a plus button to display them.

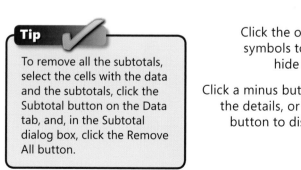

Tip

To remove all the subtotals, select the cells with the data and the subtotals, click the Subtotal button on the Data tab, and, in the Subtotal dialog box, click the Remove All button.

Summarizing the Data with a PivotTable

A PivotTable is a dynamic and powerful analysis tool that lets you look at relationships among your data and enables you to extract only the portions of the data that are of interest to you. It can sometimes be a bit difficult to figure out the proper arrangement of the data fields, but once you've created the PivotTable, you'll find it easy to work with and very useful.

Create the PivotTable

① Select the range of cells you want to use as the data for the PivotTable.

② On the Insert tab, click the PivotTable button to display the Create PivotTable dialog box. Select the source of the data, specify where you want the PivotTable to appear, and click OK.

③ Select each data field that you want to use. Each item will be placed in the location that appears to be the most appropriate for the type of data it contains.

④ To modify the locations to which the fields are assigned, drag items between the different areas.

⑤ If you want to change the names or any other display settings for field headings, click the down arrow, choose Field Settings from the drop-down menu, and make your changes in the Field Settings dialog box.

⑥ If you want to change what type of value is calculated, click the down arrow, choose Value Field Settings, and, in the Value Field Settings dialog box, specify how you want to summarize the data. Click OK.

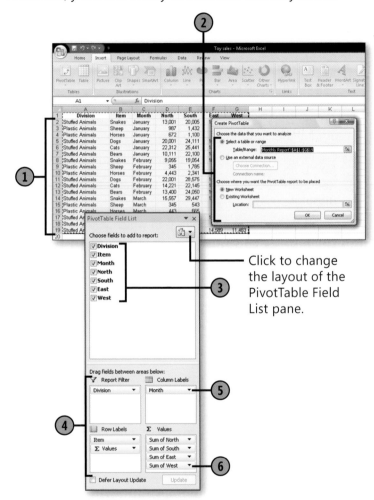

Click to change the layout of the PivotTable Field List pane.

Use the PivotTable

1 Click the down arrow in the Report Filter field, select the item you want to be displayed, and click OK.

2 Click in a Column or Row field, and clear the Select All check box.

3 Select the items you want to be displayed, and click OK.

4 Continue selecting the items you want to be displayed in the other fields.

5 Use any of the tools on the PivotTable Tools Options and Design tabs to modify the PivotTable.

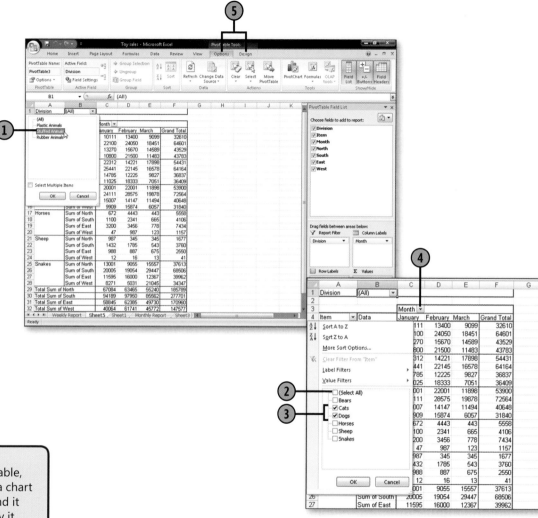

Tip

A PivotChart works just like a PivotTable, except that the data is displayed as a chart instead of as numbers. You might find it easiest to create a PivotTable, modify it, and then use it as the source for a chart. The chart will be a PivotChart in which you can change the data that's displayed.

Displaying Relative Values

Some people can glance at a column and create a visual image of the relationships among the numbers. However, if all you see is a bunch of numbers, you can add displays that indicate the relationships of the numbers to each other. For example, you can include bars that show the relative value of each number, you can color-code entries by their ranking, and you can even use icons to indicate the relative values.

Show the Relative Value

① Select the cells you want to include. Each value will be compared with all the other data in the selection.

② On the Home tab, click the Conditional Formatting button, point to the type of indicator you want, and, in the gallery that appears, click the indicator you want.

③ If you want any additional indicators or another type of conditional formatting, repeat step 2.

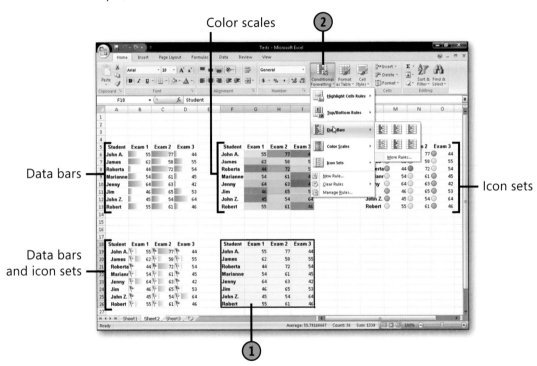

Color scales

Data bars

Data bars and icon sets

Icon sets

Tip

To see how each indicator looks, point to the different indicators, but don't click any of them; then select the one you want to use.

Automatically Highlighting Certain Data

When you use conditional formatting, you can tell Excel to apply specific formatting to any cells that meet the specific criteria you've set. For example, you can tell Excel to format a cell whenever the number of sales falls below a certain minimum or whenever the cost rises above a certain figure. Excel will apply the cell formatting only when the conditions you set are found to be true.

Set the Conditional Formatting

① Select the cells, columns, or rows to which the formatting will apply.

② On the Home tab, click the Conditional Formatting button, point to Highlight Cells Rules or Top/Bottom Rules, and, in the gallery that appears, click the item you want.

③ Enter the value or values to use for the evaluation.

④ Specify the formatting you want.

⑤ Click OK.

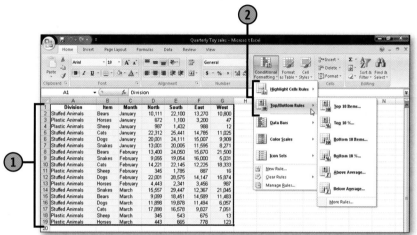

Tip ✓

You can apply multiple conditions and formatting to a selection of cells. Make sure, however, that you use different formatting for each criterion so that you're able to distinguish the different conditions.

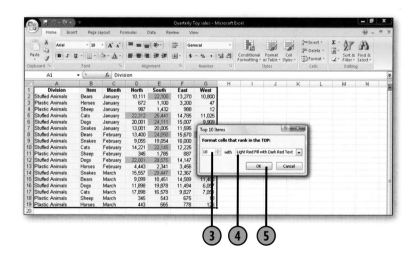

Customizing Conditional Formatting

Excel's preset conditional formatting is great for most conditions, but if you want to set your own parameters and formatting, you can do so by creating a new rule.

Create a Rule

① Select the cells to which you want to apply your conditional formatting.

② On the Home tab, click the Conditional Formatting button, and choose New Rule from the gallery to display the New Formatting Rule dialog box.

③ Select the type of rule you want to use.

④ Enter the information required for that rule, using the values and formatting you want. Each rule requires different types of information.

⑤ Select the formatting you want to apply to the cells that meet the conditions you've set. If the dialog box contains a Format button, click it, and, in the Format Cells dialog box that appears, specify the formatting you want. Click OK.

⑥ Click OK.

⑦ Apply any additional rules to the selection.

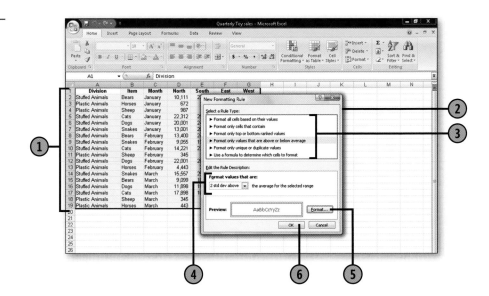

Tip

To remove conditional formatting, click the Conditional Formatting button on the Home tab, point to Clear Rules, and, from the submenu, choose where you want to remove the rules.

The Anatomy of a Chart

You can create and customize many different types of charts. In addition to adjusting the scale of the axes and changing their color, you can create an additional X and/or Y axis, each with a different scale from that of the primary X and/or Y axis. You can also create a three-dimensional image by adding a Z axis.

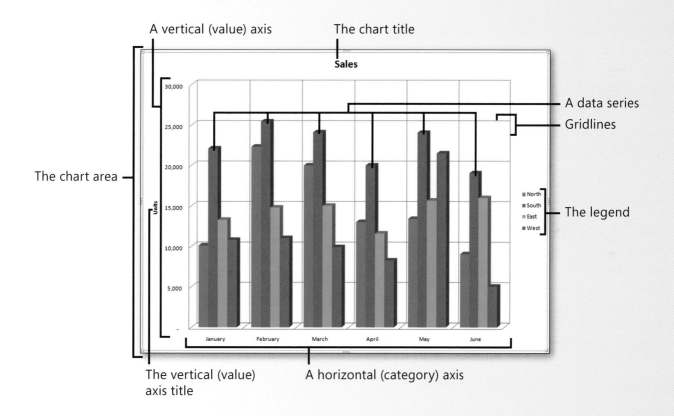

Charting Your Data

One of the best ways to present your data in a clear and understandable form is to use a well-designed chart. A chart provides the clarity and visual impact that make your data come alive in such a way that difficult concepts and comparisons become immediately understandable. You'll need to decide what you want to include in the chart, where to put everything, and the type of chart that will best illustrate the information.

Create a Chart

1. Select the data you want to use in the chart.

2. On the Insert tab, click the type of chart you want to use.

3. In the gallery that appears, click the chart design you want.

4. Click the chart to select it, and, on the Chart Tools Design tab, select a layout for the chart.

5. If you don't like the way the chart looks, do either of the following:

   - Click the Change Chart Type button, and choose a different type of chart in the Change Chart Type dialog box.

   - Click the Switch Row/Column button to change the way the data will be plotted.

6. If you want the chart to appear in its own worksheet, click Move Chart, and, in the Move Chart dialog box, click select New Sheet. Click OK.

Tip ✔

Your data doesn't have to be contiguous. To select non-contiguous data, hold down the Ctrl key while you're dragging over the data.

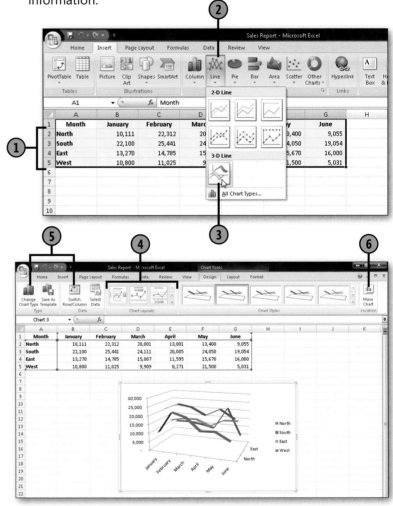

Complete the Layout

① On the Chart Tools Layout tab, with the chart selected, click any of the Labels buttons. Specify whether you want a label, and, if so, where you want it. Type the text for any labels you've created.

② Click the Axes button, and select the style and/or scale for any axis you want to modify.

③ Click the Gridlines button, and, if you want to display gridlines for an axis, specify the types of gridlines you want.

④ Click any of the Background buttons, and choose to hide or display background elements or to modify the 3-D rotation.

⑤ Click to show a trendline, drop lines, up/down bars, or error bars. Note that not all line types are available for all chart types.

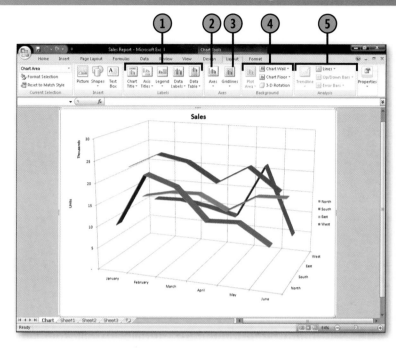

Tip ✓

The numbers and/or the text on the chart's axes are based on the worksheet data you're using. To make changes to these elements, you'll need to make the changes in your worksheet.

Tip ✓

There are numerous types of lines you can display. For example, the trendline can be linear, exponential, linear forecast, or a two-period moving average. The error bars can be based on standard error, percentage, or one standard deviation. Make sure that you choose the correct type of line for the information that you're presenting.

Formatting a Chart

When you create a chart, Excel uses the default settings for the chart design. You can change the overall appearance of the chart by changing the chart style or by changing the theme. You can also modify the appearance of individual parts of the chart.

Change the Chart Style

① Click the chart to select it

② On the Chart Tools Design tab, click the style you want for the chart.

Change the Theme

① On the Page Layout tab, with the chart visible, click the Themes button, and point to the different themes to see how the appearance of the chart changes with each theme.

② Click the theme you want for your chart.

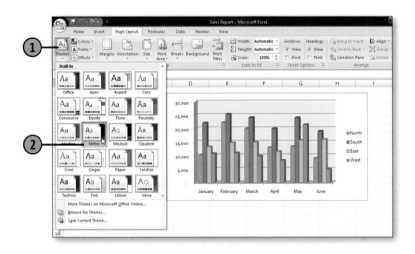

Format an Element

① On the Chart Tools Format tab, select the chart element you want to format.

② Select the style you want to apply to that element.

③ Click the appropriate button to modify the formatting applied by the style.

④ If the selection contains text that you want to format using WordArt, click the WordArt style you like. Click the appropriate button to modify the formatting.

⑤ Use the Size tools to adjust the dimensions of the selected element.

⑥ Click the Format Selection button, and, in the Format dialog box, click the various categories to make changes to the formatting of the element.

⑦ Click Close when you've finished.

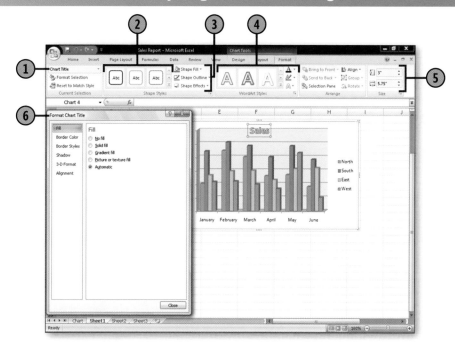

Tip

To format text without using WordArt, use the font and alignment tools on the Home tab.

Tip

You can select an element for formatting by clicking that element in the chart. You can also resize an element by selecting it and dragging its Sizing handles.

Customizing a Chart

Sometimes a series of columns, bars, or lines doesn't properly express your data. To create the most informative chart possible, you might want to combine different chart types within a single chart. You can even add one or more axes so that your data can be presented with different scales.

Change a Data-Series Chart

① Click to select the chart if it isn't already selected.

② Click to select the data series you want to change (or, on the Chart Tools Format tab, select the data series in the Chart Elements list box).

③ On the Chart Tools Design tab, click the Change Chart Type button to display the Change Chart Type dialog box.

④ Select the chart type that you want to use for the selected series.

⑤ Click OK.

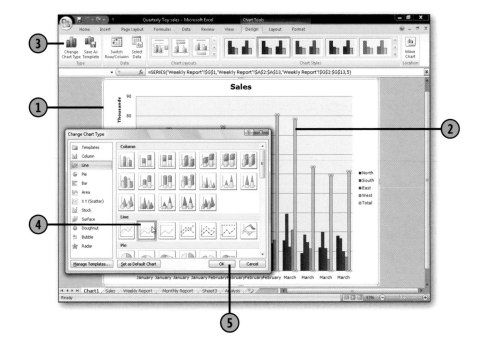

Caution

Some chart types are incompatible, so Excel might not allow you to add one type of chart to another. In this case, you'll need to experiment with different combinations of chart types to find out which ones work together.

Add an Axis

1 Click to select the chart if it isn't already selected.

2 On the Chart Tools Format tab, select the data series in the Chart Elements list box.

3 Click the Format Selection button to display the Format Data Series dialog box.

4 Select this option to have the data plotted against a second axis, and then click Close.

5 Format the axis just as you'd format any other element in the chart.

A data series using a different chart format

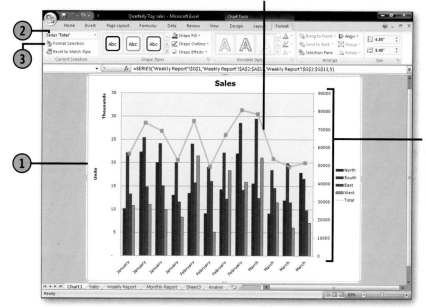

A second vertical (values) axis provides a different scale for this data series.

Tip

Clicking the Format Selection button displays different options, depending on the chart element you've selected. This button is a powerful tool for customizing individual items in a chart.

Reviewing the Data

Worksheets can quickly become huge and unwieldy. When you need to review your data, you can "freeze" certain parts of the worksheet—the column and/or row titles, for example—so that they'll remain in view while you scroll through other parts of the worksheet. You can also split the window into several sections if you want different parts of the worksheet to be visible so that you can compare them.

Freeze the Columns and/or Rows

① Click in a single cell that's at the right of the columns and/or below the rows to freeze the columns and/or the rows.

② On the View tab, click the Freeze Panes button.

③ Choose whether you want to freeze both the rows above and the columns to the left, or to freeze just the top row or the first column.

> **Tip** ✓
>
> If your data is contained in a table, the table headings will replace the standard column labels (such as A and B) at the top of the window when you scroll the window and the table headings move off the screen.

View Multiple Sections

① Click where you want to split the worksheet.

② On the View tab, click the Split button.

③ Use the scroll bars to scroll the contents of the different panes.

④ Click the Split button again to remove the multiple panes.

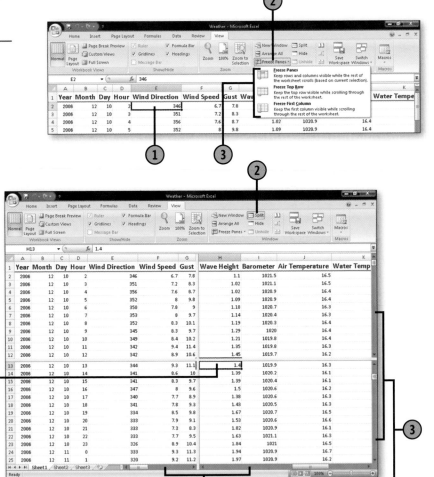

9

Creating a PowerPoint Presentation

In this section:

- What's Where in PowerPoint?
- Creating a Presentation
- Converting Text into SmartArt Graphics or WordArt
- Including a Slide from Another Presentation
- Inserting Multimedia
- Formatting a Slide
- Animating Items on a Slide
- Editing a Presentation
- Repeating Content on Every Slide
- Adding Transition Effects to Slides
- Modifying the Default Layout
- Creating a Photo Album

When you attend a company meeting, a talk, a school presentation, a sales pitch, or just about any other type of gathering where information is being presented, it's a sure bet that you'll see at least one slide presentation. Microsoft Office PowerPoint 2007 has made creating slide presentations so simple that we *almost* don't need to write about it—but we will anyway, because PowerPoint has so many great features that we want you to know about.

As with most Office programs, you can use one of PowerPoint's existing layouts, or you can create your own slide presentation from scratch. You can choose a theme to create a unified design throughout all the slides in your presentation; modify a theme; or design your own customized theme, choosing the background, the colors, and the fonts to complement the mood of the presentation. You can add tables and SmartArt graphics to your slides, and make them sparkle with some WordArt or animation. You can add a video, a sound clip, or some CD music to your presentation, and apply some of PowerPoint's stunning transitions between clips to enhance your show with that extra touch of professionalism. And if you need to do a bit of editing and tweaking, you'll find PowerPoint's Outline view and Slide Sorter extremely simple to use and very helpful.

What's Where in PowerPoint?

Microsoft Office PowerPoint 2007 is designed to create slide presentations. A presentation can have several components—the main one, of course, being the slides that display your pictures, text, charts, videos, and so on. PowerPoint can help you create the other components: handouts that include printed versions of your slides with accompanying text, and a script—that is, printed notes to assist you with your presentation. You'll spend most of your time, however, working with the slides—modifying them to achieve the consistent look that results in a polished presentation, and rearranging them so that they're shown in the most logical order. You create the individual slides in Normal view (shown below), adding text and graphics to content boxes (which are just plain text boxes ready to receive text or other content), tweaking the color scheme, and adding new slides.

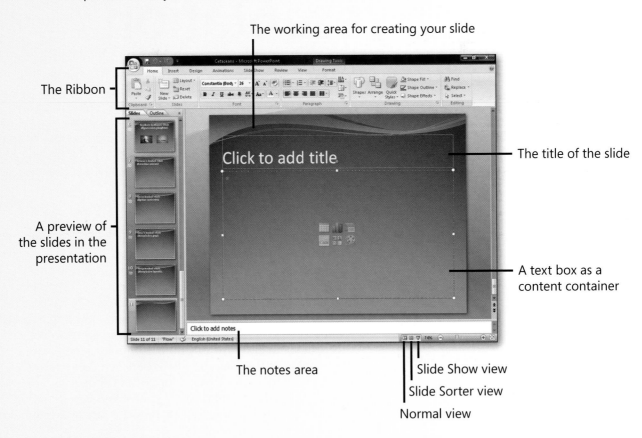

The working area for creating your slide

The Ribbon

A preview of the slides in the presentation

The title of the slide

A text box as a content container

The notes area

Slide Show view

Slide Sorter view

Normal view

You use Slide Sorter view (shown below) to organize your entire presentation and to make sure that all the design elements have a consistent look. You can also use Slide Sorter view as a kind of "storyboard" for reviewing your presentation: Just double-click a slide in Slide Sorter view, and the slide will open in Normal view, ready for editing. Slide Sorter view is also the view to use when you're setting up your slide show's properties—for example, the animation scheme, if you're using one for your slides, and/or the transition effects as one slide advances to the next.

There are other views—Slide Show view and Notes Page view, as well as the view of the Slide Master, the Handout Master, and the Notes Master—that we haven't shown here. Slide Show view is self-explanatory and Notes Page view is similar to Normal view except that it's formatted as a printed page; it shows a printed version of the slide and includes an area where you can type your notes. The three Master views allow you to set up the overall layout and look of your slides, handouts, and notes.

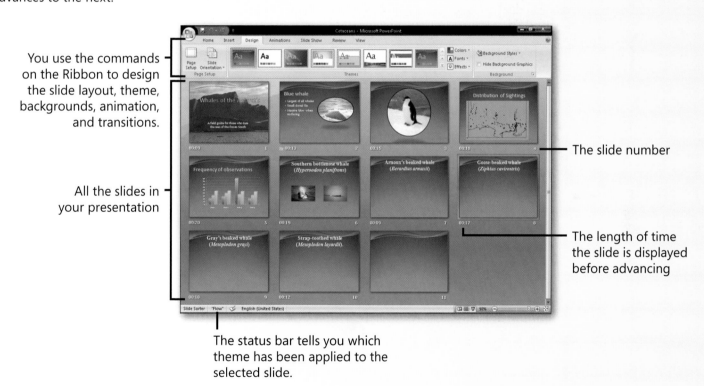

You use the commands on the Ribbon to design the slide layout, theme, backgrounds, animation, and transitions.

All the slides in your presentation

The slide number

The length of time the slide is displayed before advancing

The status bar tells you which theme has been applied to the selected slide.

Creating a Presentation

When you start the PowerPoint program, it displays the default design for a title slide. You can use the existing layout or change it to any layout you want. Then you add your text or other content, and keep adding slides and content as you develop your presentation.

Set Up the Presentation

① Start PowerPoint, or start a new, blank presentation.

② If you need to use settings for your slides other than the standard default size and orientation, on the Design tab, click the Page Setup button to display the Page Setup dialog box, change your settings, and click OK.

③ Point to the various themes to preview the way your slides will look with each theme. Click the theme you want to apply to all the slides in your presentation.

④ Click the Background Styles button, and, in the gallery that appears, point to the different styles to preview the effect each has on your slides. Click the style you want.

Tip

Every presentation has a default theme that defines the color scheme, the default fonts, and the graphics effects.

Tip

If you're creating a presentation using an existing template, the slides in the New Slide and the Layout galleries will probably look different from those you see when you start a blank presentation because custom templates contain modified master slides, which control the layout.

Add Your Content

(1) Click in a text box and add your text. Use the tools on the Home tab and the Drawing Tools Format tab to modify any text or paragraph formatting. If there are other text boxes, click in each, and add and format your text.

(2) When you're ready to create the next slide, click the bottom part of the New Slide button, and, in the gallery that appears, select the layout you want for the new slide.

(3) If you don't like the current layout, click the Layout button and choose a different layout for the slide.

(4) If your slide contains content boxes, either type the text you want, or click one of the buttons to add a table, a chart, a SmartArt graphic, a picture, a piece of clip art, or a media clip.

(5) Continue clicking the bottom part of the New Slide button, selecting the layout you want for each slide, and adding content to each slide until your presentation is complete.

(6) Click the Save button, and name and save your presentation.

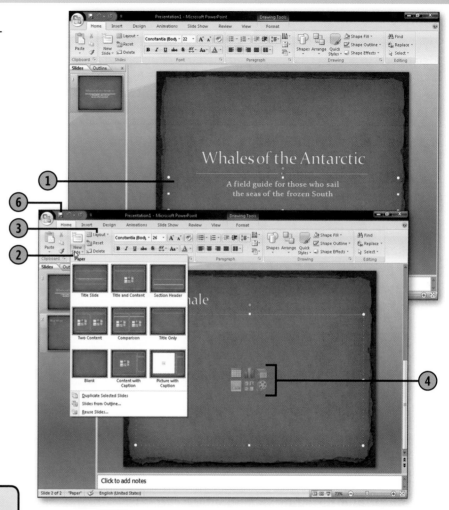

See Also

"Inserting Pictures" on page 24, "Adding Shapes" on page 28, "Adding Clip Art" on page 29, "Creating Stylized Text" on pages 32–33, and "Inserting a Relational Diagram" on pages 34–35 for information about inserting these elements into your slide presentation.

See Also

"Using Word to Prepare PowerPoint Text" on page 296 for information about using a Word document for PowerPoint content.

Inserting a Table

If you want to insert a large table into a slide, it's a good idea to create it in Word or Excel and then copy it into your PowerPoint presentation. However, you can easily create a small table directly on the slide.

Create the Table

(1) On the Insert tab, in a slide with a content box, click the Table button, and, in the Insert Table dialog box that appears, specify the number of rows and columns you need for your table. Click OK.

(2) Use the tools on the Table Tools Layout tab to modify the table as you want.

(3) On the Table Tools Design tab, select the items you want to include in the table.

(4) Use any of the Table Styles to format the table.

(5) Use the Shading, Borders, and Effects buttons to customize the table.

(6) Enter your content in the table.

(7) Apply WordArt styles and settings to your text if you want.

(8) Drag the borders of the table if you need to resize it, and then drag it to the location you want.

Tip

To insert a table into any slide, click the Table button on the Insert tab, and select the dimensions you want for the table.

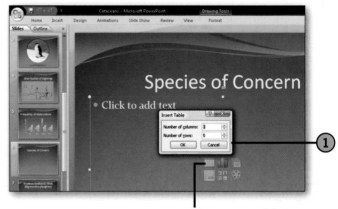

The Insert Table button

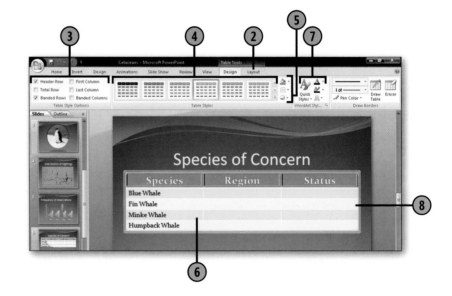

Converting Text into a SmartArt Graphic

An excellent way to dramatically improve the appearance of the slides in your presentation is to convert headings and bulleted lists into SmartArt graphics. That way, you'll have an organized structure and professional-looking graphics.

Create the Graphic

(1) Place all the text that you'll be using in the graphic in one text box, and click in the text box to select it if it isn't already selected.

(2) On the Home tab, click the Convert To SmartArt Graphic button, and choose the design you want from the gallery that appears. If you don't see a design you want, click More SmartArt Graphics in the gallery, and use the Choose A SmartArt Graphic dialog box to select the graphic you want.

(3) Use the SmartArt Tools Design and Format tabs to modify the SmartArt to the look you want.

(4) Drag a Sizing handle on the border of the SmartArt graphic if you want to change its size, and then drag a border to move the SmartArt to the location you want.

> **See Also**
>
> "Inserting a Relational Diagram" on pages 34–35 for information about working with SmartArt graphics.

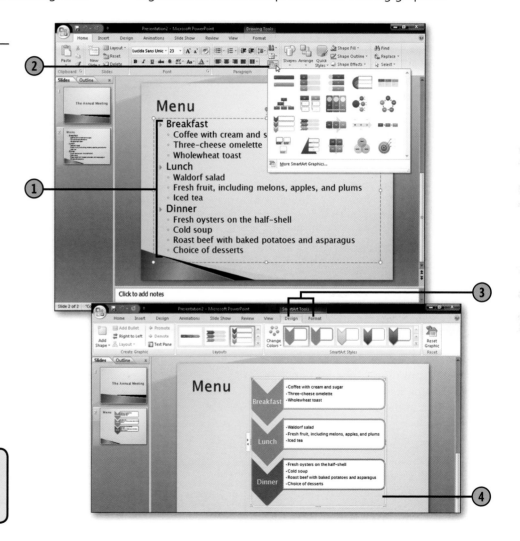

Converting Text into WordArt

Some slide presentations are just fine with plain text, but others can benefit from a little livening up. That's where WordArt comes in. It's easy and fun to add interest to titles or any special parts of your presentation with WordArt formatting. Just don't go overboard with the dazzle factor!

Convert the Text

① Select the text that you want to convert into WordArt.

② On the Drawing Tools Format tab, click the More button in the WordArt Styles section to open the gallery. Point to each WordArt style that you like to see how your text will look with that style. Note that the items in the upper part of the gallery affect only the selected text, and that the items in the lower part affect all the text in the text box. Click the style you want.

③ Use the Text Fill, Text Outline, and Text Effects buttons to modify the appearance of the selected text.

④ On the Home tab, use the Font settings to modify the font, its size and color, its kerning, and other aspects of the selected text.

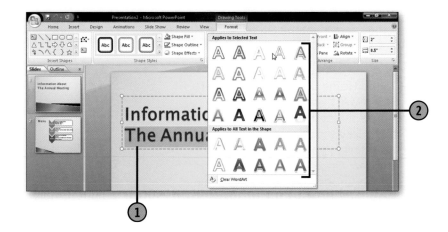

The More button

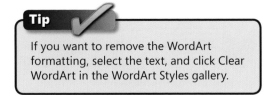

Tip

If you want to remove the WordArt formatting, select the text, and click Clear WordArt in the WordArt Styles gallery.

Including a Slide from Another Presentation

If a slide that's part of one presentation would work well in another presentation, you can copy the slide to your new show and use it wherever you need it.

Include the Slide

① On the Home tab, click the bottom part of the New Slide button, and click Reuse Slides in the gallery to display the Reuse Slides pane.

② Click the Browse button, and choose Browse File from the drop-down menu. In the Browse window, locate and select the presentation that contains the slide you want to copy, and click Open.

③ In your current presentation, click the slide that you want to precede the slide or slides to be inserted.

④ Select this check box if you want the slide to retain its formatting from the original presentation, or clear the check box if you want the slide or slides to take on the formatting of the current presentation.

⑤ Click the slide or slides that you want to add.

⑥ Repeat steps 2 through 5 to insert any slides you want from other presentations.

⑦ Close the Reuse Slides pane when you've finished.

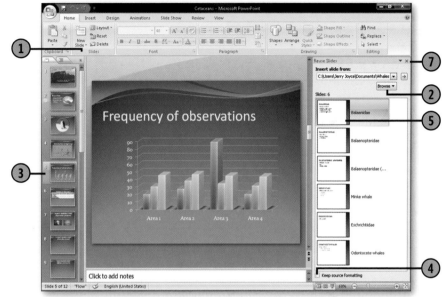

Tip

To use the Slide Library, you need access to a slide library that's on a Microsoft Office SharePoint Server 2007 server.

Tip

You can use the same slide more than once in a presentation. To do so, select the slide or slides to be duplicated, click the bottom part of the New Slide button, and click Duplicate Selected Slides in the gallery.

Inserting Multimedia

You can use a video, a sound clip, or an audio CD to enhance your presentation. When you incorporate multimedia items directly into the presentation, you don't need to switch to a different program to run your show.

Insert a Video

① Select the slide that will contain the video, and, on the Insert tab, click the Movie button. In the Insert Movie window that appears, find and select the movie you want, and click OK.

② In the Microsoft Office PowerPoint dialog box that appears, click Automatically if you want the movie to play when the slide is displayed, or click When Clicked to have the movie play only when clicked.

③ Drag the Sizing handles of the image to set the size of your video, and then drag it to the location you want.

④ Use the tools on the Movie Tools Options tab to modify your settings.

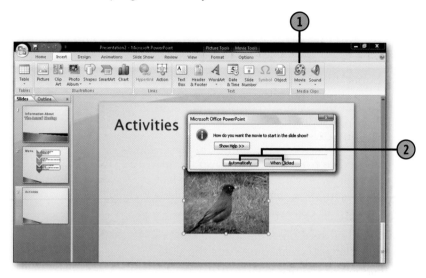

Tip

To insert a movie clip from the Clip Organizer, click the bottom part of the Movie button, and choose Movie From Clip Organizer from the drop-down menu.

See Also

"Adding an Action to a Slide" on page 175 for information about playing any file or running any program from within a PowerPoint presentation.

Insert a Sound

① Select the slide that will contain the sound, and, on the Insert tab, click the bottom part of the Sound button. Choose the sound source from the drop-down menu:

- Sound From File to display the Insert Sound window, where you can locate and select the sound file

- Sound From Clip Organizer to display the Clip Art pane with sound clips displayed

- Play CD Audio Track to display the Insert CD Audio dialog box

- Record Sound to display the Record Sound dialog box

② If you chose to play the sound from a CD, with the CD in the computer's disc drive, select the starting and ending tracks, specify any other options, and then click OK.

③ If you chose to use a sound from a file or from the Clip Art Organizer, insert the file from the Insert Sound window or the Clip Art pane.

④ In the Microsoft Office PowerPoint dialog box that appears, click Automatically if you want the sound to play when the slide is displayed, or click When Clicked to have the sound play only when clicked.

⑤ If you chose to record sound with a microphone or other sound-input setup, enter a name for the recording, click the Record button, record your sounds, and then click the Stop button. Click OK to insert the sound into your presentation.

⑥ Use the tools on the Sound Tools Options tab or the CD Audio Tools Options tab to modify your settings if necessary.

Formatting a Slide

Although the theme that you choose for your presentation applies the default color and font schemes, you can modify the individual elements and change the background to customize the appearance of each slide. The content boxes on the slides are text boxes, which are just another type of Shape.

Format the Content

1. Click a text box to select it.

2. Use the Sizing handles to resize the text box or the Rotation handle to rotate it, and then drag it to the location you want.

3. On the Home tab, with the text box selected, click the Quick Styles button, and, in the gallery that appears, click the style you want for the text box.

4. Click Shape Effects in the gallery that appears, point to the various types of effects, and then click the one you want.

5. Select the text you want to modify, and use any of the font tools to change the font and its size or color, and to add or remove any emphasis.

6. Select any paragraphs you want to modify, and use any of the paragraph tools to change the horizontal or vertical alignment, the line spacing, or the text direction; to add or remove bullets or numbering; or to create multiple columns.

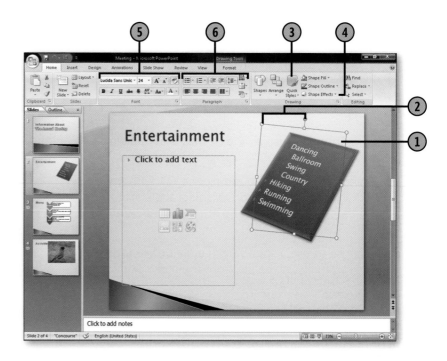

Tip

If you want to include some identifying content that will appear on each slide—a company logo or a watermark, for example—you can do so by using a background picture file. If necessary, increase the transparency value to prevent the background from interfering with the slide's content.

Format the Background

(1) On the Design tab, with the slide you want to modify selected, click the Background Styles button, and click Format Background in the gallery to display the Format Background dialog box.

(2) If you want to use a single color, select this option, and specify the color and the degree of transparency you want.

(3) If you want to use a gradient fill, select this option, and specify the colors, the type of gradient, and its direction and angle.

(4) Use these settings if you want to create a customized gradient.

(5) If you want to use a texture or a picture file, select this option, and specify the source you want to use.

(6) Select this check box if you want to use multiple copies (tiling), or clear the check box if you want to use a single copy that's resized to fit the slide (stretch).

(7) Set the tiling or stretch options.

(8) If you chose to use a picture, click the Picture category, and modify the picture as needed.

(9) Click Close to use the settings on the selected slide, or click Apply To All to use the settings on all the slides in your presentation.

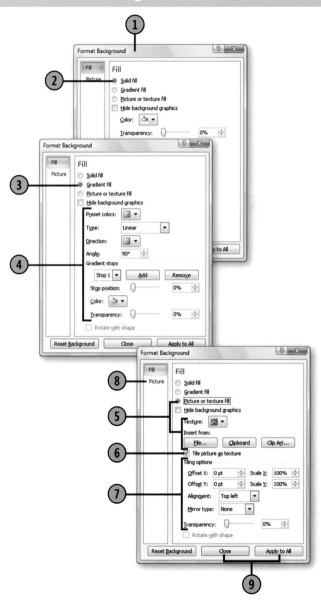

Animating Items on a Slide

Animation can make an onscreen slide presentation come alive with some very professional-looking effects. You can animate the appearance of items on your slide with just a few clicks.

And, when you're presenting your slide show, you start the animation simply by clicking your mouse.

Animate the Text

1. Click the title text box to select it.

2. On the Animations tab, click the Animate list box, and select the type of animation you want for the title.

3. Click the text box that contains the body text of the slide.

4. Click the Animate list box again, and select the animation you want for the body text:

   - All At Once to have all the content of the slide animated and to have it all appear at the same time

   - By 1st Level Paragraphs to have each first-level paragraph and all its accompanying paragraphs appear one at a time

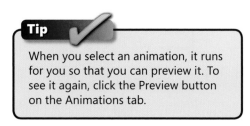

Tip

When you select an animation, it runs for you so that you can preview it. To see it again, click the Preview button on the Animations tab.

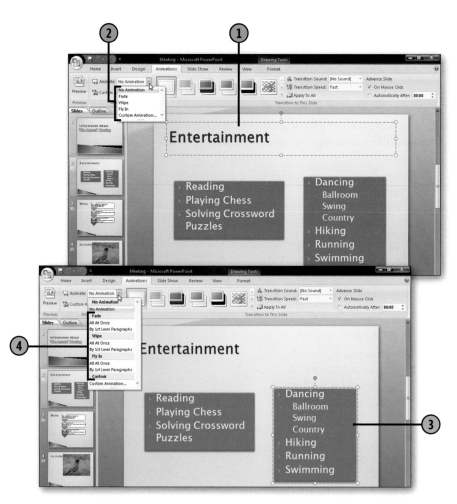

Animate a SmartArt Graphic

① Click the SmartArt graphic to select it.

② Click the Animate list box, and select the animation you want:

- **As One Object** to have all the content animated as a single unit and to have it all appear at the same time

- **All At Once** to have each element of the graphic animated and have all the elements appear at the same time

- **One By One** to have each element animated and to have the elements appear one at a time in consecutive order

- **By Level At Once** to have all the elements in the first level animated and to have them appear together, followed by all the elements of the second level, and so on

- **By Level One By One** to have each element in the first level animated and to have the elements appear one at a time in consecutive order, followed by each element of the second level, and so on

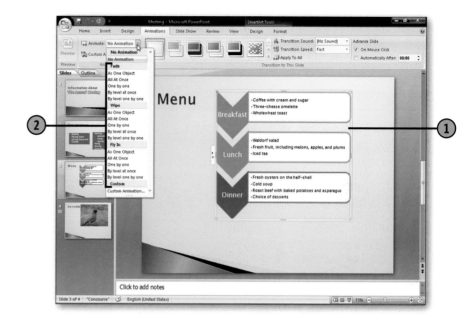

Tip

You can animate a single shape, a table, or a picture. If you're including a chart in your presentation, you can animate individual data series or individual categories, or you can animate the chart as a single item.

Customizing Your Animation

If you want to control the length of your animation effects and the order in which they occur, or add more than one effect, or have access to many different types of animations, you can create a customized animation scheme. By customizing your animations, you can make the items do a number of remarkable tricks.

Customize the Animation

① On the Animations tab, click the Custom Animation button to display the Custom Animation pane.

② Select the item whose animation you want to apply or change.

③ Click the Change button to change the type of animation you want to use. (If you haven't yet applied an animation scheme, this button will appear as the Add Effect button. Click it, and choose the animation you want from the drop-down menu.)

④ Select the Start, Direction, and Speed settings you want.

⑤ To further customize the animation, click the item's down arrow, and customize the animation to your liking.

⑥ Select the next item, and customize the animation.

⑦ Use the Re-Order buttons if you want to change the order in which the items are animated.

⑧ Click the Custom Animation button again to close the Custom Animation pane.

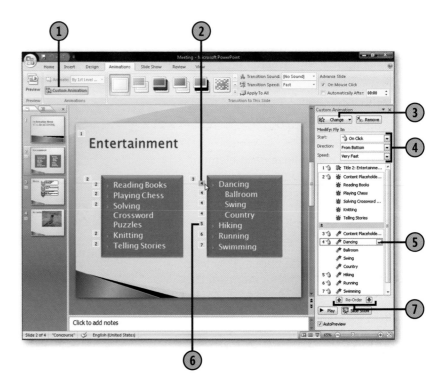

Tip

To add sound to the transition, to dim or hide the item, or to animate text by the letter or by the word, click the down arrow for the transition, and choose Effects Options from the menu.

Adding an Action to a Slide

Sometimes, in the middle of a presentation, you might want to jump to a different part of the presentation, run a different program as a demonstration, open a file, or even have a little sound clip added. You can do this by assigning an action to the text or to some other item in your presentation.

Assign an Action

① Select the item you want to use to trigger the action.

② On the Insert tab, click the Action button to display the Action Settings dialog box.

③ If you want the action to occur when you click the item, on the Mouse Click tab, select the type of action and then the action itself.

④ Select this check box if you want a sound to play when the item is clicked, and then select the sound.

⑤ Select this check box if you want the item to be animated when you click it.

⑥ If you want the action to occur when you move the mouse pointer over the item rather than clicking it, make your settings on the Mouse Over tab.

⑦ Click OK, and run your slide presentation to make sure the action you want occurs when you click the mouse or move the mouse over the item.

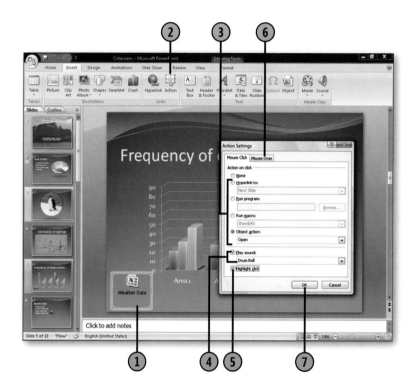

Tip ✔

The Run Macro option is available only if your presentation contains at least one macro. The Object Action is available only if you've selected an OLE (Object Linking and Embedding) object, such as an Excel workbook, that was inserted by using the Object button on the Insert tab.

See Also

"Using Navigation Buttons" on page 197 for information about adding navigation buttons to a slide show.

"Linking to a File or to a Web Page" on page 313 for information about inserting hyperlinks to files or Web pages.

Editing a Presentation

You'll probably go back into your slide presentation many times to add, delete, or tweak a few elements until you're satisfied that your show is ready for prime time. PowerPoint provides two extremely helpful organizational tools that make editing and modify your presentation a breeze: the Outline view and the Slide Sorter.

Change the Content of the Slides

(1) In Normal view, with your presentation open, click the Outline tab.

(2) Click a slide to preview it.

(3) Select any text you want to change, and type the new text. Select and delete an entire entry if you want to remove it from the slide.

(4) Click at the left of an item to select it, and, using the four-headed-arrow mouse pointer, drag the item to a new location on the slide, to a new location on a different slide, or to the left or right to promote or demote the item in a list.

(5) Make any changes to non-text items directly on the slide.

(6) Continue through the text and the slides to modify the content as desired.

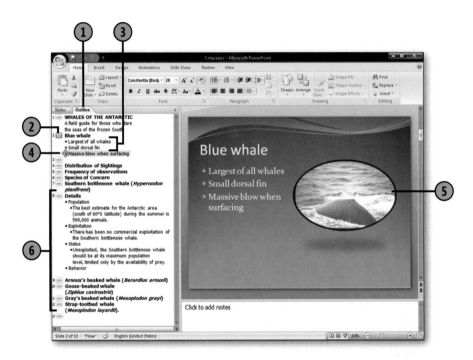

See Also

"Using Word to Prepare PowerPoint Text" on page 296 for information about creating and editing the content of a PowerPoint presentation in Word.

Change the Order of the Slides

① Click the Slide Sorter View button to switch to Slide Sorter view.

② Drag a slide that you want to display in a different part of your slide presentation to the spot where you want it.

③ If there's a slide that you don't want to include in this presentation but that you don't want to delete, select it, and, on the Slide Show tab, click the Hide Slide button. To return the hidden slide to the presentation, select it, and click the Hide Slide button again.

④ To permanently delete a slide, select it, and press the Delete key.

⑤ To add a blank slide, click the slide that will precede the new slide in the presentation, and, on the Home tab, click the New Slide button.

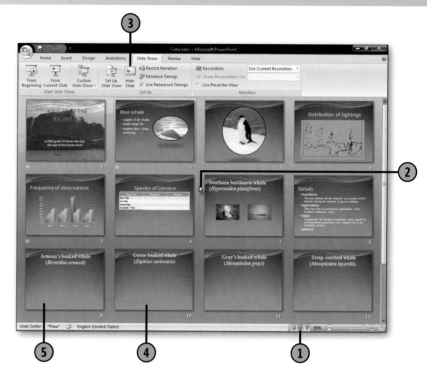

Tip

You can change the order of slides in Normal view by selecting a slide on either the Slide tab or the Outline tab and then dragging the slide to a new location on that tab. Slide Sorter view, however, lets you see more of your slides at one time than are visible in Normal view.

Repeating Content on Every Slide

If you want to add information to all your slides for your audience to see, such as the slide number, the date, your name, or any other information, you can create a footer—that is, an area at the bottom of the slide in which to put the item.

Add the Footer

① If you want to add the footer to only a single slide, select the slide. If you want to add the footer to all the slides, you can select any slide.

② On the Insert tab, click the Header & Footer button to display the Header And Footer dialog box.

③ On the Slide tab, select this check box if you want the date to appear.

④ Select this option if you want the date to be updated automatically for each slide show. Select the format for the date.

⑤ Select this option if you want to enter a specific date and have that date always displayed.

⑥ Select this check box if you want the slide number displayed.

⑦ Select this check box, and enter your text if you want to customize the text in the footer.

⑧ Select this check box if you want the footer to appear on every slide except the title slide, or clear the check box if you want the footer to appear on all slides.

⑨ Click Apply to have the footer appear only on the selected slide, or click Apply All to have it appear on all slides.

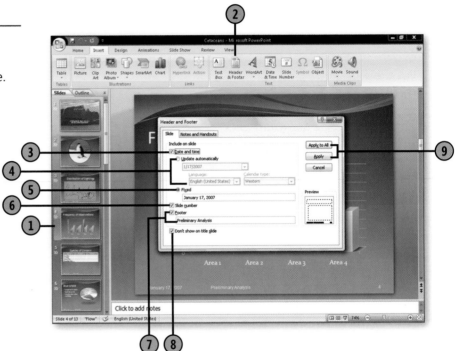

See Also

"Format the Background" on page 171 for information about adding a background graphic, and "Modifying the Default Layout" on pages 180–181 for information on how to add the same content to different presentations.

Adding Transition Effects to Slides

When you develop a slide show, you might want to include some special effects as you make the transition from one slide to the next. When a new slide appears, your audience sees a transition effect—for example, a dissolve, a checkerboard, a "newsflash" effect—and/or a sound. You can also specify whether you want the next slide to advance automatically after a preset time or whether you want to switch to the next slide manually with a mouse-click.

Set the Transitions

① Click the slide to which you want to add the transition.

② On the Animations tab, point to the various transitions to see how they look, and then click the one you want.

③ Select a sound if you want one.

④ Select a speed for the transition.

⑤ Specify how you want to advance to the next slide. If you want the slide to advance automatically, specify how long each slide is to be displayed before it advances.

⑥ Click Apply To All if you want all the slides in your presentation to have the transition you just selected. If you don't want the same transition for all the slides, repeat steps 1 through 5 to add transitions to the other slides in your presentation.

⑦ Click to preview the transitions for all the slides.

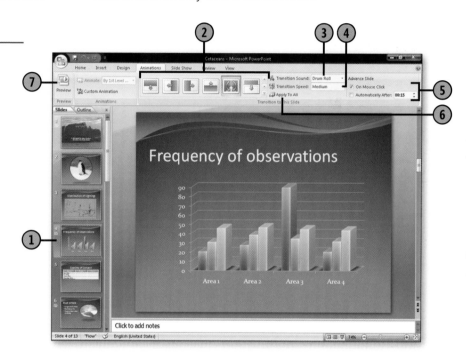

Tip

Although you can add the transition effects at any time, it's usually best to apply them after you've added all the slides to your show.

Caution

As with the text effects, don't use a lot of different transitional effects. They can make your presentation seem chaotic, and an audience might find them quite distracting.

Modifying the Default Layout

The layouts of your slides are based on the layouts of your slide master and your layout master. If you want to create your own designs, you can modify the slide master and the layout and then save the design as a template for future use. The different slide layouts are the basis for the various slide types you see in the New Slide gallery.

Modify the Layout

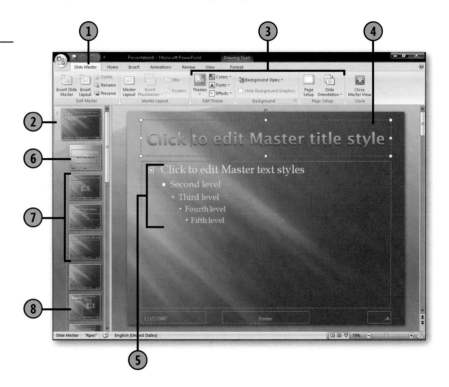

1. On the View tab, click the Slide Master button to display the Slide Master tab.

2. Click the first slide, which is the slide master. Changes you make to this slide will be used by the other layout slides that are shown below the slide master.

3. Use the tools on the Slide Master tab to set the slide dimensions, the theme, and the background styles.

4. Click in the title text box, and use the tools on the Drawing Tools Format tab and the Home tab to modify the text style.

5. Click in the content text box, and modify the styles for the different levels of text.

6. Click a slide layout, and modify the contents of the slide, including adding or deleting any text boxes or placeholders. Most changes will apply only to the selected slide, but theme and page setup changes apply to all slides.

7. Continue modifying the layouts to create your design.

8. If there's a slide layout you don't want, select it, and then click Delete on the Slide Master tab.

Tip

You can also modify the default layout for your handouts and notes. To do so, click the Handout Master button or the Notes Master button on the View tab, and modify the handout master or the notes master.

Create a New Layout

1. Click the Insert Layout button to insert a new slide.

2. Modify any content in the slide to the way you want it.

3. Click the Insert Placeholder button, and select the type of placeholder you want. Drag out the placeholder, adjust its size if necessary, and move it to the location where you want it. Add any other placeholders you want, and format the slide and the slide elements.

4. With the slide selected, click the Rename button; in the Rename Layout dialog box that appears, type a descriptive name, and click Rename.

5. Continue adding and modifying any slide layouts you want.

6. Click the Close Master View button when you've finished.

7. If you want to use this layout for future presentations, choose Save As from the Office menu; in the Save As dialog box, type a file name, save the file as a PowerPoint Template, and click Save.

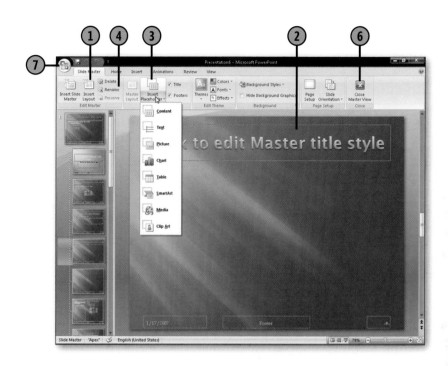

Tip

If you want to create a second series of slide layouts based on a new slide master, click Insert Slide Master on the Slide Master tab, and then add the slide layouts.

Creating a Photo Album

A PowerPoint photo album is a great way to display a collection of pictures. All you need to do is select the pictures and the layout, and PowerPoint will put together a new presentation that contains your photo album.

Create the Album

(1) On the Insert tab, click the Photo Album button to display the Photo Album dialog box.

(2) Click to open the Insert New Pictures window, locate and select the pictures you want to use, and click Insert.

(3) Click to include a blank text box in place of a picture.

(4) Use the Order buttons to re-order the pictures and any text boxes, or the Remove button to remove a picture from the album.

(5) Use the picture controls to rotate a selected picture or to change its contrast or brightness.

(6) Select a layout, the shape of the frame you want for each picture, and a design template if you want to add extra design elements to your photo album.

(7) Specify whether you want the file names to be included as captions under all your pictures, and whether you want to convert your color pictures into black-and-white versions. Note that you can't include a caption if the picture is set to fill the entire slide.

(8) Click to assign a theme.

(9) Click Create to have PowerPoint create a new presentation. Edit the photo album, adding text and changing styles and/or the theme. The completed photo album is now ready to be shown as an onscreen slide show or to be printed and bound.

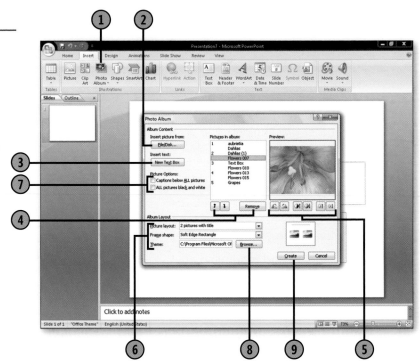

Tip

To modify the photo album layout after you've created it, click the bottom part of the Photo Album button, choose Edit Photo Album from the drop-down menu, make your changes in the Edit Photo Album dialog box, and click Update.

10

Presenting a PowerPoint Slide Show

In this section:

- Adding Speaker Notes
- Printing Handouts
- The Perils of Presentation
- Running Your Slide Show
- Recording a Narration
- Timing a Presentation
- Creating Different Versions of a Slide Show
- Creating a Show for Distribution
- Taking Your Show on the Road
- Creating Pictures of Your Slides
- Reviewing a Presentation
- Changing Slide-Show Settings

Now that you've created your slide show, the next step is to present it to an attentive and interested audience. Of course, your audience won't remain attentive if, in the middle of your show, your computer goes to sleep or your screen saver appears! With Microsoft Office PowerPoint 2007 and the Windows Vista Mobility Center, you won't have to deal with such disasters.

In this section, we'll show you how to create and print speaker notes that can serve as reminders or as a complete script. You can print handouts that contain pictures of your slides and other details so that your audience can refer back to them later. If you've been allotted a certain amount of time for your presentation, you can time the entire show as you rehearse it, and then apply that timing so that the slides advance automatically within the given time. If your computer system is set up with dual monitors, you can run your presentation from one computer and use Presenter view on the other monitor to run the full-screen show for your audience. If you want, you can also record a narration for your show so that you don't even need to be there! You can easily modify a show for different audiences, and, if you need to take the show on the road, you can create a package that contains all the files you need so that your show will run properly on an unfamiliar computer.

Adding Speaker Notes

Speaker notes are designed to help you, or the person who's presenting the show, with the details of the presentation. Your notes can be quick reminders about what to say, or they can be as organized as a detailed script. You can add the notes as you design each slide or as you review the finished slide show. You can print out the notes or view them on the screen, either in Normal view or—if you're using two monitors for your presentation—in Presenter view.

Create the Notes

(1) In Normal view, click the slide to which you want to add notes.

(2) Click in the Notes area, and type your notes as you develop the slide.

(3) On the View tab, click the Notes Page button.

(4) If you want to change the color scheme for the picture of the slide, select the color setting you want.

(5) Verify that the correct slide is shown, adjust the zoom so that you can see your text, and click in the Notes text box. Add, edit, and format the text as you want. You can also format the text box and the background of the notes page if you want.

See Also

"Running a Slide Show with Dual Monitors" on page 190 for information about using Presenter view.

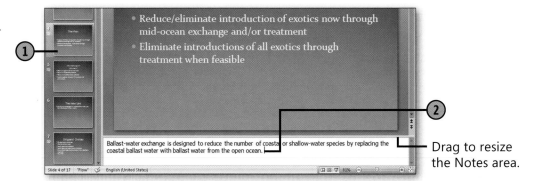

Drag to resize the Notes area.

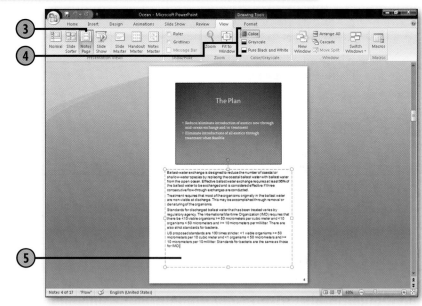

Set Up and Print the Notes

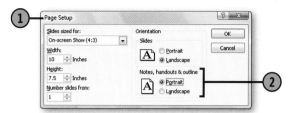

① On the Design tab, click the Page Setup button to display the Page Setup dialog box.

② Specify the orientation you want for your notes, and click OK.

③ On the Insert tab, click the Header & Footer button to display the Header And Footer dialog box.

④ On the Notes And Handouts tab, specify what you want to include in your notes, and type any custom header or footer text.

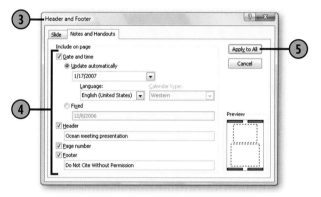

⑤ Click Apply To All.

⑥ Choose Print from the Office menu to display the Print dialog box.

⑦ Select Notes Pages in the Print What list.

⑧ Specify whether you want to print your notes in color, grayscale, or black and white.

⑨ Make whatever other print settings you want, and click OK to print your notes.

Tip

Click the Preview button in the Print dialog box to see how the notes pages will print to make sure you have the settings you want.

Tip

To print the text of your presentation as it appears in the outline, select Outline View in the Print What list.

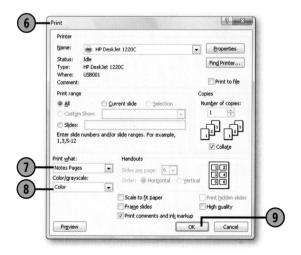

Printing Handouts

Handouts are printed copies of your presentation that PowerPoint can generate automatically. The handouts show a small image of each slide. You can specify the number of slides you want to be printed on each page, and the slides will be scaled to fit on the page.

Create the Handouts

1. With your presentation completed, point to Print on the Office menu, and, in the gallery that appears, click Print Preview to display your handout page in Print Preview.

2. Click the Orientation button if you want to change the orientation of the page.

3. Select Handouts, and specify the number of slides you want per page.

4. Click Options, and specify whether you want to include header and footer content, hidden slides, comments, and frames around the slides, and whether you want to print in color. If you've specified four or more slides per page, point to Printing Order, and specify the way you want the slides to be arranged in the columns.

5. Click Next Page, and check the way that page will print. Continue going through the handout pages to verify that the layout appears as you want.

6. Click Print. In the Print dialog box that appears, make whatever print settings you want, and, with Handouts selected in the Print What list, click OK to print the handouts.

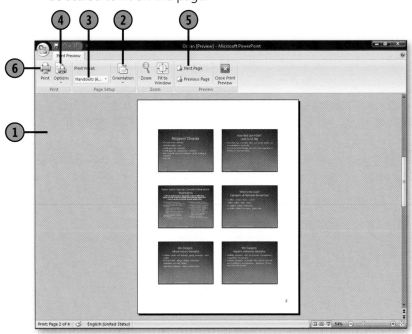

Tip

If you select three slides per page, PowerPoint prints blank lines next to each slide image so that people have room to jot down notes about the slides.

See Also

"Preparing PowerPoint Handouts in Word" on page 297 for information about using Word to create custom handouts for a PowerPoint presentation.

The Perils of Presentation

Most of us have witnessed the embarrassment of someone who's struggling to get a slide presentation to run from a projector or on a second monitor. Why is there no video signal from the computer to the projector? Why is only part of the screen visible? Or—oops!—once the show finally gets going, a screen saver suddenly pops up, or the computer goes to sleep. It's awful! The flustered presenter has to log back on and resume the presentation, only to be sabotaged yet again by the screen saver or the power settings. Fortunately, PowerPoint and Windows Vista have teamed up to help you or your presenter avoid such disasters.

If you're using a portable computer with Windows Vista to run your slide show, you have access to the Windows Mobility Center, where you can make settings that prevent most of the problems we've mentioned. To run the Windows Mobility Center, open the Vista Start menu, type **mob** in the Search box, and click Windows Mobility Center. Now you can set up the way your computer will behave when you're giving a presentation. When you click the Presentation Settings button, you can prevent the screen saver from appearing, set the sound volume, and include a background picture if your presentation doesn't fill the entire screen. When you turn on the presentation settings, you can also prevent the computer from going to sleep and can stop system messages from appearing.

The Windows Mobility Center also helps you set up the connection to a second monitor or to a projector. Provided the monitor or projector is connected and turned on, when you click the Connect Display button, Vista searches your computer for a second display connection. Once you're connected, you can set different arrangements by clicking the Change Display Settings button.

In most versions of Windows Vista you can also use a tool to help you connect to a network projector. By using the Connect To A Network Projector Wizard, you can search for any projectors on the network or, if you've been given the projector's address, connect by entering the address and, if necessary, the password.

Whether you're using a portable computer or a desktop model, PowerPoint can control your display by changing the *resolution* (the size) of the presentation if it's too big or too small on the screen (or if the display can't use a certain resolution). PowerPoint also lets you specify which monitor to use to present the slide show. If your computer has multiple-monitor capability, you can also use Presenter view, which provides controls to run the show and access to all your notes.

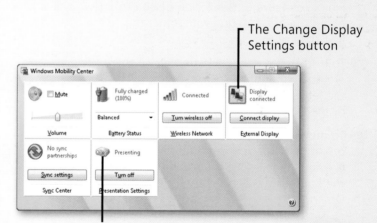

The Change Display Settings button

The Presentation Settings button

Running a Slide Show

You've finished putting your presentation together and you're ready to show it. Now what? A large part of a successful slide show is the way you deliver the presentation. Fortunately, a slide presentation is easy to set up, and PowerPoint provides some handy tools to help you run the show smoothly.

Run the Presentation

(1) On the Slide Show tab, with PowerPoint running and your slide show open, select the resolution you want to use.

(2) If you have more than one monitor attached to your computer, select the one you want to use to show your presentation.

(3) Click the From Beginning button (or press F5) or the From Current Slide button to begin the presentation with either the first slide or the currently selected slide.

(4) To display the next animation or—if there are no animations—the next slide, click the left mouse button or press the Right or the Down arrow key.

(5) To move back to the previous animation or—if there are no animations—the previous slide, move the mouse, and click the Back arrow, or press the Left or the Up arrow key.

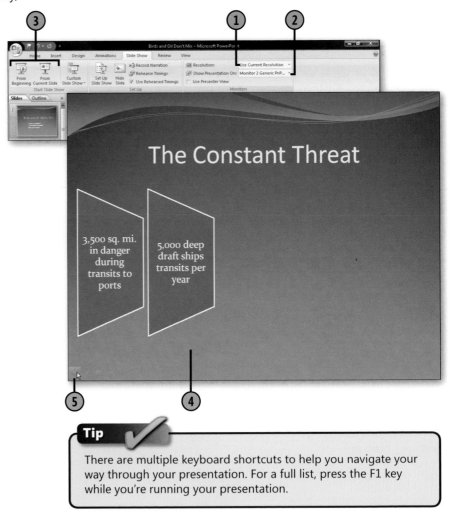

See Also

"Changing Slide-Show Settings" on page 200 for information about customizing the way you work in a slide show.

Tip

There are multiple keyboard shortcuts to help you navigate your way through your presentation. For a full list, press the F1 key while you're running your presentation.

Modify the Presentation

① Click the right mouse button or press the shortcut-menu key on the keyboard (if there is one on your keyboard). From the shortcut menu, choose the navigation command you want.

② Move the mouse to display the mouse pointer and the toolbar buttons, and click the Pointer button.

③ Choose an annotation tool.

④ Click the Pointer button again, point to Ink Color, and, in the gallery that appears, click the color you want for your annotation.

⑤ Hold down the left mouse button and drag to highlight or to annotate the slide.

⑥ Continue to go through the show, making whatever modifications you want. If you want to stop the presentation before you reach the end, press the Esc key, or right-click and choose End Show from the shortcut menu. If you've used any of the annotation tools, choose to save them when prompted if you want the annotations to be saved with the presentation.

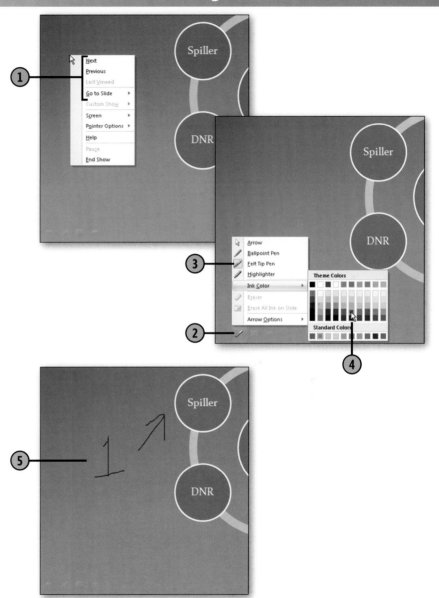

Running a Slide Show with Dual Monitors

If the computer system you're using for your slide show is set up with dual monitors, you can run your presentation using Presenter view on one monitor. Presenter view gives you a variety of tools with which to present the slide show, as well as a view of all your notes, while the second monitor displays the full-screen slide presentation for the audience. To be able to use Presenter view, your computer system must be able to have the Windows Desktop extended across both monitors. For a desktop computer, this usually means having two graphics adapters. If you're using a portable computer, it must have multiple-monitor capability.

Control the Show

① On the Slide Show tab, with PowerPoint running and your presentation open, select the Use Presenter View check box, and specify which monitor you want to use to display the slide show. Press the F5 key or click the From Beginning button to start the show.

② Preview the slide that's being shown, and then use your prepared notes to talk about the slide.

③ Use the Next or the Previous button to go to the next or the previous animation, or—if there are no animations—to the next or the previous slide.

④ Click any slide in the presentation to display that slide.

⑤ Click to select which slide to go to, to show a white or black blank screen, to show or hide annotations, to switch to a different program, or to end the show.

⑥ Click to use the annotation tools. Any annotations you make on your copy of the slide will appear in the full-screen slide show.

⑦ Press Esc if you need to end the show before you've reached the end of your presentation.

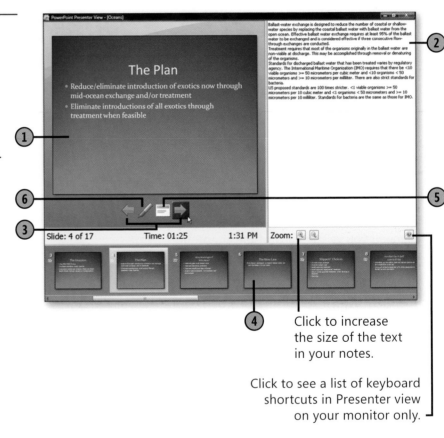

Click to increase the size of the text in your notes.

Click to see a list of keyboard shortcuts in Presenter view on your monitor only.

Customizing the Presentation

When you've finished putting all the bits and pieces of your slide show together, you'll probably want to make a few tweaks to customize the show so that it will run exactly as you want it to. After you've made your customizations, the settings are saved with the presentation and will be used unless you decide to change them.

Set Up the Show

① On the Slide Show tab, click the Set Up Slide Show button to display the Set Up Show dialog box.

② Specify the way you want the show to be displayed.

③ Select this check box to have the slide show run continuously until you (or a presenter) press the Esc key.

④ Select either of these check boxes if you want to omit from the slide show any narration or animation that exists in the presentation.

⑤ Select the range of slides you want to include in the show, or specify which custom show to use.

⑥ Specify the way you want each slide to be advanced.

⑦ If your computer system is equipped with two or more monitors, specify which monitor is to display the show.

⑧ Select this check box if you want to use Presenter view and you know that the computer is properly equipped.

⑨ Click OK.

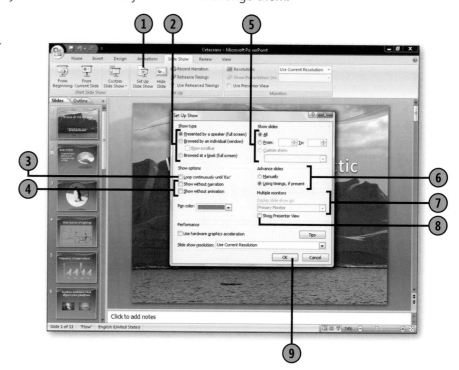

See Also

"Running a Slide Show with Dual Monitors" on the facing page for information about using Presenter view.

"Creating Different Versions of a Slide Show" on page 194 for information about creating a custom show.

Recording a Narration

If you're tired of saying the same old thing every time you present your slide show, why not record your talk so that your presence isn't required for the presentation? When you record a narration, you're also setting the length of time each slide is displayed.

Narrate Your Presentation

① Click the first slide to select it.

② Click the Record Narration button on the Slide Show tab to display the Record Narration dialog box.

③ If you haven't previously set up a narration on this computer, click each button in the dialog box, and make your recording settings; or, if you have recorded a narration on this computer, change any existing settings if you want to, and then click OK.

④ When the slide show starts automatically, record your narration as you go through the slides. Continue recording your narration until you've completed the slide show.

⑤ When PowerPoint asks you whether you want to save the timings for the slide show, click Save to save the length of time each slide was displayed, or click Don't Save to keep the narration but not the timing used to automatically advance the slides. (To run the presentation with the narration but without the slides automatically advancing on the Slide Show tab, clear the Use Rehearsed Timings check box.)

⑥ Run the slide show to make sure it's being presented exactly the way you want.

Tip

To delete a narration from a slide, in Normal view, click the sound icon at the bottom-right of the slide, and press the Delete key.

Timing a Presentation

Quite often, your slide presentation is limited to a specific length of time. Unfortunately, the allotted time might expire before you get through your entire presentation. To avoid delivering an incomplete show, rehearse your presentation and record the length of time it takes to display each slide. Then, when you've completed your rehearsal within the allotted time, you can apply that timing to your presentation and have each slide advance automatically so that your show will end exactly on time.

Time the Presentation

1. On the Slide Show tab, with your presentation complete and your notes or script in hand, click the Rehearse Timings button to start the slide show and to begin recording the timing.

2. Rehearse the presentation of each slide, noting the elapsed time for each slide and the elapsed time for the entire presentation.

3. If you encountered a problem during the presentation of a slide, click the Repeat button to restart the timing for that slide.

4. If you need to suspend your rehearsal, click the Pause button. Click the button again to resume the rehearsal. Continue rehearsing the presentation until you've reached the end of the show.

5. When you've completed the slide show, and if the total time for the rehearsal was within the allocated time, click Yes to keep the recorded timing. Otherwise, click No, and keep repeating steps 1 through 5.

6. With the Use Rehearsed Timings check box selected, start the slide show from the beginning, and make sure that the timing for the display of the slides is correct.

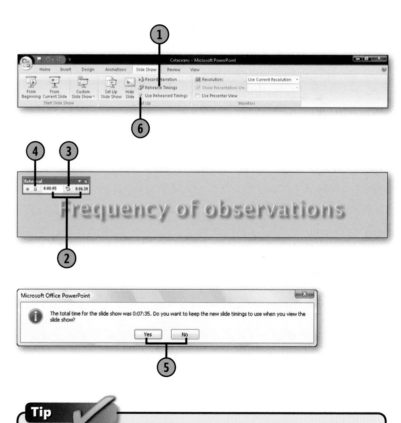

Tip ✔

To pause a timed presentation, right-click in the slide show, and choose Pause from the shortcut menu. To resume the timed presentation, right-click again, and choose Resume.

Creating Different Versions of a Slide Show

Sometimes you might need to adjust a slide show to make it suitable for a different audience or for a change of venue. Instead of creating a whole new show, or deleting slides, hiding slides, or rearranging the slide order for a different presentation, you can create one or more custom slide shows while keeping the original presentation intact.

Create a Custom Slide Show

① On the Slide Show tab, with your entire presentation completed and saved, click the Custom Slide Show button, and choose Custom Shows from the drop-down menu to display the Custom Shows dialog box.

② Click New to display the Define Custom Show dialog box.

③ Type a descriptive name for the show.

④ Hold down the Ctrl key, and click the slides that you want in the show to select them.

⑤ Click Add.

⑥ Click a slide, and use the Up or Down arrow button to change the slide's position in the show. Continue moving the slides around until they're in the order you want.

⑦ Click OK.

⑧ Click Show to preview your show.

⑨ The next time you want to view the custom show, on the Slide Show tab, with the original presentation open, click the Custom Slide Show button, and choose the show from the drop-down menu.

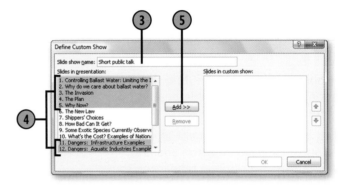

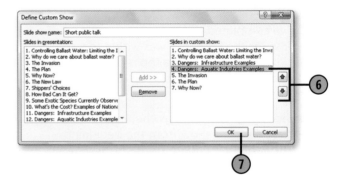

Creating a Show for Distribution

If you've created a presentation that you want friends or coworkers to run and view, you can set up the show so that it runs automatically. You can save it either in the PowerPoint 2007 format, which requires the user to have PowerPoint 2007 installed to be able to view the show, or in the PowerPoint 97–2003 format, which allows the show to be viewed with earlier versions of PowerPoint or with the PowerPoint Viewer.

Save the Show

① With your show completed, and saved, point to Save As on the Office menu, and, in the gallery that appears, click PowerPoint Show to display the Save As window.

② Type a descriptive name for the show.

③ In the Save As Type list, select the appropriate format:

  • PowerPoint Show to save the show in the PowerPoint 2007 format

  • PowerPoint 97–2003 Show to convert the show to the earlier format

④ Click Save.

⑤ If you saved the show in the 97–2003 format, inspect the results of the Compatibility Checker that was run automatically. Click Continue to complete the conversion if the changes are acceptable; otherwise, click Cancel. Distribute the file, and have your viewers double-click the show's file to run the show.

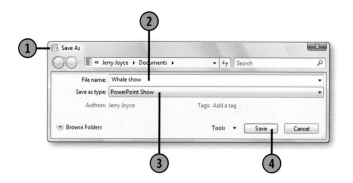

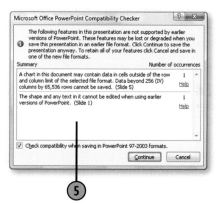

See Also

"Taking Your Show on the Road" on page 196 for information about packaging a show if it includes links to other files as well as information about including the PowerPoint Viewer with the show.

"Checking the Compatibility" on page 334 for information about saving files in previous formats and using the Compatibility Checker.

Tip

You can open a PowerPoint Show file for editing by choosing Open from PowerPoint's Office menu.

Taking Your Show on the Road

If you need to take your show on the road and run your presentation on a computer other than the one on which you created it, you might find that either the show doesn't run at all or that some of its components—the narration, the video, or the background sound—don't work. To avoid this problem, you can create one of two *packages* that each contain all the files you need. The Archive package includes all the show's PowerPoint files and any other support or linked files; the Viewer package include all the show's files and the PowerPoint Viewer, but it saves the presentation files in the PowerPoint 97–2003 Presentation format.

Package Your Presentation

① With PowerPoint running and your presentation open, point to Publish on the Office menu, and, in the gallery that appears, click Package For CD to display the Package For CD dialog box.

② Type a descriptive name for the CD.

③ Click to include any files that you want on the CD, including any other PowerPoint presentations.

④ Click to display the Options dialog box.

⑤ Select the type of package you want:

- The Viewer Package (and then specify the way you want the CD to play)

- The Archive Package

⑥ Specify which types of files you want to be included.

⑦ Set the security settings you want.

⑧ Click OK.

⑨ Click either of the following:

- Copy To Folder to store the files in a folder

- Copy To CD to copy directly to a CD

⑩ Click Close to complete the process.

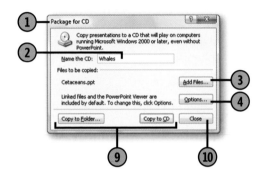

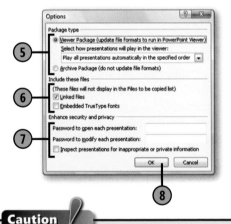

Caution

If you save the files in the PowerPoint 97–2003 Presentation format, some features, such as the animation of graphics, might be lost.

Using Navigation Buttons

One way to guide someone who's viewing a slide show on a computer is to add navigation buttons to the show. That way, your viewer can click a navigation button and go exactly where you want him or her to go.

Add Navigation Buttons

① On the Insert tab, in Normal view, with the slide to which you want to add a navigation button selected, click the Shapes button. In the gallery that appears, click one of the Action Buttons navigation shapes.

② Drag out the button on the slide.

③ In the Action Settings dialog box that appears, do any of the following:

- Confirm that the preset hyperlink is the one you want.

- Set a different hyperlink.

- Set a different action for the button.

- Include a sound.

④ Click OK.

⑤ Select the button, use the standard formatting techniques you'd use on any Shape, and then position the button where you want it.

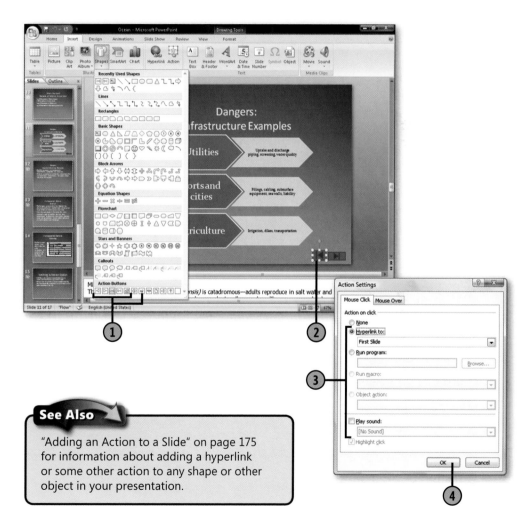

See Also

"Adding an Action to a Slide" on page 175 for information about adding a hyperlink or some other action to any shape or other object in your presentation.

Creating Pictures of Your Slides

Although pictures of your slides are printed in your notes or handouts, you might need a picture of a slide, or even pictures of your entire presentation, for other purposes— to be included in a report or for a design review, for example. Fortunately, you can save pictures of your slides in just about any picture format you want.

Create the Pictures

1 If you want to create a picture of a single slide, click that slide to select it; to create pictures of all the slides in the presentation, select any slide.

2 Choose Save As from the Office menu to display the Save As window.

3 Type a descriptive name for the picture or pictures.

4 In the Save As Type list, select the picture format you want, and then click Save.

5 In the Microsoft Office PowerPoint dialog box that appears, click the appropriate button:

- Every Slide to create a separate picture file for each slide in the presentation

- Current Slide Only to create a single picture file for the selected slide

Reviewing a Presentation

When a slide presentation is a collaborative project, the nearly finished slide show can be circulated for comments. You can then review the presentation and add your comments, and you can edit or delete existing comments.

Review the Presentation

(1) On the Review tab, with the presentation open in Normal view, click the Show Markup button if it isn't already selected. (If the button isn't available, the document doesn't yet contain any comments.)

(2) Click or select where you want to insert a comment.

(3) Click the New Comment button.

(4) Type your comment, and then click outside the comment when you've finished. Continue adding your comments to the presentation.

(5) Click the Next or the Previous button to find your own or other people's comments.

(6) To edit a selected comment, click Edit Comment, make your changes to the comment, and then click outside the comment.

(7) To delete a selected comment, all the comments on the slide, or all the comments in the presentation, click Delete, and, from the drop-down menu, choose what is to be deleted.

(8) Click the Show Markup button when you've finished. Any comments remaining in the presentation will be hidden until you're ready to review them.

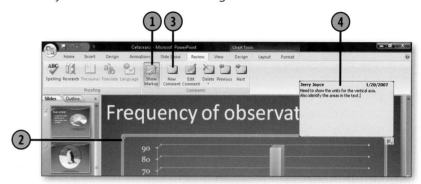

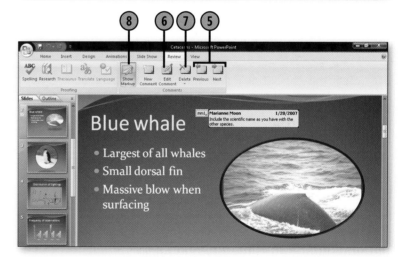

> **See Also**
>
> "Changing Your User Information" on page 321 for information about changing the initials that are used to identify your comments.

Changing Slide-Show Settings

A PowerPoint 2007 slide show is set up to work and look exactly like the slide shows that were created in earlier versions of PowerPoint. However, you can customize the way a slide show appears on your own computer. Note, though, that these changes you make to the PowerPoint options apply only on your computer; they don't affect the way this particular slide show will appear if you show it on another computer.

Change the Settings

1. Choose PowerPoint Options from the Office menu to display the PowerPoint Options dialog box.

2. Click the Advanced category.

3. Clear this check box if you want to use the right mouse button to move backward in your presentation, or select the check box to display the shortcut menu with navigation and display controls.

4. Clear this check box if you don't want the toolbar that contains the Previous, Pointer, Show, and Next buttons at the bottom of the slide-show screen to be visible. Select the check box if you want those controls to be visible.

5. Clear this check box if you always want to discard any annotations you make during the slide show, or select the check box if you want the option of keeping or discarding the annotations.

6. Clear this check box if you want the slide show to end when you move past the last slide, or select the check box if, at the end of the show, you want to see the black screen displaying a notice that the show has ended.

7. Click OK.

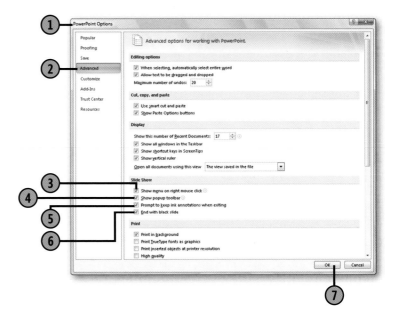

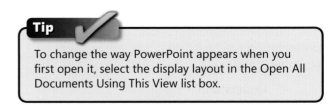

Tip

To change the way PowerPoint appears when you first open it, select the display layout in the Open All Documents Using This View list box.

Working with Messages in Outlook

In this section:

- **What's Where in Outlook Messages?**
- **Sending E-Mail**
- **Receiving and Reading E-Mail**
- **Replying to and Forwarding a Message**
- **Sending or Receiving a File**
- **Formatting E-Mail Messages**
- **Managing Messages**
- **Signing Your E-Mail**
- **Setting Up RSS Subscriptions**
- **Reading RSS Items**
- **Setting Up E-Mail Accounts**
- **E-Mailing Your Schedule**
- **Understanding E-Mail Encryption**

Microsoft Office Outlook 2007 is designed to help you manage your e-mail correspondence and more. This chapter shows you the basics of using Outlook for e-mail, such as how to add an e-mail account and compose and send e-mail messages.

Outlook lets you create e-mail messages containing much more than plain text. You can format the text in your e-mail using styles and even add your own pictures to your messages. A variety of graphical objects such as shapes, charts, and SmartArt are available to help you create attractive and effective e-mail. You can also include a file with your message or share your calendar as an e-mail message with just a few clicks.

You can use Outlook to quickly set up RSS (Really Simple Syndication) subscriptions and then read each RSS feed in its own Outlook folder. With Outlook, you can sort, search, and send RSS feeds to other people just like e-mail messages.

What's Where in Outlook Messages?

The Outlook new message form has many commands that help you create attractive and effective e-mail. The Message tab contains many frequently used commands such as text formatting, copy and paste, and spellcheck. Additional tabs contain groups of commands that enable you to include graphics and other objects; control options such as message format, delivery receipts, and other tracking options; and apply themes and advanced text formatting. Even though the Ribbon is new and offers a wide range of commands, the basics of composing a message in Outlook are much the same as in earlier versions.

Overview of New Message Window

- Create, print, export, and manage Outlook items with the Office Button.

- Save a message, undo and redo actions, and page through the messages in a folder with the Quick Access Toolbar.

- Use commands on the Ribbon to work with the currently selected text or object.

- Choose a tab to display different groups of commands.

- Compose your e-mail in the body of the message form.

- Choose recipients for your message.

- Click the Send button to mail your message.

- Enter a subject in the Subject field.

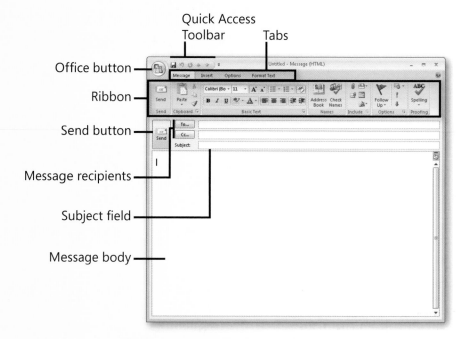

Quick Access Toolbar

Tabs

Office button

Ribbon

Send button

Message recipients

Subject field

Message body

Tip

If you need more text formatting options than are available on the Message tab, check the Format Text tab. Although many commands are available in both locations, some very useful options, such as Styles, are on only the Format Text tab.

Overview of the Message Window's Insert Tab

You can add much more than text to your e-mail messages using Outlook. This message uses commands from several tabs to achieve the effects that you see. The Insert tab has commands that enable you to add many types of objects to your e-mail messages.

Insert a picture or other graphical object using the Illustration group.

Add a Word table or an Excel spreadsheet using the Table command.

Insert Outlook items and files using commands in the Include group.

Add text and text objects like Word-Art with commands in the Text group.

Insert a picture in your message and use preset frame and shadow effects to enhance its appearance.

Format text using predefined styles from a visual gallery.

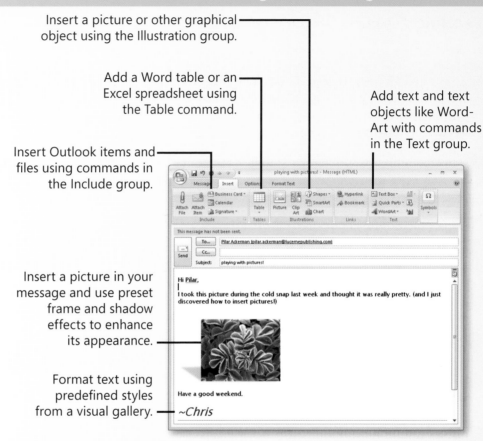

Try This!

Insert a picture in an e-mail message. Open a new e-mail message and place your cursor in the body of the message. Click the Insert tab and then click Picture. In the Insert Picture dialog box, locate a picture (you can open the Sample Pictures folder and use one of those images) and then click Insert. The picture will be displayed in your message, and you can use the commands on the Picture Tools to format it.

Tip ✓

You can send a copy of an e-mail message to people without displaying their e-mail addresses, or any other indication that they received a copy, by sending a blind carbon copy (Bcc). You can add the Bcc field to your e-mail messages by clicking on the Options tab and then, in the Fields group, clicking Bcc. Although you set this in an individual message, this setting will then be used by all new messages you create.

Sending E-Mail

When you write new messages in Outlook, you use the Message window. This window has a line for recipients (called the To line), a line for "carbon copied" recipients (the Cc line), a Subject line, and an area for the text of the message. Every new message must have at least one recipient. If you want, you can leave the Cc and Subject lines blank, but it's a good idea to give your messages a subject.

Address an E-Mail Message

① In Outlook, click New on the Standard toolbar to display a new Message window.

② To open the Select Names dialog box, click To.

③ Click the Address Book drop-down arrow.

④ Click the name of the address book you want to use, such as Contacts. The addresses in the selected address book appear in the box.

⑤ Click the name of the person to whom you want to send the new message.

⑥ Click To, Cc, or Bcc; Outlook copies the name to the specified message recipients list.

⑦ Repeat steps 5 and 6 until the message recipients list includes all the recipients you want to send the message to.

⑧ Click OK.

Tip ✓

You can set up several different address books to store your e-mail recipients' contact information. For example, you might have a company-wide address book that stores addresses and contact information for all internal employees. A second address book can be set up for external contacts, such as vendors, suppliers, and customers. A third address book could store personal contact information.

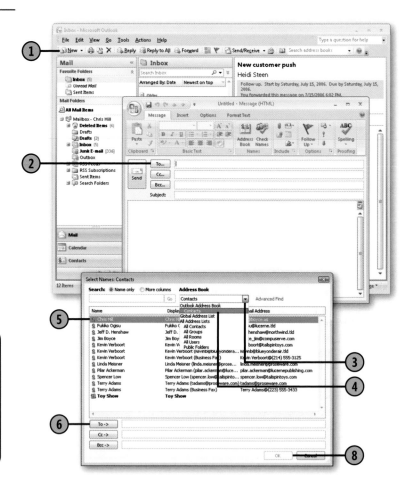

Type Your Message
Subject and Text

① In the New Message window, type a subject for the new message in the Subject field.

② Press Tab or click in the message body area.

③ Type your message.

④ Click Send.

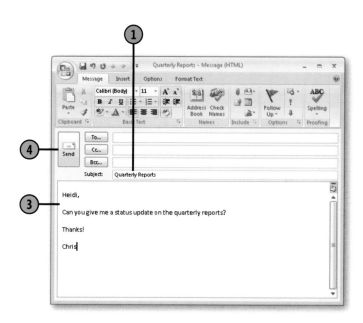

Tip

As you write your message, you do not have to press Enter at the end of each line. Keep typing and Outlook wraps the text to the next line. To create a new paragraph, press Enter. If you want each paragraph to be separated by two blank lines, press Enter twice at the end of each paragraph. This makes your messages easier to read than single-spaced messages.

Caution

You can apply special formatting to your message (see "Formatting E-Mail Message Text" on page 210), but you might not want to. If you send mail to people who use a different e-mail program, they might not see the formatting that you intended. When in doubt, it's usually a good policy to keep your messages simple so nothing gets lost in the translation.

Receiving and Reading E-Mail

Outlook makes it easy for you to receive your incoming messages and preview them or read their contents. The Inbox folder displays the sender's name, the message subject, the date the message was received, the size of the message, and whether the message has an attachment.

Locate New Messages

① Click the Mail button on the Navigation Pane to display your new messages.

② Choose Reading Pane from the View menu, then choose Bottom from the submenu.

③ Click the Newest On Top column to sort your new messages by the date you received them. Messages you have not read appear in boldface.

Open Message Items

① Click the Inbox icon on the Navigation Pane to display your new messages.

② Click the message you want to read to show its contents in the Reading Pane.

③ Double-click the message to open it in its own window.

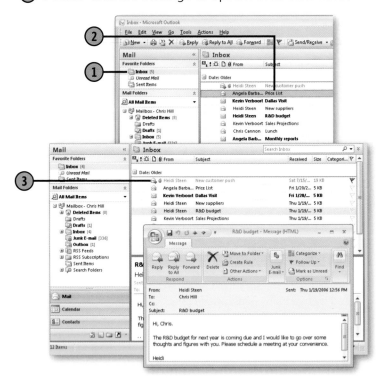

Replying to and Forwarding a Message

When you receive a message, you can reply directly back to the sender. You also have the option of forwarding the message or sending a response to everyone who receives the message. When you reply to a message, Outlook keeps the original message text and lets you add your new text above the original text. The sender's name becomes the recipient name, and the subject line begins with "RE:" to denote that the message is a reply.

Reply to an E-Mail Message

① Click the Inbox icon on the Navigation Pane to display messages in your Inbox folder.

② Click the message to which you want to reply.

③ Click Reply on the Standard toolbar.

④ Click in the space above the original message line, and type your reply.

⑤ Click Send.

Forward an E-Mail Message

① Click the Inbox icon on the Navigation Pane to display messages in your Inbox folder.

② Click the message you want to forward.

③ Click Forward on the Standard toolbar.

④ Add the address to which you want to forward this message.

⑤ Click in the space above the original message line, and type a message, if desired.

⑥ Click Send.

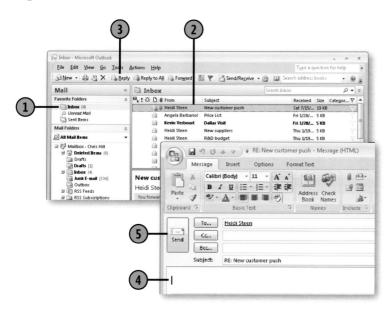

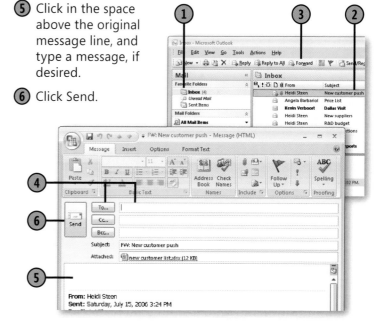

Sending or Receiving a File

Sometimes when you create an e-mail message, you want to send along a file as well. Files sent with e-mail are called message attachments. When you send the message, the file goes along with the message so the recipient can open it on his or her computer. When you receive an e-mail attachment, you can open it directly from the message, save it to your hard drive and open it from there, or print it straight from the message to a printer. Messages that have attachments display a paper clip icon to the left of the message author's name or below the message received date, depending on the location of the Reading Pane and the width of the display.

Attach a File

① Open a new message, and click the Insert tab on the Ribbon.

② Click Attach File on the Attach group.

③ Click the file you want to attach.

④ Click Insert.

Caution

The recipient of an attached file must have an application on his or her computer that can open the attached file. If not, you may need to save the file in an agreed-on format before sending the file.

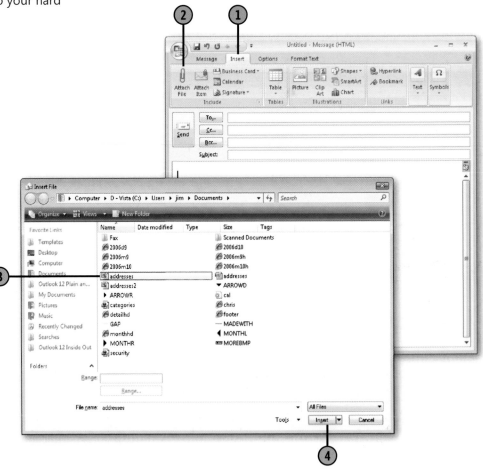

Open an Attachment

① Click the Inbox icon on the Navigation Pane to display messages in your Inbox folder.

② Click the message with the attachment.

③ Double-click the attachment in the Attachments field.

④ If asked if you want to open or save the attachment, click Open.

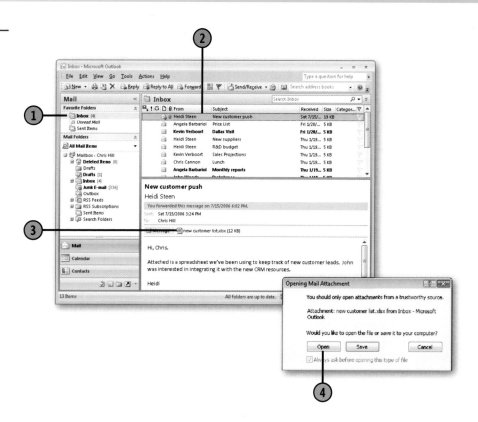

Tip

To open an attachment, you must have an application that supports the attached file. For example, if you receive a PowerPoint file (.ppt or .pptx), you must have PowerPoint, the PowerPoint Viewer, or some similar application installed on your system to view the file.

Caution

Some files that you receive from another user, such as programs, Web pages, and script files, can be infected with a computer virus. You should save all executable files to your system and run an antivirus program that checks the file for a virus before you open it. If you receive an attachment from someone you do not know (as happens a lot with junk e-mail), you should never open it. Just delete the message.

Formatting E-Mail Messages

Outlook lets you format text so that it looks more attractive to you and your recipients. For example, you can apply bold, italic, underline, colors, and other rich formatting to your mes- sages. You also can add HTML formatting to your messages, including tables, hyperlinks, heading levels, and more. Plain text messages cannot be formatted.

Use a Rich Text or HTML Message Format

1. Create a new message, and add some text.

2. Click the Options tab in the ribbon.

3. Choose HTML or Rich Text from the Format group on the Ribbon.

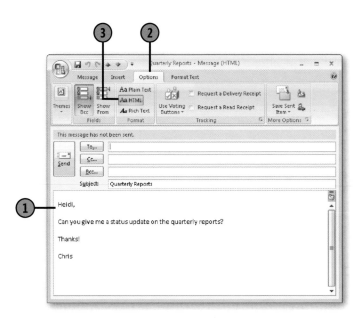

Add Formatting to a Message

1. Select the text you want to format.

2. Click the Format Text tab on the ribbon.

3. Click Bold in the Font group to bold the text.

4. Click Italic to italicize the text.

5. Click Underline to underline the text.

6. Select a font name from the Font drop-down list to change the text font.

7. Select a color from the Font Color drop-down list to change the text font color.

8. Select a value from the Font Size drop-down list to change the text font size.

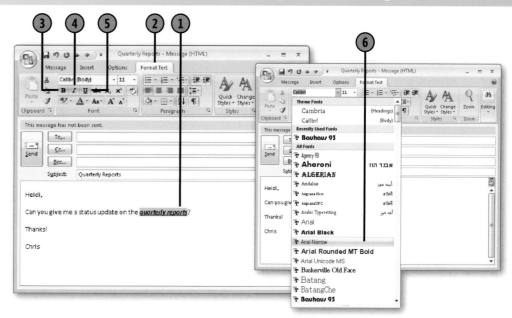

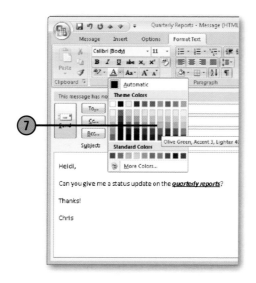

Managing Messages

You can mark messages as read or unread, delete them, and move them between folders.

Mark, Unmark, and Delete Messages

(1) Right-click a message.

(2) Choose Mark As Unread to mark the message as unread. Choose Mark As Read to mark the message as having been read.

(3) Choose Delete to move a message to the Deleted Items folder.

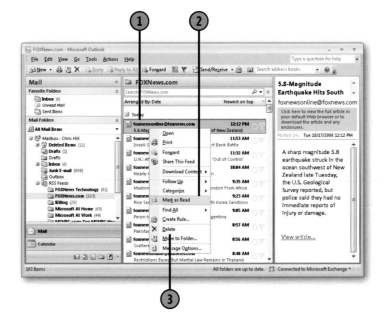

Move Messages
Between Folders

1. Click the message you want to move.

2. Drag and drop the message on the target folder, or...

3. Right-click the item and choose Move To Folder.

4. Select the target folder.

5. Click OK.

Tip

You can copy a message rather than move it, preserving the message in the original location. To copy a message, right-drag the message to the destination and choose Copy from the pop-up menu.

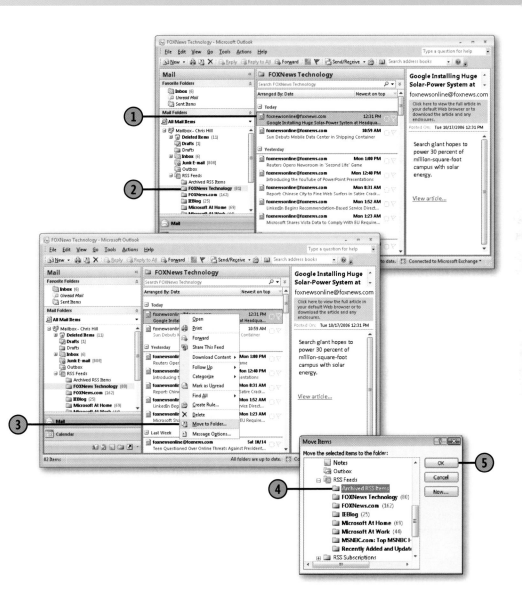

Signing Your E-Mail

A signature is boilerplate text or a file that is attached to any new messages you compose. The signature appears at the bottom of your messages, much like the signature that you would write on paper documents. Often, the signature includes your phone number and other information.

Using Your Signature

1. In Outlook, choose Options from the Tools menu.

2. Click the Mail Format tab.

3. Click Signatures to open the Signatures And Stationery dialog box.

4. From the E-Mail Account drop-down list, select the account for which you want to assign the signature.

5. Select a signature from the New Messages drop-down list.

6. Click OK twice and close the Options dialog box.

Tip
If you want your signature to appear in messages you reply to or forward, select the appropriate signature from the Replies/ Forwards drop-down list.

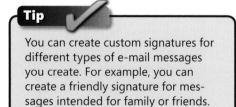
Tip
You can create custom signatures for different types of e-mail messages you create. For example, you can create a friendly signature for messages intended for family or friends.

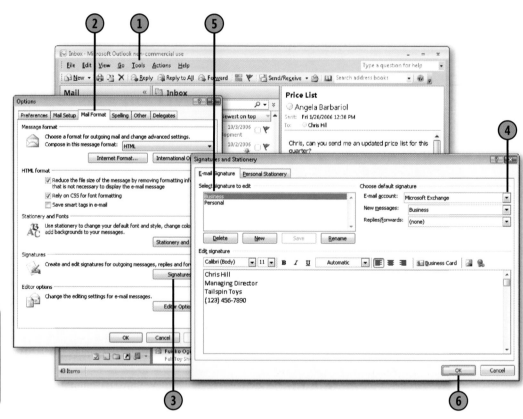

Setting Up RSS Subscriptions

Outlook makes it easy to add RSS feeds. When your computer is connected to the Internet, Outlook offers a page of quick links you can use to add a feed with a single click, or you can add feeds by typing the URL for the feed.

Add an RSS Feed from a Quick Link

1. Open Outlook, right-click on RSS Feeds in the Navigation Pane, and then select Add A New RSS Feed.

2. Type the address of the RSS Feed.

3. Click Add.

4. Click Yes.

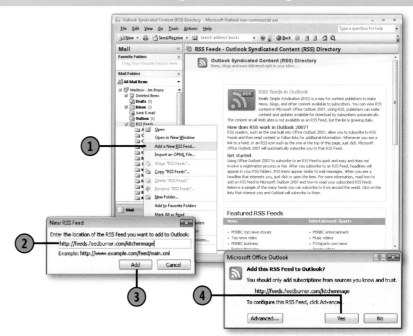

Reading RSS Items

Because Outlook separates your RSS feeds into individual folders, you can easily locate and view content from a specific feed.

Read RSS Feed

1. In the Outlook Navigation Pane, click to expand the RSS Feeds folder.

2. Click the feed you want to view.

3. Look through items to find the one you want to read and click it.

4. Preview the item in the Reading Pane.

5. Click to view the full item.

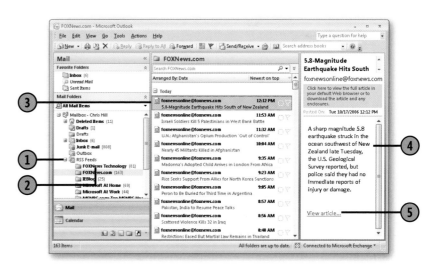

Setting Up E-Mail Accounts

You can use Outlook to send and receive messages for several different types of e-mail accounts. Outlook supports Microsoft Exchange Server, POP3 services such as a typical account from an Internet service provider (ISP), IMAP services such as CompuServe 2000, and HTTP-based e-mail services such as Hotmail. You can easily add a new account or import e-mail account settings from Microsoft Outlook Express, Windows Mail, or Eudora. (Outlook 2007 does not support import from other applications such as Thunderbird or Opera.)

Add an E-Mail Account

1. Open Outlook, and choose Account Settings from the Tools menu.

2. Click New.

3. Select Microsoft Exchange, POP3, IMAP, Or HTTP.

4. Click Next.

(continued on the next page)

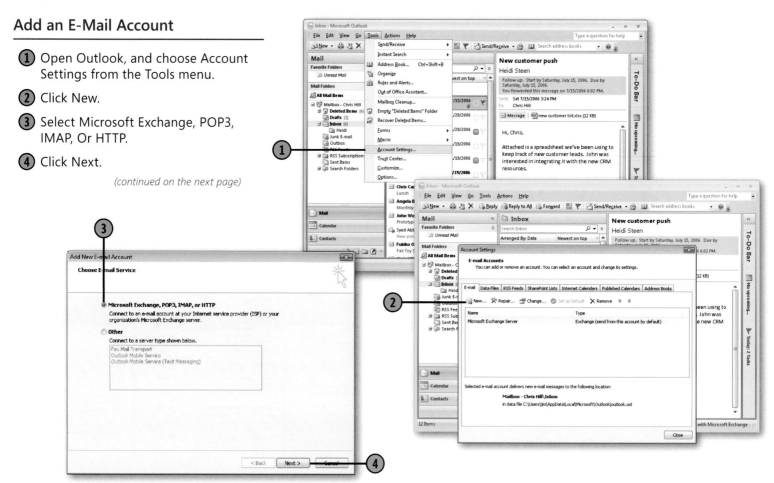

Add an E-Mail Account *(continued)*

⑤ Select Manually Configure Server Settings Or Additional Server Types, and then click Next.

⑥ Select Internet E-Mail, and click Next.

⑦ Type your name and e-mail address.

⑧ Choose the account type.

⑨ Type the incoming and outgoing mail server names.

⑩ Type your user name and pass-word for the server.

⑪ Click Test Account Settings to have Outlook test your settings, then close the test window when the test is completed success-fully. Click Next, and then Finish to return to the Account Settings window.

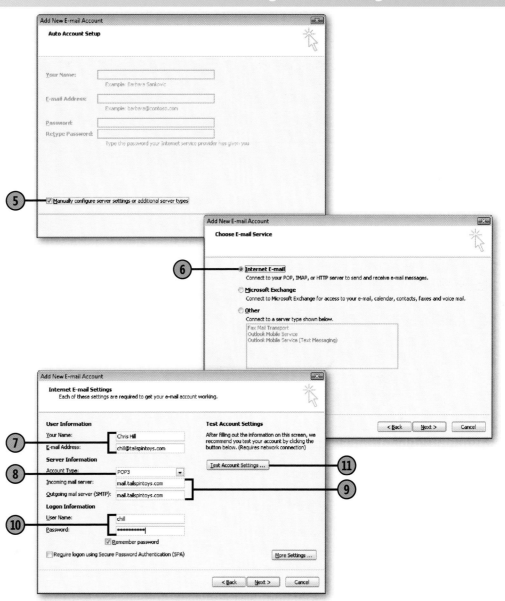

E-Mailing Your Schedule

You can send your calendar to other people via e-mail. You can choose just how much information about your schedule you want to share.

Send Your Schedule via E-Mail

① With your calendar open, click Send A Calendar Via E-mail.

② Choose the Date Range.

③ Choose the level of Detail.

④ Select the checkbox to Show Time Within My Working Hours Only if you want to limit the calendar to your usual work hours.

⑤ Click OK.

(continued on the next page)

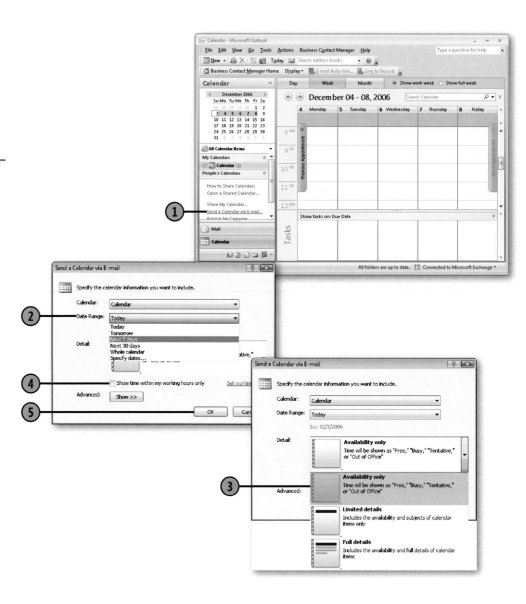

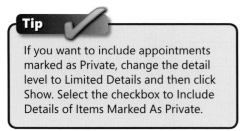

Tip

If you want to include appointments marked as Private, change the detail level to Limited Details and then click Show. Select the checkbox to Include Details of Items Marked As Private.

Send Your Schedule
via E-Mail *(continued)*

6 A message will open with your calendar in the body. Enter an e-mail address in the To field.

7 Add text to the message if you wish.

8 Click Send.

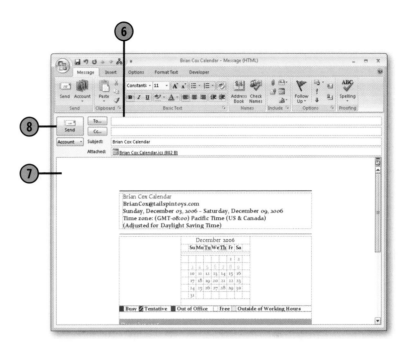

Try This!

Select a specific date range for the calendar you send. Choose Specify Dates in the Date Range drop-down list and then select the Start date and End date.

Tip

You can include files you have saved in your calendar. First, change the detail level to Full Details and then click Show. Select the checkbox to Include Attachments Within Calendar Items.

See Also

If you are using Exchange Server, read "Viewing Your Group's Schedule" on page 228 to learn how to view the calendars of people with whom you work.

Understanding E-Mail Encryption

Your e-mail may contain sensitive or confidential information that you need to protect from unauthorized disclosure by someone who manages to intercept your messages. Encrypting your e-mail ensures that only you and the intended recipients are able to read it.

E-mail encryption makes use of digital IDs, which are essentially certificates used in Public Key encryption. Public

Key encryption uses a pair of certificates—a private key certificate and a public key certificate. The private key enables you to create a public key that you can share with others so that they can read the e-mail you encrypt. Others can use your public key to encrypt e-mail to you that you can decrypt and read using your private key.

Choose the default settings for e-mail encryption and digital signatures.

Control how Outlook handles e-mail encryption in the e-mail security settings area of the Trust Center.

Manage your digital IDs and share your public key with others.

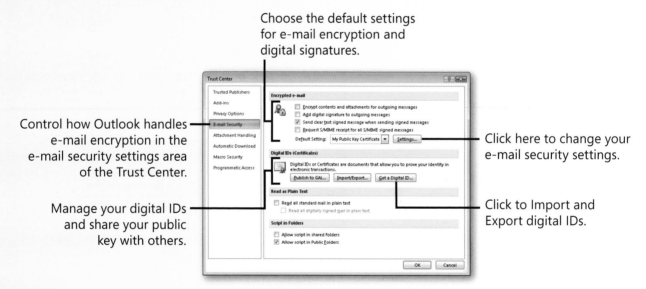

Click here to change your e-mail security settings.

Click to Import and Export digital IDs.

Tip

Encryption is a powerful tool, but with all those unfamiliar acronyms, it can also be intimidating. If you are using a digital ID, however, you will find that the default settings work just fine in almost every circumstance. This means you can simply obtain and install a certificate to start sending encrypted e-mail, without worrying about too many details.

Tip

While you can have Outlook encrypt all of your e-mail, it is more likely that you will only want to encrypt a few messages. You can encrypt a single message using commands on the Options tab of the new message form.

Organizing with Outlook

In this section:

- What's Where in Outlook?
- Keeping Track of Your Schedule
- Sharing Calendars
- Viewing Your Group's Schedule
- Scheduling a Meeting
- Managing Your Contacts
- Keeping Track of Your Tasks
- Assigning Tasks
- Tacking Up Notes
- Creating and E-Mailing Contact Business Cards
- Customizing Outlook

Beyond providing full-featured e-mail communications, Microsoft Office Outlook 2007 helps you manage the scheduling of appointments, meetings, and tasks, as well as all of the associated information. You can identify free time, schedule your appointments, and invite people to meetings, as well as quickly determine what is on your schedule for any day, week, or month.

Outlook makes it easy to document your own tasks and assign tasks to others, tracking their progress, and receiving an automatic notification when the task is complete. You can also easily share information about your contacts, by creating customized contact business cards that you can attach to your e-mail.

What's Where in Outlook?

Although Outlook is easy to use, the Outlook program window can seem overwhelming to new users because it contains so much information. Once you understand how Outlook organizes and presents that information, however, you'll have no trouble moving from folder to folder to view and manage your information. The main program window organizes all of your Outlook folders for easy access, and individual windows help you work with the different types of Outlook items.

Select commands from the Menu bar.

Preview a message without opening it.

Review your calendar, upcoming appointments, and tasks.

Perform common tasks from the toolbar.

Move between folders with the Navigation Pane.

Use other folders in Outlook.

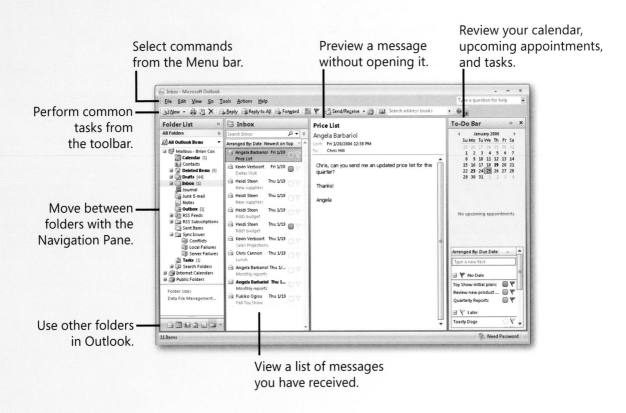

View a list of messages you have received.

Calendar

Outlook 2007 sports a new look for its Calendar folder with additional color and visual elements. The Calendar also adds a Daily Task List pane at the bottom of the window. The Daily Task List shows the tasks that are due on the current date, such as tasks with that day's due date or e-mail messages with a follow-up date of that day.

You can view your calendar and make appointments complete with reminders, so you won't forget. Upcoming events are listed in the To-Do bar in the main Outlook window, so you can check your schedule with a glance.

If you are using Outlook with Exchange Server, you can schedule meetings with other people and, if your network administrator has configured it, even reserve rooms. All without leaving Outlook!

Contacts

The Contacts folder acts as an address book but also does much more. Contacts can contain a wide range of information: personal things like birthday, names of spouse and children; work-related information such as office location, title, and manager's name; and Internet-related information such as IM identity and web page addresses.

You can also create customized business cards for your contacts, selecting the information and picture to use and then formatting it as you wish. Business cards can be shared with others, making it simple to build a network of business or personal connections.

Outlook lets you view your contacts as a series of single address cards or all at once, moving through your Contacts folder as if it were an electronic phone book or address book.

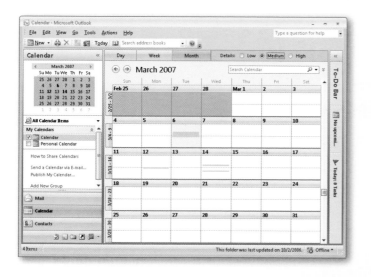

Keeping Track of Your Schedule

With Outlook's calendar you're not stuck with one view—you can view your calendar in several different formats. Day view is an hour-by-hour view of your daily schedule, while Month view shows your schedule for the entire month. The Date Navigator is a small calendar with which you can navigate quickly to a specific day, week, or month, while the To-Do Bar consolidates all of the features of task list, Date Navigator, and appointment list into one task pane.

Use the Date Navigator

1. Click the Calendar icon on the Navigation Pane.

2. Click the Day tab at the top of the calendar.

3. Click a day on the Date Navigator to display it in the Calendar view.

4. Click to the left of a week on the Date Navigator to display that week in the Calendar view.

5. Click the right arrow on the Date Navigator to move to the next month.

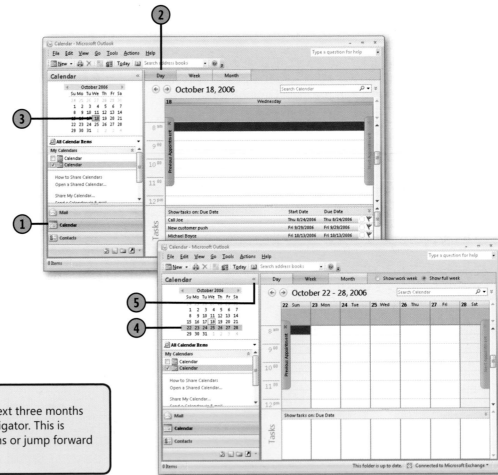

Tip ✓

You can access the current, last three, and next three months by clicking the month name in the Date Navigator. This is handy if you want to jump back a few months or jump forward a month or two.

Use the Calendar View

① Click the Calendar icon on the Navigation Pane.

② Choose a type of view from the View menu.

- Click Day to see an hourly break-down of your day.

- Click Work Week to see a work week's schedule by hour.

- Click Week to see a week's schedule.

- Click Month to see a month's schedule.

Use the To-Do Bar

① Click the Calendar icon on the Navigation Pane.

② Choose View, then choose Normal from the To-Do Bar submenu.

③ Click a date on the Date Navigator to view appointments for that date.

④ View upcoming appointments.

⑤ View current tasks.

Tip

Depending on the options you set for the To-Do Bar, portions of the Appointments or Tasks areas of the To-Do Bar might be blank.

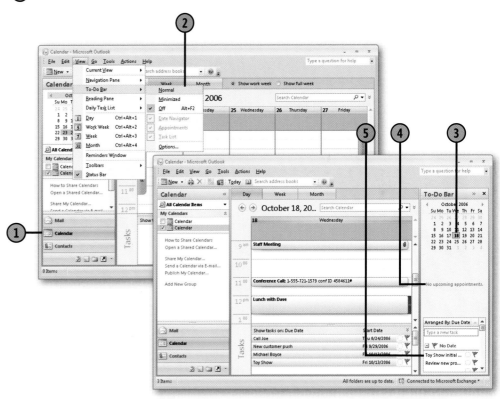

Sharing Calendars

Outlook enables you to share Calendar information with others. You can forward a Calendar item by e-mail to other Outlook users, or you can forward an iCalendar to any user over the Internet. You should use iCalendar when you schedule meetings with people who do not use Outlook.

Forward a Calendar Item

① Open an existing meeting item.

② Click the Meeting tab of the ribbon.

③ Click the Forward button.

④ Type the e-mail address of the recipient in the To box.

⑤ Click Send.

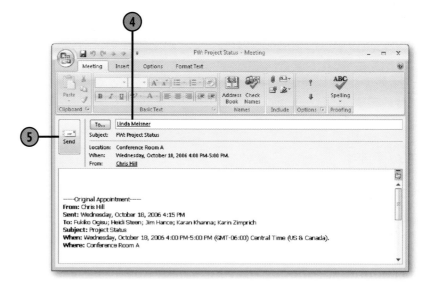

Forward an Item as an iCalendar

① Open a meeting item by double-clicking it in the Calendar.

② Click the Meeting tab on the ribbon.

③ Click the arrow beside the Forward button and choose Forward as iCalendar.

④ Type the e-mail address of the recipient in the To box.

⑤ Click Send.

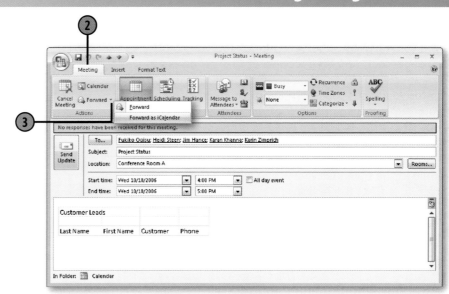

If you forward a calendar item that has an attachment, that attachment is forwarded along with the calendar item.

iCalendar is for communicating with people who do not use Outlook. If you want to forward a Calendar item to someone who uses Outlook, use the Forward command on the Actions menu or click Forward in the Actions group on the meeting form's ribbon.

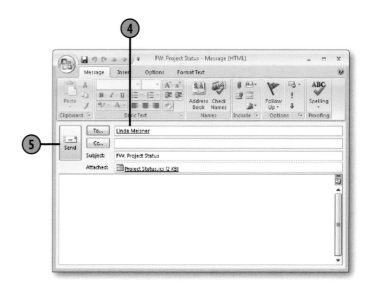

Viewing Your Group's Schedule

If you are using Exchange Server, Outlook lets you create a group of contacts and then view all of their schedules at the same time. You can create a number of groups to make it easier for you to see the information you need. After you create a group, you can quickly look at the calendars in it.

Create a New Group

(1) While in the Calendar view, choose View Group Schedules from the Actions menu.

(2) Click New.

(3) Give the group a name.

(4) Click OK.

(5) Click Add Others.

(6) Choose Add From Address Book.

(continued on the next page)

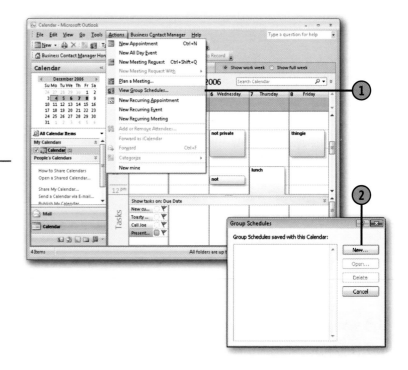

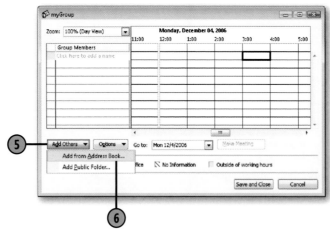

Create a New Group *(continued)*

(7) Select a contact name.

(8) Click To. Repeat for each person you want in the group.

(9) When you are finished, click OK.

(10) Click Save and Close.

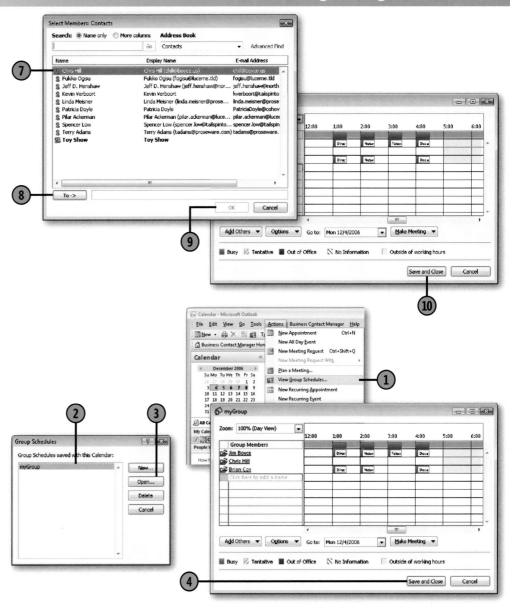

View a Group Schedule

(1) While in the Calendar view, choose View Group Schedules from the Actions menu.

(2) Select the Group Schedule.

(3) Click Open.

(4) The schedule is displayed. When you are done, click Save and Close.

See Also

If you do not use Exchange Sever, you can e-mail your schedule to people using Outlook as described in "E-Mailing Your Schedule" on page 218.

Scheduling a Meeting

A meeting is an activity that involves other people and sometimes resources. A resource can be a conference room, VCR, slide projector, conference call equipment, laptop computer, or other equipment. Usually a meeting involves you and at least two other people (but can certainly be just you and one other person). Outlook sends a meeting invitation to every person you designate, and they have the option of accepting or rejecting the request, or even proposing a new time for the meeting.

Create a Meeting in a Block of Time

① Click the Calendar icon on the Navigation Pane.

② Highlight a block of time on the meeting day for the meeting.

③ Choose New Meeting Request from the Actions menu.

④ Click To.

⑤ Select attendees and resources from the Address Book, or type addresses manually.

⑥ Click OK when you are done.

⑦ Type a description of the meeting in the Subject box.

⑧ Type the location of the meeting in the Location box.

⑨ Add notes, directions, or comments for the meeting as needed.

⑩ Click Send.

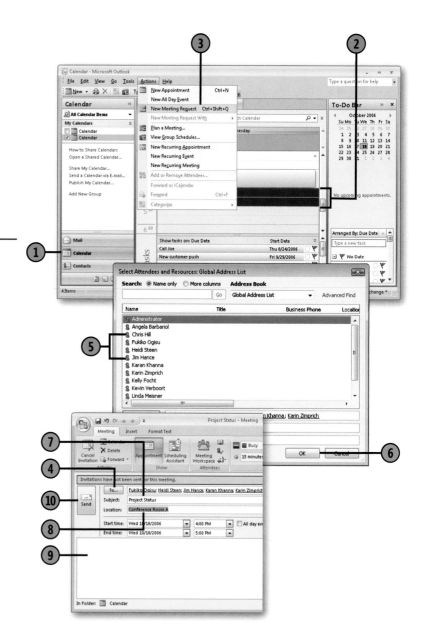

Specify a Meeting Date and Time Manually

① Create a new meeting.

② Add attendees, a subject, and a location for the meeting.

③ Click the down arrow in the Start Time date field, and select the starting date.

④ Click the down arrow in the Start Time hour field, and select the starting time of the meeting.

⑤ Click the down arrow in the End Time hour field, and select the ending time of the meeting.

⑥ Click Send.

Caution

Make sure that your attendee list has correct e-mail addresses. If you attempt to send the meeting request to someone not in one of your address books, Outlook prompts you that the person cannot be validated.

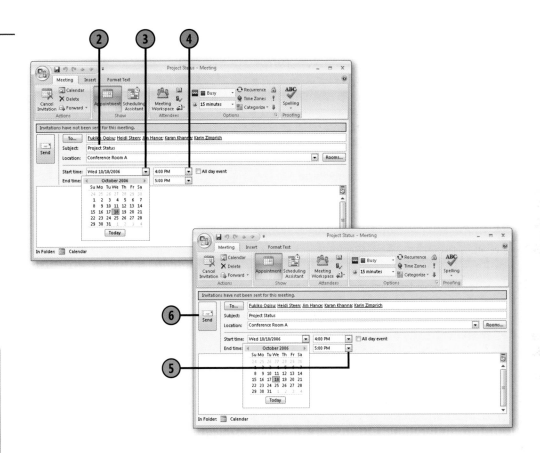

Managing Your Contacts

You can add contacts to Outlook's Contacts folder in three ways: by typing new information about someone, by using information you've entered for another contact, or by using information from an e-mail message. In the latter case, for example, you can quickly create a new contact by using the information from a message that you've received.

Use E-Mail Message Information

(1) With the Inbox showing, select the message that has the contact information you want to save. If you don't have the Reading Pane displayed, open the message to access the From field.

(2) Right-click the name or address that appears in the From field.

(3) Choose Add To Contacts from the shortcut menu that appears. A new contact card opens, with some of the new contact's information already entered.

(4) Type the pertinent information into the remaining fields.

(5) Click Save & Close to save the contact information.

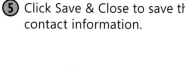

Click Full Name on the address card to open the Check Full Name dialog box. In this box, fill in the complete name and any appropriate prefix (such as "Dr.") or suffix (such as "Jr."). Click OK.

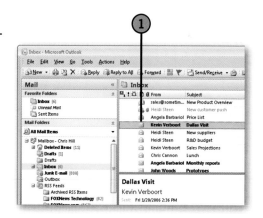

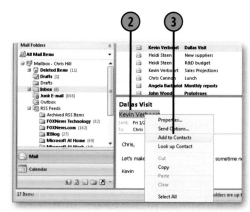

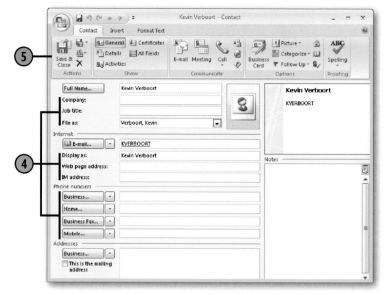

Use the Contact Window

① Click the Contacts icon on the Navigation Pane to display the Contacts folder.

② Double-click the contact you want to open.

③ Type information about your contact in the appropriate fields.

④ From the File As drop-down list, select one of the choices of how Outlook can display the contact's name, such as last name first, first name last, and so on.

⑤ Type any additional useful information in the Notes box at the bottom of the address card.

⑥ Click Save & Close to save your changes.

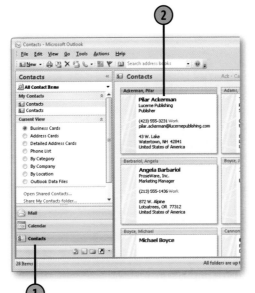

Caution

When typing a contact's e-mail address, be sure you type it correctly. An incorrect address will prevent your messages from being sent successfully. Take the time when typing a contact's e-mail address to double-check it for accuracy. You can, of course, change it later, but it's best to make sure it's correct the first time.

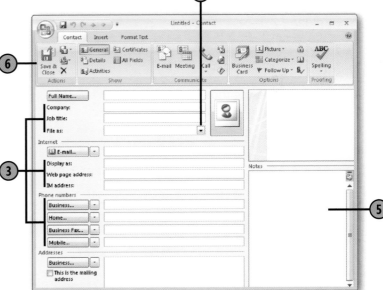

Tip

To ensure the AutoDialer feature works correctly, type phone numbers as numbers, rather than using any acronyms or letters.

Tip

If you want to keep the Inbox open and also open Contacts, right-click Contacts on the Navigation Pane and choose Open In New Window.

Keeping Track of Your Tasks

Tasks can be added to your Tasks folder in one of two ways: you can create the task yourself or accept a task that someone else assigns to you. If you create the task yourself, you can create it using the New menu, or you can create it through the Tasks folder.

Outlook includes a Tasks folder that you can use to store your tasks and tasks that you assign to others. The Tasks folder offers a handful of ways to view and work with your tasks, including the Daily Task List that appears at the bottom of the Calendar, and the Tasks List in the To-Do Bar. The default view for the Tasks folder is the Simple List view, which shows whether the task is complete, the name (subject) of the task, and the due date.

Set the Task Name and Due Date

1. Click the Tasks icon on the Navigation Pane to open the Tasks folder.

2. Click New to start a new task.

3. Type a subject for the task.

4. Click the arrow beside the Due Date field and select a date from the Date Navigator.

5. Click Save & Close.

Tip

With any folder open, you can use the New menu to open a new task form and create the task. Click the arrow beside the New button on the Standard toolbar and choose Task from the submenu to open the new task form.

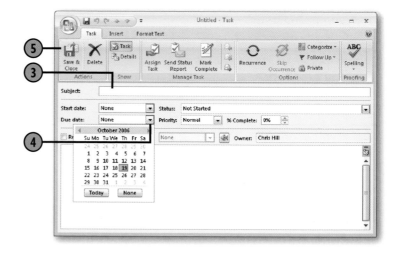

Open the Task Item Window

① Click the Tasks icon on the Navigation Pane to open the Tasks folder.

② Double-click a task to open the task's form. If you don't have a task created yet, just double-click in the Tasks folder to start a new task.

③ Click Details in the Show group of the Ribbon's Task tab to display additional task information.

④ Click Save & Close to close the form.

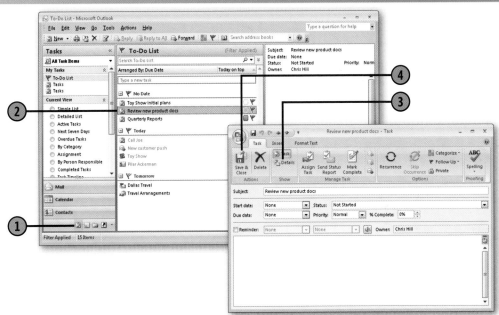

Use the Task List

① Click the Tasks icon on the Navigation Pane to open the Tasks folder.

② When the Tasks folder opens, click the Arranged By column and choose an item by which to sort the list.

③ Click Arranged By again, and click Due Date to restore the default sort method.

④ Click the flag beside the task's subject to mark the task as complete.

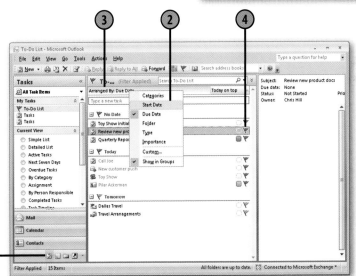

Assigning Tasks

If you manage others and use Outlook in your organization for e-mail and collaboration, you'll probably want to assign tasks to others. Outlook sends the task assignment as an e-mail message and the assignee has the option of accepting or rejecting the task. When you assign a task you define a status update distribution list. The people on that list receive status reports when the assignee makes changes to the task.

Assign a Task

① Click the arrow beside New on the Standard toolbar and choose Task Request to open a new task form that includes message address fields.

② Use the fields on the Task tab to define the task.

③ Select Keep An Updated Copy Of This Task On My Task List to have Outlook keep track of the assigned task with a copy on your own task list that updates as the assignee works on the task.

④ Select Send Me A Status Report When This Task Is Complete to have Outlook send you a status report when the assignee completes the task.

⑤ Type the assignee's name, or click To and select the person to whom you want to assign the task from your Contacts list.

⑥ Click the Details button.

⑦ Add other information for the task.

⑧ Click Task to return to the task form.

⑨ Click Send.

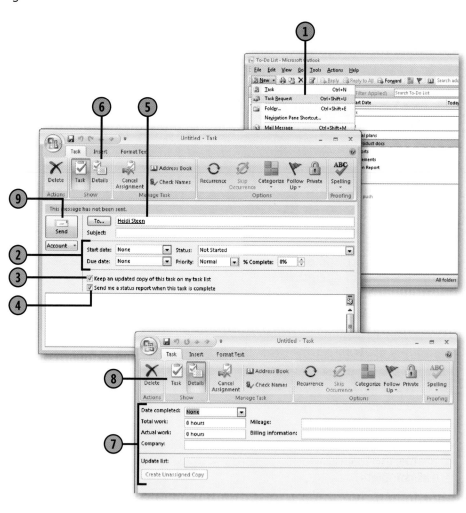

Tacking Up Notes

Working with notes is one of the easiest tasks in Outlook. Notes are little more than text files, and creating a new note is as easy as creating a file with Notepad or WordPad. Outlook opens an empty window when you start a new note, ready for your text. You can easily edit a note to change its contents or add more text. Finally, when you don't need the note anymore you can simply delete it.

Add a Note

1 Click the Notes icon on the Outlook Bar to open the Notes folder.

2 Click New on the Standard toolbar to open a new note window.

3 Start typing the note text in the note window.

4 Click the Close button to save the changes and close the note window.

5 Outlook adds an icon to the Notes window for the new note.

Tip

To place a copy of a note on the Windows desktop, just drag it from the Notes window in Outlook and drop it on the desktop.

Tip

You can insert blank lines in a note simply by pressing Enter twice.

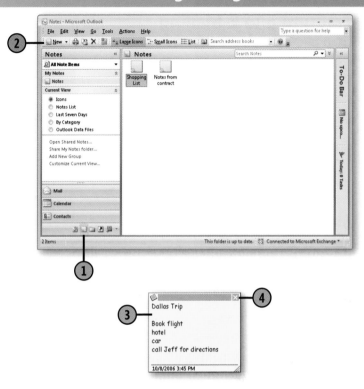

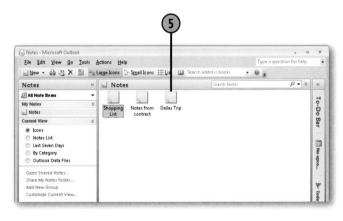

Creating and E-Mailing Contact Business Cards

You can create customized business cards for people in your Contacts folder. You can share these business cards by sending them to others via e-mail.

Create a Contact Business Card

① In the Contacts folder, double-click on a contact to open it.

② Click on Business Card.

③ View a thumbnail preview of the business card.

④ In the Card Design area, you can add a picture and control how the picture appears.

⑤ Choose the information that is displayed on the business card.

⑥ You can change the text formatting for the currently selected field.

⑦ When you are done, click OK.

Try This!

You can add fields to a business card. Many people have more than one phone number or e-mail address. To add information to a business card during editing, under Fields, click Add. Choose a category from the menu and then choose the field to add.

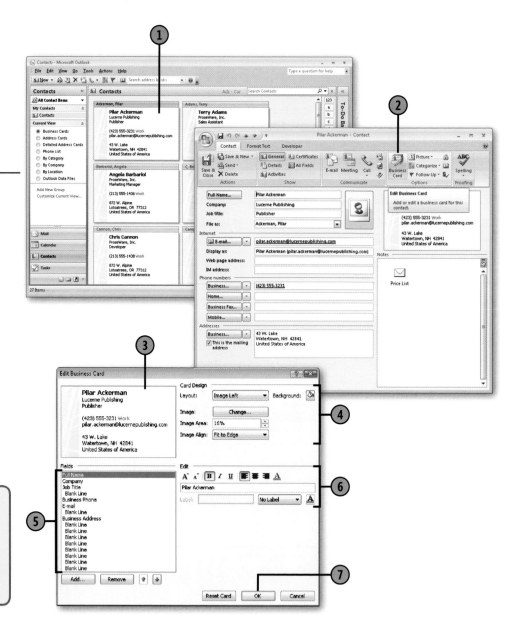

E-Mail a Contact Business Card

(1) In your Mail folder, click New.

(2) Click Insert.

(3) Click Business Card.

(4) Select a name if it is on the menu; otherwise, choose Other Business Cards.

(5) Select the contact whose business card you want to send.

(6) Click OK.

(7) Enter a recipient's e-mail address.

(8) Add a message.

(9) Click Send.

Try This!

Send a business card from the Contacts folder. Open the Contacts folder and locate the person whose business card you want to send. Right-click on the contact and choose Send As Business Card. An e-mail message will open so that you can choose a recipient and add a message. When you are finished, click Send.

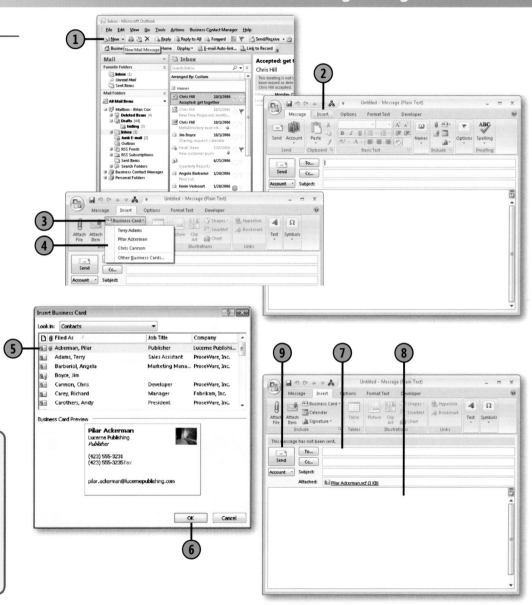

Customizing Outlook

Outlook includes several toolbars that contain dozens of toolbar buttons. Most users, however, use only a handful of toolbar buttons during any given Outlook session. Outlook enables you to add or remove toolbar buttons, and even add or remove an entire toolbar.

Add or Remove a Toolbar

1 Choose Toolbars from the View menu.

2 If a toolbar is displaying, it will have a checkmark next to it. Select the toolbar to hide it.

3 Select a nonchecked toolbar to display it.

Tip

To quickly toggle toolbars on and off, right-click the toolbar and choose the toolbar's name from the submenu.

Tip

To quickly add or remove a button from a toolbar, click the Toolbar Options arrow at the far-right end of the toolbar. Select Add Or Remove Buttons, and then select the name of the toolbar (such as Standard) you want to edit. You can then add or remove buttons from the list that appears.

Caution

Be selective when choosing the number of buttons you add to a toolbar. Unless you use a high screen resolution and have a large monitor, Outlook may not be able to display all the toolbar buttons at once.

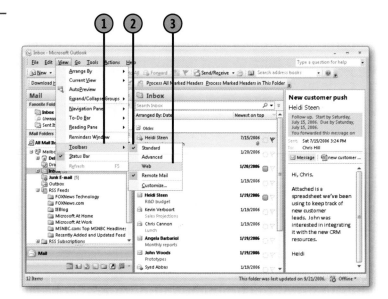

Try This!

To move a toolbar, click and hold the vertical dashed bar at its left end and drag it to a different location.

Creating a Publication in Publisher

In this section:

- What's Where in Publisher?
- Creating a Publication
- Flowing Text Among Text Boxes
- Tweaking Your Text
- Adding a Table
- Repeating Objects on Every Page
- Formatting and Arranging Objects
- Stacking and Grouping Objects
- Flowing Text Around an Object
- Inserting Your Business Information
- Creating a Web Site in Publisher
- Sending a Publication as E-Mail
- Printing Your Publication

Microsoft Office Publisher 2007 is a layout program for creating a vast assortment of publications. As you start working with it, you'll find that Publisher is a very scalable program—that is, it's quite easy to use when you're creating newsletters, greeting cards, or flyers and printing them on your printer or e-mailing them. However, because Publisher is powerful enough to include commercial-printing features such as *trapping, overprinting*, and setting *spot colors*, you'll have the opportunity to venture into the complexities of professional layout features if you really want to embark on that adventure! However, in this section of the book, we'll deal only with the basics; if you want to go further, we trust that you'll find the right sources to guide you.

Perhaps the first thing you'll notice about Publisher 2007 is that it looks different from most of the other Office programs in that it uses a menu layout and multiple toolbars instead of the Ribbon and the single Quick Access toolbar. Of course, if you've used Publisher before, you're already familiar with this interface. Otherwise, the best way to get to know Publisher is to start it up and look around. You'll see dozens of different ready-made designs, and all you have to do is choose a design and insert your own content. If you're creative and you'd prefer to design your own publications from scratch, go right ahead.

What's Where in Publisher?

When you work in Publisher, you work with *objects*. What, exactly, *is* an object? Let's say you want to insert some text. In Publisher, you'll need to create a container for it—a *text-box object*—and you'll place your text inside that object. To include a picture, you'll create a *picture-frame object*, and you'll place your picture inside that object. Some objects, however, come with their own containers: When you insert a piece of clip art or WordArt, for example, it goes onto the page as a Clip Art

or WordArt object, already nestled in its own container. On a larger scale, each page of your publication is a container for all the objects you place on it. After you've created these self-contained objects, you can move each one around and/or resize it to create your arrangement on the page. The result is a polished publication that your readers see as an integrated whole rather than a collection of separate objects.

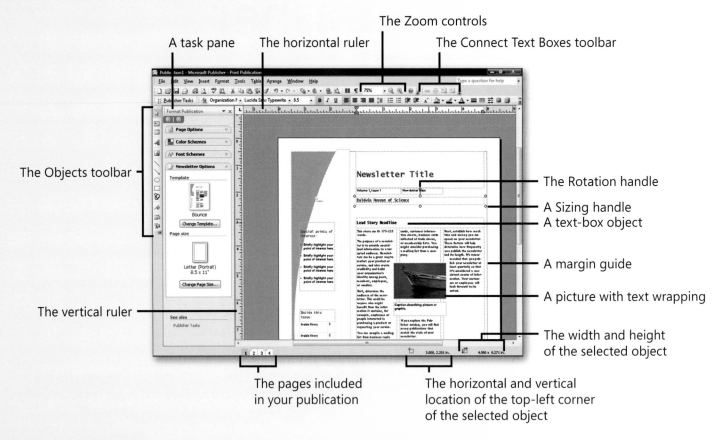

- The Zoom controls
- A task pane
- The horizontal ruler
- The Connect Text Boxes toolbar
- The Objects toolbar
- The Rotation handle
- A Sizing handle
- A text-box object
- A margin guide
- A picture with text wrapping
- The vertical ruler
- The width and height of the selected object
- The pages included in your publication
- The horizontal and vertical location of the top-left corner of the selected object

Creating a Publication from a Design

Consistency of design is critical in producing an attractive publication that will be inviting enough to command your readers' attention. No matter how compelling the content of your story, its credibility will suffer if it's poorly presented. If you need some assistance in the area of design, you can use one of Publisher's many predesigned publications, each suited to a specific purpose. To use a design, simply select it, and then replace the placeholder items with your own material.

Use a Design

(1) Start Publisher, or, if it's already running, choose New from the File menu to open the Microsoft Publisher window.

(2) Select a publication type.

(3) Click the design you want to use.

(4) Select the customizations and any other options you want.

(5) Click Create.

(6) In the publication that appears, replace the placeholder text and pictures with your own content, and then name and save the publication.

Tip

If you start creating a publication but decide you don't like the design, click the Change Template button in the Options section of the Format Publications task pane, and select a different template. If you want to change the paper size, click the Change Paper Size button and specify the page dimensions.

Search the computer and look on line for additional designs.

Click to see your saved templates.

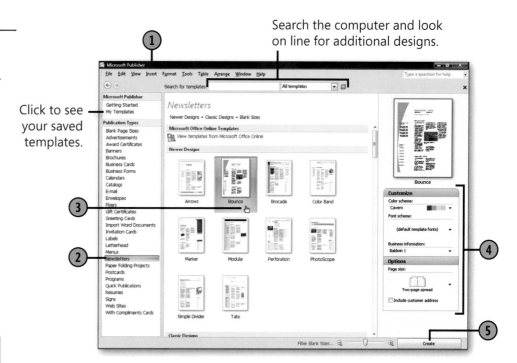

Tip

If the printer you're going to use isn't your default printer, choose Printer Setup from the File menu, and select your printer so that only the features that are supported by the printer will be available as you create your publication.

Creating a Publication from Scratch

If none of the designs Publisher provides (or any design you've saved as a template) meets your needs, you can start with a blank publication, add the elements you want, and arrange them for the best effect.

Set Up Your Publication

① Start Publisher, or, if it's already running, choose New from the File menu to open the Microsoft Publisher window, and select Blank Page Sizes in the Publication Types list. Specify your page size and orientation, select a different color scheme if you want, and click Create to start your publication.

② In the Format Publication task pane, if you want to modify the appearance of items in the publication, click to expand the Color Schemes area, and select the color scheme you want.

③ Click to expand the Font Schemes area, and select the font pair you want for the title and body text.

④ Click here if you want to apply an existing template to this page.

⑤ Click here if you want to change the dimensions of the page or the margin guides.

⑥ Add the objects, such as text boxes and pictures, to your publication.

⑦ Choose Background from the Format menu, and use the Background task pane to apply a background to the active page.

⑧ Save the publication.

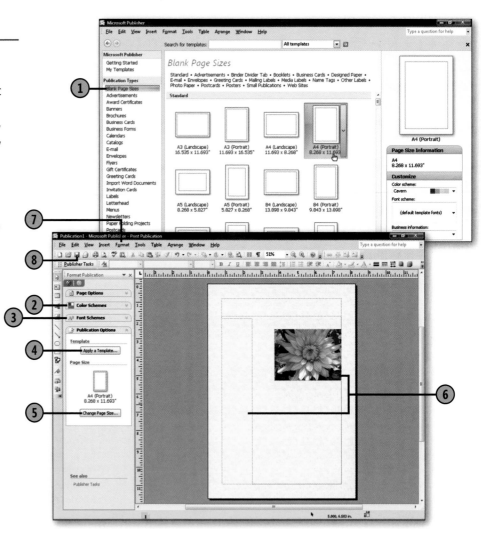

Adding Text

All the text in a Publisher publication is contained in text boxes. To add text to your publication, you first insert a text box and then put your text inside the text box. If there's too much text to fit into the text box, you can make the text box bigger, reduce the size of the text, or have the text continue in another text box—possibly on a different page if there's not enough space on the current page.

Add Text

(1) With your publication open in Publisher, click the Zoom In or the Zoom Out button so that you can see the entire area in which you're going to place the text box.

(2) Click the Text Box button on the Objects toolbar.

(3) In your publication, drag out a text box to the approximate dimensions you want.

(4) Click in the text box to activate it.

(5) Type or paste your text. Resize the text box to fit the text if necessary.

(6) Use any of the tools on the Formatting toolbar to format the text the way you want, and, once again, resize the text box if necessary.

(7) Drag a border to move the text box into the location you want.

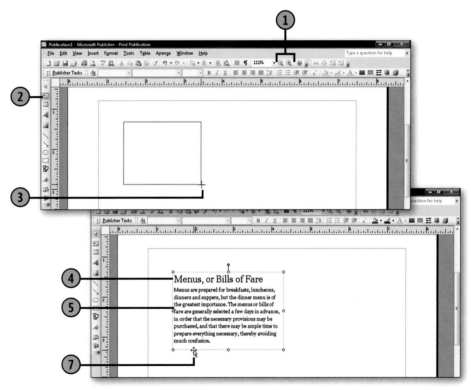

See Also

"Using Word to Prepare Publisher Text" on page 300 for information about preparing and editing your text in Word.

See Also

"Flowing Text Among Text Boxes" on pages 246–247 for information about having text continue from one text box to another if all the text doesn't fit into the first text box.

Flowing Text Among Text Boxes

You can position a long story in a publication by using two or more connected text boxes that allow the story to flow from one text box to another. In that way, you can continue a story from one side of a page to the other, from one sidebar to the next, or from one page to another. You can use the AutoFlow feature to automatically flow text that's too long for one text box into the next one, or you can flow the text manually by connecting the text boxes that will contain the rest of your story.

AutoFlow the Text

1. Copy the text of your story (press Ctrl+C) from its source—a Word document, for example.

2. With your publication open in Publisher, create the text boxes you'll need for the story.

3. Click in the first text box, and paste your text (press Ctrl+V).

4. When Publisher asks whether you want to use AutoFlow, click Yes.

5. When Publisher asks whether you want to use a specific text box, click Yes if it's the one you planned to use for the extra text, or click No if Publisher selected the wrong text box. Continue clicking Yes or No until Publisher has flowed all the text into the appropriate text boxes.

6. If you have some leftover text but no more available text boxes, click Yes when Publisher asks you whether you want it to create additional text boxes to fit the text; click No if you want to include the remaining text by manually flowing it or by resizing the existing text boxes.

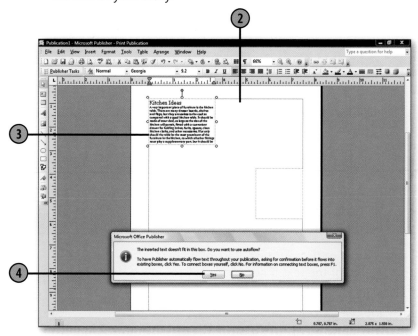

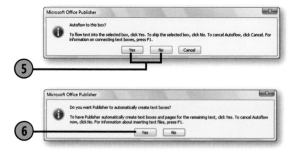

Manually Flow the Text

(1) If you selected No when prompted to have Publisher AutoFlow the text, create a second text box, if you haven't already created one.

(2) Click in the first text box (the one that contains the text that's too long).

(3) Click the Create Text Box Link button on the Connect Text Boxes toolbar.

(4) Click in the second text box to flow the text into that text box.

(5) If the text is long enough that you need another text box to contain it, create a third text box. Then click in the second text box, click the Create Text Box Link button, and click in the third text box.

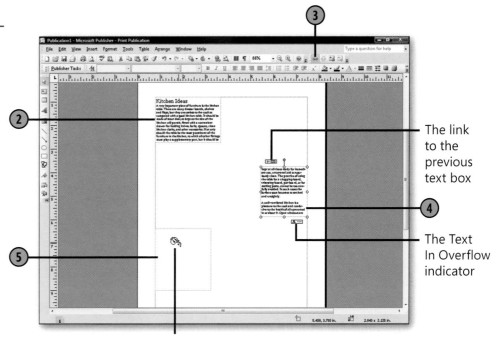

The link to the previous text box

The Text In Overflow indicator

The Text Flow pointer

Tweaking Your Text

The text is usually the largest part of most publications, and if the text doesn't look good, the publication doesn't look good. Of course, you need to start by choosing a clear, easy-to-read font for your story—for example, you wouldn't use a script font or any other fancy font because large blocks of such fonts are difficult to read. Then you can improve the overall look of your text by tweaking some subtle but important details: namely, the *scaling*, *tracking*, and *kerning* of the characters. Sometimes it's the small details that make a big difference.

Improve the Look of the Text

(1) Select the text whose appearance you want to improve.

(2) Choose Character Spacing from the Format menu to display the Character Spacing dialog box.

(3) Adjust the percentage if you want to scale—that is, shrink (condense) or stretch (expand)—the width of the selected characters and their spacing without changing the height of the characters.

(4) Select a type of tracking, or enter a percentage, to adjust the distance between all the characters of the selected text.

(5) Select a type of kerning, and the amount of kerning, to fine-tune the space between two selected characters without changing the dimensions of the characters themselves.

(6) Select the Kern Text At check box, and set the minimum point size for character pairs that tend to look "gappy" because of their shapes (for example, VA, WA, To, Te) so that they'll always be automatically kerned.

(7) Click OK.

Adding a Table

Using a table is often the best way to organize and present certain types of information with the greatest possible clarity in a publication. Publisher comes with a series of design formats that help you create exactly the type of table you need for your specific purpose.

Insert the Table

1 With your publication open in Publisher, click the Insert Table button on the Objects toolbar, and drag out a table with the approximate dimensions you need.

2 In the Create Table dialog box that appears, select the number of rows and columns you want for the table.

3 Select a table format.

4 Click OK.

5 Add your content to the table.

6 Select the content, and use the tools on the Formatting toolbar to modify the formatting of the table.

7 Select rows or columns, and use the commands on the Table menu to add or delete any rows or columns.

8 Use the Sizing handles to change the size of the table, or use the Rotation handle to change the orientation of the table.

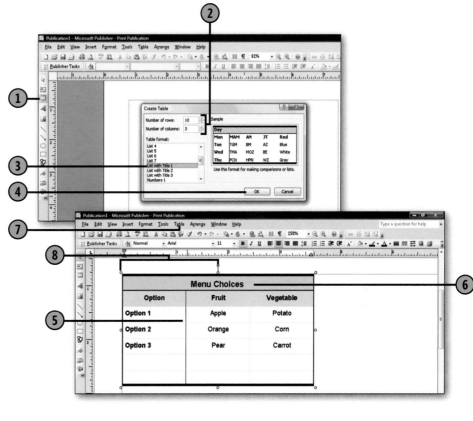

Tip

To change the format of the table, choose Table AutoFormat from the Table menu.

Repeating Objects on Every Page

If you want certain design objects to repeat on every page of your publication—for example, a picture, a logo, a background pattern, and so on—you can place the object on a *master* *page*. Then, whenever you create a new page, the material on the master page will be included on the new page.

Add the Repeating Objects

① With your publication open in Publisher, choose Master Page from the View menu.

② Click here if you want to create a two-page-spread master page instead of a single-page master page.

③ Add the object or objects that you want to be repeated on every page.

④ Click the New Master Page button if you want an additional master page so that you can create a different layout in part of the publication, and place on that second master page the objects you want to be repeated.

⑤ Click the Close Master View button to return to your publication's Normal view.

⑥ With a page of your publication selected, specify which master page you want to be applied to that page or whether you want the master page to be ignored in this instance. If the Apply Master Page task pane isn't displayed, choose Apply Master Page from the Format menu. Continue selecting pages and applying the master page you want to use.

> **Tip** ✓
>
> A master page contains more than repeating objects; it controls the margins, the layout grid, the background color, and any headers and footers that you're using.

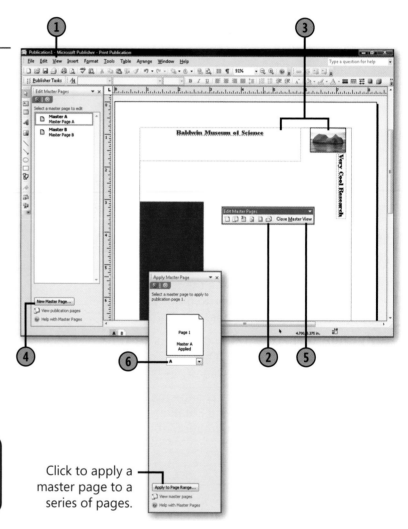

Click to apply a master page to a series of pages.

Modifying a Picture

After you've placed a picture in your Publisher publication, you can make substantial modifications to the picture (but not to the picture file itself) to make the picture look exactly the way you want.

Modify the Picture

① With the picture selected in your publication, click the Color button, and choose one of the following to specify how you want the image to appear:

- Automatic to use the original color
- Grayscale to use shades of gray instead of color
- Black & White to use only those two colors
- Washout to create a faint image

② Click to use these tools to adjust the contrast and the brightness in the picture.

③ Drag a Sizing handle at one of the corners or sides of the picture. Use a corner handle to resize the picture proportionally, or use a side handle to distort the image.

④ Drag the Rotation handle to rotate the picture.

⑤ Click the Crop button to use the Cropping tool.

⑥ Place the Cropping pointer over a Sizing handle at one of the corners or sides of the picture, and drag the pointer inward to crop the picture. Click outside the picture to turn off the cropping tool.

See Also

"Inserting Pictures" on page 24 for information about inserting pictures, and "Managing and Editing Your Pictures" on page 312 for information about editing the picture files.

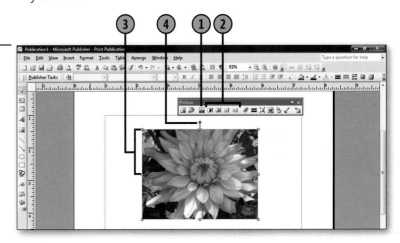

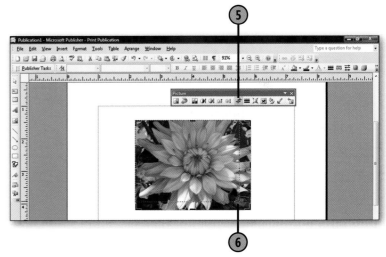

Formatting an Object

When you insert any item into your publication, that item is inserted as an object, whether it's a picture, a piece of clip art, an AutoShape, or a text box. Although you can format all these items, the type of formatting you use varies by the type of object, so you'll need to play around with each type to see all the options.

Format the Object

① Click the object to select it.

② Use the tools on the Formatting toolbar to adjust the fill color, the line color and style, the arrow style (if appropriate), the shadow style, and/ or the 3-D style. Some options aren't available for every type of object.

③ To adjust the settings, choose the object that appears at the bottom of the Format menu (Format Text Box, Format Picture, or AutoShape, for example) to display the Format dialog box. (The name of the dialog box changes depending on the type of object chosen.)

④ On the various tabs, adjust the items you want. Some tabs aren't available for every object.

⑤ Click OK.

⑥ Use the Sizing handles to adjust the size and shape of the item, use the Rotation handle to change the orientation, and then drag the item to the location you want.

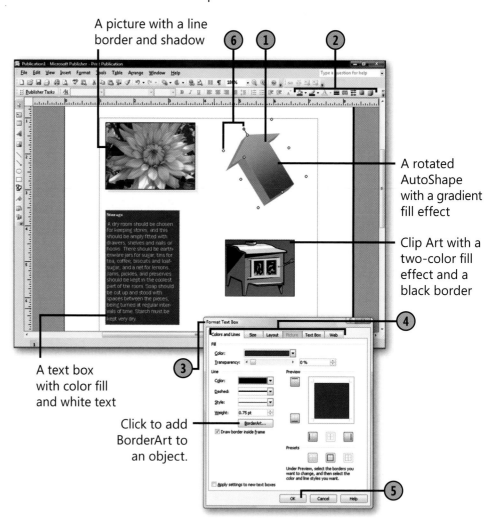

A picture with a line border and shadow

A rotated AutoShape with a gradient fill effect

Clip Art with a two-color fill effect and a black border

A text box with color fill and white text

Click to add BorderArt to an object.

Adding a Design Object

If you need some fresh ideas, take a look at Publisher's Design Gallery! It provides a huge variety of design objects that were created to complement Publisher's design themes. You'll find that some of these objects are inserted automatically when you apply a design theme to a publication, but you can add any of the objects yourself, even if you're not using the design for which that particular object was intended.

Insert the Design Object

1. With your publication open in Publisher, click the Design Gallery Object button on the Objects toolbar to display the Design Gallery dialog box.

2. Select the type of object you want to insert.

3. Use the Zoom Controls to preview the objects if necessary.

4. Click the object whose appearance will fit with your publication's design.

5. Click the Insert Object button.

6. Move and size the object to fit into your publication.

7. If necessary, ungroup the object, edit any text, modify or replace any clip art, and format any other objects to fit the design of your publication.

See Also

"Formatting an Object" on the facing page for information about formatting objects.

"Stacking and Grouping Objects" on page 256 for information about grouping and ungrouping objects.

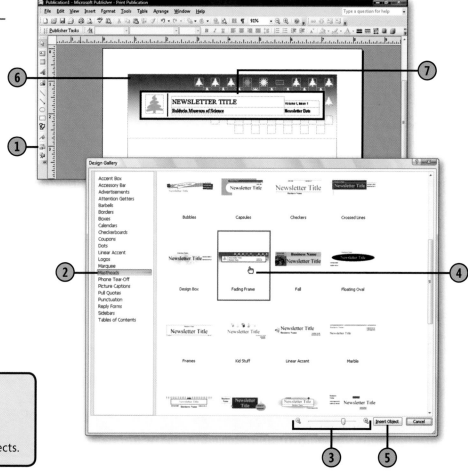

Arranging Objects on the Page

Misalignment of the items on a page can make your publication look sloppy and amateurish. By using Publisher's arranging tools, you can produce a professional-looking publication whose objects are precisely placed for maximum design impact. Use the margin guides to specify the amount of space between your content and the edge of the page; use the grid guides to line up objects either horizontally or vertically; use the baseline guides so that the lines of text align horizontally across the page even if they're in different text boxes; and use the ruler guides to align each object to a specific measurement.

Set Up Your Grid

1. With your publication open in Publisher, choose Layout Guides from the Arrange menu to display the Layout Guides dialog box.

2. On the Margin Guides tab, set the margins you want for the page.

3. On the Grid Guides tab, select the number of column guides and row guides you want, and set the spacing (the distance from the guide with which an object will align) for both column guides and row guides.

4. On the Baseline Guides tab, specify the spacing for the baseline of your text—that is, the imaginary nonprinting line the text sits on—and set the offset distance that you want between the first baseline and the top margin guide.

5. Click OK.

6. Point to Snap on the Arrange menu, and choose To Guides from the submenu.

7. On the View menu, make sure that the Boundaries And Guides item is selected, and, if you want the baseline guides to be displayed, make sure the Baseline Guides item is selected.

8. Drag or resize an object in your document, and note the way it aligns with the grid guidelines.

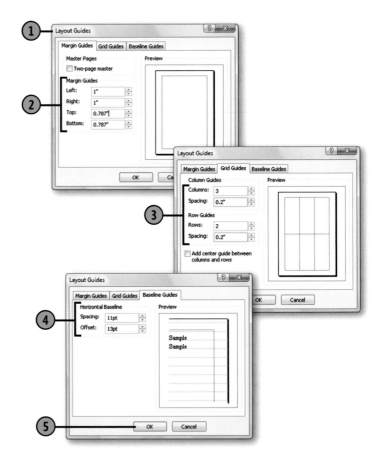

Position an Object at an Exact Location

(1) Point to the horizontal ruler, and drag out a horizontal ruler guide to the location you want, as shown on the vertical ruler. Drag out and position as many horizontal ruler guides as you want.

(2) Point to the vertical ruler, and drag out a vertical ruler guide to the location you want, as shown on the horizontal ruler. Drag out and position as many vertical ruler guides as you want.

(3) Point to Snap on the Arrange menu, and choose To Ruler Marks from the submenu.

(4) Move or resize an object so that its boundaries snap to a horizontal or a vertical ruler guide, or to the intersection of a horizontal and a vertical guide.

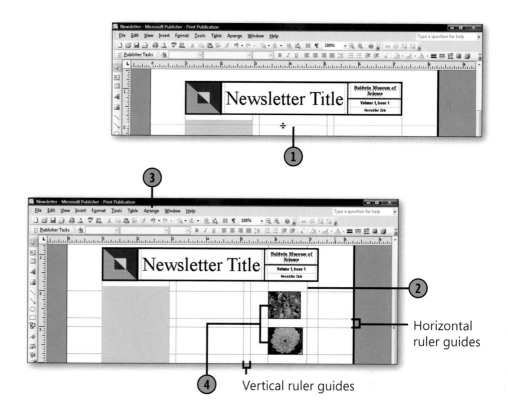

Horizontal ruler guides

Vertical ruler guides

Tip

To be able to align text to the baseline guide, you must set the paragraph formatting to use the baseline guides. The easiest way to do this is to create a style that includes alignment to the baseline guides. Click the Styles button on the Formatting toolbar, and, in the Styles task pane that appears, choose New Style to create the new style.

Try This!

Point to Toolbars on the View menu, and choose Measurement from the submenu. Click to select an object, and note the information about its position, dimensions, and font characteristics. Point to Nudge on the Arrange menu, and drag the top of the submenu so that it becomes a floating toolbar. Move the selected object by clicking the Nudge buttons.

Stacking and Grouping Objects

One of Publisher's most powerful features is the ability it gives you to *stack*, or *layer*, several different objects, and to adjust the order in which they're stacked. After you've assembled the objects you've chosen into the arrangement you like, you can group them so that they function as a single unit that you can then easily move around or resize.

Arrange the Objects

① In a publication that contains all the objects you want to stack and arrange, point to Order on the Arrange menu, and drag the submenu away from the menu to create the Order toolbar.

② Drag one object on top of another object.

③ With the first object still selected, click an Order button to set the relative stacking order of the two objects.

④ Repeat steps 2 and 3 until all the objects are placed in the positions you want and are in the desired stacking order.

⑤ Hold down the Ctrl key, and click each object that you want to be grouped into a single unit with the other objects.

⑥ Click the Group Objects button. To change the arrangement of objects you've grouped, select the group, and choose Ungroup from the Arrange menu.

> **Tip** ✓
>
> When you're working with several stacked objects that you want to group, it can be difficult to select an object that's stacked underneath other objects by clicking it. To select all the objects, use the mouse to drag a selection rectangle around all the objects, and then group them.

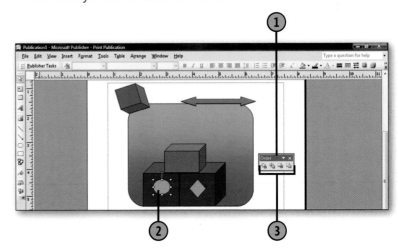

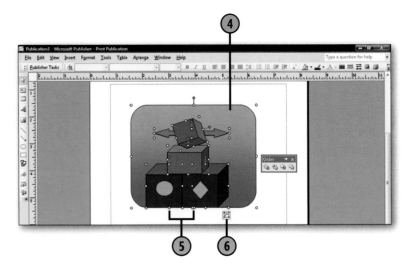

Flowing Text Around an Object

You can add style and sophistication to your publication by flowing the text of your story around an object—a picture or an AutoShape, for example. You do this by setting the text wrapping for the object that the text wraps around.

Set the Text Wrapping

(1) In a publication that contains a text box and the object you want the text to wrap around, right-click the object, and choose Format from the shortcut menu to display the Format dialog box. (The name of the dialog box changes depending on the type of object selected.)

(2) On the Layout tab, select the text-wrapping style you want.

(3) Specify how you want the text to wrap around the object.

(4) If you selected the Square wrapping style and would rather not use the automatic setting, clear the Automatic check box, and set the values for how closely the text will wrap around the object.

(5) Click OK.

(6) Drag the object into a text box that contains text, and adjust the position of the object so that the text wraps around the object in exactly the way you want.

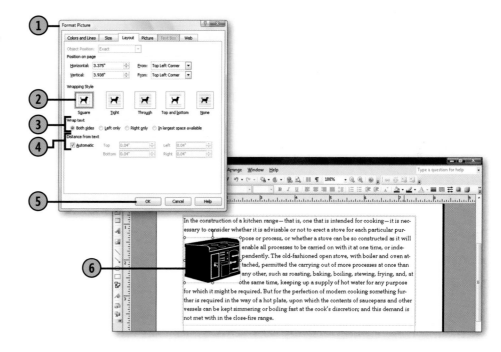

Try This!

Set the text wrapping to Tight for an object, and drag the object into a text box that contains text. Point to Text Wrapping on the Arrange menu, and choose Edit Wrap Points from the submenu. Drag a square black wrapping point into a new location to change the way the text wraps around the object. Continue moving wrapping points until you get the wrapping effect you want. Click outside the object when you've finished.

Reusing Content

When you're creating a long publication or several related publications, you might want to duplicate certain items—a picture, a design, a logo, or a slogan, for example—and place them in several different locations. Instead of returning to the first use of the item and copying and pasting it where you need it, you can place it in the Content Library and then insert it wherever you want it with just a couple of mouse-clicks.

Use the Content Library

① In your publication, select the item you want to add to the Content Library.

② Click the Item From Content Library button to display the Content Library task pane.

③ Click Add Selected Items To Content Library.

④ In the Add Item To Content Library dialog box that appears, type a descriptive name for the item, select the check box for each category you want it classified as, and click OK.

⑤ To find an item in the Content Library, select the category and/or the type of item you want.

⑥ Point to the item in the library, click the down arrow, and, from the drop-down menu that appears, choose Insert to insert the item onto the current page, or choose Copy to copy the item to the Clipboard so that you can paste it into the location you want when you're ready to do so.

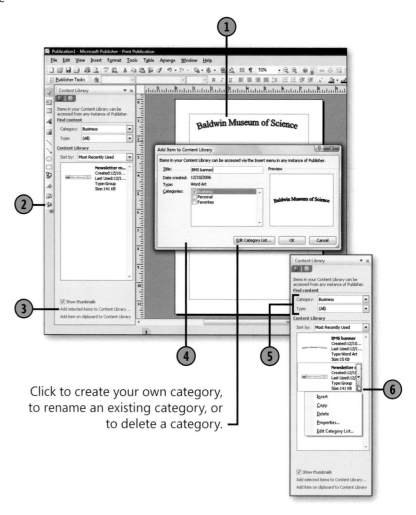

Click to create your own category, to rename an existing category, or to delete a category.

Inserting Your Business Information

Publisher's Business Information feature lets you store your business contact information, which you can then automatically insert into a publication using the appropriate *fields*. Fields are special tools that place data from an information source into a publication so that you don't need to type the material each time. Additionally, once the fields are placed in the publication, other people can use the publication, and their business information will be inserted automatically.

Use Business Information

1. If you haven't yet created a Business Information Set, choose Business Information from the Edit menu to display the Create New Business Information Set dialog box.

2. Enter the information, including a picture of your logo if you want. Type a descriptive name for this profile, and click Save. In the Business Information dialog box that appears, confirm that the information is correct, and click the Update Publication button.

3. Choose Business Information from the Insert menu to display the Business Information task pane.

4. Select an item, and drag it into the location in your publication where you want it. Continue adding any further information you want.

5. If you want to use a different Business Information Set, click Change Business Information in the Insert Business Information task pane, and, in the Business Information dialog box that appears, select a different set.

6. If you need to create a new Business Information Set, click New, complete the information in the Create New Business Information Set dialog box, and click Save.

7. With the correct Business Information Set selected, click Update Publication.

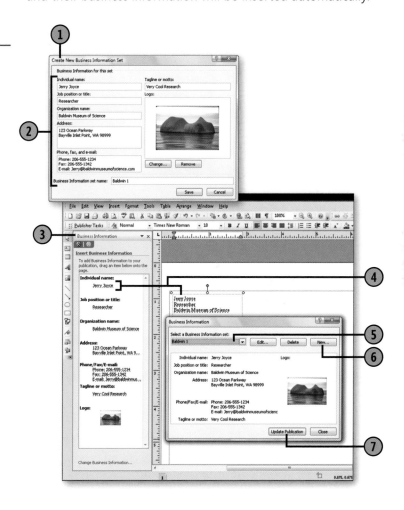

Creating a Web Site in Publisher

Publisher provides some excellent tools for creating your own Web site, even if the site has only one page. You create the Web site as a Publisher publication, but you publish it to the Web as HTML and supporting files. Although you won't be able to edit the Web site in Publisher once you've published it to the Web, you can edit the Publisher publication, make changes to the pages, and then publish the edited files to the Web again.

Create the Web Site

1. Start Publisher, or, if it's already running, choose New from the File menu to open the Microsoft Publisher window, and select Web Sites as the publication type. Select a Web-site design and any other options you want. Click Create.

2. In the Easy Web Site Builder dialog box that appears, select the check boxes for the items you want to add to the Web site, and click OK.

3. Click Page Options if you want to change the page layout, the name of the page, the background, or the background sound.

4. Use the tools on the Web Tools toolbar to customize your Web page. If your site has more than one page, switch to the other pages and customize them.

5. Replace the placeholder text and graphics on each page with your own content.

6. Click the Save button on the Standard toolbar to save the publication as a Publisher file so that it will be available for any later modifications.

7. Click the Web Page Preview button on the Web Tools toolbar to preview the site in your Web browser.

8. Return to your publication, make any changes you want, and save the publication again.

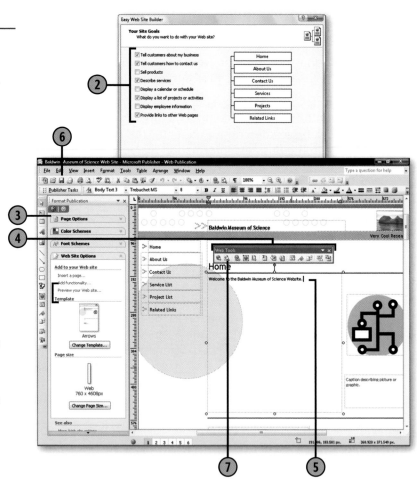

Publish It!

① Choose Publish To The Web from the File menu. If a dialog box appears and tells you that you need a Web-hosting service, click OK to continue if you already have a Web service. Otherwise, click the link to find a host on line, or press the Esc key to cancel the publishing until you've signed up for a Web-hosting service.

② In the Publish To The Web dialog box, do either of the following:

- If your Web host supports FTP publishing directly from Publisher, type the location of the site in the form **ftp:\\websitename.com** (where *websitename.com* is the address of your Web site), and click Save. Log on to your site when requested, and then, if the Publish To The Web dialog box appears again with a proposed file name, click Save without changing any settings.

  - If your Web host doesn't support direct publishing, if you can't connect to the host, or if you want to publish to a different location, locate the folder for the files, and click Save.

③ If the Microsoft Office Publisher dialog box appears telling you that a filtered HTML version has been created, read the notice, and click OK.

④ Wait for the files to be uploaded.

⑤ If your Web host doesn't support publishing directly to the Web, transfer the files from the folder in which you saved them to your Web site, using the directions your Web host has provided.

⑥ Go to your Web site, and make sure that everything is working properly.

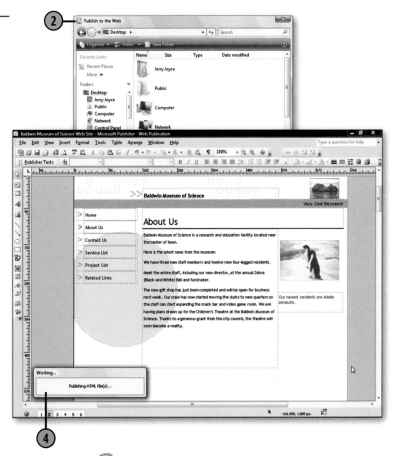

Tip
You can publish your Web site to a folder on your computer, to a network location or an intranet, or to an Internet Web-hosting site. Provided the location has the Windows IIS component installed, you'll see the full functioning of your Web site and can test and evaluate it.

Double-Checking Your Publication

You worked long hours on a publication that you thought would be a joy to behold, but what you got when you printed it was a woefully misaligned mess. Your eyes fill with tears of anger and despair as you wail, "What happened?" Don't give up! At this point, you could scroll through your publication to try to detect the problems, but there's a lesson to be learned here: *Before you print,* let Publisher do a comprehensive check through your publication to identify any problems.

Check the Design

① In your completed and saved publication, choose Design Checker from the Tools menu to display the Design Checker task pane.

② Point to a problem that Design Checker has identified, click the down arrow button, and choose

- Go To This Item to jump to the problem item and adjust the problem manually.

- Fix... to automatically fix the problem, bearing in mind that not every problem can be fixed automatically.

- Never Run This Check Again to discontinue using the specific check that reported the problem.

- Explain... to display Publisher Help, read why this is a problem, and learn about any automatic or manual fixes.

③ Repeat step 2 for any other identified problems.

④ Click Close Design Checker when you've finished.

Select or clear check boxes to change which items are checked.

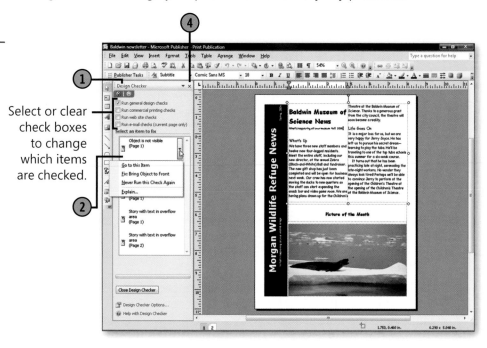

Sending a Publication as E-Mail

If you want to send an unusually elaborate e-mail message, a newsletter, or an announcement, consider creating it in and sending it from Publisher. You have two choices: You can send the publication itself as the message, or you can enclose the publication file as an attachment to an e-mail message. If you send the publication itself as the message, it will be sent in the HTML format. If you send the publication as an attachment, the recipient must have Publisher on his or her computer to be able to view the file.

E-Mail Your Publication

① Create and save your publication. Point to Send E-Mail on the File menu, and choose E-Mail Preview from the submenu.

② In the Web-page preview that appears, verify that the publication contains the information you want, and then close the preview window.

③ Point to Send E-Mail on the File menu again, and, from the submenu, choose the way you want to send the e-mail:

- Send As Message to send the publication itself as an e-mail message

- Send Publication As Attachment to send the Publisher file as an attachment

④ Address the message, and add a subject.

⑤ If Publisher detected any errors, click the Design Checker button, and fix the error or errors using the Design Checker task pane.

⑥ Click Send.

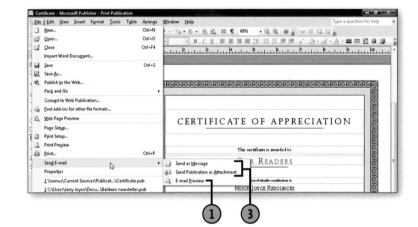

Printing Your Publication

Although you can use Publisher to produce Web pages and e-mail messages, chances are that you're going to print most, if not all, of your publications on paper. You'll find that Publisher gives you exceptionally fine control of the printing process so that you can designate exactly what's printed and how it's printed.

The Final Step: Print It!

(1) With your publication proofread, checked by Design Checker, and saved, choose Print from the File menu to display the Print dialog box.

(2) Select the printer you're going to use if it isn't already selected. Specify the pages to be printed, the number of copies, and whether the copies are to be collated.

(3) On the Printer Details tab, click the Advanced Print Settings button to display the Advanced Printer Setup dialog box.

(4) On the Separations tab, specify whether you want to print a *composite copy* of the publication (a final copy showing all the colors together on each page), or the *separations* (a separate page for each color to check that the color has been applied correctly to every element). Complete the other printing specifications.

(5) On the Page Settings tab, specify how you want the pages to be printed, which printer's marks you want, and whether there are any bleeds (color that extends beyond the edge of the page).

(6) On the Graphics And Fonts tab, specify how the graphics are to be printed and whether you'll allow the printer to substitute its fonts for the fonts in your publication.

(7) On the Printer Setup Wizard tab, use the tools to set up two-sided printing or envelope printing. Click OK, and click Print to print your publication.

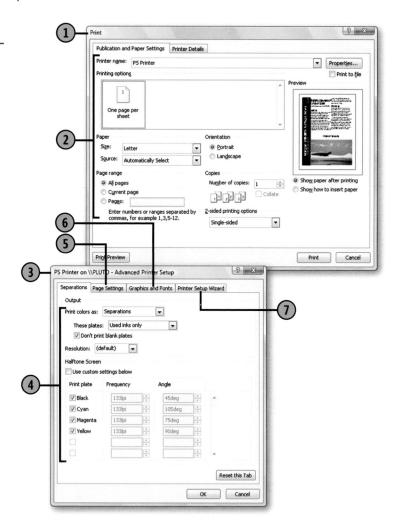

14

Working in Access

In this section:

- **What's Where in Access?**
- **Using an Existing Database**
- **Creating a Database from a Template**
- **Creating and Modifying Tables**
- **Adding Data to a Table**
- **Access File Formats**
- **Importing and Exporting Data**
- **Defining Relationships Among Tables**
- **Creating Forms, Reports, and Queries**
- **Analyzing Data with a PivotChart**
- **Collecting Data Using E-Mail**
- **Customizing Access**

Microsoft Office Access 2007 is designed to help you store, combine, and ask questions of large collections of data relevant to your business or your home life. You can create databases to track products and sales for a garden supply company, or, just as easily, build databases to keep track of your books and holiday card lists. Regardless of the specific use you have in mind, Access is a versatile program you can use to store and retrieve data quickly.

Working with Access is pretty straightforward. The program has a number of templates you can use to create entire databases or just parts of them. You also have the freedom to create databases and their components from scratch, giving you the flexibility you need to build any database.

What's Where in Access?

Surveying the Access Window

- The title bar displays the name of the database and the window control buttons.

- The tabs on the Ribbon enable you to display different types of commands based on the category you select.

- The ribbon contains comands that reflect the active contextual tab, your position in the database, and the selected objects.

- The Navigation pane displays database objects of the type you select.

- The object window displays any open database objects.

- The status bar indicates the progress of any ongoing processes.

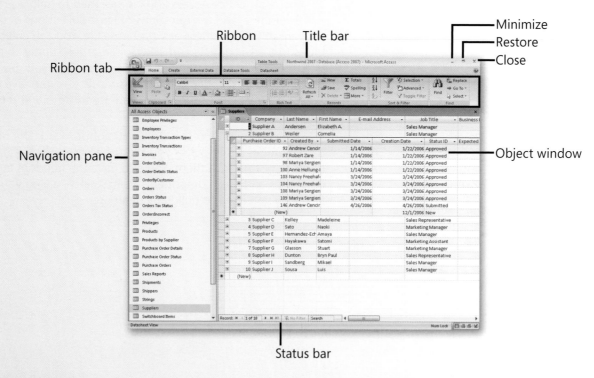

Surveying the Object Window

- The object tabs display the names of all open database objects.

- The Close button enables you to close the active database object with a single mouse click.

- Opening a database object in Design view displays contextual tabs that contain design and formatting tools.

- The horizontal scroll bar enables you to move side to side within your object.

- The vertical scroll bar enables you to move up and down within your object.

- Right-clicking a control on the body of a database object while you display the object in Design view displays a contextual menu that enables you to edit the selected control.

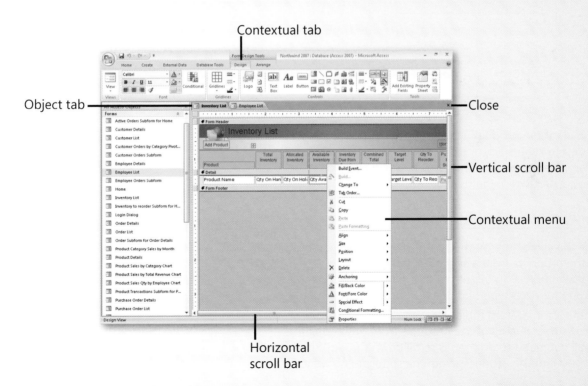

Contextual tab

Object tab

Close

Vertical scroll bar

Contextual menu

Horizontal scroll bar

What is a Relational Database?

Storing Data on Index Cards

Before computers, a popular way to store data was on index cards. If you ran a gardening supply store, you could keep track of your products by creating a card for each product, dividing the cards into product categories, and then alphabetizing the cards in each section by product name. Each card would contain relevant data such as the product's name, unique identifier, category, price, description, and the supplier's name and phone number.

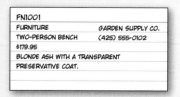

To find all of the products from a specific supplier, you either needed to keep track of the products on a separate sheet of paper or go through the cards and pull every one representing a product made by that supplier.

Storing Data on the Computer

If you store the same data on the computer, however, you can find all of the products from a specific supplier much more easily. As an example, you might create a Microsoft Word table with a column for each type of data you want to store.

With the list in a Word table, you can change the order of the table rows to group all of the products from one supplier together...all you need to do then is scroll down through the table until you find the products from the supplier you want.

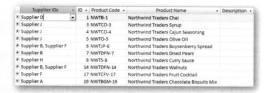

Using Word to store your data isn't the best solution, however. One limitation is that there's no way to combine information from two tables, so you need to write the supplier's phone number in every row representing a product from that supplier. If that phone number changes, you need to change the phone number entry in every table row representing a product from that supplier.

Storing Data in a Database

Databases, by contrast, are designed to combine data from several sources into a single table. After data is entered into a table, it can be combined with other tables in the database to produce valuable information. It's possible, for example, to store information about suppliers in one table and information about purchase orders in another table. If a supplier changes its phone number, you need to change the phone number only once.

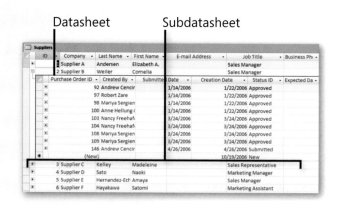

Datasheet   Subdatasheet

Using an Existing Database

When you start Access, the Getting Started with Microsoft Office Access screen appears in the Access window. A list of recently opened files appears at the right of the window, in the Open Recent Database section. You can select the file you want to open from the list that appears. If the file you want isn't on that list, click More to display the Open dialog box. From the Open dialog box, you can navigate to the folder with the database you want to open.

Open a Database on Startup

① Start Microsoft Office Access 2007.

② Click More.

③ Navigate to the folder with the database you want to open.

④ Double-click the file you want to open.

Open a Recently Used Database

① Start Microsoft Office Access 2007.

② In the Open Recent Database section, click the name of the database you want to open.

Creating a Database from a Template

The developers of Microsoft Office Access 2007 have one primary goal: to make it as easy as possible for you to create powerful and useful databases that help you get your work done quickly. You must have a great database program to meet that goal, but it also helps if the developers draw on the rest of the Microsoft community to design databases you can use without modification (for tasks such as tracking your contacts, sales, or workouts) or to use as the basis for your own custom databases. You can find those preexisting databases, called templates, installed on your computer and also on the Office Online Web site.

Create a Database from a Template

1. If necessary, click the Microsoft Office button and then choose Close Database to close any open database.

2. Click a Template Category.

3. Click the desired template.

4. Type a name for your database.

5. Click the folder icon.

6. Navigate to the folder where you want to store your database.

7. Click OK.

8. Click Download.

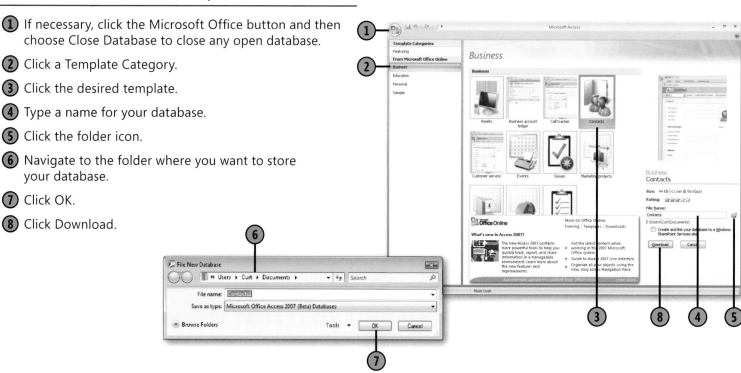

Find Database Templates Online

(1) If necessary, click the Microsoft Office button and then click Close Database to close any open database.

(2) Click an Office Online template category.

(3) Click the desired template.

(4) Type a name for your database.

(5) Click the folder icon.

(6) Navigate to the folder where you want to store your database.

(7) Click OK.

(8) Click Download.

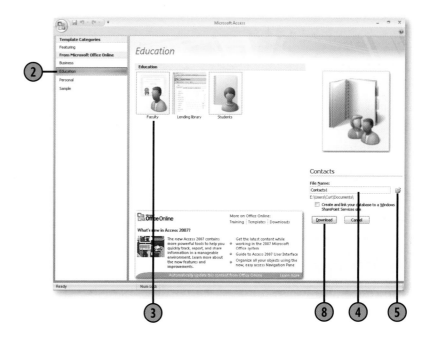

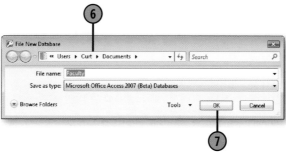

Adding a Table to a Database

It might seem strange to want to enter data into a table without first defining the table's structure, but there's one scenario in which it makes perfect sense: when you're in a hurry and you have to get the data into the database quickly. When you type data into a blank table, Access assigns generic names to the fields, such as Field1, Field2, and so on. After the data's in the table, you can open the table in Design view and name the fields, define data types, and so on.

Create a New Table by Typing

1. Click the Create tab.

2. In the Tables group, click Table.

3. Type the data for the first new field and press Tab.

4. Repeat step 3 until you have typed all of the data for one record, and then press Enter twice to return to the first field.

5. Click Save.

6. Type a name for your table.

7. Click OK.

8. Click the Close box for the table.

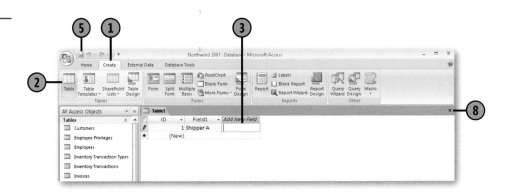

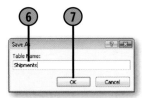

Tip

When you create a field by typing, Access defines the table's first field as a sequentially numbered field named ID, which serves as the table's primary key field. It's a good idea to leave the field in the table, but you should rename it to something more descriptive so you can identify it if you use it as a foreign key. If the table's name is Warehouses, for example, you could name the field WarehouseID.

Modifying a Table

It's easy to create tables in Access, but you're not stuck with the first version of a table. After you create a table, you can modify it by adding, deleting, and reordering fields. Although the order of your fields doesn't affect how your table functions within the database, changing their order can make it easier for you and your colleagues to understand your table's structure

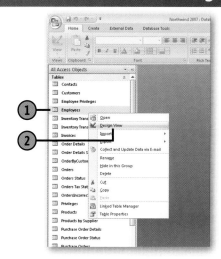

Change a Table

① Right-click the table you want to modify.

② Click Design view.

③ Follow any of these steps:

- ■ To delete a field, click the row selector of the row you want to delete, click the Delete Rows button, and then click Yes to confirm that you want to delete the row.

- ■ To add a field, click the row selector of the row below where you want the new field to appear, click the Insert Row button, type a name for the field, click the row's Data Type cell, click the down arrow that appears, and then click the desired data type.

- ■ To reorder the fields in your table, click the row selector of the row you want to move, and then drag the row selector to the desired position.

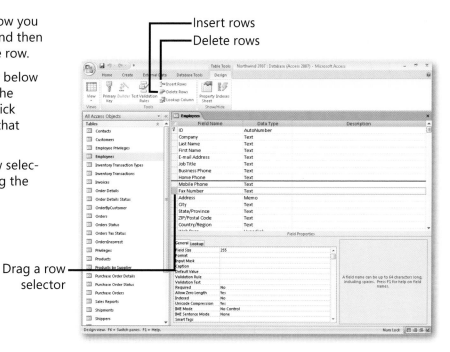

Insert rows
Delete rows

Drag a row selector

Adding Data to a Table

After you open a table, you can edit the existing data, add new data, or copy data from one cell and paste it into another. You can edit text using the same techniques that you use in other Microsoft Office 2007 applications. When you cut or copy table data, the Office Clipboard keeps track of the last 24 items you cut or copy. If you want Access to undo the last change you made, you can do so by pressing Ctrl+Z or by clicking the Undo button on the Quick Access Toolbar.

Select Text

- Move the mouse pointer over a cell until the pointer turns into a white cross and then click in the cell.

- Double-click a word to select it.

- Drag the mouse pointer over text to select it.

Delete Text

- Click to the right of the text to be deleted and press Backspace to delete it one character at a time.

- Select the text and press Delete.

Undoing Operations

- To undo an operation, click the Undo button in the Quick Access Toolbar.

Move the mouse ...

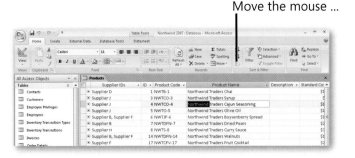

Copy and Paste Text

① Select the text you want to copy.

② Click the Home tab.

③ Click the Copy button.

④ Click the position where you want to paste the text.

⑤ Click the Paste button.

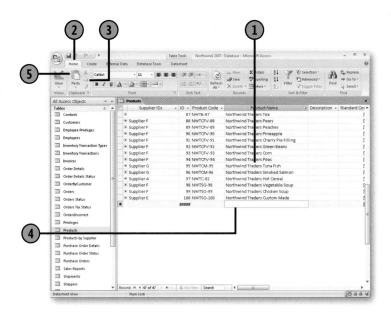

Access File Formats

Access 2007 uses a new file format that supports a number of new capabilities. Access 2007 database files, which end with the .accdb file extension (e.g., Northwind2007.accdb), enable you to use these new capabilities:

- Multivalued fields enable you to select multiple values from a list of acceptable choices.

- Attachment data type enables you to store files, such as images or Word documents, as part of a database record.

- Improved integration enables you to interact effectively with Windows SharePoint Services and Microsoft Office Outlook 2007. The new Access 2007 file system includes security capabilities that enable the 2007 Microsoft Office system programs to disable databases that contain programming code from an unknown source. These new security capabilities make it possible to integrate Access 2007 with Outlook 2007 and Windows SharePoint Services sites.

- Append-only memo fields allow users to add data to a field but prohibit editing or deleting information previously entered into the field. Requiring users to record changes in an append-only memo field helps preserve data integrity and establishes a chain of events.

- Improved encryption helps protect your database from intruders who attempt to gain unauthorized access to your data.

The Access 2007 file format doesn't support database replication or the user-level security model, both of which were available in the Access 2003 file format. However, you can open a database in the Access 2003 file format in Compatability Mode, which enables you to use those capabilities if you absolutely must have them.

Importing Data

Many times you find that data from another database would be nice to have in the database you're working on. You can bring tables (or other objects) into your database using the controls on the External Data tab. Copying tables from another database enables you to use the data as it exists at the time you make the copy, so any updates you make to the original table are not reflected in the copy, and vice versa.

Copy a Table from Another Database

① Click the External Data tab.

② Click Access.

③ Click Browse.

④ Double-click the database from which you want to import the table.

(continued on the next page)

Tip

You can import data from other types of database objects by clicking the object type (for example, Queries) in the Import Objects dialog box and then clicking the object from which you want to get your data.

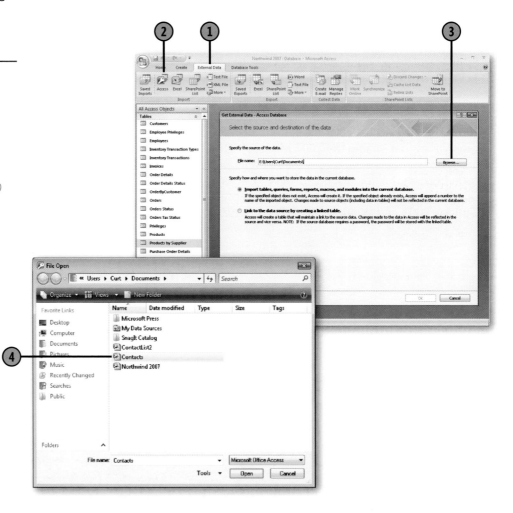

Copy a Table from Another Database *(continued)*

⑤ Select the Import Tables, Queries, Forms, Reports, Macros, And Modules Into The Current Database option.

⑥ Click OK.

⑦ Click the table or tables to import.

⑧ Click OK.

Tip

If you clicked a table to include it in the list of tables to be imported, but have changed your mind, you can click the table again to deselect it.

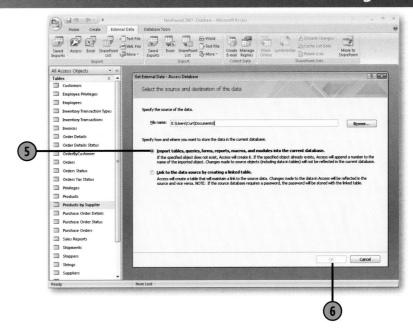

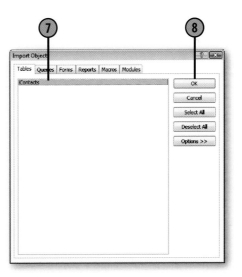

Exporting Data

Access enables you to store and summarize data stored in your database tables, but Excel provides a much wider range of analytical tools. Exporting your Access table or query data to an Excel workbook takes just a few steps, after which you can analyze your data using all of the capabilities Excel has to offer.

Exporting Data to Excel

① Click the table or query you want to export.

② Click the External Data tab.

③ In the Export group, click the Export to Excel Spreadsheet button.

④ Type a name for the file.

⑤ If desired, select the Export Data With Formatting And Layout option.

⑥ Click OK.

⑦ Click Close.

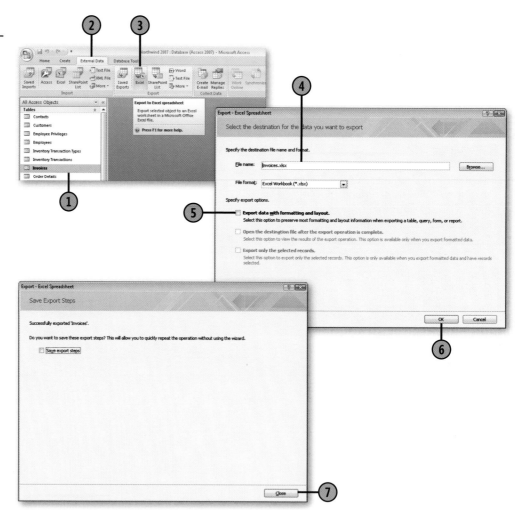

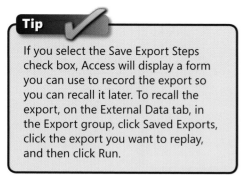

Tip ✓

If you select the Save Export Steps check box, Access will display a form you can use to record the export so you can recall it later. To recall the export, on the External Data tab, in the Export group, click Saved Exports, click the export you want to replay, and then click Run.

Defining Relationships Among Tables

When the primary key from one table is present in another table, you can create a relationship between the two tables. This ability to link two (or more) tables together is one reason why relational databases are so powerful—you make your data easier to read by creating simple tables and then use your computer's processing power to combine tables of data into useful information you can use to make business decisions.

Define a Relationship

① Click the Database Tools tab.

② Click Relationships.

③ If one or more of the tables you want to relate don't appear in the Relationships window, click the Show Table button.

④ Click the first table to add to the Relationships window.

⑤ Click Add.

⑥ Repeat steps 4 and 5 as necessary.

⑦ When you finish adding tables, click Close.

⑧ Drag the primary key field from the first table to the corresponding foreign key field in the second table.

⑨ Click Create.

⑩ Click the Close button to close the Relationships window.

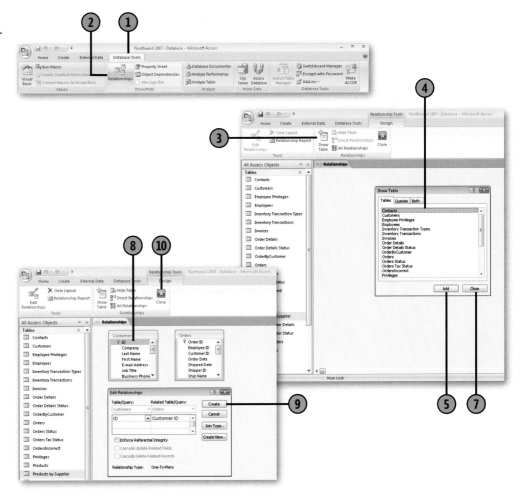

Creating a Form

Access makes it possible for you to create powerful and complex forms, but there will be plenty of occasions when a simple form that contains all of the fields from a table will meet your needs. Creating a simple form is a straightforward process. You simply select the table from which you want to create your form, then tell Access you want to create a simple form based on that table and you're done. If you'd like more control over the form you create, you can use the Form Wizard, which enables you to choose the data source, the type of the form, and the form's appearance.

Create a Simple Form

① In the Navigation pane, click a table.

② Click the Create tab.

③ Click Form.

Step through the Form Wizard

① Click the Create tab.

② Click More Forms.

③ Click Form Wizard.

(continued on the next page)

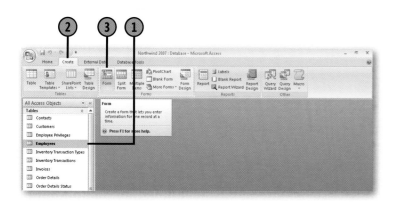

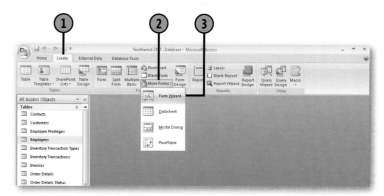

Step through the
Form Wizard *(continued)*

(4) Click the Tables/Queries down arrow.

(5) Click the table to provide the values and structure for the form.

(6) Click a field in the Available Fields box and then click either of the following:

- Click Add to add the selected field.

- Click Add All to add all fields to the form.

(7) Click Next.

(8) Select the layout for the form.

(9) Click Next.

(10) Click the name of the style for the form.

(11) Click Next.

(12) Type a name for the form.

(13) Click Finish.

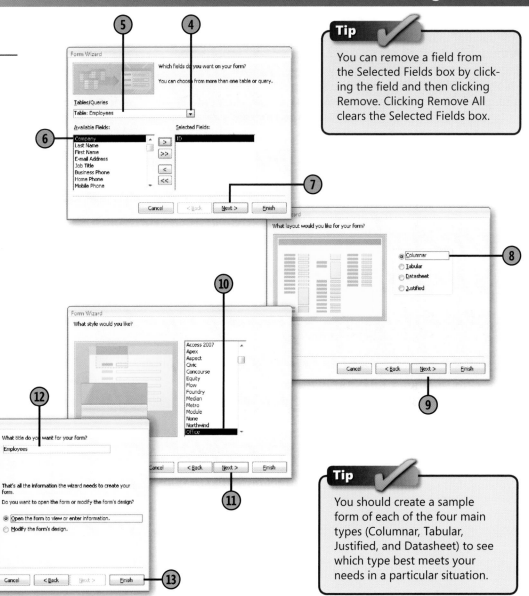

Tip ✓

You can remove a field from the Selected Fields box by clicking the field and then clicking Remove. Clicking Remove All clears the Selected Fields box.

Tip ✓

You should create a sample form of each of the four main types (Columnar, Tabular, Justified, and Datasheet) to see which type best meets your needs in a particular situation.

Creating a Report from the Data

Although it might be possible to generate useful reports from the data in a single table or query, it's very likely that you'll want to combine data from more than one table or query into a single report. For example, you might have product data in one table and supplier data in another table, and then want to create a report where full supplier contact information accompanies the product information. You can do that by creating a report using the Report Wizard.

Step through the Report Wizard

① Click the Create tab.

② Click Report Wizard.

③ Click the down arrow and then choose the first table or query from which you want to draw values for the report.

④ Click a field in the Available Fields box and then click either of the following buttons:

- Add to add the selected field.
- Add All to add all fields to the report.

⑤ Click Next.

- If you created a report based on a query that reads in primary key values from more than one table, a wizard page appears asking you to select a preliminary grouping criteria for the report's records. Click the name of the field by which you want to group and then click Next.

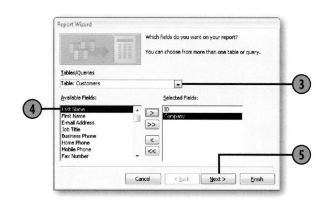

(continued on the next page)

Step through the Report Wizard *(continued)*

(6) If necessary, click the first field by which you want to group the report's contents and then click Add. Repeat to add grouping levels.

(7) Click Next.

(8) Click the first field's down arrow, and click the first field by which you want to sort the report's contents.

(9) If necessary, click the sort options to toggle between Ascending or Descending.

(10) Click Next.

(11) Use the controls on the remaining wizard pages to select a layout, page orientation, style, and name for the report. When you're done, click Finish.

Tip

You can remove fields from the Selected Fields pane of the Report Wizard by clicking the field name and then clicking either Remove, to remove the selected field, or clicking Remove All, to remove all fields.

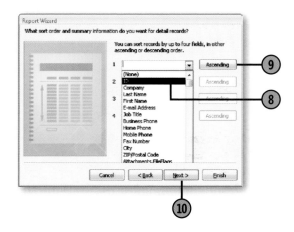

Extracting Information from a Database (Queries)

When you create a basic select query, you identify the table (or tables) with the data you want to find, name the fields to appear in the query results, and then save the query. The Query Wizard walks you through the process, making it easy to identify the tables and fields to appear in your query. What's more, you can choose whether to have Access display detailed results (that is, the individual query rows) or summarize the query's contents.

Create a Detail Query

1. Click the Create tab.
2. Click Query Wizard.
3. Click Simple Query Wizard.
4. Click OK.

(continued on the next page)

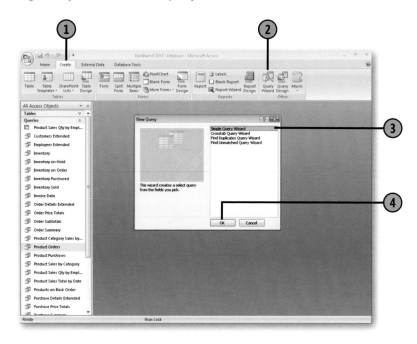

Create a Detail Query (continued)

⑤ Click the Tables/Queries down arrow and then click the table or query with the fields you want to use in your query.

⑥ Click the first field to include in the query's results.

⑦ Click Add.

⑧ Repeat steps 6 and 7 to add more fields (and step 5 to change the table or query from which you draw fields).

⑨ Click Next.

⑩ Click the Detail option button.

⑪ Click Next.

⑫ Type a name for your query.

⑬ Click Finish.

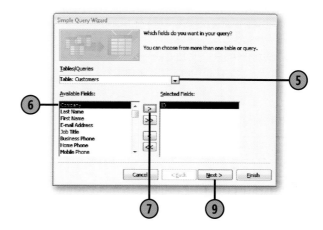

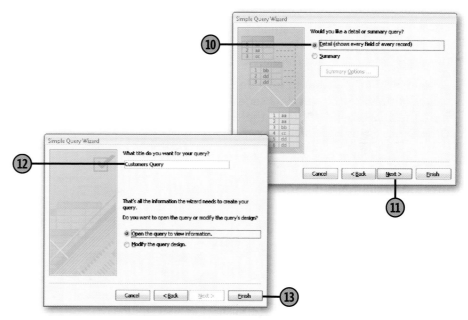

Analyzing Data with a PivotChart

Just as you can create tables that you can reorganize on the fly to emphasize different aspects of your table and query data, you can also create dynamic charts, or PivotCharts, to summarize your data effectively. By changing the grouping order of the fields used to create your PivotChart, or by limiting which values are presented in the PivotChart, you answer specific questions posed by you and your colleagues. In addition to letting you change how your data appears in the chart, you can even change the type of chart you use to display your data!

Step through the PivotChart Wizard

① Click the database object that contains your PivotChart data.

② Click the Create tab.

③ Click PivotChart.

④ Drag fields that you want to provide values for the PivotChart's category axis rows from the Chart Field List box to the Drop Category Fields Here area.

⑤ Drag fields that you want to provide values for the PivotChart's data series from the Chart Field List box to the Drop Series Fields Here area.

⑥ Drag the fields that you want to provide values for the body of the Pivot-Chart from the Chart Field List box to the Drop Data Fields Here area.

⑦ Click the Save button.

⑧ Type a name for your PivotChart.

⑨ Click OK.

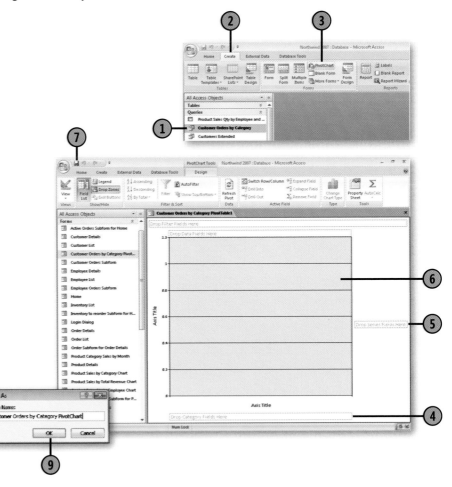

Change a PivotChart Chart Type

1 Display the forms in your database.

2 Double-click the form that contains your PivotChart.

3 If necessary, click the Design tab.

4 Click the Change Chart Type button.

5 Click the Type tab.

6 Click the new chart type.

7 Click the subtype of the chart you want to create.

8 Click the Close box.

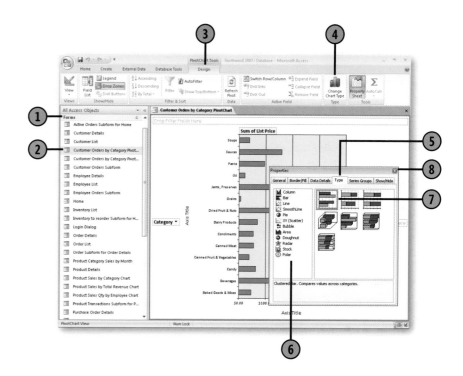

Collecting Data Using E-Mail

Gathering data from one's colleagues, vendors, and customers can be a frustrating process. When you ask a question by phone, in person, or over e-mail, you end up transcribing the responses and typing them into your database. The potential for inaccuracies, mistranscriptions, and other mistakes abound. One of the most useful new things you can do in Access 2007 is to create Outlook 2007 messages that contain Access forms. You send the form to a colleague as an e-mail message, which the recipient fills out and sends back. You can then read the data directly from Outlook into your Access table. You never have to touch the data with your hands, which means that you don't have to worry about making a mistake as you type the data. Yes, it's possible your colleague made a mistake while entering the data, but you reduce the number of steps in the process and eliminate many opportunities to introduce errors.

Send a Data Collection E-Mail Message

1. Click the table for which you want to collect data.

2. Click the External Data tab.

3. In the Collect Data group, click Create E-Mail.

4. Click Next to advance past the first Collect Data Through E-Mail Messages wizard page (not shown).

5. Select the HTML Form option.

6. Click Next.

7. Select the Collect New Information Only option.

8. Click Next.

(continued on the next page)

Caution

Both you and your recipient must have Microsoft Office Outlook 2007 installed to exchange data collection e-mail messages.

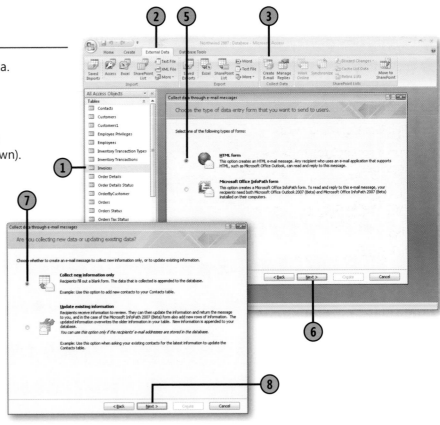

Send a Data Collection E-Mail Message *(continued)*

⑨ Click the first field you want to add to the form.

⑩ Click the Add button.

⑪ Repeat Steps 9 and 10 to add all applicable fields.

⑫ Click Next.

⑬ Verify that the Automatically Process Replies And Add Data To *Invoices* option is deselected.

⑭ Click Next.

⑮ Select the Enter The E-mail Addresses In Microsoft Office Outlook option.

⑯ Click Next.

⑰ Type a subject for the e-mail messages.

⑱ Type an introduction for the e-mail messages.

⑲ Click Next.

⑳ Click Create.

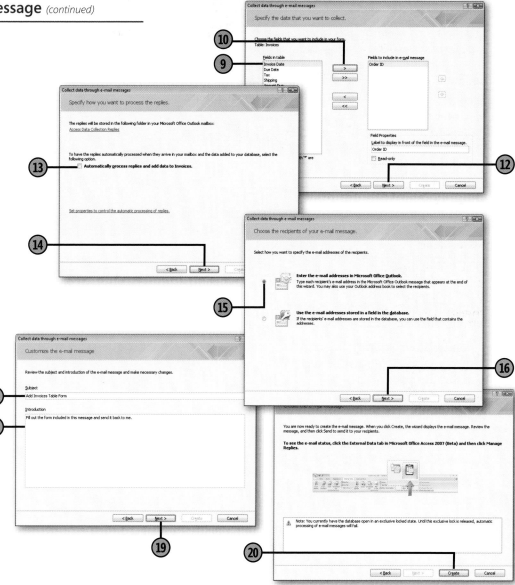

Customizing Access

A macro is a series of automated steps, such as opening a report or form or displaying a message box that you create and save. After you save the macro, you can run it whenever you want, either by right-clicking it and clicking the Run option, or by running it when something specific happens, such as clicking a button on a form. If you export Access tables to other formats, print records, or search for records and are tired of going through the process manually, you can create a macro that does it for you.

Create a Macro

① Click the Create tab.

② Click the top part of the Macro button.

③ Click the down arrow in the first Action cell.

④ Click the desired action.

⑤ Fill in the arguments for the action. The arguments you can set will be different for every action.

- Repeat Steps 3 through 5 on subsequent table rows to add actions to your macro.

⑥ On the Quick Access Toolbar, click the Save button.

⑦ In the Save As dialog box that appears, type a name for your macro.

⑧ Click OK.

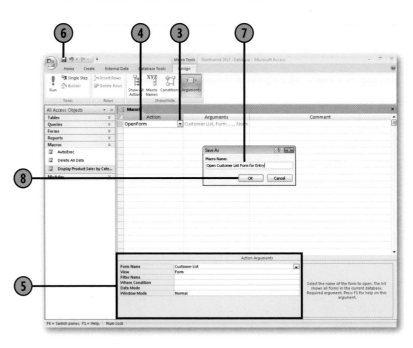

15 Exchanging Information Among Programs

In this section:

- Inserting Excel Data or an Excel Chart into a Document, Publication, or Presentation
- Analyzing a Word Table in Excel
- Using Word to Prepare PowerPoint or PublisherText
- Preparing PowerPoint Handouts in Word
- Inserting a PowerPoint Slide Show into a Document, Worksheet, or Publication
- Using Publisher to Present a Word Document
- Using Access Data in a Mail Merge
- Converting a Scanned Document into Text

Each of the programs in the 2007 Microsoft Office System was designed to do a specific job, and to do it superbly. However, there are times when the *interoperability* of the programs—that is, the way they work together to enhance each other's performance—can give you even better results than using a single program. And, because of the similarities in structure and functionality among most of the Office programs, working with more than one program at a time is just as simple as working in a single program. The interaction among programs is almost seamless, and the results are well worth a few extra clicks!

In this section, we'll describe why you might want to exchange information among programs, and then we'll walk you through a few procedures so that you can see how well the programs work together. Let's say that every month you write a company newsletter in Word. It looks fine, but you'd like to give it a more polished look. You could do that in Word, but you don't know much about designing a layout and you don't have time to experiment. Just choose one of Publisher's layout designs for newsletters, and insert your newsletter's text and pictures. The result is a professional-looking publication that you'll be proud of. This is just one example of many more good ideas you'll find in the pages that follow.

Inserting Excel Data into a Document, Publication, or Presentation

Microsoft Office Excel is a great tool for collecting and analyzing data, but the information contained in an Excel worksheet is often easiest to understand when it's presented along with some explanations or supplemental information.

To that end, you can integrate Excel information into a Microsoft Office Word document, a Publisher publication, or a PowerPoint presentation.

Copy the Data

(1) In the Excel worksheet, select and copy the cells you want.

(2) In Word, PowerPoint, or Publisher, click where you want to insert the data. In Word or PowerPoint, on the Home tab, click the bottom part of the Paste button, and choose Paste Special from the drop-down menu to display the Paste Special dialog box. In Publisher, choose Paste Special from the Edit menu.

(3) Specify whether or not you want the inserted table to be linked to the original Excel file. The Paste option inserts data without any connection to the original Excel file. The Paste Link option inserts the data and creates a link to the original Excel file. (You can use only certain formats to insert a linked file.)

(4) Select the format you want for the inserted item. Each program offers different choices for the formatting of the inserted data. Use the information in the Result area to determine the effect of each format.

(5) Click OK.

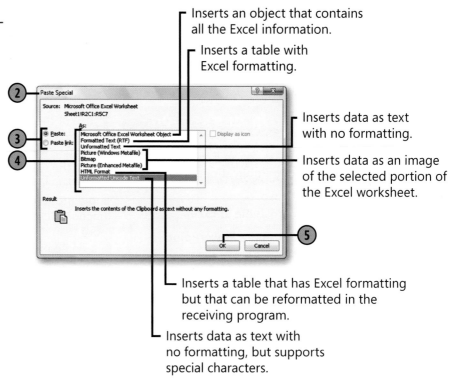

Inserts an object that contains all the Excel information.

Inserts a table with Excel formatting.

Inserts data as text with no formatting.

Inserts data as an image of the selected portion of the Excel worksheet.

Inserts a table that has Excel formatting but that can be reformatted in the receiving program.

Inserts data as text with no formatting, but supports special characters.

Tip ✓

You can also use the Paste Special dialog box to insert Excel content into an Outlook mail message.

Edit the Data

① Do any of the following:

- If you pasted the data as an Excel object, double-click the object to open it in your program, and edit the data in the worksheet that appears. Click outside the object to close it.

- If you paste-linked the data as an Excel object, double-click the object to open the original Excel file in Excel, and make your changes in that worksheet. Save and close the workbook when you've finished.

- If you paste-linked the data into Word using a different format—Formatted Text, for example—open the original Excel file, make your changes to the worksheet, and save the workbook.

- If you pasted the data in any other format, make the changes to the data in your program. The changes won't be made automatically in the original Excel worksheet, nor will changes to the Excel worksheet be reflected in the data in your document, publication, or presentation. Note that you can't modify the data if it was inserted as a picture.

② Position and format the inserted table or object as desired.

③ Save your document, publication, or presentation.

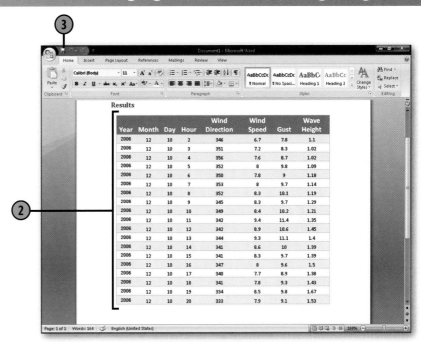

Tip ✓

When you insert an Excel object, you can work with the worksheet in an Excel window by right-clicking the object in your document, publication, or presentation, pointing to Worksheet Object on the shortcut menu (Microsoft Office Excel Worksheet Object in Publisher), and choosing Open from the submenu. When you've finished, choose Close & Return from the File menu.

Inserting an Excel Chart into a Document, Publication, or Presentation

If the final results of your data are contained in an Excel worksheet but you want to display the data as a chart, you can copy the chart into your Word document, Publisher publication, or PowerPoint presentation. You can insert the chart in one of three ways: as a picture; as a linked Excel object so that changes to the chart in the Excel file will be updated in the chart in your document, publication, or presentation; or as an unlinked (or *embedded*) Excel object so that the chart resides in your Word, Publisher, or PowerPoint file. The last option lets you edit the chart as necessary, and you no longer need the original Excel file.

Insert the Chart

1. In Excel, create and format your chart. Select and copy it. In your Word, Publisher, or PowerPoint file, click where you want the chart to appear. On the Home tab, click the bottom part of the Paste button, and choose Paste Special from the drop-down menu to display the Paste Special dialog box. (In Publisher, choose Paste Special from the Edit menu.)

2. In the Paste Special dialog box, choose one of the following to specify how you want to insert the chart:

   - Microsoft Office Excel Chart Object, with the Paste option selected, to incorporate all the Excel data so that you can edit the data without access to the original Excel file.

   - Microsoft Office Excel Chart Object, with the Paste Link option selected, if you'll need to edit the data and if you have access to the original Excel file. If you're linking to the Excel chart, make sure that you've named and saved the Excel file before you insert it.

   - Picture or Bitmap if you're not going to edit the chart and its data.

3. Click OK. Position and format the object, and then save the document, publication, or presentation.

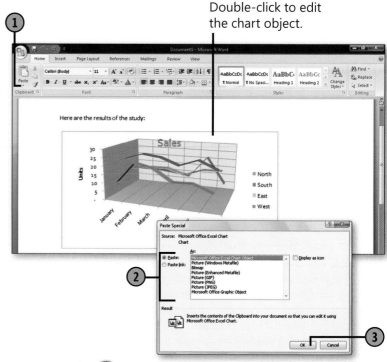

Double-click to edit the chart object.

Tip

Excel provides many powerful formatting tools. Be sure to format the chart so that it looks the way you want before you insert it. You might need to change the size of the inserted chart to clearly see all the formatting you've applied.

Analyzing a Word Table in Excel

You can use Microsoft Office Word to generate professional-looking tables that present your data cleanly and clearly. However, Word isn't the best tool for summarizing and analyzing that data. If, after you've created a table in Word, you realize that you need to do a bit more analysis of the data, take it to the data-analysis expert: Excel.

Analyze the Table

① In Word, on the Home tab, select the table, and click the Cut button (or press Ctrl+X).

② Switch to a blank Excel worksheet, and, on the Home tab, click the Paste button (or press Ctrl+V) to insert the data from Word.

③ Make whatever changes you want to the table, and save the file.

④ Select the cells that contain the data you want to return to your Word document, and, on the Home tab, click the Copy button (or press Ctrl+C).

⑤ Click in the Word document to place the insertion point where you want to insert the table, and click the Paste button (or press Ctrl+V).

⑥ Click the Paste Options button, and choose one of the following to specify how you want to paste the table:

- Match Destination Table Style to insert the table without staying connected to the Excel worksheet

- Match Destination Table Style And Link To Excel to maintain the connection to Excel so that you can continue to make changes in Excel that will appear in the Word table

⑦ Make any changes you want to the formatting of the table, and save the document.

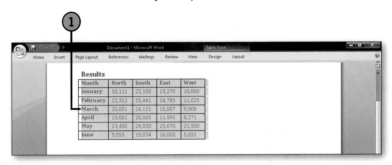

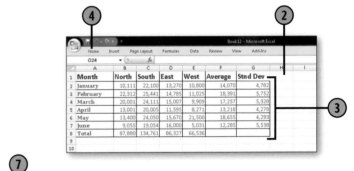

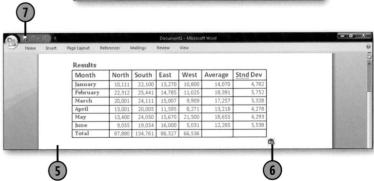

Using Word to Prepare PowerPoint Text

When you're developing a PowerPoint presentation, you'll find that preparing the text (but not content such as tables and pictures) in Word and then sending it to PowerPoint is the easiest and most flexible way to go. You can take advantage of Word's multitude of features to create exactly the look you want for the text of your presentation. As you create your document in Word, you can use the heading styles to tell PowerPoint how you want the information to be interpreted.

Create the Presentation

① In Word, create the outline for the presentation, using styles that have the following outline levels assigned to them:

- Outline Level 1 (such as Heading 1) for a slide title

- Outline Level 2 (such as Heading 2) for the text on the slide

- Outline Level 3 (such as Heading 3) for second-level text under Outline Level 2 text

- Outline Levels 4 through 9 for third- through eighth-level text

② Save and close the document.

③ In PowerPoint, choose Open from the Office menu to display the Open window. In the File Type list, choose All Outlines, and double-click the Word file you just created.

④ On the Home tab in PowerPoint, with the Outline tab displayed in the left pane, make any changes you want to the order of the slides.

⑤ With the Slides tab displayed in the left pane, make any changes you want to the formatting of your slides.

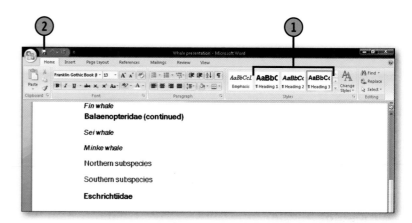

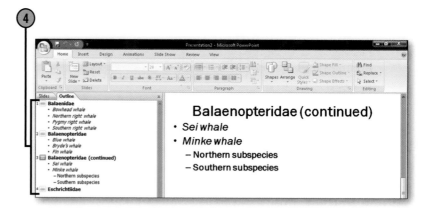

Preparing PowerPoint Handouts in Word

You can easily create printed handouts for your PowerPoint slide show, and the handouts can include thumbnail images of your slides. However, if you want to add more information about the slides and have full control of customizing the handouts, you can easily send the PowerPoint presentation to Word. In Word, you can include notes, add more text, modify the arrangement of the items, and make any other customizations you want to the handouts.

Publish the Slides to Word

① In PowerPoint, with your slide show finalized and saved, point to Publish on the Office menu, and click Create Handouts In Microsoft Office Word in the gallery that appears.

② In the Send To Microsoft Office Word dialog box that appears, select the basic layout you want.

③ Specify the way you want to insert the slide images:

- Paste to use images that are static and won't change

- Paste Link to have the images updated if you make changes to the slides in PowerPoint

④ Click OK.

⑤ Switch to the new Word document and add and/or modify the content.

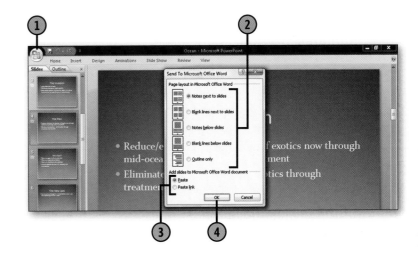

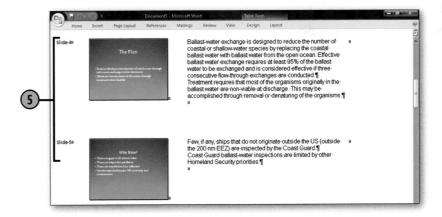

Inserting a PowerPoint Slide Show into a Document, Worksheet, or Publication

An ingenious way to create a file that contains a great deal more information than it appears to is to insert one or more PowerPoint presentations into a Word document, an Excel worksheet, or a Publisher publication. With the presentation's only visible sign of existence being an icon, it's hardly noticeable on the page, but double-click the icon, and, presto, there's a slide show! The person viewing the slide show, however, must have PowerPoint 2007 installed on his or her computer to be able to view the show.

Insert the Presentation

1. In your saved document, worksheet, or publication, click where you want to insert the PowerPoint presentation.

2. On the Insert tab, click the Object button to display the Object dialog box. In Publisher, choose Object from the Insert menu.

3. In Word or Excel, click the Create From File tab in the Object dialog box. In Publisher, click the Create From File option. Click Browse, and use the Browse dialog box to locate the PowerPoint presentation. Double-click the presentation.

4. Select the Display As Icon check box to display an icon for the presentation instead of displaying the entire presentation.

5. Click Change Icon if you want to use a different icon, and, in the Change Icon dialog box, select the icon you want. Change the caption that will appear below the icon, and click OK.

6. Click OK.

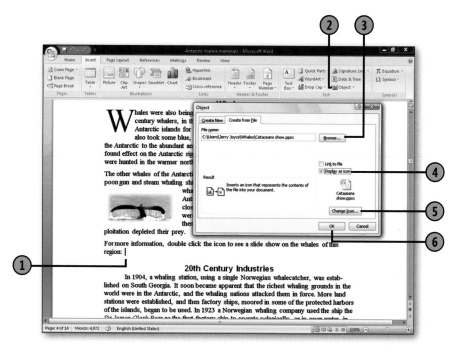

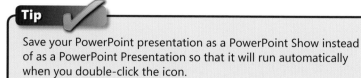

> **Tip**
>
> Save your PowerPoint presentation as a PowerPoint Show instead of as a PowerPoint Presentation so that it will run automatically when you double-click the icon.

Using Publisher to Present a Word Document

You can do all sorts of tweaking in a Word document to give it a really professional look. However, you'll find that you can do a lot more—and do it more easily—by using Publisher to enhance and fine-tune your document's appearance and design. Be sure, though, to double-check your document, especially if it contains tables or pictures, and then reposition those objects if necessary.

Publish Your Document

1. In Word, if you haven't done so already, create the document, using the formatting and styles you want. Save and close the document.

2. Start Publisher, or, if it's already running, choose New from the File menu to open the Microsoft Publisher window.

3. Select the Import Word Documents category.

4. Select the design you want

5. Select or change any of the options.

6. Click Create. In the Import Word Document window that appears, locate and double-click the document you want to use.

7. If an item from the document wasn't properly inserted, in the Extra Content section of the Format Publication task pane, click the item, and then choose to insert it, delete it, or add it to the Content Library.

8. Use the Publisher tools and techniques to complete the publication.

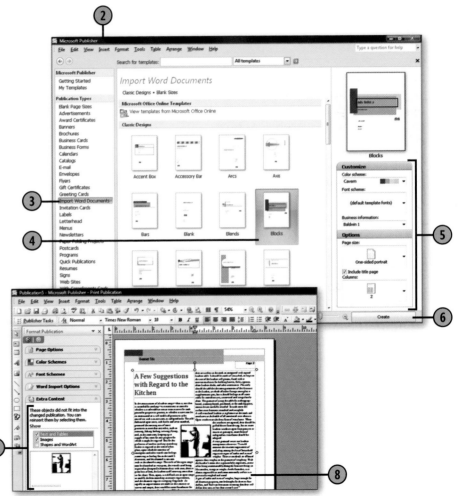

Using Word to Prepare Publisher Text

Trying to compose a lengthy story from scratch in Publisher would be akin to writing a long speech on index cards: impossible to fit everything on one card, and a frustrating waste of time and energy shuffling the cards around. It's a bad idea. Here's a good one: Compose the entire story in Word, using all of Word's tools, and then put the finished, formatted story into Publisher. Then, if you need to, you can do any small edits in Publisher, or you can return to Word for more substantial edits.

Create Your Story

(1) In Publisher, design and save the type of publication you want, and lay out your page, with an empty text box (or a text box with placeholder text) ready to contain your story.

(2) Right-click the text box, point to Change Text on the shortcut menu, and choose Edit Story In Microsoft Word from the submenu.

(3) In Microsoft Word, delete any existing placeholder text, and write your story, using all the features of Word. Note that some features, such as SmartArt graphics, are not fully supported in Publisher. A SmartArt graphic will be inserted as a picture.

(4) When you've finished writing, choose Close & Return To from the Office menu.

(5) In your Publisher publication, modify the dimensions of the text box, and add any formatting you want.

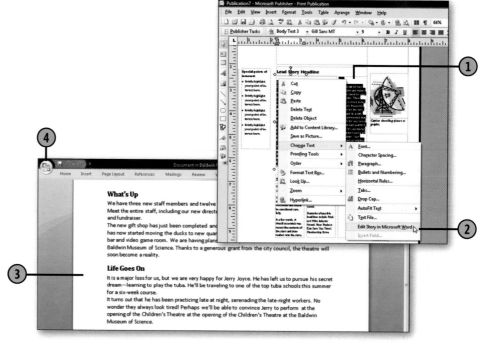

Tip

To insert part of an existing Word file as a story, select the text in Word, copy it, and paste it into the Publisher text box. To insert an entire Word file, right-click the text box, point to Change Text on the shortcut menu, and choose Text File from the submenu. Double-click the document file in the Insert Text File dialog box.

Using Word to Present Access Data

Microsoft Office Access 2007 is the perfect tool for analyzing relational data and for generating good-looking reports on the data. However, when it's time to present the data in a customizable form, along with other relevant information, Access leaves something to be desired. To improve your presentation, you can send the data to Word, where you can manipulate the presentation so that it looks the way you want.

Publish Your Data

(1) In Access, open the table, query, form, or report that you want to present in Word. If you want to export only selected records, select them.

(2) On the External Data tab, click the Export to RTF File button.

(3) In the Export Wizard, specify where you want the file to be located.

(4) Select this check box if you want the file to open automatically in Word.

(5) If you selected certain records, select this check box if you want to export only those records, or clear the check box to export all the records.

(6) Click OK. In the Save Export Settings page of the Export Wizard, specify whether you want to save the export settings, and then click Close.

(7) In Word, if necessary, open the document and modify it as you want. Choose the Convert command from the Office menu to save the document in the Word 2007 format.

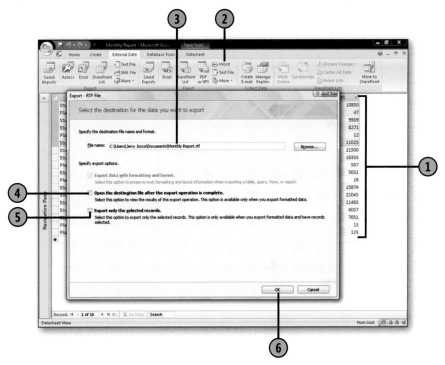

Tip

Any changes you make to the Word document won't affect the data or the format in the Access database, so you can feel free to delete any rows or columns you don't want.

Analyzing Access Data in Excel

The power of Access is its ability to extract information from, and look at relationships in, sets of data. The power of Excel is its ability to easily perform statistical and other types of analyses on sets of data. You can combine the power of both programs by gathering a data set in Access and then analyzing it in Excel. You can use either a table or a query as the source of the data you send to Excel, but, if you use a query, you're using the power of Access to customize your data set before you export it.

Analyze Your Data

1. In Access, open the item you want to export if it isn't already open, and click it to select it. If you want to export only selected records, select them.

2. On the External Data tab, click the Export To Excel Spreadsheet button.

3. In the Export Wizard that appears, specify whether you want to include formatting with the data; whether you want Excel to open with the data; and, if you selected certain records, whether you want to export only the selected records. Click OK, and on the Save Export Settings page of the Export Wizard, specify whether you want to save the Export settings. Click Close.

4. In Excel, use any of the powerful functions to conduct your statistical or other analysis of the data.

Adding Excel Data to an Access Database

If you want to use a large or complex Excel worksheet in an Access database, you don't have to reenter the data in order to use it in Access. You can simply import the data into Access and use it as you'd use any other Access table. When you import the data, you're creating a copy of the Excel worksheet data. The imported data is independent of the original Excel workbook file, so any changes you make to the data in Access won't change the information in the Excel file.

Get the Excel Data

1. On the External Data tab in Access, with the database you want to use open, click the Import Excel Spreadsheet button.

2. In the Get External Data Wizard, specify the Excel workbook you want to use; whether you want to place the imported data in a new table; whether you want to append to an existing table; and whether you want the data to be linked. Step through the wizard, specifying

   • Which worksheet or named range is to be imported, and whether the first row contains column names.

   • The destination of the table.

   • The field name and data type for each column in the worksheet, whether the selected column is to be indexed, and whether the column should be included when the data is imported.

   • The field for the primary key, if any, and the name of the new Access table.

3. In the Navigation pane, double-click the new table that you imported to display it. Examine the table to verify that it's correct, make any modifications you want, and then save the table.

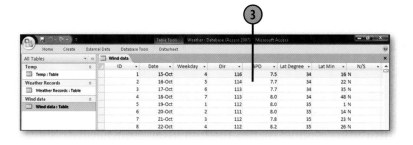

Using Access Data in a Mail Merge

Word and Publisher both have mail merge capabilities that work in similar ways. When you couple a mail merge with an Access database, you can create a highly selective mail merge much more easily than you could if you tried to do a selective mail merge directly in Word or Publisher.

Create a Mail Merge Using Access Data

① In Access, create and save a query that displays only the records you want to use, and then close Access.

② In Word or Publisher, create the document or the publication that you'll use for your mail merge.

③ Start the mail merge: In Word, on the Mailings tab, click the Start Mail Merge button, and choose the type of merge you want. In Publisher, point to Mail And Catalog Merge on the Tools menu, and choose the type of merge you want.

④ Step through the mail merge process, specifying that you'll be using an existing list as the data source.

⑤ In the Select Data Source dialog box that appears, locate and double-click the Access database that contains the query you created.

⑥ In the Select Table dialog box that appears, double-click the query.

⑦ In the Mail Merge Recipients dialog box that appears in Publisher (or that appears in Word when you click the Edit Recipient List), make any necessary changes to specify which records you want to be included. Click OK.

⑧ Insert the fields from the database table or query into your document or publication, and format the fields as you want them to appear in the final document or publication. Complete the mail merge setup, check for errors, and then execute your merge.

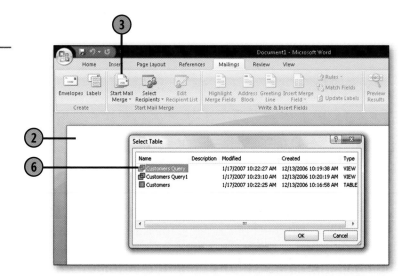

Using Your Contacts List in a Mail Merge

If you have a substantial number of individuals in your Outlook Contacts list, you can use that list as the data source for your mail merge in Word or Publisher. Using your Contacts list as your data source is especially efficient if the list contains detailed contact information, including complete addresses; or if you're creating a mail merge that will be distributed via e-mail.

Create a Mail Merge Using Your Contacts List

1. In Word or Publisher, create the document or the publication that you want to use as the basis for your mail merge.

2. Start the mail merge. In Word, on the Mailings tab, click the Start Mail Merge button, and choose the type of merge you want. In Publisher, point to Mail And Catalog Merge on the Tools menu, and choose the type of merge you want.

3. Step through the mail merge process, specifying that you'll be using your Outlook Contacts list as your data source. If prompted, specify the Outlook *profile* (the Outlook account) you want to use, and, in the Select Data Source dialog box, double-click the Contacts folder you want to use.

4. In the Mail Merge Recipients dialog box that appears in Publisher (or that appears in Word when you click the Edit Recipient List), make any necessary changes to specify which records you want to be included. Click OK.

5. Insert the fields from the Contacts list into your document or publication, and format the fields as you want them to appear in the final document or publication.

6. Complete the mail merge setup, check for errors, and then execute your merge.

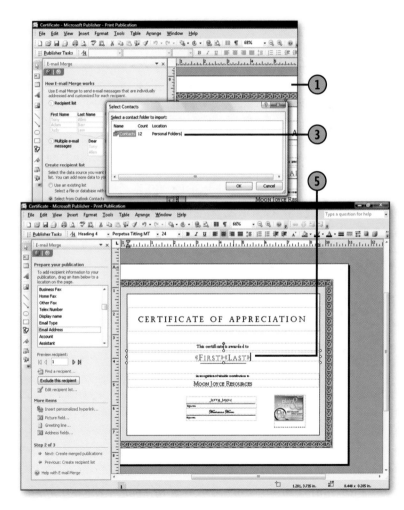

Creating PDF or XPS Documents

Wouldn't it be great if you could send out a document that would look exactly the same as its original version regardless of the configuration of the computer that it's viewed on? There are two types of formats available that can make this happen. The PDF (Portable Document Format) is a long-established format that requires a free, downloadable reader to view the file. The XPS (XML Paper Specification) Format is a new format that's integrated into Windows Vista and that you can view using Internet Explorer. To use either of these formats, you'll need to download and install an add-in for Office. You can create PDF and XPS documents using Access, Excel, PowerPoint, Publisher, and Word.

Create a Document in Access, Excel, PowerPoint, or Word

① In Access, Excel, PowerPoint, or Word, with your document completed, proof-read, saved, and absolutely the way you want the world to see it, point to Save As on the Office menu, and, in the gallery that appears, click PDF Or XPS.

② In the Publish As PDF Or XPS window that appears, enter a name for the document.

③ In the Save As Type list, select either PDF or XPS Document.

④ Select the optimization option you want.

⑤ Click Options.

⑥ Select any other items or options that you want to include. The items will differ depending on the program you're using. Click OK when you've finished.

⑦ With the correct destination selected, click Publish.

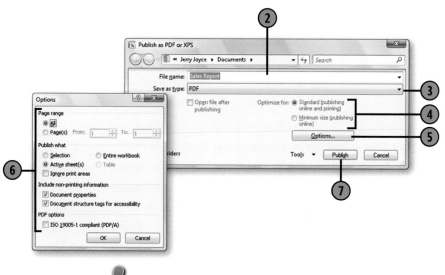

Caution

You can't open a PDF or an XPS Document for editing in any of the Office programs; be sure to keep a copy of the original Office document so that you can edit it if necessary.

See Also

"Downloading Add-Ins and Other Free Software" on page 332 for information about obtaining and installing add-ins and other free software.

Create a Document in Publisher

(1) With your publication completed and saved, choose Publish As PDF Or XPS from the File menu to display the Publish As PDF Or XPS window.

(2) Type a name for the document.

(3) In the Save As Type list, select either PDF or XPS Document.

(4) Click Change, and, in the Publish Options dialog box that appears, click the Advanced button if the entire dialog box isn't displayed.

(5) Select the level of quality you want.

(6) Modify any other settings, as necessary.

(7) Click Print Options if you want to change the page size and orientation, the pages that are to be published, and the printer marks you want to include. Click OK when you've finished.

(8) Click OK.

(9) With the correct destination selected, click Publish.

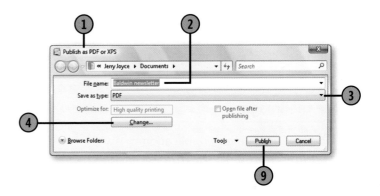

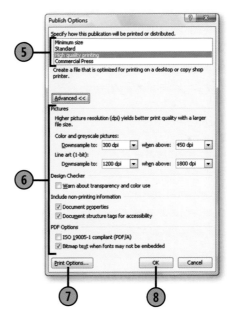

> **Tip**
>
> Many commercial printers prefer to use PDF files as their printing source rather than using an application (such as Publisher) file. Before you create your PDFs, make sure that the printer gives you all the printing settings you'll need.

Creating an Image of Your Work

If you want to distribute a monochrome picture of a document, a publication, or any content that can normally be printed instead of printing and scanning it, you can create an electronic image of the item and then save the image as a .tif file. You can then view the file in the Microsoft Office Document Imaging program or in another graphics viewing program. This is also an excellent way to prepare a document for faxing.

Create the Image

1 With your document, publication, presentation, workbook or whatever other type of file you want to use completed and saved, choose Print to display the Print dialog box.

2 Select Microsoft Office Document Image Writer in the Name list.

3 Click Properties to display the Microsoft Office Document Image Writer Properties dialog box.

4 On the Advanced tab, select the format you want to use. If you chose the TIFF format, specify the resolution, and then click OK.

5 Make any changes you want to the print settings.

6 Click OK.

7 In the Save As dialog box that appears, specify where you want to store the image, type a name for it, and click Save.

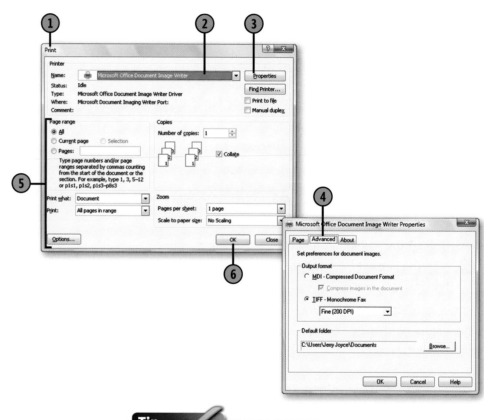

Tip

You can use this technique not only with Microsoft Office programs but with any program that can use a printer.

Viewing and Annotating a Scanned Image or a Fax

If you have an electronic image—a scanned document or picture, or a fax saved in the .tif format, for example—you can view it on your screen and can add annotations if you like.

View and Annotate an Image

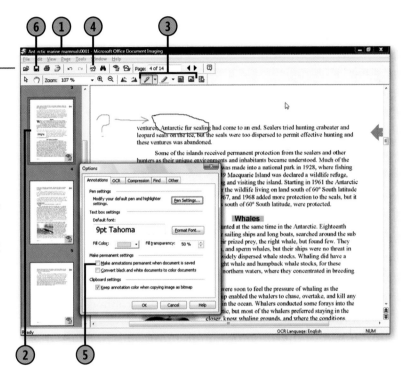

(1) On the Windows Start menu, click All Programs, click the Microsoft Office folder, click the Microsoft Office Tools folder, and choose Microsoft Office Document Imaging. In the Microsoft Office Document Imaging window that appears, click the Open button, and open your scanned document's image file.

(2) If the file contains multiple pages, click the page you want to view, and adjust the zoom so that you can easily read the page.

(3) To annotate the image, click any of the annotation tools:

- Pen to write or draw by dragging the mouse

- Highlighter to highlight text by dragging the mouse

- Insert Text Box to create a text box in which you can type notes

- Insert Picture to add a picture

(4) To view the page in Reading view, click the Reading View button on the Standard toolbar. Press Esc to exit Reading view.

(5) If you want to save your annotations with the document, choose Options from the Tools menu. On the Annotations tab of the Options dialog box, select this check box to make the annotations permanent, and then click OK.

(6) To save any other changes you've made, click the Save button.

Tip

To edit annotations, click the Select Annotations button on the Annotations toolbar, and click the annotation to select it. Once you've selected the annotation, you can resize it by dragging a Sizing handle, change its color by choosing Format Ink from the Edit menu, or delete it by pressing the Delete key.

Converting a Scanned Document into Text

When you scan a document, it's saved as a picture, not as text. You can use the Optical Character Recognition (OCR) feature in Microsoft Office Document Imaging to convert the scanned image into text and then export the text into a Word document.

Convert the Image

1. Open Microsoft Office Document Imaging from the Windows Start menu, if it isn't already open. In the Microsoft Office Document Imaging window that appears, click the Open button, and open your scanned document's image file.

2. If you want to convert a single page or several pages of a multiple-page scanned document, select the page or pages in the left pane of the window. Hold down the Ctrl key and click to select multiple pages.

3. Click the Recognize Text Using OCR button.

4. In the Recognize Text Using OCR dialog box that appears, specify whether you want to convert the selected page(s) or all the pages of the scanned document into text, and then click OK.

5. Click the Send Text To Word button.

6. In the Send Text To Word dialog box that appears, specify whether you want to send the selected text, the selected page(s), or all the pages of the scanned document to the Word document.

7. Select this check box to have pictures in the scanned document included in the Word document.

8. Specify where you want the new Word document to be stored.

9. Click OK, and then edit the text in the Word document that appears.

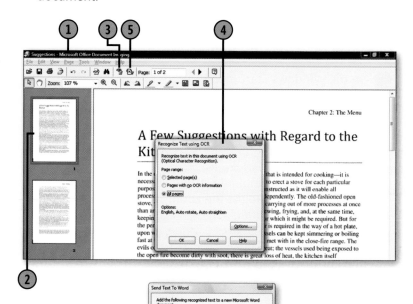

Tip

You can open any image that has been saved in the .tif file format that's used by many different scanners and electronic fax programs. You can also open the files in the Microsoft Document Interface (MDI) format that can be created in Microsoft Office Document Imaging.

Scanning a Document

If you want to create an electronic image of a letter, an article, or any other type of printed item, you can use the Microsoft Office Document Scanning program to scan the item. By default, when the item is being scanned, the Optical Character Recognition (OCR) feature is automatically activated so that when you're viewing the document in Microsoft Office Document Imaging after completing the scan, you can also send the content of the document to Microsoft Word for editing.

Scan a Text Document

(1) With the document in the scanner, and with the scanner turned on and properly configured for your computer, start Microsoft Office Document Scanning from the Office Tools folder of the Windows Start menu to display the Scan New Document dialog box.

(2) Specify the type of scanning you want.

(3) If you want to customize the scan, click Preset Options, and, from the drop-down menu that appears, choose to create a new setting or click to edit the selected preset option.

(4) Select the check boxes for the options you want.

(5) If you have more than one scanner configured on your computer, or if you want to use the scanner's driver dialog box to make your settings, click the Scanner button. In the Choose Scanner dialog box, select the scanner you're using, specify whether you want to show the scanner's driver dialog box, and click OK.

(6) Click Scan.

(7) If you're scanning more than one document, click Continue. When you've finished scanning, click Done.

(8) Review and save your document or documents in the Microsoft Document Imaging window that appears.

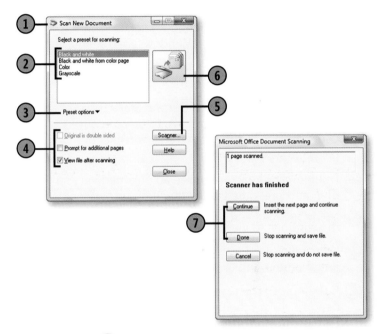

Tip

Microsoft Office Document Scanning requires that your scanner use a Windows Imaging Acquisition (WIA) driver to scan your documents. If your scanner uses a TWAIN driver, use the program that came with the scanner to scan and save the images as .tif or TIFF files, and then open them in Microsoft Office Document Imaging.

Managing and Editing Your Pictures

The Microsoft Office Picture Manager is a program you can use to organize all your pictures, edit them, and then share them with family, friends, or coworkers.

Work with Your Pictures

1. Start Microsoft Office Picture Manager from the Office Tools folder of the Windows Start menu.

2. Click one of the picture shortcuts to view the pictures in that folder.

3. Use the commands in the Getting Started task pane to add picture shortcuts; to search your computer for pictures; or to edit, rename, or distribute your pictures.

4. Double-click a picture to see an enlarged version of it, and press the Left or the Right arrow key (or use the Previous or Next button at the bottom of the window) to view other pictures in that folder.

5. If the color and/or the brightness of the picture aren't quite right, click the AutoCorrect button.

6. If the AutoCorrect feature doesn't work or if you need to make other adjustments, click the Edit Pictures button, and use the tools in the Edit Pictures pane to adjust the brightness, contrast, color, rotation, and size; to remove "red eye"; or to crop the picture.

7. Choose Save or Save As from the File menu to save your edits of the picture.

8. To change the view of the picture or pictures, choose Thumbnails or Filmstrip from the View menu.

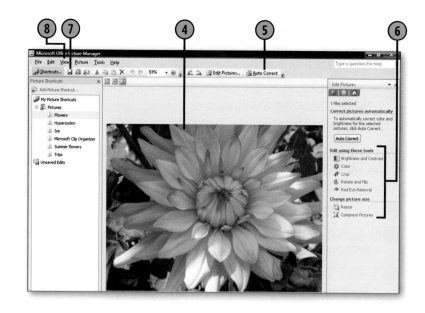

Linking to a File or to a Web Page

A hyperlink, often called a *link* or a *jump,* creates a connection from your document, workbook, publication, presentation, database, or message to other files or to Web pages.

Link to the File or to the Web Page

1. Type and select the text you want to use as a hyperlink.

2. On the Insert tab, click the Hyperlink button. In Publisher, click the Insert Hyperlink button on the Standard toolbar.

3. In the Insert Hyperlink dialog box, click Existing File Or Web Page.

4. Click a category to locate the file you want to link to:

   - Current Folder to link to a file in your default document folder, or to locate a file in another folder on your computer or network

   - Browsed Pages to link to Web pages you've visited or files you've opened

   - Recent Files to link to files you've used recently

5. Use the Browse tools to locate a Web page or to move to the correct folder if the file you want is in a different folder.

6. Click the file or the Web page you're linking to.

7. Click the ScreenTip button, type a short description of the link, and click OK.

8. Click OK.

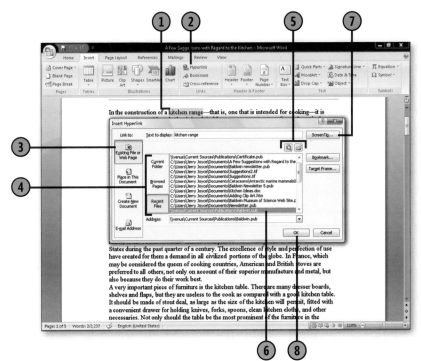

Managing Pictures, Videos, and Sound Files

The Microsoft Clip Organizer catalogs and provides easy access to your media files. The Clip Organizer uses the folders on your computer that contain the media as the basis for cataloging the files, treating each folder as a separate collection. You can add custom collections and can rearrange the catalog as you want, after which you'll be able to access your media files directly from the Clip Art pane in your program.

Organize Your Clips

① Start the Microsoft Clip Organizer from the Windows Start menu.

② To add picture files and other media files to the Clip Organizer, point to Add Clips To Organizer on the File menu, and choose the way you want to add the clips:

- Automatically to have the Clip Organizer search the hard drive or drives for all your picture files and media files

- On My Own to manually select all the picture files and media files that you want to add

- From Scanner Or Camera to add scanned pictures or to download pictures from your camera

③ In a collection, right-click a media file, and choose Edit Keywords to display the Keywords dialog box.

④ Modify the caption and keywords for the current media file, and click Apply. Click Next to preview the next media file in the collection, and make any changes you want to the caption and keywords. Continue going through all the media files in the collection, and click OK when you've finished.

⑤ Close the Clip Organizer.

⑥ In your Office programs, use the Clip Art pane to locate a media file by searching for its keyword or keywords, just as you'd search for a piece of clip art.

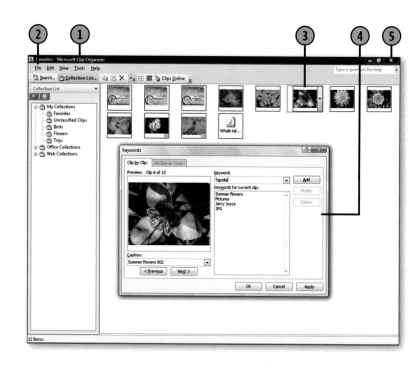

16

Customizing and Securing Office

In this section:

- Customizing the Quick Access Toolbar
- Customizing the Window
- Changing Your User Information
- Customizing the Spelling and Grammar Checkers
- Customizing Your Spelling Dictionaries
- Protecting a Document, Workbook, or Presentation with a Password
- Signing a Document or Workbook with a Visible Signature
- Downloading Free Software
- Adding or Removing Office Components
- Checking the Compatibility
- Fixing Office

You can customize almost anything in the 2007 Microsoft Office System programs. You can load up the Quick Access toolbar with items you use frequently; customize the program windows to have each file open in its own window, or use only one window to switch among files; show or hide items on the status bar; and change the overall color scheme for the program window. You can change the editing settings to suit your working style; change the user information that Office inserts into your files; customize the spelling and grammar checkers so that they're appropriate for the type of work you do; customize your spelling dictionaries; and change the locations where the programs store your files.

If people who use earlier versions of Office need access to your files, you can save those files in a compatible format. You can protect your files with a password, using various levels of protection that dictate the type of access you'll allow. You'll find information in this section about using *digital IDs* and *digital certificates* as well as ways to protect your system from malicious macros and other evils. We'll also show you how to add or remove Office components, download free software, check compatibility issues, and run diagnostics to fix Office if or when something goes wrong.

Customizing the Quick Access Toolbar

In Word, Excel, PowerPoint, and Access, and in the Outlook Editor, the Quick Access toolbar is the place to keep the items that you not only need to access quickly but want to be immediately available regardless of which of the Ribbon's tabs you're working on. If you put so many items on the Quick Access toolbar that it becomes too big to fit on the title bar, you can move it onto its own line.

Add or Remove Items Common to the Quick Access Toolbar

① Click the down arrow at the right of the Quick Access toolbar.

② On the Customize Quick Access Toolbar menu, click to select any unchecked items that you want to add to the toolbar.

③ Click any checked items that you want to remove from the toolbar.

④ Right-click any item anywhere on the Ribbon that you want to add to the toolbar, and choose Add To Quick Access Toolbar from the shortcut menu.

⑤ If the toolbar becomes too large to fit on the title bar or if you want easier access to it, click the down arrow at the right of the toolbar, and click Show Below The Ribbon on the menu.

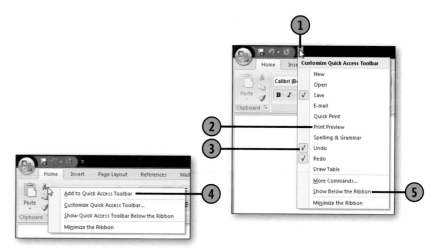

The Quick Access toolbar on its own line

See Also

"Using the Ribbon" on pages 10–11 for information about minimizing the Ribbon when you don't need it.

Control the Customization

(1) Click the down arrow at the right of the Quick Access toolbar, and, on the Customize Quick Access Toolbar menu, click More Commands to display the program's Options dialog box with the Customize category selected in the left pane.

(2) Specify where you want to save the changes to the toolbar.

(3) Specify the category of commands you want to select from.

(4) Click a command that you want to add to the toolbar.

(5) Click Add.

(6) To remove a command you don't use, select it, and click Remove.

(7) To change the order in which commands will appear on the toolbar, click a command, and use the up or down arrow to move the command.

(8) Repeat steps 3 through 7 to make any further customizations to the Quick Access toolbar. Click OK when you've finished.

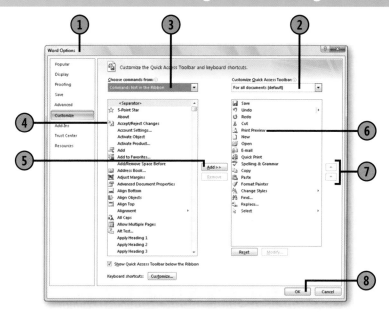

Tip

You're not limited to standard commands on the Quick Access toolbar. You can include styles, fonts, macros, and many items that aren't available from the Ribbon.

Tip

When you add or delete items using the Customize Quick Access Toolbar menu or the shortcut menu on the Ribbon, you'll see that version of the toolbar in all your documents. If you want to see that version of the toolbar in the current document only, use the program's Options dialog box to specify that you want to save these changes in the current document only.

Customizing the Window

The program window is where you do your work, so you'll probably want to customize it to fit your work habits and working style. In Word, Excel, PowerPoint, and Access, and in the Outlook Editor, you can show or hide items on the status bar, set the Ribbon to appear only when you need to use it, change the overall color scheme for the window, and so on.

Show or Hide Items on the Status Bar

① Right-click anywhere on the status bar.

② Review the information on the Customize Status Bar menu.

③ To show an item that isn't currently displayed on the status bar, click the item.

④ To hide an item that's currently displayed, click the item.

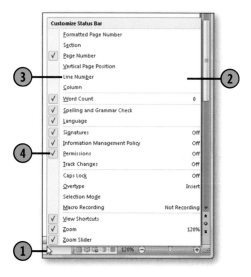

Change the Window's Color Scheme

① Click the Office button, and click the program's Options button on the menu to display the program's Options dialog box.

② With the Popular category selected in the left pane, specify the color scheme you want.

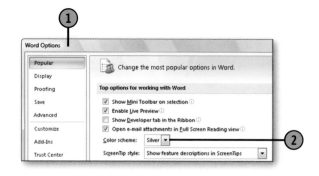

Change What's Shown

① Click the Advanced category in the left pane.

② In the Display category, select the number of files you used recently that are displayed on the Office menu.

③ In Word and Excel, and in the Outlook Editor, select the units of measurement if you want to use units different from the default units for your country or region.

④ Select this check box if you want each open file in this program to have its own window and its own button on the Windows taskbar; clear the check box if you want only one window for the program so that you can switch among open files.

⑤ Make any other display settings that are specific to your program.

⑥ In Word or in the Outlook Editor, click the Display category, and select the formatting marks you want to be displayed. In Word, select any other items you want to be displayed.

⑦ Click OK.

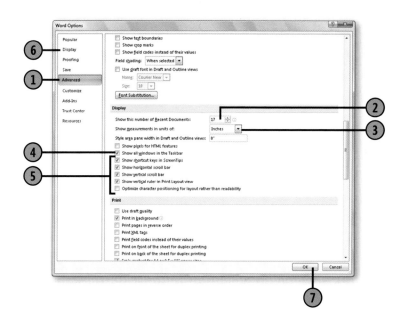

Tip

Each program has different settings in its Display section because each program displays different types of information in its own way. Explore the different areas of the Advanced category to see the extent to which you can customize each program.

Customizing Your Editing

Your Office programs are set up to use the most common editing settings that, in most cases, make your work easy and produce fine results. However, if there are some settings that aren't exactly right for your working style, or if you need to adjust settings to comply with a design or some other specification, you can easily modify the editing settings. Each Office program has its own type of settings, but some universal settings apply to all or most of the programs.

Adjust the Settings

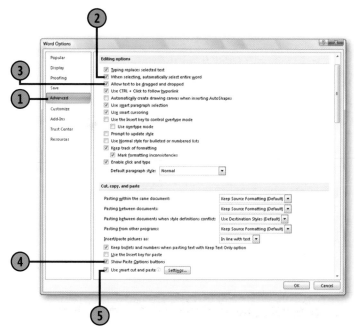

1. Click the Office button, click the program's Options button on the menu, and, in the program's Options dialog box, click the Advanced category. In Publisher, choose Options from the Tools menu to display the Options dialog box, and click the Edit tab.

2. In Word, PowerPoint, and Publisher, and in the Outlook Editor, select this check box to select whole words when only a part of a word is selected but the selection extends outside of a word. Clear the check box to select portions of adjacent words.

3. In Word, Excel, PowerPoint, and Publisher, and in the Outlook Editor, select this check box to allow dragging content to a new location. In Excel, select the Enable Fill Handle And Cell Drag-And-Drop check box.

4. In Word, Excel, PowerPoint, and Publisher, and in the Outlook Editor, select this check box to display the Paste Options actions button that lets you modify the way content is pasted into your files.

5. In Word and PowerPoint, and in the Outlook Editor, select this check box to use the Smart Cut And Paste feature so that the formatting of the pasted content will match the formatting in the destination file. In Word or in the Outlook Editor, click the Settings button to adjust the way the Smart Cut And Paste feature works. Continue adjusting any program-specific settings, and then click OK.

Changing Your User Information

Office programs routinely insert certain information into your files, using data that you've supplied. For example, when you're reviewing a file, your name and/or your initials are used to identify your comments. However, all that automation is useless if the information you supplied is incorrect or nonexistent. Fortunately, you can easily correct or add the information.

Change Your Name and Address

① In Word, Excel, PowerPoint, and Access, and in the Outlook Editor, click the Office button, click the program's Options button on the menu, and, in the Options dialog box, click the Popular category in the left pane, if it isn't already selected.

② If your name is incorrect, select it, and type your correct name.

③ To change or correct your initials in any program except Excel, select the initials, and then type the initials you want to use.

④ In Word, click the Advanced category.

⑤ In the General section, enter, correct, or replace your mailing address.

⑥ Click OK.

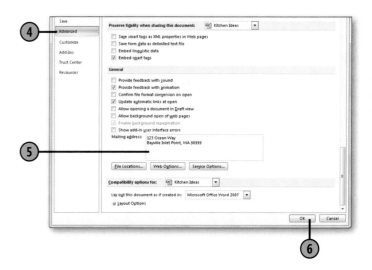

> **See Also**
>
> "Inserting Your Business Information" on page 259 for information about entering your name and business information in Publisher.

Customizing the Spelling and Grammar Checkers

Depending on the type of file you're creating, you might need to tailor the levels of spelling and grammar checking to make them appropriate for that type of file. You can customize the types of checking the program does, and you can even designate certain text not to be checked at all.

Specify What's to Be Checked

(1) Click the Office button, click the program's Options button on the menu, and, in the program's Options dialog box, click the Proofing category. In Publisher, point to Spelling on the Tools menu, and choose Spelling Options from the submenu.

(2) In Word, PowerPoint, and Publisher, and in the Outlook Editor, select this check box to instruct the program to check the spelling of each word as you type it.

(3) In Word and PowerPoint, and in the Outlook Editor, select this check box to instruct the program to check spelling based on the context in which a word is used (for example, to detect whether "form" should be used instead of "from").

(4) Select the options to be included in the spelling check.

(5) In Word or in the Outlook Editor, select these check boxes to have each phrase and sentence checked for proper grammar as it's completed and to have your grammar checked whenever the program checks your spelling. Specify whether you want the program to check grammar alone or grammar together with writing style. Click Settings to define the grammar rules you want Word to use to check your document.

(6) In Word, PowerPoint, and Publisher, and in the Outlook Editor, specify if and when you want spelling errors not to be displayed; and, in Word or in the Outlook Editor, if and when you want grammar errors not to be displayed.

(7) Click OK to use your new settings.

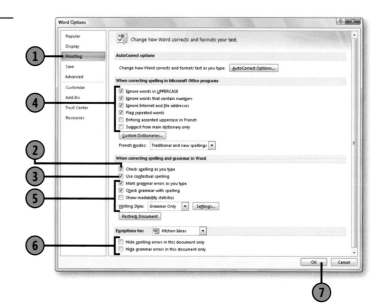

Tip

Click the Recheck Document button if you previously told Word to ignore misspellings or grammatical errors in this document but you now want any errors to be marked.

Customizing Your Spelling Dictionaries

The Office programs use one or more dictionaries to check your spelling. When there's a word in your file that's correct but that isn't recognized—an unfamiliar technical or scientific term, for example—you can tell your program to add that word to your custom dictionary. If you already have a custom dictionary that includes those words or terms, you can add that dictionary to the list of dictionaries you're using. Also, if you discover any incorrectly spelled words in your dictionary, replace them with the correct spelling; otherwise, your program will consider the incorrect spelling to be correct.

Add a Dictionary

① Click the Office button, click the program's Options button on the menu, and, in the program's Options dialog box, click the Proofing category in the left pane. In Publisher, point to Spelling on the Tools menu, and choose Spelling Options from the submenu. Click the Custom Dictionaries button to display the Custom Dictionaries dialog box.

② If there's an existing dictionary you want to use, click Add, and, in the Add Custom Dictionary dialog box that appears, locate the dictionary file. Click Open.

③ Select the language for an added dictionary if you want it to be used only for that specific language.

④ To create a dictionary by adding entries, click New, use the Create Custom Dictionary dialog box to name the dictionary file, and click Save.

⑤ To add or delete words in a dictionary, select the dictionary, and click Edit Word List.

⑥ Do either of the following:
- Type a word you want to add, and click Add.
- Select a word you want to remove, and click Delete.

⑦ Click OK.

⑧ Verify that the dictionaries you want to use are checked and that those you don't want to use aren't checked.

⑨ Click OK.

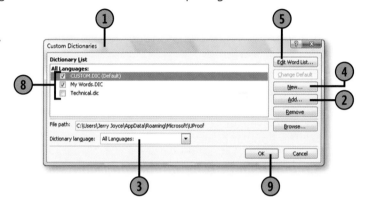

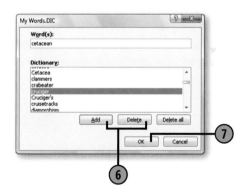

Changing the Location and Type of Saved Files

If you don't like the locations where Word, Excel, PowerPoint, or Access proposes to store your files, you can change those locations and create the organization that works best for you. And if you're working with other people who require access to your files in a different version of Office, you can set the default format so that your files are in a format that's fully compatible with earlier versions of these programs. If you consistently save your Word files in a format other than the Word 2007 format, you should modify the Compatibility settings on the Advanced tab of the Word Options dialog box so that your documents have the correct layout for the format in which you save them.

Change the File Locations and Formats

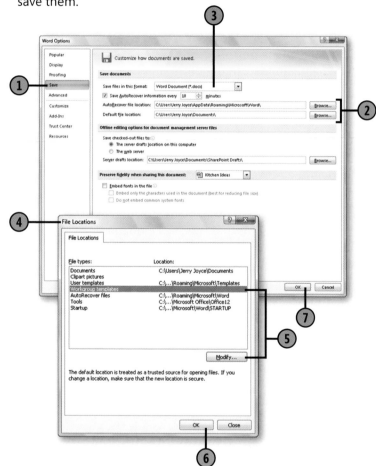

(1) Click the Office button, and click the program's Options button on the menu to display the program's Options dialog box. In Word, Excel, and PowerPoint, click the Save category in the left pane. In Access, click the Popular category.

(2) For each file location you want to change, enter the new location; or click the Browse button (if there is one), locate the destination folder, and click OK.

(3) Select the default format in which you want to save your files.

(4) In Word, to change the location of other types of files, click the Advanced category in the left pane, and, in the General section, click the File Locations button to display the File Locations dialog box.

(5) Click the item whose location you want to change, click Modify, and, in the Modify Location dialog box, locate and select the folder that you're designating as the new location; click OK.

(6) Specify the location for any other file types, and click OK when you've finished.

(7) Click OK to close the program's Options dialog box.

Safeguarding a Document

At one time or another, you've probably lost some work on your computer. Whether you forgot to save a file or were the victim of a power outage, it's a frustrating and depressing experience that you vow will never happen again. You can safeguard your work and prevent most losses by using the AutoRecover feature, which remembers to save files even when you don't.

Set Up the Safeguards

① In Word, Excel, and PowerPoint, click the Office button, click the program's Options button on the menu, and, in the program's Options dialog box, click the Save category in the left pane. In Publisher, choose Options from the Tools menu, and click the Save tab of the Options dialog box.

② Select this check box if it isn't already selected.

③ Set a short interval to specify how often you want the AutoRecover information to be saved.

④ Make any program-specific settings for AutoRecover.

⑤ Click OK.

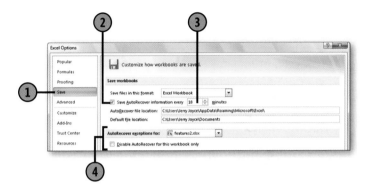

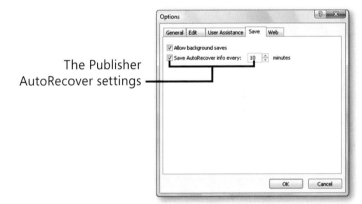

The Publisher AutoRecover settings

Tip ✓

In Word, you can further safeguard your files by automatically creating a backup copy of your document each time you save it. You can also create a local copy of a document that you've opened from a network location. Make these settings in the Save section of the Advanced category in the Word Options dialog box.

Protecting a Document, Workbook, or Presentation with a Password

If your file contains sensitive information that you don't want anyone else to see, you can *encrypt* the file so that no one can access its contents unless you give them the password you've created. You can further protect the file by allowing access to it but requiring a password to control who may make and save changes to the document, workbook, or presentation.

Encrypt the Document, Workbook, or Presentation

1. With your document, workbook, or presentation completed and saved, click the Office button, point to Prepare on the menu, and choose Encrypt Document to display the Encrypt Document dialog box.

2. Enter a password.

3. Click OK, enter the password again in the Confirm Password dialog box that appears, and click OK.

4. Make any changes you want, saving the file occasionally, and then close it.

5. When you want to work on the document, workbook, or presentation again, open it and, in the Password dialog box that appears, enter the password.

6. Click OK to gain access to the file.

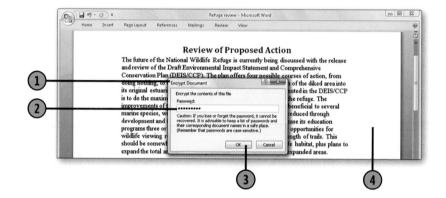

Caution

You won't be able to open an encrypted file without the password, so either keep an unencrypted copy of the file in a secure location or write down the password and store it in a safe place.

Protect the Document, Workbook, or Presentation from Modifications

(1) With your document, workbook, or presentation completed, click the Office button, and choose Save As from the menu to display the Save As window.

(2) Enter a name for the file.

(3) Click Tools, and choose General Options from the drop-down menu.

(4) In the General Options dialog box that appears, enter a password if you want to require a password to open the document, workbook, or presentation. Enter the password again when prompted, and click OK.

(5) Enter a different password if you want to require a password to save changes to the document, workbook, or presentation. Enter the password again when prompted, and click OK.

(6) Click OK.

(7) Click Save.

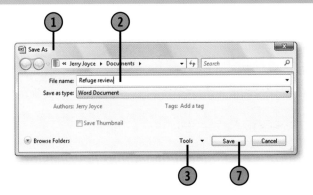

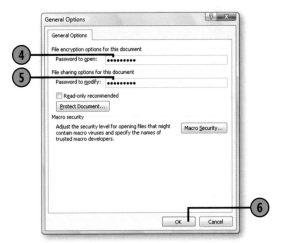

Signing a Document or Workbook with a Visible Signature

In the world of business and commerce, certain documents need to be signed and, often, witnessed. When a document is transmitted electronically, not only does it need to be signed, but the signature must be verifiable. Word and Excel take care of this in two ways. Each provides an easy way to set up an electronic document for a signature by either typing the signature or using a scanned image of the signature inserted as a picture. Additionally, both Word and Excel attach a *digital certificate* that has been issued to the signer from a reliable source. The digital certificate verifies the identity of the signer. With the digital certificate attached, the document or workbook is considered digitally signed. To prevent any alterations to the file after it has been signed, the digital signature is invalidated if any changes are made.

Set Up the Signature

(1) On the Insert tab, with your document or workbook completed and saved, and with the insertion point where you want the signature to appear, click the Signature Line button to display the Signature Setup dialog box.

(2) Enter the name and, optionally, the title and e-mail address of the suggested signer.

(3) Modify the instructions to the signer if you want.

(4) Specify whether you want to allow the signer to add comments when signing the file.

(5) Specify whether you want to include the date on which the file was signed.

(6) Click OK. Save and close the document or workbook. If the file is intended for someone else's signature, send it to that person.

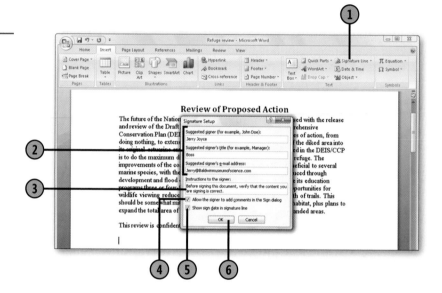

> **Tip**
>
> The typed or scanned image of a signature is used only to visually indicate who signed the document. It's the digital certificate that accompanies the document that provides the proof that the document is digitally signed.

> **Tip**
>
> You need a digital certificate (also called a digital ID or a digital signature) to be able to digitally sign a document. If you try to sign a document without one, you'll be prompted either to purchase one from a third party or create your own. If you create your own certificate, it will be available to validate your signature on your computer only.

Sign the Document

① Open the file that has been prepared for your signature, and double-click the signature line.

② In the Sign dialog box that appears, do either of the following:

- Type your name in the box.

- Click Select Image, and use the Select Signature Image dialog box to locate the picture file that contains your signature. Click Open in the dialog box to insert the signature image.

③ If the text box that states the purpose of signing is shown, click in the box, and enter any information you want.

④ Verify that this digital signature name is the name of the digital certificate you want to use to verify your identity. If it isn't, click Change, and, in the Select Certificate dialog box, select the digital certificate you want. Click OK.

⑤ Click Sign, and save the file.

⑥ Send the digitally signed file to whoever required you to sign it. The digital certificate will accompany the file, and the recipient will be able to examine the certificate to verify that you signed it and that the file hasn't been altered since you signed the certificate.

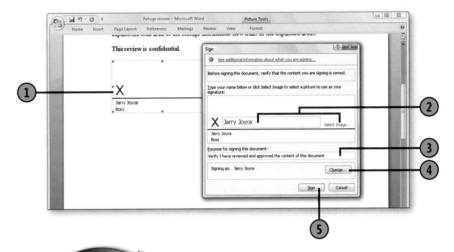

See Also

"Signing a Document, Workbook, or Presentation with a Digital Certificate" on page 330 for information about verifying that the digital signature is valid in a digitally signed document you've received.

Caution

A digital signature might or might not be recognized as a legal signature, depending on the type of document and your local laws.

Tip

There are various providers of digital signing certificates and other methods of digitally signing documents that might be legally recognized in many instances. To investigate these, click the down arrow at the right of the Signature Line button, and choose Add Signature Services from the menu.

Signing a Document, Workbook, or Presentation with a Digital Certificate

If you want to prove that a document, workbook, or presentation you're sending or sharing really does come from you and hasn't been changed by anyone since you finished it, you can include an invisible digital signature by attaching a digital certificate that verifies who you are. You'll need to have a digital certificate issued to you to be able to digitally sign a document, workbook, or presentation. In most cases, digital certificates are issued through a third-party certificate provider or a corporate network.

Attach a Digital Signature

1. With your document, workbook, or presentation completed and saved, and with the insertion point where you want the digital signature to appear, click the Office button, point to Prepare on the menu, and choose Add A Digital Signature from the gallery to display the Sign dialog box.

2. If you want, type a note stating the reason for signing the file.

3. Verify that the digital signature is the one you want. If it isn't, click Change, and, in the Select Certificate dialog box, select the certificate you want. Click OK.

4. Click Sign. Close the document, workbook, or presentation, and then distribute or share it.

5. To verify that the digital signature is valid, open the file, click the Office button, point to Prepare, and choose View Signatures from the gallery to display the Signatures pane.

6. In the Signatures pane, point to the signature name, click the down arrow that appears, and choose Signature Details to display the Signature Details dialog box to verify the signature. Close the dialog box when you've finished.

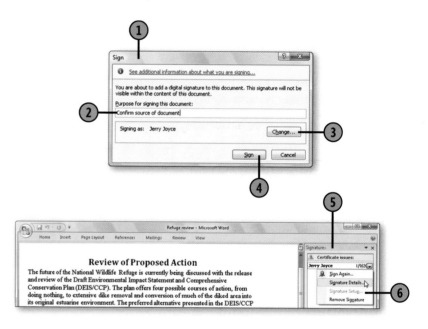

See Also

"Signing a Document or Workbook with a Visible Signature" on pages 328–329 for information about obtaining a digital certificate to digitally sign a document, workbook, or presentation.

Controlling Macros, Add-Ins, and ActiveX Controls

Macros are programs you use to automate actions in other programs—repeating a series of commands, for example. *Add-ins* are programs or other items—more smart tags, for example—that you can add to your program to extend its capabilities. *ActiveX controls* are items that provide extra functionality—displaying special dialog boxes or toolbars, for example. Unfortunately, sometimes these items either are so poorly written that they cause operational problems or are

written maliciously with the explicit intention of causing harm. To combat these risks, Word provides very strong protections against malfunctioning and malicious macros, add-ins, and ActiveX controls. However, these protections sometimes prevent good and effective tools from being used, so you might need to adjust your security settings to balance security and functionality.

Modify the Settings

1 In Word, Excel, PowerPoint, and Access, click the Office button, and click the program's Options button on the menu. In the Options dialog box, click the Trust Center category in the left pane, and click the Trust Center Settings button to display the Trust Center dialog box. In Outlook and Publisher, choose Trust Center from the Tools menu.

2 Click the Add-Ins category, and select this check box if you want to require that all add-ins come from a trusted source. Each time an add-in from another source tries to be used, you'll be asked whether you want to use it.

3 In Word, Excel, and PowerPoint, click the ActiveX Settings category, and select the level of security you want for ActiveX controls.

4 Select this check box if it isn't already selected.

5 Click the Macro Settings category, and select the level of security you want for macros.

6 Click any categories that are specific to the program, and make the changes you want.

7 Click OK to close the Trust Center dialog box, and, in Word, Excel, PowerPoint, and Access, click OK again to close the Options dialog box.

Downloading Add-Ins and Other Free Software

Microsoft and its partners are continually developing tools, utilities, and other items that make it possible for Office to work better, run more effectively, and just do more things. Many such items are available as free downloads from the Microsoft Office Online Web site. Your search can yield some pretty interesting items related to just about any Office product, including trial versions of many of Microsoft's programs.

Download the Software

① In Word, Excel, PowerPoint, and Access, click the Office button, and click the program's Options button on the menu. In the Options dialog box, click the Resources category, and, in the Go To Microsoft Office Online section, click the Go Online button to open the Microsoft Office Online Web page.

② Click the Downloads tab to review the available downloads.

③ Click a download. If you don't see the download you want, either click a category to browse for downloads, or enter the name of the download in the Search box and click Search.

④ Review the information about the download and the instructions for downloading and installing the item.

⑤ If you receive a warning in the Information bar, click the bar, and select the action you want to take. In most cases at these Microsoft sites, the warning asks you to install the ActiveX control required for the download.

⑥ Click Download, and follow the directions on the screen.

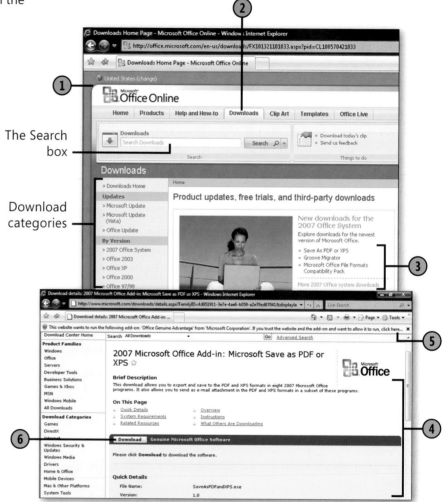

The Search box

Download categories

Adding or Removing Office Components

Office 2007 provides such a multitude of components that you probably haven't needed or wanted to install all of them on your computer. You can install additional components on an as-needed basis or remove components that you never use so as to save some hard-disk space.

Add or Remove Components

1 With all your Office programs closed, open the Control Panel from the Windows Start menu, click Programs, and then click Programs And Features to display the Programs And Features window. Click your Office program in the list, and click the Change button to display the Microsoft Office window. In the Change Your Installation Wizard that appears, click the Add Or Remove Features option, and click Continue.

2 Click the plus signs to expand the outline of the components until you find the item you want to add or remove.

3 Click the down arrow to display the installation choices, and specify a choice. Repeat for any other components you want to change.

4 Click Continue, and wait for the installation to be completed.

5 Start each of the Office programs to which you've made changes, and verify that the component or components have been installed or uninstalled.

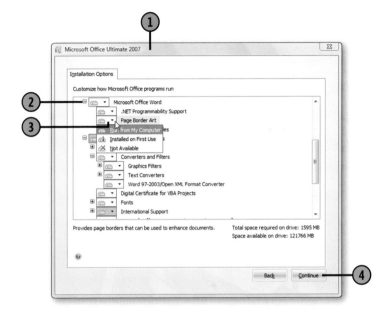

Tip

If a component is set to be installed on first use, it will be automatically installed when you need it, provided you have access to the Microsoft Office disc or the network installation files.

Tip

If you're running Windows XP, click the Add Or Remove Programs category in the Control Panel to display the Add Or Remove Programs window. With the Change Or Remove Programs tab selected, click your Office program.

Checking the Compatibility

The Word, Excel, and PowerPoint 2007 file formats and some of their features aren't fully compatible with earlier versions of the programs. Although people running earlier versions will be able to open these Office 2007 files using a converter (provided they've installed it, of course), some features and/or content might be changed or lost. To see which features aren't fully compatible and will be changed or lost, run the Compatibility Checker before you distribute the document, workbook, or presentation.

Run the Check

1. With your document, workbook, or presentation completed and saved, click the Office button.

2. On the Office menu, point to Prepare, and choose Run Compatibility Checker to display the Microsoft Office Compatibility Checker dialog box for that program.

3. Scroll through the list of items that will be changed or lost.

4. Click OK.

5. If you're not sure whether the changes are acceptable, point to Save As on the Office menu, and click the program's 97–2003 format in the gallery that appears. In the Save As dialog box, enter a different name for the file, and click Save. Scroll through your file and examine the changes to see whether they're acceptable. If they are, distribute your original file; if they aren't, edit the file to eliminate the incompatibilities.

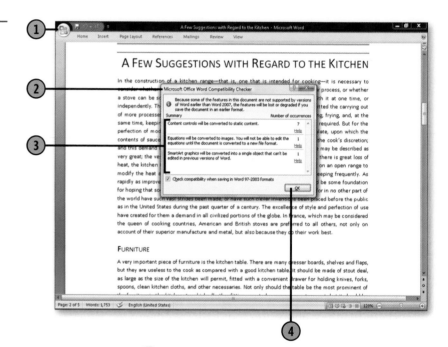

See Also

"Finalizing Your Document" on page 104 for information about preparing a file for distribution.

Tip

If you select the check box for checking compatibility in the Compatibility Checker dialog box, this compatibility check will be run automatically any time you save a file that was created in the Office 2007 format in an Office 97–2003 format.

Fixing Office

Although the Microsoft Office programs are robust programs, once in a while things can go wrong. Sometimes a problem might be severe enough to cause your computer to crash— that is, to shut down. This type of problem might be caused by a program or a support file on your hard disk being corrupted, or there might be something wrong with your computer itself. When any Office component isn't working properly, you can run a series of diagnostic tests to find out what's wrong and, usually, learn how to fix the problem, unless Office fixes it automatically.

Run the Diagnostics

(1) Close any running programs except for a single blank Word, Excel, or PowerPoint file.

(2) Click the Office button, click the program's Options button on the menu to display the program's Options dialog box, and click the Resources category. Click the Diagnose button to display the Microsoft Office Diagnostics Wizard.

(3) Click Run Diagnostics, and wait for the series of diagnostic tests to be completed.

(4) Review the results, and note any item where the wizard found a problem.

(5) Click Continue if you need to go to the Office Online Web site for additional help and tools.

(6) If no cause was found for the problem you're having, and if the Office Online Web site didn't offer a solution, try using the tools in Windows to diagnose and solve your problem and to run full scans for viruses, spyware, and other malware.

Caution

Running the diagnostics can take a long time, so make sure that you won't need to use your computer immediately after you start the diagnostics.

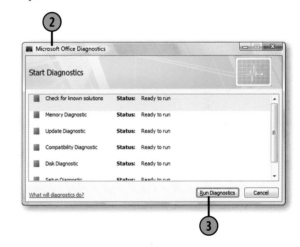

Index

* (asterisk), 132, 134
^ (caret), 134
= (equal sign), 132, 134
- (minus sign), 134
( ) (parentheses), 134
% (percent sign), 134
+ (plus sign), 134
/ (slash), 132, 134
1-page spreads, 250
2-page spreads, 250
2-sided documents, 66, 79
2-sided printing, 264
3-D effects
    charts, 153
    Publisher options, 252
    WordArt options, 32
3-D rotation, 27

A

absolute cell references, 109, 133, 137
.accdb files (Access), 275
accepting
    changes in Word, 55
    tasks, 236
Access. *See also* databases
    add-ins, 331
    analyzing data in Excel, 302
    customizing windows, 318–19
    default file formats, 324
    default file locations, 324
    downloading add-ins and utilities, 332
    Export Wizard, 301, 302
    exporting data for mail merge, 304
    file formats, 275, 324

Get External Data Wizard, 303
    importing Excel data into, 303
    integration with other products, 275
    macros, 290, 331
    overview, 8
    PivotCharts, 286–87
    presenting data in Word, 301
    relational database overview, 268
    Ribbon, 10
    saving files, 19
    screen elements, 266–67
    user information, 321
accounting number formats, 113
accounts, e-mail, 216–17
Action Buttons in presentations, 197
actions
    assigning to slides, 175
    compared to smart tags, 91
    order of, 134
ActiveX controls, 331, 332
adding numbers, 136
add-ins
    downloading, 332
    security, 331
addition, 134, 136
addresses. *See also* mail merge feature
    business cards, 238
    business information in Publisher, 259
    Contacts folder, 223
    editing, 321
    e-mail, 204, 233
    envelopes, 99
    mail merge, 101, 102
    mailing labels, 100
    meeting invitations, 230
    RSS feeds, 215

separating mailing lists into
    columns, 144
    smart tags and, 91
    user information, 321
    validating, 231
Adjustment handles, 28, 33
advertising blurbs, 28
alerts. *See* troubleshooting
aligning
    chart elements, 155
    keyboard shortcuts for, 15
    paragraphs in Word, 63
    snapping items to grids and guides, 254
    text in Excel cells, 111, 120
    text in Publisher, 255
    text in Word, 58
    text on slides, 170
alphabetical order
    sorting Excel data, 142
    sorting Word tables or lists, 85
animation
    adding to presentations, 161
    customizing, 174
    running in presentations, 188
    slide effects, 172–73
    transitions between slides, 179
    turning on or off, 191
annotations and comments
    balloon comments, 54
    copying, 115
    deleting, 199, 309
    discarding, 200
    displaying, 190
    editing, 309
    in faxes, 309
    Full Screen Reading view, 16

annotations and comments, *continued*
  hiding, 190
  inserting into presentations, 199
  inserting into reviewed documents, 54
  inserting into scanned or faxed files, 308, 309
  inserting into slides, 189
  inserting into worksheets, 128
  resizing, 309
antivirus programs, 209
append-only memo fields, 275
appointments, scheduling 218, 222, 223, 225
Archive Packages, 196
archiving presentations, 196
arguments
  in functions, 139
  in macros, 290
arithmetic, 134–35
arranging. *See* moving; re-ordering
arrow styles, 30, 252
arrows for Excel cell references, 140
ascending sort orders, 85
assigning tasks, 236
asterisk (*), 132, 134
attachments, 208–9, 219, 227, 275
attendees for meetings, 230–31
audio clips
  Action Buttons, 197
  assigning actions, 175
  in Clip Organizer, 169, 314
  narration, 192
  playing in presentations, 168, 169
  playing during transitions, 174, 179
auditing formulas, 140–41
AutoCorrect feature (Picture Manager), 312
AutoCorrect feature (Word), 50, 91
AutoDialer feature (Outlook), 233

AutoFill feature (Excel), 115, 118, 131, 133, 137
AutoFit feature (Excel), 121
AutoFlow feature (Publisher), 246
AutoRecover feature (Office), 325
AutoShapes feature (Office), 28, 30, 252
AutoSum feature (Excel), 136
averaging numbers, 136
axes in Excel charts, 151, 153, 157

B

backgrounds
  Excel charts, 153
  Excel pictures, 120
  PowerPoint slides, 161, 170, 171
  Publisher master pages, 250
  Publisher publications, 244
backing up files, 325
back-to-back page layouts, 79
back-to-back printing, 264
balloon comments, 54
bar tabs, 67
baseline guides, 254, 255
bibliographic notes, 96–97
binary files, 20
Binary Workbook file format, 20
bitmaps, 294
black-and-white pictures, 251
black screens in presentations, 200
blank documents, 40
blank e-mail messages, 204
blank lines for handout notes, 186
blank lines in Outlook notes, 237
blank presentations, 161
blank publications, 244
blank slides, 177
blank workbooks, 107
bleeds, 264

blue squiggles, 48, 49
bold text, 15, 58, 68, 206, 210, 211
BorderArt, 252
borders
  BorderArt, 252
  Excel cells, 111
  graphics, 27
  paragraphs, 58
  shapes, 30
  slide tables, 164
  SmartArt, 35, 165
  Word table cells, 76
  WordArt, 33, 166
bound documents, 79
brightness of pictures, 26, 182, 251, 312
Browser, 39
browsing Help topics, 18
bulleted lists
  bullet shapes, 58
  converting to SmartArt, 165
  creating, 70
  formatting, 71
  on slides, 170
business cards, 223, 238–39
Business Information Sets, 259
buttons
  presentation navigation buttons, 197
  on toolbars. *See* toolbars and toolbar buttons

C

calculations
  averaging, counting, or summing, 136
  formulas, 132–33
  functions, 138–39
  mathematical, 134–35
  performing series of, 137
  PivotTables and, 146
  subtotals, 145

Calendar folder, 223, 230–31
Calendar view, 225
calendars
    iCalendars, 226–27
    reviewing, 222
    selecting, 31
    sending via e-mail, 218–19
    sharing, 226–27
callouts, 28, 30
canceling
    dialog-box choices, 9
    keyboard-shortcut selections, 14
captions
    media files, 314
    photos in PowerPoint, 182
capturing pictures of slides, 198
caret (^), 134
cases of text, 15
categories
    clip art, 29
    Content Library, 258
    databases, 271
    templates, 41
category axes in charts, 151
cautions
    buttons on toolbars, 240
    collecting data with e-mail, 288
    combining chart types, 156
    contact e-mail addresses, 233
    converting older files, 22
    copying formatting, 69
    deleting portions of tables, 75
    digital signatures, 329
    e-mail attachments, 208
    e-mail formatting, 205
    errors in formulas, 135
    hyperlinks, 210
    paragraph spacing, 65
    passwording files, 326–27

PowerPoint 97–2003 file format, 196
research services, 36
restoring pictures, 27
Rich Text formatting, 210
running diagnostics, 335
scheduling meetings, 231
viruses, 209
CDs
    accessing in presentations, 168, 169
    packaging slide shows on, 196
cell notation, 129
cell ranges
    PivotTables, 146
    selecting, 132, 139
cell references, 109, 132–33, 140
cells (Excel)
    addresses, 132
    cell notation, 129
    cell ranges, 132, 139, 146
    cell references, 109, 132–33, 140
    conditional formatting, 149
    copying contents, 114–15
    defined, 105, 109
    deleting contents, 117
    dragging and dropping, 320
    editing, 108
    formatting, 111
    highlighting, 149
    moving contents, 114–15
    naming, 132
    numeric values, 135
    resizing, 120–21
    selecting, 106
    sorting, 142
    text alignment, 120
    values, 135
cells (Word tables)
    formatting, 76
    moving to, 72

centered tabs, 67
centered text, 63
certificates, digital, 220, 328–30
chapters in Word documents, 82
character formatting, 60, 69
character spacing, 58
character styles
    bulleted and numbered lists, 71
    formatting text with, 58
    symbols for, 61
characters
    kerning, 248
    selecting, 52
    spacing between, 248
    symbols. See special characters and
        symbols
charges for research services, 36
charts
    adding axes, 157
    animation, 173
    combining multiple types in one
        chart, 156
    creating, 152–53
    customizing, 156–57
    editing data in, 153
    formatting, 154
    formatting elements, 155
    illustrated, 106
    inserting into slides, 163
    layouts, 152–53
    moving to separate pages, 152
    overview, 151
    pasting into other programs, 294
    PivotCharts, 147, 286–87
    selecting elements, 155
    switching types, 287
    themes, 154
check boxes, 9

checking spelling. *See* spelling
circular references, 140
citations, 96–97
classifications. *See* categories
clearing Clipboard, 17
clicking
    assigning actions for, 175
    navigating through slides by, 200
clip art
    Clip Organizer, 8, 169, 314
    Clip Art objects, 242, 314
    formatting, 252
    inserting, 29, 163
Clip Organizer, 8, 169, 314
Clip Art objects, 242, 314
Clipboard, 16–17
clips, media. *See* media clips
closing
    dialog boxes, 9
    menus, 12
collaboration
    combining changes from different
      reviewers, 55
    comments in Excel workbooks, 128
    comments in Word documents, 39
    comparing versions of documents, 55,
      56
    converting older files, 20, 22, 34, 275,
      324, 334
    creating groups for Outlook
      scheduling, 228
    reviewing presentations, 199
    reviewing publications, 262
    sharing calendars, 226–27
    tracking changes, 54–55
    viewing group schedules, 228–29
collapsing outlines, 86
Collect Data Through E-Mail Messages
    Wizard, 288–89

color schemes
    publications, 244
    windows in programs, 318
color separations, 264
colors
    annotation ink, 309
    e-mail text, 210, 211
    graphics, 26, 251, 312
    modifying themes, 112
    in publications, 244, 252
    shading in Excel tables, 164
    shapes, 30
    slide backgrounds, 171
    slide schemes, 161
    slide text, 170
    speaker-note schemes, 184
    text in Excel cells, 111, 112, 148
    text in Word, 58, 68
    themes, 58, 59
    windows in programs, 318
    WordArt, 33
    worksheet tabs, 122
column breaks (Word text), 81
column guides (Publisher), 254
Columnar forms, 281
columns (Excel)
    adding or deleting, 116–17
    cell references and, 132
    defined, 109
    filtering, 143
    freezing, 158
    headings, 106, 158
    height, 120–21
    hiding or displaying, 119
    PivotTables, 147
    separating data into, 144
    sorting, 142
    subtotals, 145
    switching rows and columns, 143
    tables, 130–31

columns (PowerPoint slides), 170
columns (Word tables)
    deleting, 75
    formatting, 76
    sorting content, 85
columns (Word text), 81
combining
    changes from different reviewers, 55
    chart types in one chart, 156
command tabs, 7, 10–11, 14, 106
commands
    keyboard shortcuts, 14–15
    on menus, 12
    on Quick Access toolbar, 317
    on Ribbon, 7, 10–11, 14, 106
comma-separated data, 144
comments. *See* annotations and
    comments
commercial printers, 307
company logos on slides, 170
comparing documents, 55, 56
Compatibility Checker, 334
Compatibility mode, 22, 275, 324
Compatibility Pack, 22
completed tasks, 235, 236
composite printouts, 264
CompuServe 2000, 216
computers in meeting rooms, 230
condensing characters, 248
conditional expressions in mail merge,
    101, 102
conditional formatting in Excel, 148,
    149, 150
conference and meeting rooms, 223, 230
Connect Text Boxes toolbar, 242
Connect To A Network Projector
    Wizard, 187
connecting
    monitors, 187
    text boxes, 246–47

consistency in formatting, 63
contacts
    adding to groups, 228–29
    business cards, 238–39
    creating, 232–33
    e-mail address books, 204
    mail merging data from, 305
Contacts folder, 223, 232–33
content controls, 92, 97
Content Library, 5, 258
contextual spelling errors, 49
continuing text on later pages, 247
continuously cycling slide shows, 191
contrast in pictures, 26, 182, 251, 312
Convert Text To Columns Wizard, 144
converting
    cells into Excel tables, 130
    footnotes and endnotes, 95
    older files, 20, 22, 34, 275, 324, 334
    presentations to older file formats, 195
    scanned documents into text, 310
    SmartArt into pictures, 34
    tables into normal Excel cells, 131
    text documents into scanned
      images, 311
    text into Excel columns, 144
    text into SmartArt, 165
    text into Word tables, 74
    text into WordArt, 166
copying
    Access data, 274
    Access database tables, 276–77
    calculations, 137
    to Clipboard, 16–17
    comments, 115
    Content Library items, 258
    data into databases, 276–77
    e-mail messages, 213
    Excel cell contents, 115

Excel charts, 294
Excel data, 114–15, 292
Excel formulas, 115
Excel values, 115
    keyboard shortcuts, 15
    multiple items, 17
    notes, 237
    slides, 167, 297
    with Smart Cut And Paste feature, 320
    Word tables, 295
    Word text, 53, 300
    Word text formatting, 69
correcting spelling and grammar. *See*
    grammar; spelling
costs for research services, 36
cover pages, 88
crashing programs, 335
criteria
    in conditional formatting, 149
    filtering Excel data with, 143
cropping graphics, 25, 251
currency
    formatting in Excel, 113
    symbols, 23
customizing
    dictionaries, 323
    editing options, 320
    e-mail signatures, 214
    Excel charts, 156–57
    Excel data series, 118
    Outlook toolbars, 240
    paths to saved files, 324
    PowerPoint animation effects, 172–74
    PowerPoint presentations, 191, 194, 200
    PowerPoint slide layout, 180–81
    Quick Access toolbar, 316–17
    Ribbon display, 11
    spelling and grammar options, 322
    user information, 321

Word cover pages, 88
Word templates, 41
cutting
    Clipboard options, 16–17
    Excel data, 114
    with Smart Cut And Paste feature, 320

D

Daily Task List pane, 223, 234
data
    collecting with e-mail messages,
      288–89
    data sources for mail merge, 101, 102
    editing in Excel, 108
    series. *See* data series
    sorting in Word tables, 85
data bars (Excel), 148
data points, 109
data series
    animating, 173
    averaging, counting, or summing, 136
    creating in Excel, 118
    customizing charts, 156–57
    displaying in charts, 151
data sources for mail merge, 101, 102
databases. *See also* Access
    adding tables to, 272
    containing programming code, 275
    defining table relationships, 279
    encryption, 275
    entering data, 274
    exporting data to Excel, 278, 302
    exporting data to Word, 301
    forms, 280–81
    gathering data with e-mail, 288–89
    hyperlinks and, 313
    importing data from tables, 276–77
    importing Excel data, 303

databases, *continued*
  macros, 290
  modifying tables, 273
  Object window display, 267
  opening existing, 269
  PivotCharts, 286–87
  presenting data in Word, 301
  querying data, 284–85
  relational, 268
  reports, 282–83
  saving data as PDF or XPS files, 306
  security, 275
  starting from templates, 270–71
Datasheet forms, 281
Date Navigator feature, 224, 234
dates and times
  e-mailing schedules, 218–19
  filling Excel data series, 118
  inserting automatically, 31
Day view (Outlook), 224, 225
decimal tabs, 67
default file formats and locations, 324
default printers, 243
default workbook settings, 110
deleting
  annotations, 200, 309
  buttons from toolbars, 240
  cell contents, 117
  comments, 199
  conditional formatting, 150
  cover pages, 88
  data in Excel, 108
  database fields, 273
  duplicated data in Excel, 131
  e-mail, 212
  Excel data, 108, 114, 131
  Excel rows and columns, 117
  fields from queries, 284
  fields from reports, 283

fields on forms, 281
footnotes or endnotes, 95
formatting with keyboard shortcuts, 15
heading numbers, 89
items from Quick Access toolbar,
  316–17
narration, 192
Office components, 333
Outlook toolbars, 240
paragraph numbers, 70
passwords, 327
slides, 177
SmartArt elements, 34
subtotals, 145
tab stops, 67
text accidentally, 45
text in databases, 274
text in Word table cells, 75
watermarks, 94
Word-table rows or columns, 75
WordArt formatting, 166
words in dictionaries, 323
worksheets, 123
delimited files, 144
delivery addresses on envelopes, 99
demoting
  items in SmartArt, 34
  slide bullets, 176
  topics in outlines, 86
descending sort orders, 85
Design Checker feature, 262
Design Gallery, 253
Design view (Access), 267, 273
Desktop, extending, 190
detailed queries, 285
diagnosing problems. *See* troubleshooting
Diagnostics Wizard, 335
diagrams (SmartArt), 34–35, 165
dialing telephone numbers, 233

dialog boxes, 9
dictionaries, 323
digital certificates, 220, 328–30
digital IDs, 220, 328
digital signatures, 328–30
direct formatting, 58
direction
  of animation, 174
  of copying in Excel, 115
  of selection in Excel, 108
displaying
  customized windows, 318–19
  data in Excel tables, 131
  details for subtotals, 145
  faxes, 309
  formatting marks, 319
  formulas, 140
  group schedules, 228–29
  hidden buttons, 13
  hidden Excel rows and columns, 119
  hidden worksheets, 123
  items with keyboard shortcuts, 15
  line numbers, 90
  markups, 199
  media in presentations, 168
  outlines, 86
  Outlook toolbars, 240
  pages side by side, 44
  relationships between numbers, 148
  Ribbon, 10–11
  ScreenTips, 13
  slides, 177
  split-window view of worksheets, 158
  styles, 61
  two versions of documents, 55–56
  watermarks, 94
displays, secondary, 187, 188, 190
dissolves, 179
distributing slide shows, 195

dividing
    Excel data into columns, 144
    numbers, 132, 134
    windows in Excel, 158
Document Image Writer, 308
Document Imaging program, 8, 308, 309, 310
Document Inspector feature, 104, 119
Document Scanning program, 8, 311
documents. *See also* files; Word
    breaking into chapters, 82
    combining changes from different reviewers, 55
    comparing versions of, 55, 56
    Compatibility Checker, 334
    creating, 40
    creating stories for Publisher, 300
    digital signatures, 328–30
    display options, 42–43
    file formats, 20
    finalizing, 104
    hyperlinks and, 313
    importing into Publisher, 299
    inserting Access data into, 301
    inserting Excel charts into, 294
    inserting Excel data into, 292
    inserting slide shows into, 298
    outlines, 86
    page numbers, 51
    passwording, 326–27
    Reading view, 44
    reorganizing elements of, 86
    reviewing changes in, 54–55
    saving, 19
    saving as PDF or XPS files, 306
    saving as TIFF images, 308
    scanning, 311
    selecting everything in, 52
    sending or receiving in e-mail, 208–9

    specialized, 41
    starting with templates, 41
    tracking changes in, 54–55
.docx files, 20
double-sided documents, 79
double-sided printing, 264
double-spaced text, 64
double-strikethrough text, 55
double-underlined text, 55
downloading
    add-ins, 332
    database templates, 270–71
    free software, 332
    themes, 59, 112
Draft view (Word), 38, 43
dragging. *See* moving
drawing. *See also* graphics and pictures
    shapes, 28
    text boxes, 93
drawing canvas, 83
Drawing Tools Format tab, 28
drop lines in charts, 153
dual-display monitors, 187, 188, 190
due dates for tasks, 234
duplex printing, 264
duplicated data, removing, 131
duration
    animation, 174
    slide display, 179

E

earlier versions of Office
    Access databases and, 275
    Compatibility Checker, 334
    file formats and, 20
    Office Compatibility Pack, 22
    opening files from, 22
    saving files for, 324

    saving presentations for, 195
    SmartArt and, 34
    upgrading files from, 22
Easy Web Site Builder dialog box, 260
editing
    animation effects, 174
    annotations, 309
    charts, 153
    citations, 97
    comments in Excel, 128
    comments in PowerPoint, 199
    comparing versions of documents, 55, 56
    customizing settings for, 320
    dictionaries, 323
    equations, 92
    Excel data, 108
    in Full Screen Reading view, 44
    graphics and pictures, 26, 251, 312
    keyboard shortcuts, 15
    pasted Excel data, 293
    photo albums, 182
    presentations, 176–77, 189
    preventing, 327
    recipient lists for mail merge, 102, 103
    return addresses, 99
    slide layout, 180–81
    slide masters, 180–81
    slides, 176–77
    text, 45, 52–53
    text-wrap appearance, 83
    tracking changes, 54–55
    user information, 321
    WordArt, 33
effects
    animation, 172–73, 174
    graphics, 27, 251
    presentation themes, 161
    in Publisher, 251

effects, *continued*
  shapes, 30
  slide transitions, 179
  slides, 170
  SmartArt, 35
  tables, 164
  text wrapping, 257
  washout, 251
  WordArt, 32–33, 166
elapsed time in presentations, 193
electronic postage, 99
e-mail messages
  attachments, 208–9, 219, 263
  business cards, 238–39
  copying, 213
  creating contacts from, 232
  data collection, 288–89
  deleting, 212
  displaying in Full Screen Reading
    view, 44
  encryption, 220
  formatting, 210–11
  forwarding, 207
  hyperlinks and, 313
  illustrated, 202–3
  inserting items into, 203
  marking as read, 212
  organizing in folders, 213
  previewing, 222
  receiving and reading, 206
  replying to, 207
  responses in replies, 207
  sending, 204–5
  sending calendars, 226–27
  sending pictures, 203
  sending Publisher files, 263
  setting up accounts, 216–17
  signatures, 214
  sorting, 206
  subscribing to RSS feeds, 215

  task assignments, 236
  testing accounts, 217
  unread, 206, 212
embedding charts into other
    programs, 294
encryption, 220, 275, 325
endnotes, 95
entering
  data from e-mail, 288
  data in Access, 274
  data in Excel, 107
  text in e-mail, 205
envelopes. *See also* mail merge feature
  mail merged, 101
  printing, 99
E-Postage, 99
equal sign (=), 132, 134
equations, 92
equipment in meeting rooms, 230
error bars in charts, 153
Error Checking feature (Excel), 140
errors. *See also* cautions; troubleshooting
  chart indicator bars, 153
  checking final documents, 104
  checking for before mail merging, 103
  checking for before publishing, 262
  Excel formulas, 135, 140–41
Eudora program, 216
evaluating formulas, 141
even-numbered pages, 79
Excel. *See also* workbooks and worksheets
  analyzing Access data in, 302
  analyzing Word tables in, 295
  AutoRecover feature, 325
  cell references, 132–33
  charts. *See* charts
  Compatibility Checker, 334
  copying information into other
    programs, 292
  copying or moving data, 114–15

  customized windows, 318–19
  default file formats and locations, 324
  default settings, 110
  digital signatures, 328–30
  downloading add-ins and utilities, 332
  editing options, 320
  entering data, 107
  exporting data for Access, 303
  file formats, 20, 324
  formulas, 132–33
  freezing columns and rows, 158
  functions, 132–33
  inserting charts into other
    programs, 294
  inserting slide shows into
    worksheets, 298
  interface elements, 106
  large worksheets and, 158
  macros, add-ins, and ActiveX
    controls, 331
  overview, 8
  page setup, 124–25
  passwording files, 326–27
  PivotTables, 146–47
  Ribbon, 10
  saving files as TIFF images, 308
  templates, 110
  troubleshooting formulas, 140–41
  user information, 321
  worksheet overview, 109
Exchange Server, 216, 223, 228
exchanging information
  analyzing Access data in Excel, 302
  analyzing Word tables in Excel, 295
  converting scanned documents into
    text, 310
  copying Excel data into other
    programs, 292
  creating Publisher stories in Word, 300
  importing Access data into Word, 301

importing Access mail merge data, 304
importing Excel data into Access, 303
importing Outlook data for mail
    merges, 305
importing Word documents into
    Publisher, 299
importing Word outlines into
    PowerPoint, 296
inserting Excel charts into other
    programs, 294
inserting hyperlinks, 313
inserting slide shows into other
    programs, 298
Picture Manager, 312
preparing presentation handouts in
    Word, 297
saving files as PDF or XPS, 306–7
saving files as TIFF images, 308
scanning files, 311
viewing or annotating faxes, 309
executable files, 209
expanding outlines, 86
exponential trendlines, 153
exponentiation, 134
Export Wizard, 301, 302
exporting. See also exchanging
    information
    Access data to Word, 301
    data from databases, 278
    digital IDs, 220
    Excel data to other programs, 292
    PDF or XPS files, 306–7
    TIFF images, 308
extending Windows Desktop, 190
Extensible Markup Language (XML), 20,
    306–7
external data
    exporting, 301, 302
    importing, 276–77
    saving as spreadsheets, 278

F

false values, 135, 139
faxes, 308, 309
fees for research services, 36
fields
    business-card information, 238
    Business Information Sets, 259
    citations as, 96
    collecting data in with e-mail, 289
    database reports, 282–83
    foreign keys, 279
    form information, 280–81
    form-letter information, 102
    header and footer content, 84
    mail merge and, 101, 304, 305
    memo information, 275
    multivalued, 275
    new databases and, 272
    PivotCharts and, 286–87
    PivotTables and, 146
    primary keys, 272, 279
    queries and, 284, 285
    removing from forms, 281
    re-ordering in database tables, 273
    tables of content as, 98
file extensions, 22, 275
file formats
    97–2003 Office files, 20
    Access files, 275, 324
    binary files, 20
    Binary Workbook files, 20
    Compatibility Checker, 334
    customizing saving options, 324
    default formats and locations, 324
    e-mailed attachments, 208
    Excel files, 20, 324
    HTML files, 20, 261, 263
    macro-enabled templates, 20

new features, 5
Office files, 20
older Office files, 20, 22, 34, 275,
    324, 334
older presentation files, 195
Portable Document Format (PDF),
    306–7
PowerPoint files, 20, 195, 324
Publisher HTML files, 263
Rich Text Format files, 20, 210
saving in specified formats, 324
Single File Web Page files, 20
SmartArt and, 34
text files, 20
TIFF files, 308
Web HTML files, 20, 261
Web Page files, 20
Web Page Filtered files, 20
Word files, 20, 324
XML files, 20
file locations, 324
file names, 19
files. See also specific types of files
    (databases, documents, etc.)
    attached to e-mail, 208–9, 219, 227, 275
    AutoRecover feature, 325
    file formats. See file formats
    linking to. See linking
    locations of, 324
    media. See media clips
    older versions of, 20, 22, 34, 275,
        324, 334
    saving. See saving
fill effects. See also colors; filling cells
    gradient fills, 171, 252
    Publisher, 252
    shapes, 30
    slide backgrounds, 171
    SmartArt, 35
    WordArt, 33, 166

fill handles, 115, 137, 320
filling cells
    AutoFill feature, 115, 118, 131, 133, 137
    with copied content, 115
    data series, 118
    fill handles, 115, 137, 320
filmstrip view of pictures, 312
filtered HTML versions of files, 261
filtering
    addresses for mail merge, 101
    Excel data, 143
    Excel tables, 130, 131
    PivotTable data, 147
finalizing documents, 104
finding. *See* searching
first-line indents, 66
first-use installation, 333
fixed-width data, 144
fixing problems. *See* errors;
        troubleshooting
flipping rows and columns in charts, 152
flow charts, 34
flowing text
    around objects. *See* wrapping text
    in Publisher, 246–47
folders
    copying presentation files to, 196
    e-mail messages and, 212, 213
    in Outlook, 222, 223
fonts
    chart elements, 155
    e-mail text, 211
    Excel cells, 111
    presentation themes, 161
    publication schemes, 244
    Quick Access toolbar and, 317
    resizing, 62
    Ribbon and, 10
    slides, 170

special symbols in, 23
substitution, 264
themes, 112
Word, 58, 62
Word themes, 59
WordArt, 32, 166
footers on pages. *See* headers and footers
footnotes, 95
foreign-key fields, 279
form letters, 101, 102
Form Wizard, 280–81
Format Painter feature, 69
formatting
    annotation ink, 309
    AutoShapes, 252
    baseline-guide alignment and, 255
    business cards, 238
    chart axes, 157
    chart elements, 155, 157
    charts, 154
    clip art, 252
    conditional, 148, 149, 150
    consistency in, 63
    copying in Excel, 115
    copying in Word, 69
    dates and times, 31
    e-mail text, 202, 205, 210–11
    Excel cells, 111
    Excel cells as tables, 130
    Excel rows and columns, 120–21
    fonts, 58
    formatting marks, 40, 319
    marking inconsistencies in, 49
    numbers, 113
    page numbers, 51
    pasted text, 17
    pictures, 252
    Publisher tables, 249
    Publisher text, 245

shapes, 30
slide backgrounds, 171
slide text, 163
slides, 170
slides from other presentations, 167
SmartArt graphics, 35
special characters, 68
text boxes, 93, 252
themes, 58, 59, 112
watermarks, 94
WordArt effects, 166
Word styles, 58
Word tables, 76
formatting marks, 40, 319
forms (databases), 280–81
Formula bar, 106
formulas (Excel)
    copying, 115
    copying in Excel, 137
    displaying, 140
    evaluating, 141
    functions, 138–39
    overview, 132–33
    troubleshooting, 140–41
formulas (Word tables), 74
forwarding
    e-mail messages, 207, 214
    iCalendars, 226–27
frames
    e-mailed graphics, 203
    photos, 182
free software, 332
freezing Excel rows and columns, 158
FTP publishing, 261
full names in contacts, 232, 233
Full Screen Reading view (Word), 38,
        42, 44
functions
    arguments in, 139
    defined, 129

finding and using, 138–39
overview, 132–33
Word tables and, 74

G

galleries
  accessing, 10
  Action Buttons, 197
  charts, 152
  colors, 122
  conditional formatting, 148, 150
  Design Gallery, 253
  digital signatures, 330
  e-mail text formatting, 203
  equations, 92
  Excel themes, 112
  handouts, 186
  illustrated, 38
  new features, 5
  presentation templates, 162
  Quick Styles, 170
  sidebars and pull quotes, 93
  slide layouts, 163, 180
  SmartArt, 165
  styles in, 61
  tables of contents, 98
  View Options, 44
  watermarks, 94
  WordArt, 32, 166
gaps in text, 248
Get External Data Wizard, 303
glowing effects, 27
gradient fills, 33, 171, 252
grammar, 48–49, 140, 322
graphic effects. *See* effects
graphics and pictures
  adding to slides, 163
  animating, 173

AutoShapes, 28, 30, 252
behind Excel worksheets, 120
borders, 27
capturing pictures of slides, 198
clip art, 29
Clip Organizer, 8, 169, 314
converting scanned images into
  text, 310
cropping, 25, 251
editing, 26, 251
effects for, 27
fax files, 308, 309
formatting, 252
formatting lists with, 71
glowing, 27
handles, 25
inserting, 24, 203
linking to, 24
Office Picture Manager, 8, 312
pasting charts as, 294
photo albums, 182
picture-frame objects in Publisher, 242
reflections, 27
resizing, 25, 251
restoring to original appearance, 27
rotating, 26, 182, 251
saving files as printable TIFF
  images, 308
scanned images, 308, 309
sending in e-mail, 203
shadows, 27
shapes, 28
slide backgrounds, 171
SmartArt, 165
soft edges, 27
storing in Content Library, 258
stretching, 171
tiling, 171

watermarks, 94
  wrapping text around, 83, 242, 257
grayed commands or buttons, 13
grayed options in dialog boxes, 9
grayscale pictures, 251
green squiggles, 49
gridlines (Excel)
  charts, 151, 153
  illustrated, 106
  printing or hiding, 124
grids in Publisher, 254, 255
grouping
  data in PivotCharts, 286–87
  database records, 282
  objects in Publisher, 256
groups
  collaboration. *See* collaboration
  creating for Outlook scheduling, 228
guides, 254, 255
gutters, 78, 79

H

handles
  Adjustment, 28, 33
  fill, 115, 137, 320
  graphics, 25
  Publisher objects, 242
  Rotation, 28, 33, 35, 242
  Sizing, 28, 35, 165, 242
  shapes, 28
  WordArt, 33
Handout Master view, 161
handouts
  masters, 161, 180
  preparing in Word, 297
  printing, 186
hanging indents, 66

headers and footers
    dates or times in, 31
    Excel pages, 125
    PowerPoint handouts, 186
    PowerPoint slides, 178
    PowerPoint speaker notes, 185
    Word pages, 82, 84
headings
    Excel tables, 130, 158
    scrolling in Excel and, 158
    Word numbering, 89
    Word tables of content and, 98
height
    of objects in Publisher, 242
    of rows in Excel, 120–21
Help
    diagnostics, 335
    Excel functions, 139
    Help button, 39
    keyboard shortcuts, 15
    searching for, 18
Help button, 39
hibernation settings, 187
hiding
    annotations, 190
    details for subtotals, 145
    Excel rows and columns, 119
    formulas, 141
    items with keyboard shortcuts, 15
    slides, 177
    status-bar items, 318
    worksheets, 123
highlighting
    cells with conditional formatting, 149
    text in reviewed documents, 54
Home tab, 38
horizontal axes of charts, 151
horizontal pages, 78, 80

HTML (Hypertext Markup Language)
    e-mail formatting, 210
    e-mailed Publisher files, 263
    file formats, 20
    publishing to the Web, 261
HTTP–based e-mail services, 216
hyperlinks
    Action Buttons, 197
    e-mail, 210
    linking to files or Web pages, 313
hyphenation adjustments, 77

I

iCalendars, 226–27
icons
    Excel sets, 148
    toolbars. *See* toolbars and toolbar
      buttons
IF function, 139
If... statements in mail merge, 101
ignoring misspellings, 48
IM identities, 223
IMAP e-mail services, 216
importing. *See also* exchanging
    information
    Access data into Word, 301
    data into databases, 276–77
    digital IDs, 220
    e-mail account settings, 216
    Word documents into Publisher, 299
Inbox, 206, 207
incoming mail servers, 217
indents
    bulleted lists, 70
    markers, 38
    paragraphs, 66
    styles and, 58
index-card metaphor, 268

initials for users, 321
ink colors, 309
Insert tab, 39
inserting
    attachments, 208–9, 219, 227, 275
    charts, 152–53
    citations, 96–97
    clip art, 29
    data series, 118
    dates and times, 31
    Design Gallery objects, 253
    digital signatures, 328
    Excel comments, 128
    Excel data into other programs, 292
    Excel rows and columns, 116
    footnotes and endnotes, 95
    functions, 138
    graphics, 24
    hyperlinks, 313
    items from Content Library, 258
    items into e-mail messages, 203
    media clips into presentations, 168–69
    movies, 168
    photos, 182
    PivotTables, 146
    placeholders, 181
    PowerPoint tables, 164
    Publisher tables, 249
    pull quotes, 93
    shapes, 28
    sidebars, 93
    slide layouts, 181
    slides, 163, 167
    smart tags, 91
    SmartArt, 34–35
    special characters and symbols, 23
    tables of contents, 98
    watermarks, 94
    Word tables, 72

WordArt, 32–33
worksheets, 123
insertion points, 39, 108
inside margins, 79
inspecting documents, 104
installed templates, 41
installing Office components, 333
interfaces. *See* screen elements
Internet service providers, 216. *See also*
SharePoint Services
interoperability. *See* exchanging
information
interruptions in presentations, 187
invitations to meetings, 230–31
ISBLANK function, 139
ISPs (Internet Service Providers), 216
italic text, 15, 58, 68, 210, 211

J

jumping forward or backward in
Calendar, 224
jumps. *See* hyperlinks
Justified forms, 281
justified text, 63, 77

K

kerning text, 248
keyboard shortcuts
activating commands and menus
with, 14–15
identifying on menus, 12
opening menus with, 12
special characters, 23
KeyTips, 14
keywords for media files, 314

L

labels
chart elements, 153
mailing. *See* mail merge feature
landscape page orientation, 78, 80, 124
Language Settings, 8
languages, 8, 323
laptops
meeting-room equipment, 230
resolution for presentations, 187
layers of objects in Publisher, 256
layout masters, 180–81
layouts, charts, 152–53
leader characters for tabs, 67
left indents, 66
left-aligned tabs, 67
left-aligned text, 63, 77
left-hand pages, 79
leftover text, 246
legends on Excel charts, 151
length
animation, 174
slide display, 179
letters. *See* mail merge feature
levels
multilevel sorting in Excel, 142
numbered headings in Word, 89
tables of contents and, 98
line breaks in text, 77
line spacing, 15, 58, 64–65, 170
line styles in Publisher, 252
linear forecast trendlines, 153
lines
on handouts, 186
numbering in text, 90
selecting, 52
lining through text, 55, 68
lining up. *See* aligning

linked styles, 58, 61
linking
databases, 279
documents to pictures, 24
Excel charts into other programs, 294
Excel data into other programs, 292
inserting hyperlinks to files or Web
pages, 197, 210, 313
slide shows into other programs, 298
text boxes, 246–47
Word tables into Excel, 295
lists
converting into SmartArt, 165
creating, 70
formatting, 71
sorting data in, 85
styles, 58
Live Preview feature, 10
locations of files, 324
logical tests, 135, 139
logos
business information, 259
inserting on slides, 170
storing in Content Library, 258
watermarks, 94

M

macro-enabled templates, 20
macros
Access, 290
file formats and, 20
macro-enabled templates, 20
Quick Access toolbar, 317
running in presentations, 175
security and, 331
viruses, 209
magazine-like columns, 81

magnifying
   picture views, 312
   text, 40, 184
mail merge feature
   Access data in, 304
   data sources for, 103
   form letters, 102
   Mail Merge Wizard, 103
   Outlook's Contacts List and, 305
   overview, 101
Mail Merge Wizard, 103
Mail program, 216
mailing addresses. *See also* addresses
   editing, 321
   envelopes, 99
   separating mailing lists into
      columns, 144
mailing labels, 100. *See also* mail
     merge feature
mapping cell references, 140
margins
   Excel pages, 124
   Publisher guides, 242, 254
   Publisher pages, 244
   Word markers, 38
   Word settings, 78
marking
   documents as final, 104
   e-mail as read, 212
   inconsistencies in formatting, 49
   moved paragraphs, 55
   tasks as completed, 235
markup
   PowerPoint slides, 199
   Word documents, 54–55
master documents in mail merge, 101
master pages, 250
master slides, 180–81
Master view, 180–81

mathematical calculations, 134–35
mathematical equations, 92
mathematical functions. *See* functions
mathematical symbols, 23
MDI (Microsoft Document Interface)
    format, 310
measurement units, 319
media clips
   adding to slides, 163, 168–69
   Clip Organizer, 314
   sound clips, 169
meeting rooms, 223, 230
meetings
   forwarding invitations, 227
   meeting rooms, 223, 230
   scheduling, 223, 230–31
memo fields, 275
Menu bar (Outlook), 222
menus
   customizing, 319
   exploring, 12
   keyboard shortcuts and, 12
   shortcut menus, 12, 13
message recipients. *See* recipients
messages. *See* e-mail messages
microphones, 169
Microsoft Access. *See* Access
Microsoft Clip Organizer, 8, 169, 314
Microsoft Document Interface (MDI)
    format, 310
Microsoft Excel. *See* Excel
Microsoft Exchange Server, 216, 223, 228
Microsoft Office. *See* Office
Microsoft Office 2007 Language
    Settings, 8
Microsoft Office Access. *See* Access
Microsoft Office Clipboard, 16–17
Microsoft Office Compatibility
    Checker, 334

Microsoft Office Compatibility Pack, 22
Microsoft Office Diagnostics, 8
Microsoft Office Diagnostics Wizard, 335
Microsoft Office Document Image
    Writer, 308
Microsoft Office Document Imaging, 8,
    308, 309, 310
Microsoft Office Document Scanning
    program, 8, 311
Microsoft Office Excel. *See* Excel
Microsoft Office Online Web page, 96,
    112, 270–71, 332, 335
Microsoft Office Outlook. *See* Outlook
Microsoft Office Picture Manager, 8, 312
Microsoft Office PowerPoint. *See*
    PowerPoint
Microsoft Office Publisher. *See* Publisher
Microsoft Office SharePoint Server
    2007, 167
Microsoft Office Tools. *See* Office Tools
Microsoft Office Word. *See* Word
Microsoft Trust Center, 220, 331
Microsoft Windows Clipboard, 16
Microsoft Windows Desktop, 190
Microsoft Windows Mail, 216
Microsoft Windows Mobility Center, 187
Microsoft Windows Photo Gallery, 26
Microsoft Windows SharePoint
    Services, 275
Microsoft Windows Vista, 6
Microsoft Windows XP, 6, 19, 333
Microsoft Word. *See* Word
Mini toolbars, 39
minimizing Ribbon, 11, 15
minus sign (-), 134
mirroring margins, 79
misspellings, correcting. *See* spelling
mistakes. *See* errors; grammar; spelling;
    troubleshooting

Mobility Center, 187
modifying. *See* editing
monitors, 187, 190
Month view (Outlook), 224, 225
mouse-clicks
    assigning actions for, 175
    navigating through presentations
        with, 200
movies
    Clip Organizer, 314
    presentations, 168
moving
    around onscreen. *See* navigating
    charts to separate pages, 152
    e-mail messages into folders, 212, 213
    Excel data, 114–15
    nudging objects into alignment, 255
    page numbers, 51
    paragraphs, 55
    Publisher objects, 252
    Quick Access toolbar, 316
    shapes, 28
    slide elements, 176
    slide elements with animation, 172–73
    SmartArt, 165
    tables, 164
    text, 53
    text boxes, 245
    toolbars, 240
moving averages, 153
multilevel lists, 89
multilevel sorting, 142
multimedia
    Clip Organizer, 8, 169, 314
    presentations, 168–69
multiple monitors, 187, 188, 190
multiple versions of slide shows, 194
multiplication, 132, 134

N

Name Box (Excel), 106
#NAME! errors, 140
names
    cells, 132
    contacts, 232, 233
    slide designs, 181
    smart tags, 91
    styles, 60
    user information, 259, 321
    workbooks and worksheets, 122
narration, 191, 192
navigating
    in Access, 266
    in Calendar, 224
    to Excel cells, 107
    in Excel worksheets, 106
    slide-show navigation buttons, 197
    through slide shows, 188, 190
    to Word pages, 44
    in Word table cells, 72
navigation buttons for presentations, 197
Navigation pane (Access), 266
negation, 134
networks, projectors on, 187
newspaper-like columns, 81
noncontiguous blocks of text, 52
noncontiguous data in charts, 152
nonlinear data series, 118
Normal paragraph styles, 71
Normal view (Excel), 106
Normal view (now Draft view in Word),
    38, 43
Normal view (PowerPoint), 160
notebook computers
    meeting-room equipment, 230
    resolution for presentations, 187

notes
    Excel comments, 128
    Outlook feature, 237
    PowerPoint note masters, 180
    PowerPoint slides, 160
    PowerPoint speaker notes, 184–85
    Word footnotes and endnotes, 95
Notes folder, 237
Notes Master view (PowerPoint), 161
Notes Page view (PowerPoint), 161
NOW function, 139
NPER function, 139
nudging objects into alignment, 255
numbered lists (PowerPoint), 170
numbered lists (Word), 70, 71
numbering
    double-sided pages, 79
    footnotes and endnotes, 95
    headings, 89
    lines, 90
    pages, 51
    slides, 161
numbers
    addition, 136
    displaying relationships, 148
    filling Excel data series, 118
    formats, 113
numeric order, sorting in, 85, 142
numeric values in cells, 135

O

Object Linking and Embedding (OLE), 175
Object window (Access), 266–67
objects
    animating, 173
    charts. *See* charts
    Design Gallery, 253
    grouping, 256

objects, *continued*
  pictures. *See* graphics and pictures
  Publisher definitions, 242
  stacking in layers, 256
  ungrouping, 256
  wrapping text around. *See* wrapping text
Objects toolbar, 242
OCR (Optical Character Recognition), 310, 311
odd-numbered pages, 79, 82
Office
  adding or removing components, 333
  Compatibility Checker, 334
  Compatibility Pack, 22
  dialog boxes, 9
  dynamic appearance, 6
  file formats, 20
  interface. *See* screen elements
  interoperability of programs, 291
  macros, add-ins, and ActiveX controls, 331
  Office button, 5
  Office menu, 5
  Office Online Web page, 96, 112, 270–71, 332, 335
  Office tools. *See* Office Tools
  programs included in, 8
  repairing installation, 335
  versions of, 8
Office Access. *See* Access
Office button, 5
Office Clip Organizer, 8, 169, 314
Office Compatibility Pack, 22
Office Diagnostics program, 8
Office Diagnostics Wizard, 335
Office Document Image Writer, 308
Office Document Imaging program, 8, 308, 309, 310

Office Document Scanning program, 8, 311
Office Excel. *See* Excel
Office menu, 5
Office Online Web page
  add-ins and free software, 332
  databases, 270–71
  diagnostic help, 335
  templates, 96, 270–71
  themes, 112
Office Outlook. *See* Outlook
Office Picture Manager, 8, 312
Office PowerPoint. *See* PowerPoint
Office Publisher. *See* Publisher
Office SharePoint Server 2007, 167
Office Tools
  Clip Organizer, 8, 169, 314
  Document Imaging program, 8, 308, 309, 310
  Document Scanning program, 8, 311
  Office 2007 Language Settings, 8
  Office Diagnostics, 8
  Picture Manager, 8, 312
Office Word. *See* Word
older versions of files
  Access databases and, 275
  Compatibility Checker, 334
  file formats, 20
  Office Compatibility Pack, 22
  opening, 22
  saving as, 324
  saving presentations as, 195
  SmartArt and, 34
  upgrading, 22
OLE objects, 175
one-page spreads, 250
online resources. *See* Office Online Web page

opening
  e-mail attachments, 209
  e-mail messages, 206
  Excel templates, 110
  existing databases, 269
  menus, 12
  new Word documents, 40
  older versions of files, 20, 22, 34, 275, 324, 334
  presentations, 195
  slides, 161
operators, mathematical, 134–35
order of actions in Excel, 134
organization charts, 34–35
orientation
  Excel pages, 124
  landscape, 78, 80, 124
  portrait, 78, 80, 124
  PowerPoint handouts, 186
  PowerPoint speaker notes, 185
  Word pages, 78, 80
outgoing mail servers, 217
Outline view (PowerPoint), 176
Outline view (Word), 38, 43
outlines (graphic). *See* borders
outlines (PowerPoint)
  preparing in Word, 296
  printing, 185
  viewing, 176
outlines (Word)
  numbered headings and, 89
  numbering, 71
  preparing for PowerPoint, 296
  reorganizing documents with, 86
  tables of contents and, 98
outlining (subtotaling) in Excel, 145

Outlook
    business cards, 238–39
    Calendar folder, 223
    Contacts folder, 223, 232–33
    customizing toolbars, 240
    customizing windows, 318–19
    editing options, 320
    e-mail accounts, 216–17
    e-mail attachments, 208–9
    e-mail data collection, 288–89
    e-mail interface, 222
    e-mail organization, 212, 213
    e-mail signatures, 214
    encryption, 220
    formatting e-mail, 210–11
    forwarding e-mail, 207
    group schedules, 228–29
    mail merge and, 305
    managing contacts, 232–33
    notes, 237
    overview, 8
    receiving and reading e-mail, 206
    replying to e-mail messages, 207
    RSS subscriptions, 215
    schedule tracking, 224–25
    scheduling meetings, 230–31
    screen elements, 202–3, 222–23
    sending e-mail, 204–5
    sending schedules, 218–19
    sharing calendars, 226–27
    spelling and grammar
      checking, 322
    Tasks folder, 234–35
Outlook Express, 216
outside margins, 79
overflow text, 246
Overtype mode (Word), 45

P

packaging presentations, 196
Page Break view (Excel), 106
page breaks in Excel printouts, 106, 127
page headers or footers. *See* headers
    and footers
Page Layout view (Excel), 106, 127
page layouts (Excel), 124–25
page layouts (PowerPoint)
    handouts, 161, 180, 186
    speaker notes, 185
page layouts (Publisher). *See* publications
page layouts (Word)
    bound documents, 79
    chapters, 82
    columns of text, 81
    double-sided pages, 79
    hyphenation adjustments, 77
    standard-sized pages, 78
page numbers, 39, 51, 79
page orientation. *See* orientation
pages (Excel)
    headers and footers, 125
    margins, 124
    moving charts to, 152
    orientation, 124
    previewing page breaks, 127
    scaling, 124
    setup, 124–25
pages (Publisher)
    arranging items on, 254
    backgrounds, 250
    changing size, 244
    continuing text on, 247
    illustrated, 242
    margins, 244
    master, 250
    one-page spreads, 250
    precision placement, 255
    repeating elements on each page, 250
pages (Web). *See* Web sites and pages
pages (Word)
    cover, 88
    displaying one or two, 44
    displaying side by side, 44
    double-sided, 79
    even-numbered, 79
    headers and footers, 82, 84
    left-hand, 79
    numbering, 51
    odd-numbered, 79, 82
    orientation, 78, 80, 124
    page numbers, 51, 79
    right-hand, 79, 82
    in sections, 80
    tall, 78, 80, 124
    turning, 44
    wide, 78, 80, 124
paper size, 124
paragraph formatting, 69
paragraph marks, 39
paragraph spacing, 64–65
paragraph styles
    defined, 60
    formatting text with, 58
    symbols for, 61
paragraphs
    alignment, 63
    copying formatting, 69
    indenting, 66
    marks, 39
    numbering, 70
    selecting, 52
    spacing, 64–65
    starting new, 40
parameters (arguments), 139, 290
parentheses (( )), 134

passwording, 326–27
passwords, 325
Paste Special dialog box, 115, 292, 294
pasting
    Clipboard and, 16–17
    data into databases, 274, 276–77
    editing pasted Excel data, 293
    Excel charts into other programs, 294
    Excel data, 114, 292
    keyboard shortcuts, 15
    multiple items, 17
    slides into Word, 297
    with Smart Cut And Paste feature, 320
    text in Word, 53
    Word tables into Excel, 295
    Word text into Publisher, 300
paths to files, 324
patterns in shapes, 30
pausing presentations, 193
PDF documents, 306–7
percent sign (%), 134
percentage error bars, 153
percentages, 113, 134
phone numbers, 91, 233
photo albums in PowerPoint, 182
Photo Gallery, 26
pi value, 138
Picture Manager, 8, 312
Picture Tools Format tab, 25, 26
picture-frame objects in Publisher, 242
pictures. *See* graphics and pictures
PivotChart Wizard, 286–87
PivotCharts, 147, 286–87
PivotTables, 131, 146–47
placeholder text
    citations, 96
    Excel templates, 110
    headers, 84
    publications, 243
    Word, 300

Plain Text format, 20, 210
plain-text messages, 210
playing sounds and media, 168–69, 175
plus sign (+), 134
point measurements, 64
POP3 e-mail, 216
portable computers
    meeting-room equipment, 230
    resolution for presentations, 187
Portable Document Format (PDF), 306–7
portrait page orientation, 78, 80, 124
postage, 99
PowerPoint. *See also* presentations
    AutoRecover feature, 325
    Compatibility Checker, 334
    customizing spellchecking, 322
    customizing windows, 318–19
    default file formats and locations, 324
    digital certificates, 330
    downloading add-ins and utilities, 332
    editing options, 320
    file formats, 20
    importing Word outlines, 296
    inserting slide shows into other
        programs, 298
    keyboard shortcuts, 188
    macros, add-ins, and ActiveX
        controls, 331
    overview, 8
    passwording files, 326–27
    pasting Excel data into, 292
    preparing handouts in Word, 297
    Ribbon, 10
    saving files as TIFF images, 308
    screen interface, 160–61
    user information, 321
PowerPoint Viewer, 195
.pptx files, 20

precedence of operators, 134
precedents, tracing, 140
precision
    functions, 138
    graphic settings and positions, 27
    locations of objects in Publisher,
        242, 255
preparing final documents, 104
presentations. *See also* PowerPoint
    adding content to, 163
    adding slides to, 163
    animation effects, 172–73
    assigning actions, 175
    backgrounds, 171
    Compatibility Checker, 334
    copying slides from, 167
    creating, 161–62
    creating multiple versions of, 194
    customizing, 191
    digital certificates, 330
    distributing, 195
    editing, 176–77, 180–81, 189
    ending, 190
    file formats, 20
    formatting slides, 170
    handouts, 186
    hyperlinks and, 313
    inserting Excel charts into, 294
    inserting Excel data into, 292
    inserting slides into other
        programs, 298
    media clips in, 168–69
    narration, 192
    navigation buttons, 197
    opening files from, 175
    opening on other machines, 195
    Outline view, 176
    packaging, 196
    passwording, 326–27

pausing, 193
PDF files, 306
photo albums, 182
preparing handouts in Word, 297
preparing outlines in Word, 296
previewing, 176
rehearsing, 193
re-ordering slides, 177
reviewing, 199
running slide shows, 188–89
saving, 163, 195
saving in older formats, 195
screen interface, 160–61
screen savers and, 187
security, 196
settings, 200
slide layout, 180–81
slide previews, 160
SmartArt effects, 165
speaker notes, 184–85
tables in, 164
templates, 162
themes, 161, 170
TIFF files, 308
timing, 193
tips for, 187
transition effects, 179
traveling with, 196
WordArt, 166
XPS files, 306
Presenter view (PowerPoint), 187, 190
previewing
    animation, 172
    business cards, 238
    e-mail messages, 222
    Excel page breaks, 127
    Excel printouts, 127
    mail-merged letters, 103
    slide transition effects, 179

slides, 160, 176
    speaker-note printouts, 185
    Word headers and footers, 84
    Word styles, 61
primary key fields, 272, 279
print areas, 126
Print dialog box, 9
Print Layout view (Word), 38, 42
Print Preview feature, 43, 124, 127
printers
    commercial, 307
    targeting, 243
printer's marks, 264
printing
    at commercial printers, 307
    double-sided output, 264
    envelopes, 99
    files as TIFF images, 308
    keyboard shortcuts, 15
    mailing labels, 100
    presentation handouts, 186
    presentation outlines, 185
    publications, 264
    speaker notes, 185
    workbook sections, 126
    workbooks and worksheets, 126–27
private appointments, 218
professional print shops, 307
programs
    adding or removing components, 333
    crashing, 335
    viruses, 209
projectors
    meeting-room equipment, 230
    slide shows, 187
promoting
    items in SmartArt, 34
    slide bullets, 176
    topics in outlines, 86

protecting computers and files
    ActiveX controls, 331
    add-ins, 331
    AutoRecover feature, 325
    databases with programming code, 275
    digital signatures, 328–30
    e-mail viruses, 209
    encryption, 220
    macros, 331
    passwords, 326–27
    presentation security settings, 196
    preventing changes, 327
Public Key encryption, 220
publications
    adding text, 245
    arranging page items, 254
    AutoRecover feature, 325
    business information in, 259
    checking final design, 262
    creating from scratch, 244
    Design Gallery, 253
    editing, 320
    editing pictures, 251
    e-mailing, 263
    fine-tuning text, 248
    flowing text in, 246–47
    formatting objects, 252
    hyperlinks and, 313
    importing Word documents into,
        299, 300
    inserting Excel charts into, 294
    inserting Excel data into, 292
    inserting slide shows into, 298
    mail merging Access data, 304
    mail merging Outlook data, 305
    master pages, 250
    pages in, 242
    predesigned, 243
    printing, 264

publications, *continued*
    repeating elements on each page, 250
    reusing content in Content Library, 258
    saving as PDF or XPS files, 306–7
    saving as TIFF images, 308
    saving as Web sites, 260–61
    spellchecking, 322
    stacking and grouping objects, 256
    tables in, 249
    WordArt, 33
Publisher. *See also* publications
    AutoRecover feature, 325
    customizing spellchecking, 322
    editing options, 320
    overview, 8
    screen elements, 242
    Web-site output, 260–61
publishing to the Web, 261
pull quotes, 28, 93
punctuation marks. *See* special characters
    and symbols

Q

queries (database), 302
Query Wizard, 284–85
querying
    databases, 278, 284–85, 302
    Excel data, 143
Quick Access Toolbar, 5, 202, 316–17
Quick Styles feature, 35, 60, 61
Quick Tables feature, 73

R

R1C1 cell referencing, 132
ragged edges of text, 77
ranges of cells, 132

reading
    e-mail, 206, 212
    RSS feeds, 215
Reading Highlight option (Word), 46
Reading view (Office Document
    Imaging), 309
Reading view (Word), 44
receiving
    e-mail, 206
    files in e-mail, 208–9
recently used databases, 269
recently used files, 319
recently used functions, 138
rechecking spelling and grammar, 322
recipients
    editing list of, 103
    inviting to meetings, 230–31
    listing, 202
    mail merged letters, 102
    replying to messages, 207
    sending e-mail to, 204–5
    sending iCalendars to, 227
recognizing text in scanned images, 310
recoloring pictures, 26
recording
    appointments, 218, 222, 223, 225
    narration, 192
    sound, 169
    timing for slide shows, 193
recovering files, 325
recto pages, 79, 82
"red eye," 312
red squiggles, 48
redoing actions, 15
#REF! errors, 140
references
    citations, 96–97
    footnotes and endnotes, 95
reflections in graphics, 27
rehearsing presentations, 193

rejecting
    changes, 55
    tasks, 236
relational databases, 268, 279. *See also*
    Access
relative cell references, 109, 133, 137
reminders for appointments, 223
removing. *See* deleting
renumbering footnotes and endnotes, 95
re-ordering
    animated effects, 174
    database fields, 273
    items on Quick Access toolbar, 317
    objects in Publisher, 256
    slides, 177, 194
    worksheets, 122
repeating elements
    dates in headers or footers, 31
    Excel page headers or footers, 125
    Excel rows on printouts, 126
    PowerPoint handout headers or
        footers, 186
    PowerPoint slide headers or footers, 178
    PowerPoint speaker-note headers or
        footers, 185
    Publisher designs, 250
    times in headers or footers, 31
    Word page headers or footers, 82, 84
repeating presentations, 193
replacing
    data in Excel, 108, 109
    misspelled text, 50
    non-text items, 47
    text in Word, 45, 47
replying to e-mail messages, 207, 214
Report Wizard, 282–83
reports
    databases, 282–83
    removing fields from, 283
republishing. *See* updating

requesting meetings, 230–31
research features, 36
resetting
  graphics to original appearance, 27
  original themes, 59
reshaping
  shapes, 28
  text-wrap appearance, 83
  WordArt, 33
resizing
  annotations, 309
  chart elements, 155
  graphics, 25
  objects in Publisher, 252
  pages in Excel, 124
  pages in Word, 78
  pictures, 251, 312
  rows and columns in Excel, 120–21
  shapes, 28
  Sizing handles, 28, 35, 165, 242
  SmartArt, 35, 165
  tables in publications, 249
  text boxes in Publisher, 245
  text in e-mail, 211
  text in Help window, 18
  text in Word, 62
  text on slides, 170
  video images, 168
  WordArt, 33
resolution for slide shows, 188
resources in meetings, 230
restarting list numbering, 70
restoring
  deleted text, 45
  graphics to original appearance, 27
  original themes, 59
resuming paused presentations, 193
return addresses on envelopes, 99

reusing
  business information in
    publications, 259
  content in publications, 258
  slides, 167
reviewing
  checking Word documents for
    revisions, 104
  combining reviewers' changes in
    Word, 55
  comparing versions of Word
    documents, 55, 56
  connected text boxes in Publisher, 247
  displaying reviewers' comments in
    Word, 39
  Excel workbooks, 128
  final publications in Publisher, 262
  finalizing Word documents, 104
  inspecting Word documents, 104
  PowerPoint presentations, 199
  tracked changes in Word documents,
    54–55
revisions, checking for, 104
Ribbon
  Access use of, 266
  adding items to Quick Access
    toolbar, 316
  displaying, 10–11
  illustrated, 106, 160, 202
  keyboard shortcuts, 14
  minimizing, 11
  new features, 4–5
  Office use of, 7
  tabs and options on, 10–11
Rich Text format, 20, 210, 301
right-aligned indents, 66
right-aligned tabs, 67
right-aligned text, 63
right-hand pages, 79, 82

rotating
  3-D charts, 153
  graphics, 26, 182
  objects in Publisher, 242, 252
  pictures, 251, 312
  with Rotation handles, 28, 33, 35, 242
  shapes, 28
  SmartArt, 35
  text on slides, 170
  WordArt, 33
Rotation handles, 28, 33, 35, 242
row guides (Publisher), 254
rows (Excel)
  adding, 116
  cell references and, 132
  defined, 109
  deleting, 117
  freezing, 158
  headers, 106
  height, 120–21
  hiding or displaying, 119
  in PivotTables, 147
  repeating on printouts, 126
  sorting, 142
  switching to columns, 143
  in tables, 130–31
  totals, 131
rows (Word mailing labels), 100
rows (Word tables)
  deleting, 75
  formatting, 76
  sorting content, 85
RSS subscriptions, 215
RTF (Rich Text Format), 20, 210, 301
ruler guides, 254, 255
rulers
  in Publisher, 242, 254, 255
  in Word, 38, 66

rules

    conditional formatting, 150

    mail merge, 101

running

    diagnostics, 335

    macros, 175

    media clips in slide shows, 168, 169

    slide shows, 188–89, 191, 193, 195

    slide shows with narration, 192

running heads. *See* headers and footers

S

saving. *See also* exchanging information

    Access data as spreadsheets, 278

    annotations on images or faxes, 309

    annotations on slides, 189

    attachments, 208

    converting older files, 20, 22, 34, 275, 324, 334

    databases, 272

    files, 19

    files as TIFF images, 308

    files in specified formats, 324

    formatting as styles, 60

    keyboard shortcuts, 15

    macros, 290

    PDF or XPS files, 306–7

    presentations, 195

    slide masters, 181

    slide shows, 163, 195

    slides as pictures, 198

    tasks, 235

    Web-site pages, 260

scaling. *See* resizing

scanned documents, 308, 309, 310

scanned images of signatures, 328

scanners, 311

schedules

    Calendar folder, 223

    displaying for workgroups, 228–29

    e-mailing, 218–19

    tracking, 224–25

scheduling meetings, 230–31

screen captures of slides, 198

screen elements

    Access, 266–67

    customizing, 318–19

    Excel, 106

    Outlook, 202–3, 222–23

    PowerPoint, 160–61

    Publisher, 242

    Word, 38–39

screen savers, 187

screens, 187, 190

ScreenTips, 13, 115, 313

script files, 209

scroll bars, 39, 267

scrolling

    freezing Excel headers and, 158

    synchronous scrolling in Word, 56

searching

    for all instances of text, 46

    for citations, 96

    for clip art, 29

    for database templates, 271

    for functions, 138

    for Help topics, 18

    for marked changes in Word, 55

    for media files, 314

    for new e-mail, 206

    for pictures on hard drives, 312

    resources for information, 36

    for software downloads, 332

    for text in Word, 46–47

sections

    chapters, 82

    switching page orientation, 80

security

    ActiveX controls, 331

    add-ins, 331

    AutoRecover feature, 325

    databases with programming code, 275

    digital signatures, 328–30

    e-mail viruses, 209

    encryption, 220

    macros, 331

    passwording files, 326–27

    presentation settings, 196

    preventing changes to files, 327

selecting

    cell ranges, 139

    cells in Excel, 111

    chart elements, 155

    data series in charts, 156

    direction of selections in Excel, 108

    settings for, 320

    text in databases, 274

    text in Word, 45, 52–53

Send button, 202

sending

    business cards, 239

    calendars via e-mail, 226

    e-mail, 204–5

    e-mail replies, 207

    files in e-mail, 208–9

    schedules via e-mail, 218–19

sentences, selecting, 52

separations (color), 264

series. *See* data series

servers

    e-mail, 217

    SharePoint Server 2007, 167

    slide libraries on, 167

service providers. *See* Internet service providers; SharePoint Services

shading. *See* colors; fill effects

shadows
 applying in Publisher, 252
 applying in Word, 58
 applying to graphics, 27
 around pictures in e-mail, 203
shapes
 Action Buttons, 197
 animating, 173
 formatting, 30
 inserting, 28
 on slides, 170
 wrapping text around. *See* wrapping
  text
SharePoint Server 2007, 167
SharePoint Services
 Access integration with, 275
 SharePoint Server 2007, 167
sharing files. *See also* collaboration;
  SharePoint Services
 calendars, 226–27
 converting older files, 20, 22, 34, 275,
  324, 334
sheets of labels, 100
shortcut menus, 12, 13
shortcuts. *See* keyboard shortcuts
sidebars, 93
signature services, 329
signatures
 digital, 328–30
 e-mail, 214
Simple Query Wizard, 284
Single File Web Page file format, 20
sizing. *See* resizing
Sizing handles, 28, 35, 165, 242
slash (/), 132, 134
sleep settings, 187
Slide Library feature, 167
Slide Master view (PowerPoint), 161,
  180–81
slide masters, 161, 180–81

slide presentations. *See* PowerPoint;
  presentations
Slide Show view (PowerPoint), 160, 161
Slide Sorter view (PowerPoint), 160, 161,
  177
slides. *See also* presentations
 animation effects, 172–73
 assigning actions, 175
 backgrounds, 171
 blank, 177
 capturing pictures of, 198
 copying from other presentations, 167
 customizing, 180–81
 default layouts, 180
 deleting, 177
 duplicating, 167
 editing, 176–77
 exporting to Word, 297
 footers on, 178
 formatting, 170
 formatting shapes, 170
 hiding, 177
 inserting, 163
 masters, 161, 180–81
 moving elements, 164, 176
 numbers, 161
 Outline view, 176
 photo albums, 182
 placeholders on, 181
 previewing, 176
 re-ordering, 177, 194
 reproducing in handouts, 186
 reusing, 167
 speaker notes for, 184–85
 switching, 179
 tables on, 164
 timing, 179
 transition effects, 179
 WordArt, 166

Smart Cut And Paste feature, 320
smart tags, 91
SmartArt feature
 adding to slides, 163
 adding to Word documents, 300
 animation and, 173
 converting text to, 165
 new features, 5
 relational diagrams, 34–35
snapping objects
 to guides, 254, 255
 to ruler marks, 255
soft-edge effects, 27
software
 adding or removing Office
  components, 333
 downloading free, 332
 older versions of. *See* earlier versions
  of Office
 trial versions, 332
sorting
 data in Excel, 142
 data in Excel tables, 131
 data in Word tables, 74, 85
 database reports, 283
 e-mail messages, 206
 lists in Word, 85
 slides, 177
 tasks, 235
sound clips
 Action Buttons, 197
 assigning actions to, 175
 Clip Organizer, 169
 narration, 192
 in presentations, 168, 169
 transitions between slides, 174, 179
 volume settings, 187
source data, 101, 102

Source Manager feature, 96–97
space marks, 39
spacing
  adjusting in Word, 58
  hyphenation adjustments and, 77
  keyboard shortcuts, 65
  between lines or paragraphs, 64–65
  "space before" or "space after," 64–65
  space marks, 39
  white spaces in text, 77
speaker notes for presentations, 184–85
special characters and symbols
  in equations, 92
  in file names, 19
  in footnotes and endnotes, 95
  inserting, 23
  stock symbols, 91
  style icons, 61
special effects. *See* effects
speed
  animation, 174
  slide display, 179
  transition effects, 179
spelling
  AutoCorrect feature, 50
  contextual errors, 49
  correcting, 48–49, 50
  customizing settings, 322
  dictionaries, 323
  keyboard shortcuts, 15
splitting windows in Excel, 158
spreadsheets. *See* workbooks and
  worksheets
squiggles, 48–49
SQRT function, 139
stacking objects, 256
standard deviations, 138, 153
standard error bars, 153
status bar, 14, 106, 161, 266, 318

status reports for tasks, 236
Step By Step Mail Merge Wizard, 103
stock symbols, 91
stories, 300
storing. *See* saving
storyboards, 161
stretching
  characters, 248
  graphics, 171
strikethrough text, 55, 68
Strong character style, 71
styles
  alignment to baseline grid and, 255
  applying, 15, 61, 170
  applying to graphics, 27
  character. *See* character styles
  charts, 154
  citations, 96, 97
  creating, 60
  displaying, 61
  formatting Excel cells with, 111
  formatting Excel tables with, 130
  formatting PowerPoint tables with, 164
  formatting Word text with, 58, 60
  keyboard shortcuts, 15
  numbered headings, 89
  paragraph. *See* paragraph styles
  on Quick Access toolbar, 317
  on Ribbon, 10
  symbols for, 61
  tables of contents, 98
  in templates, 41
  WordArt, 33
subjects of e-mail messages, 202, 204
subscribing to RSS feeds, 215
subscript text, 58
substituting fonts, 264
subtotals in Excel data, 145
subtraction, 134

suggested spellings, 48
summing numbers, 136
superscript text, 58
suppressing line numbers, 90
switching
  chart types, 152, 156, 287
  Excel chart rows and columns, 152
  Excel rows and columns, 143
  to programs for demos, 190
symbols. *See* special characters and
  symbols
synchronous scrolling, 56
syntax, correcting, 140
system messages, 187

T

tab-delimited data, 144
tables (database)
  adding data to, 274
  creating, 272
  defining relationships, 279
  exporting data, 278
  exporting into Excel, 302
  importing Excel data into, 303
  importing into Access, 276–77
  including in queries, 285
  mail merging data from, 304
  modifying, 273
  relational databases and, 268
tables (Excel)
  converting into normal cells, 131
  creating, 130–31
  filtering, 131
  headings, 158
  illustrated, 106
  inserting in e-mail, 203
  sorting, 131
tables (Outlook), 210

tables (PowerPoint)
  adding to slides, 163, 164
  animating, 173
tables (Publisher), 249
tables (Word)
  adding or deleting rows or columns, 75
  analyzing in Excel, 295
  converting text into, 74
  creating, 72
  formatting, 76
  formulas in, 74
  inserting into e-mail, 203
  predesigned, 73
  sorting data in, 85
  table styles, 58, 61
  tables of contents, 98
  using instead of tabs, 67
tables of contents, 98
tabs (Ribbon), 7, 10–11, 14, 106
tabs (text), 58, 67, 72
Tabular forms, 281
tall pages, 78, 80, 124
task panes in Publisher, 242
task-oriented Ribbon tabs, 7, 10–11,
  14, 106
tasks (Outlook)
  accepting or rejecting, 236
  assigning, 236
  creating, 234
  Daily Task List pane, 223
  due dates, 234
  marking as complete, 235
  saving, 235
  sorting lists of, 235
  status reports, 236
  To-Do Bar, 224
  tracking, 234–35
  upcoming, 222, 225

team members. *See also* collaboration;
  SharePoint Services
  creating groups for Outlook
    scheduling, 228
  viewing group schedules, 228–29
telephone numbers, 91, 233
templates
  databases, 270–71
  file formats, 20
  presentations, 162
  publications, 243
  switching in Publisher, 243
  watermarks, 94
  Word documents, 41
  Word tables, 73
  workbooks and worksheets, 110
testing e-mail accounts, 217
text
  adding to publications, 245
  aligning in Excel, 120
  animating, 172–73
  baselines, 254
  business cards, 238
  chart elements, 153, 155
  converting scanned documents
    into, 310
  converting into Excel columns, 144
  converting into SmartArt, 165
  converting into Word tables, 74
  converting into WordArt, 166
  copying and pasting, 16–17, 53
  deleting in Word tables, 75
  editing, 45
  finding in documents, 46–47
  flowing in Publisher, 246–47
  fonts. *See* fonts
  formatting in e-mail, 203, 210–11
  formatting in presentations, 163
  formatting in Word, 60

  headers or footers. *See* headers and
    footers
  inserting into e-mail, 203
  justified, 63, 77
  kerning, 248
  moving, 53
  outlines. *See* outlines (PowerPoint);
    outlines (Word)
  overflow or leftover, 246
  placeholders on slides, 181
  replacing, 47
  resizing in e-mail, 211
  resizing in publications, 248
  resizing in slides, 170
  resizing in Word, 62
  rotating in slides, 170
  scanning, 311
  selecting, 45, 52–53
  in shapes, 28, 30
  sidebars and pull quotes, 93
  smart tags and, 91
  spacing. *See* spacing
  tracking, 248
  watermarks, 94
  WordArt, 32–33
  wrapping around graphics. *See*
    wrapping text
text boxes
  connecting and flowing text in
    Publisher, 246–47
  in dialog boxes, 9
  formatting in Publisher, 252
  inserting in Publisher, 242, 245
  inserting in Word, 93
  in scanned or faxed files, 309
  in slides, 160
  wrapping text around objects. *See*
    wrapping text

text files
  file formats, 20
  Outlook notes, 237
  tab-delimited data, 144
text styles. *See* styles
text wrapping. *See* wrapping text
textures, 171
themes
  changing, 59
  charts, 154
  colors in, 112
  cover pages, 88
  Excel workbooks, 112
  fonts in, 62, 112
  formatting Word text with, 58
  presentation designs, 161, 170
  Publisher designs, 253
  Quick Styles, 60
third-party digital certificate
    providers, 328
three-dimensional effects
  charts, 153
  WordArt, 32
three-dimensional rotation, 27
thumbnail view of pictures, 312
.tif files (TIFF), 308, 309, 310
tiling graphics, 171
times. *See* dates and times
timing
  animation tempo, 174
  presentations, 193
  slide-display duration, 161, 179
  transition effects, 179
title bars, 9, 266
titles
  chart axes, 151
  slides, 160
  worksheets, 126
To-Do Bar (Outlook), 5, 224, 225

toolbars and toolbar buttons
  adding or removing in Outlook, 240
  customizing in Outlook, 240
  exploring in Office, 13
  hiding in PowerPoint, 200
  moving, 240
  navigating presentations with, 200
tools, software. *See* Office Tools; software
ToolTips. *See* ScreenTips
topics, reorganizing, 86
totals rows in Excel tables, 131
tracing precedents in Excel, 140
Track Changes feature, 54–55
tracking in text, 248
transferring. *See* exchanging information;
    importing
transition effects, 161, 174, 179
transparency, 30
transposing Excel rows and columns, 143
trendlines, 153
trial versions of software, 332
troubleshooting
  Design Checker feature, 262
  e-mail formatting, 205
  finalizing Word documents, 104
  formulas, 140–41
  hyperlinks, 210
  Query Wizard steps, 284
  repairing Office installation, 335
true values, 135, 139
Trust Center
  encryption, 220
  macros, add-ins, and ActiveX
    controls, 331
Try This! exercises
  AutoFlowing text, 247
  background pictures in Excel, 120
  business cards, 238, 239
  calculations in Excel, 134
  citation placeholders in Word, 96

creating Outlook contacts, 232
e-mailing pictures, 203
e-mailing schedules, 219
measuring objects in Publisher, 255
minimizing Ribbon, 11
moving toolbars, 240
outline levels in Word, 86
Quick Styles, 61
smart tags, 91
text wrapping, 257
Word table rows and columns, 75
WordArt, 32
turning features on or off
  buttons on toolbars, 13
  disabling databases with programming
    code, 275
  Excel fill handles, 115
  passwords, 327
  Word line numbers, 90
  Word numbered headings, 89
turning pages, 44
TWAIN drivers, 311
two-page spreads, 250
two-sided documents, 66, 79
two-sided printing, 264
typefaces. *See* fonts
typing
  data into Access, 272, 274
  data into Excel, 107
  over text, 45
  text in Word, 40

U

unavailable options in dialog boxes, 9
underlined text
  applying formatting, 58, 68, 210, 211
  evaluating formulas, 141
  keyboard shortcuts, 15

moved paragraphs in Word, 55
smart tags, 91
undoing actions. *See also* restoring
in databases, 274
deleting cell contents, 117
keyboard shortcuts, 15
restoring deleted text, 45
with search-and-replace, 47
uneven text margins, 77
ungrouping objects, 256
unhiding. *See* displaying
units of measurement, 319
unnumbered paragraphs, 70
unread e-mail, 206, 212
upcoming tasks and appointments, 225
updating
business information in
publications, 259
dates and times, 31
tables of contents, 98
up/down bars in charts, 153
upgrading files from previous versions.
See earlier versions of Office
uploading Web pages, 261
URLs for RSS feeds, 215
user information, 321
utilities. *See* Office Tools; software

V

validating addresses, 231
value axes in charts, 151, 157
#VALUE! errors, 140
values
calculating in Excel, 134–35
conditional formatting and, 148–50
copying in Excel, 115
false, 135, 139
sorting by, 142

VCRs in meeting rooms, 230
versions
of documents, displaying, 55–56
of Office, 8. *See also* earlier versions
of Office
of slide shows, 194
verso pages, 79, 82
vertical axes of charts, 151, 157
vertical pages, 78, 80
videos
Clip Organizer, 314
presentations, 168
View Options gallery (Word), 44
Viewer Packages, 196
viewing. *See* displaying
views. *See names of views* (Draft view,
Month view, etc.)
viruses, 209. *See also* macros
Vista operating system, 6
volume settings, 187

W

washout effects, 251
watermarks, 94, 170
Web hosts, 261
Web Layout view (Word), 38, 42
Web Page file format, 20
Web Page Filtered file format, 20
Web sites and pages
in Contacts folder, 223
creating with Publisher, 260–61
file formats, 20
linking to, 313
on local computers, 261
Office Online, 96, 112, 270–71, 332, 335
RSS feeds, 215
SharePoint Services, 275
viruses and, 209

Week view (Outlook), 225
white spaces in text, 77
WIA (Windows Imaging Acquisition), 311
wide pages, 78, 80, 124
width
columns in Excel, 120–21
objects in Publisher, 242
windows
customizing, 318–19
freezing panes in Excel, 158
splitting in Excel, 158
Windows Clipboard, 16
Windows Desktop, 190
Windows Imaging Acquisition (WIA), 311
Windows Mail, 216
Windows Mobility Center, 187
Windows Photo Gallery, 26
Windows SharePoint Services
Access integration, 275
SharePoint Server 2007, 167
Windows Vista, 6
Windows XP, 6, 19, 333
wizards
Collect Data Through E-Mail Messages
Wizard, 288–89
Connect To A Network Projector
Wizard, 187
Convert Text To Columns Wizard, 144
Export Wizard, 301, 302
Form Wizard, 280–81
Get External Data Wizard, 303
Microsoft Office Diagnostics
Wizard, 335
PivotChart Wizard, 286–87
Query Wizard, 284–85
Report Wizard, 282–83
Simple Query Wizard, 284
Step By Step Mail Merge Wizard, 103

Word. *See also* documents
  ActiveX controls, 331
  add-ins and utilities, 331, 332
  analyzing tables in Excel, 295
  AutoRecover feature, 325
  Compatibility Checker, 334
  customizing spelling and grammar
    checking, 322
  customizing windows, 318–19
  default file formats and locations, 324
  digital signatures, 328–30
  editing options, 320
  exporting documents for Publisher,
    299, 300
  exporting outlines for PowerPoint, 296
  file formats, 20, 324
  inserting slide shows into
    documents, 298
  keyboard shortcuts, 65
  line spacing, 65
  macros, 331
  mail merging data, 304, 305
  multiple techniques for working in,
    52–53
  overview, 8
  passwording files, 326–27
  pasting Excel data into, 292
  preparing presentation handouts
    in, 297
  presenting Access data in, 301
  saving files as TIFF images, 308
  screen interface, 38–39
  "space-before" or "space after" spacing,
    64–65
  starting, 40
  storing data in, 268
  user information, 321
  viewing options, 42–43
  word counts, 39
Word 97–2003 file format, 20

WordArt
  creating and inserting, 32–33
  formatting chart text as, 155
  in publications, 242
  on slides, 166
  in tables, 164
words
  counting, 39
  in dictionaries, 323
  hyphenating, 77
  selecting, 52
Work Week view (Outlook), 225
workbooks and worksheets. *See also* Excel
  adding new worksheets, 123
  binary file format, 20
  cell references in, 132–33
  chart pages, 152
  colors, 111, 112, 148
  comments in, 128
  Compatibility Checker, 334
  copying information into other
    programs, 292
  default settings for, 110
  defined, 105
  deleting worksheets, 123
  digital signatures, 328–30
  exporting data for Access, 303
  file formats, 20
  filtering data, 143
  freezing panes in, 158
  headers and footers, 125
  hiding or displaying worksheets, 123
  hyperlinks and, 313
  illustrated, 106
  importing database data, 278, 302
  inserting data into e-mail, 203
  inserting slide shows into, 298
  interface elements, 106
  naming and arranging worksheets, 122
  overview, 109

  page breaks, 127
  passwording, 326–27
  previewing printouts, 124
  printing, 126–27
  row headers, nonscrolling, 158
  saving as PDF or XPS files, 306
  saving as TIFF images, 308
  sorting, 142
  splitting view of, 158
  tables. *See* tables (Excel)
  templates, 110
  text alignment, 120
  themes, 112
  working with large areas, 158
  worksheet tab colors, 122
working hours, 218
wrapping text
  around graphics, 83, 257
  around WordArt, 33
  in Excel cells, 111
  to new lines, 205
  in Publisher, 242, 257

X

.xlsx files, 20
XML (Extensible Markup Language)
  documents, 20
XML Paper Specification (XPS), 306–7
XML presentations, 20
XPS documents, 306–7

Z

Zoom Controls, 38, 40, 242
zooming
  magnifying text, 40, 184
  picture views, 312

About the Authors

Jerry Joyce is a marine biologist who has conducted research from the Arctic to the Antarctic and has published extensively on marine-mammal and fisheries issues. He developed computer programs in association with these studies to simplify real-time data entry, validation, and analysis that substantially enhanced the quality of the research. He has also had a long-standing relationship with Microsoft: Prior to co-authoring 15 books about Microsoft Windows, Word, and Office, he was the technical editor for numerous books published by Microsoft Press, and he wrote manuals, help files, and specifications for various Microsoft products. Jerry is a Seattle Audubon volunteer and represents Seattle Audubon on the Washington State Oil Spill Advisory Council and the Washington State Ballast Water Working Group.

Marianne Moon has worked in the publishing world for many years as proofreader, editor, and writer—sometimes all three simultaneously. She has been editing and proofreading Microsoft Press books since 1984 and has written and edited documentation for Microsoft products such as Microsoft Works, Flight Simulator, Space Simulator, Golf, Publisher, the Microsoft Mouse, and Greetings Workshop. In another life, she was chief cook and bottlewasher for her own catering service and wrote weekly cooking articles for several newspapers. When she's not chained to her computer, she likes gardening, cooking, traveling, writing, and knitting sweaters for tiny dogs. There's a children's book in her head that she hopes will find its way out one of these days.

Marianne and Jerry own and operate Moon Joyce Resources, a small consulting company. They've been friends for 25 years, have worked together for 21 years, and have been married for 15 years. They are co-authors of the following books:

Microsoft Word 97 At a Glance

Microsoft Windows 95 At a Glance

Microsoft Windows NT Workstation 4.0 At a Glance

Microsoft Windows 98 At a Glance

Microsoft Word 2000 At a Glance

Microsoft Windows 2000 Professional At a Glance

Microsoft Windows Millennium Edition At a Glance

Troubleshooting Microsoft Windows 2000 Professional

Microsoft Word Version 2002 Plain & Simple

Microsoft Office System Plain & Simple— 2003 Edition

Microsoft Windows XP Plain & Simple

Microsoft Windows XP Plain & Simple—2nd Edition

Microsoft Office Word 2007 Plain & Simple

Windows Vista 2007 Plain & Simple

If you have questions or comments about any of their books, please visit *www.moonjoyce.com*.